PRAISE FOR *GREE*
SUSTAINABLE FINA

'In 2017, I challenged Simon Thompson and the Chartered Banker Institute to create training programmes that would set the global benchmark for the knowledge and skills required by finance professionals leading the transition to net zero, emphasizing the science content needed to understand fully the relationship between finance and climate-related risk. This he has done emphatically in what I believe is a world first in green finance education. I am very proud to see these published, and recommend them to colleagues worldwide who wish to develop and demonstrate their knowledge of the science behind, and the principles and practice of, green and sustainable finance.'

Sir Roger Gifford, Chair, Green Finance Institute

'Finance professionals reading this book will not only have the knowledge about green finance they need, but the understanding to put that knowledge to practical use. An essential read as the financial and corporate world finally put climate considerations front and centre.'

Dame Susan Rice DBE

'An excellent and very timely introduction to the important subject of green and sustainable finance and how financial institutions can truly become fit for purpose for financing the needs of society. We need every finance professional to develop their knowledge of the topics covered in this book, and apply them in their work, if we are to successfully transform finance and our economies to support a sustainable, low-carbon future.'

Eric Usher, Head, UNEP Finance Initiative

'This progressive book provides a comprehensive review and explanation of the origin, content and rationale of the form, scale and scope of green finance and its implications internationally. By weaving together the theory, history, practice, significance and ramifications of green finance, this contribution provides a solid foundation and introduction to this most important topic.'

John K Ashton, Professor of Banking, Bangor University Business School

'Incredibly comprehensive and yet very easy to read and navigate. The financial services sector will have to transform rapidly to respond to the climate crisis. Building the right skills and knowledge on this topic will be key to succeed so this is a recommended read, not just for sustainability practitioners but all bankers.'
Elisa Moscolin, Head of Sustainability and ESG, Santander UK

'Over the next three decades, $3.5 trillion needs to be invested annually in infrastructure to meet the climate challenge. Mark Carney, former Governor of the Bank of England, has said the scale of that funding requirement means "we need to turn billions of public capital into trillions of private capital." That calls for exceptional standards of professionalism from financiers and others, and Simon Thompson's book is an exemplary toolkit for board members and beginners alike in this, the greatest crisis and the greatest opportunity of our times.'
Simon Culhane, Chartered FCSI, CEO, Chartered Institute for Securities & Investment

CHARTERED BANKER SERIES

Culture, Conduct and Ethics in Banking Fred Bell

Retail and Digital Banking John Henderson

Commercial Lending Adrian Cudby

Relationship Management in Banking Steve Goulding and Richard Abley

The above titles are available from all good bookshops.

For further information on these and other Kogan Page titles, or to order online, visit the Kogan Page website at: www.koganpage.com.

Chartered Banker

GREEN AND SUSTAINABLE FINANCE

PRINCIPLES AND PRACTICE

SIMON THOMPSON

First published in Great Britain and the United States in 2021 by Kogan Page Limited

2nd Floor, 45 Gee Street
London
EC1V 3RS
United Kingdom

122 W 27th St, 10th Floor
New York, NY 10001
USA

4737/23 Ansari Road
Daryaganj
New Delhi 110002
India

www.koganpage.com

Kogan Page books are printed on paper from sustainable forests.

ISBNs

Hardback 978 1 78966 457 7
Paperback 978 1 78966 454 6
Ebook 978 1 78966 455 3

British Library Cataloguing-in-Publication Data

A CIP record for this book is available from the British Library.

Library of Congress Cataloging-in-Publication Data

Names: Thompson, Simon (CEO of the Chartered Banker Institute), author.
Title: Green and sustainable finance : principles and practice / Simon Thompson.
Description: London ; New York, NY : Kogan Page Inc, 2021. | Series: Chartered banker | Includes bibliographical references and index.
Identifiers: LCCN 2020054368 (print) | LCCN 2020054369 (ebook) | ISBN 9781789664546 (paperback ; alk. paper) | ISBN 9781789664577 (hardback ; alk. paper) | ISBN 9781789664553 (ebook)
Subjects: LCSH: Finance–Environmental aspects. | Sustainable development–Finance.
Classification: LCC HG101 .T46 2021 (print) | LCC HG101 (ebook) | DDC 332–dc23
LC record available at https://lccn.loc.gov/2020054368
LC ebook record available at https://lccn.loc.gov/2020054369

Typeset by Integra Software Services, Pondicherry
Print production managed by Jellyfish
Printed and bound by CPI Group (UK) Ltd, Croydon CR0 4YY

CONTENTS

PREFACE

In the aftermath of the 2008 Global Financial Crisis, many – including many financial services professionals – felt the finance sector needed to fundamentally reconsider its strategies, operations and activities, and align these with more socially-purposeful, longer-term aims and objectives to deliver greater shared economic and social value. Finance, in short, should become more sustainable.

Following the 2015 Paris Agreement on climate change, policymakers, regulators and practitioners have focused on environmental sustainability, especially tackling global warming. Article 2.1c of the Paris Agreement requires signatories to align flows of finance with lower greenhouse gas emissions and climate resilient development. It is extremely significant that the key global climate change agreement singles out the critical role of finance.

By December 2020, 125 countries had published net zero or similar targets by 2050 at the latest, requiring systemic economic transitions on an unprecedented scale. Every economic entity will need to align their own strategies, operations and activities with below 2°C of global warming, and the finance sector – banks, fund managers, insurers, investors and a wide range of supporting professional services – must play a leading role. Green finance will power the transition, ensuring capital flows to the firms, investments, projects and technologies creating our sustainable, low-carbon world.

Mark Carney, the UN Special Envoy for Climate Action and Finance, tells us that the objective for the finance sector is simple: every professional financial decision must take climate change into account. This requires not only institutions, but also individuals to align their professional activities and behaviour with this goal. Financial decisions are not taken by institutions, but by individuals – and it is individual finance professionals, not just sustainability professionals, who must embed green and sustainable finance principles and practice into their advice, analysis, actions and decisions if we are to lead a successful transition.

There is a wider perspective to sustainable finance beyond climate change, and indeed we cannot successfully address the climate emergency without addressing broader aspects of economic and social sustainability, as well as creating a more widely shared prosperity for current and future generations. Aligning the finance sector to support a wider set of societal goals, as expressed in the 17 United Nations Sustainable Development Goals, is equally important.

Recognizing the need to develop finance professionals' knowledge and skills of green and sustainable finance, the Chartered Banker Institute – the oldest institute of bankers in the world – launched the world's first benchmark Certificate in Green and Sustainable Finance in 2018. This book is based on an updated version of that programme. Our aim is to ensure that sustainability and stewardship sit alongside credit, risk, operations, technology and ethics as key aspects of financial professionalism for all working in the finance sector, so that every professional financial decision takes sustainability into account.

I am firmly convinced that embedding green and sustainable finance principles and practice offers wonderful opportunities for finance professionals, and the finance sector. For professionals it offers the opportunity to align work and careers with personal values and play an important societal role. For the finance sector, it provides not just significant commercial opportunities to finance the transition to a sustainable, low carbon world; it gives us the opportunity to demonstrate the very positive social purpose of finance and continue to rebuild trust in our finance profession.

ACKNOWLEDGEMENTS

I am extremely grateful to Jason Lowe, Dan Williams, Ailsa Barrow and Katrina MacNeill from the UK Met Office for providing the authoritative view of climate science that underpins much of this book. In addition, I would like to thank Dr Ben Caldecott from the Smith School of Enterprise and the Environment at the University of Oxford for his many contributions, expert advice and comments throughout; our colleagues from the Finance Innovation Lab (Gemma Bone, Anna Laycock, Laurie MacFarlane and Robert Nash) for their significant contributions to the original version of the book, many of which are still included; Olga Shchehrykovich for her comments on risk; Andrew Voysey for guidance on the development of the original Green and Sustainable Finance syllabus; and my colleagues at the Chartered Banker Institute, Lynn McLeod, Madhura Pradhan, David Kennedy and Mark Roberts, for their help developing the Green Finance Certificate for which this book was originally developed.

01

An introduction to green finance

LEARNING OBJECTIVES

On completion of this chapter you should be able to:

- Define green finance, and distinguish between green finance and related terms.
- Describe the typical characteristics of green finance approaches.
- Describe the challenges and opportunities for green finance.
- Describe the UN Sustainable Development Goals.
- Outline the development of the green finance sector globally.

Green finance is a growing phenomenon, with the global transition to a low-carbon economy estimated to require approximately $6 trillion per year for the foreseeable future.[1] For the finance sector, this is not only a commercial opportunity, but also fulfils a valuable social purpose by demonstrating commitment to participating in the transition to a low-carbon, more sustainable world. In this introductory chapter, we explore the dimensions of green finance and compare it to concepts such as sustainable finance and climate finance. We also introduce the UN Sustainable Development Goals, and briefly explore their links with green finance.

Green finance, sustainable finance and related terms

Green finance is one of a number of terms that are used to label activities related to the two-way interaction between the environment and finance and investment. Related terms include: responsible banking and responsible investment; environmental, social and governance (ESG); sustainable finance; and climate finance.

These terms are often treated synonymously, but there are differences in their scope, particularly whether they include social and governance issues:

Environmental issues relate to the quality and functioning of the natural environment and natural systems including: biodiversity loss; greenhouse gas emissions, renewable energy, energy efficiency, natural resource depletion or pollution; waste management; ozone depletion; changes in land use; ocean acidification and changes to the nitrogen and phosphorus cycles.

Social issues relate to the rights, well-being and interests of people and communities including human rights, labour standards, health and safety, relations with local communities, activities in conflict zones, health and access to medicine, consumer protection; and controversial weapons.

Economic issues relate to investee impacts on economic conditions at local, national and global levels. Performance areas include direct financial performance and risk, and indirect impacts such as through employment, supply chains and provision of infrastructure.

Governance issues relate to the management of investee entities. Issues include: board structure, size, diversity, skills and independence; executive pay; shareholder rights; stakeholder interaction; disclosure of information; business ethics; bribery and corruption; internal controls and risk management; and, in general, issues dealing with the relationship between a company's management, its board, its shareholders and its other stakeholders.[2]

Approaches that embrace the full range of these issues are more likely to be termed sustainable finance, responsible banking and/or responsible investment, whereas those that only focus on environmental issues are more likely to be termed green finance. Where the concern is only with preventing or responding to climate change, the term climate finance may be used. Climate finance is also used specifically to refer to the UN climate change negotiations (the Paris Climate Agreement) and the provision of aid from developed countries to developing countries to help with climate change mitigation and climate adaptation.

QUICK QUESTION

What do you see as the main differences between sustainable finance and green finance?

Advocates for a sustainable finance approach argue that it's not possible to separate the environment from society: society depends on the environment for its existence, and human society has a major impact on the environment. Many of today's most pressing environmental issues impact disproportionately on those with the fewest resources, in both high-income and low-income countries, and the need to improve standards of living and reduce inequality cannot be separated from the need to protect our environment. In 2015, the United Nations defined and adopted the Sustainable Development Goals (SDGs) to encourage governments, business and civil society to tackle these wider issues of sustainability. The SDGs are explained in more detail below.

A sustainable financial system is one that creates, values and transacts financial assets in ways that shape real wealth to serve the long-term needs of an inclusive, environmentally sustainable economy.[3]

Defining green finance

This book, initially written to support the Chartered Banker Institute's **Certificate in Green and Sustainable Finance**, is focused on green finance. Although the term is increasingly used by multinational bodies, governments, central banks and regulators, banks, investment funds, insurers and other financial institutions, finance professionals, academics and consumers, there is no single, agreed definition of what constitutes green finance. It can refer to some or all of: green products and services offered by financial institutions (eg green bonds), identifying and managing environmental and climate risks, organizational strategies, organizations themselves, investment sectors, industry initiatives and policy and regulatory instruments. This list is by no means exhaustive; as the green finance sector grows and becomes more mainstream, more and more activities are being promoted as green. Assessing the extent to which activities are truly green and avoiding greenwashing is a major theme of this book, and is covered in depth in subsequent chapters.

Some working definitions of green finance in the national and international context include:

G20 Green Finance Study Group: 'Financing of investments that provide environmental benefits in the broader context of environmentally sustainable development. These environmental benefits include, for example, reductions in air, water and land pollution, reductions in greenhouse gas (GHG) emissions, improved energy efficiency while utilizing existing natural resources, as well as mitigation of and adaptation to climate change and their co-benefits.'[4]

Organisation for Economic Co-operation and Development (OECD): Green finance is finance for 'achieving economic growth while reducing pollution and greenhouse gas emissions, minimizing waste and improving efficiency in the use of natural resources'.[5]

European Banking Federation: 'Green Finance includes, but is not limited to:

a. environmental aspects (pollution, greenhouse gas emissions, biodiversity, water or air quality issues); and

b. climate change-related aspects (energy efficiency, renewable energies, prevention and mitigation of climate change-connected severe events).'[6]

China State Council Guidelines for Establishing the Green Financial System: 'Financial services for economic activities that improve the environment remediation, address climate change, and enhance efficiency of resource utilization. These economic activities include the financing, operation and risk management for projects in areas such as environmental protection, energy savings, clean energy, green transportation, and green buildings.'[7]

Government of Germany: 'Green finance is a strategic approach to incorporate the financial sector in the transformation process towards low-carbon and resource-efficient economies, and in the context of adaptation to climate change.'[8]

UK Green Finance Initiative: 'Funding any means of reducing carbon emissions or raising resource efficiency... It incorporates green crowdfunding for small-scale, community schemes right up to green bond issuance for major infrastructure projects or corporate energy-efficiency schemes.'

QUICK QUESTION

What are the main similarities and differences between these definitions?

While these definitions all differ in their emphasis, they generally share some or all of the following elements:

- The role of finance in allocating capital for wider, more sustainable purposes, including mitigating the impacts of climate change.
- A focus on the use of investment to either benefit the environment or reduce harm.
- A concern to manage environmental risks, including climate risks facing the finance sector and society as a whole. Climate-related financial risks can be classed as physical, transition (including stranded asset) and liability risks, which we introduce in Chapter 3 and explore in more detail in Chapter 5.
- A recognition of the policies and infrastructure required to enable green finance, which we explore in Chapter 3.
- A broader context of sustainable development and/or economic growth, which we explore throughout this book.
- Examples of products, services, sectors and projects that may be supported by green finance, which we detail in Chapters 6 to 11.

Countries including Brazil and China have developed taxonomies that seek to define what a green product, service or outcome is, and is not. In 2017, the **European Union's (EU) High-Level Expert Group on Sustainable Finance** commissioned a study to consider different definitions of and approaches to defining green and sustainable finance.[9] In March 2018, the study's recommendations were incorporated into the EU's Action Plan: Financing Sustainable Growth, which established a Technical Expert Group (TEG) on sustainable finance to develop:

- an EU Taxonomy (classification system) to determine whether an economic activity is environmentally sustainable;
- an EU Green Bond Standard;
- benchmarks for low carbon investment strategies; and
- guidance to improve corporate disclosure of climate-related information.

The development of the EU Taxonomy for Sustainable Activities is seen by many as the most important and, potentially, far-reaching activity in the Action Plan. It is intended that the classification system – which will define and provide examples for what is green – will be embedded in EU law and provide a framework for many other features of the Action Plan. The Taxonomy will be used, for example, to determine which investments will qualify as being green in the context of the proposed EU Green Bond Standard; bonds that finance cleaner coal that are currently labelled as green by some issuers would be unlikely to qualify once this is introduced. Given the EU's reach and influence, the development, publication and implementation of the Taxonomy is likely to have a significant global impact and, over time, lead to the harmonization of definitions of green finance.

For the purpose of this book, however, we require a definition of green finance that combines aspects of the above and will be generally acceptable. For the Chartered Banker Institute, green finance encompasses the finance sector's strategic approach to meeting the challenges of climate change and the transition to a low-carbon world.

Green finance is, therefore:

> any financial initiative, process, product or service that is designed to protect the natural environment and support the transition to a sustainable, low-carbon world; and/or manage climate-related and other environmental risks impacting finance and investment.

This is a broad definition that acknowledges the different dimensions of the concept of green finance, while retaining an overarching focus on enhancing and sustaining the natural environment, and managing current and future environmental risks – particularly, but not exclusively, climate change. It highlights and recognizes the two-way nature of the relationship. Finance and investment can help or harm the environment, while the environment can also positively or negatively impact the performance of investments and financial services firms.

Mitigation and adaptation

Green finance supports projects and activities that aim to reduce greenhouse gas emissions and the rate of climate change (**climate change mitigation**) and to improve resilience to the effects of climate change (**climate change adaptation**). Climate change mitigation activities seek to address the causes of climate change, for example by funding renewable energy systems to reduce carbon emissions, or cleaner transport systems. Climate change adaptation activities address the impacts of climate change, both those that are already visible (eg measures to reduce coastal community flooding caused by rising sea levels) and those that are anticipated as a result of global warming (eg developing new agricultural crops and techniques to reduce water use and vulnerability to higher temperatures).

To date, the majority of green finance funding has tended to support climate change mitigation projects and activities. The Climate Policy Initiative reported that, of the $455 billion of climate finance in 2016, only an estimated $22 billion was focused on adaptation projects and activities.[10] Whilst there is inevitably some crossover between mitigation and adaptation projects (eg new, greener infrastructure may be sited further away from coastlines), and there is a lack of consistent reporting on mitigation versus adaptation, it is clear that the latter is currently underfunded. More recently, however, major green finance institutions, particularly the Multilateral Development Banks (MDBs), are placing much greater emphasis on climate change adaptation, with the World Bank committing to an equal weighting of mitigation and adaptation project finance in its most recent 2021 to 2025 strategic plan. This is covered in more detail in Chapter 8.

The dimensions of green finance

The breadth of the term green finance means that it can be used to refer to specific green financial products and services (eg green bonds, green loans), including those designed to both directly benefit the environment and to manage environmental risks, to organizational approaches and to industry sectors. In this book, we cover all of these, and briefly introduce them below.

Green finance products and services

Green finance covers a wide range of financial products and services, which can be broadly divided into banking, investment and insurance products. Examples of these include green bonds, green-tagged loans, green investment funds and climate risk insurance. We explore the different types of green finance products in more detail in Chapters 6 to 11.

But what makes a financial product green? In many cases the green aspect of the product relates to the asset, such as investments in clean energy projects or reforestation. In other cases, the features of the product are designed to encourage or reward environmentally friendly activity, such as mortgages that are discounted in line with a property's energy efficiency, or investment that links the sustainable management of resources with funding limits or collateral requirements.

Other products labelled green may not be universally accepted as such, for example:

- financial products (eg credit cards) that offer a donation to environmental protection work in reward for a certain level of spend;
- financial products that respond to an environmental issue (such as flood insurance) but do not seek to address the causes of this issue (such as climate change);
- financial products that minimize the environmental impacts of the provider's operations (such as using recycled paper) or offset the customer's normal activities (such as the carbon emissions generated by air travel).

Such products raise the question of where the boundary lies in terms of green finance. We explore this in more detail in subsequent chapters. For now, however, note that, from our definition of green finance above, it is clear that the core of the product, service or organization should be green and that the focus should be on protecting or improving natural systems, and managing environmental (physical, transition and liability) risks. These, and other key risks associated with green finance, are covered in more detail in Chapter 5.

Green finance as an organizational approach

QUICK QUESTION

Give examples of some financial services firms that have adopted green finance as an organizational approach.

Green finance principles can be applied not just at a product or individual process level, but also across an entire financial services organization. For some such organizations, such as Ecology Building Society, Naturesave Insurance or Banca Etica, environmental sustainability has been central to their strategy, culture and decision-making for many years. A growing number of large mainstream financial institutions are also incorporating green finance principles into some or all of their activities and this trend has been accelerating, particularly after the Paris Climate Agreement was signed in December 2015 (see Chapter 2). The development of the UN's Principles for Responsible Banking also encourages financial institutions to incorporate green and sustainable finance principles into their strategies and activities and link their business plans to societal goals as expressed in the UN Sustainable Development Goals and the Paris Agreement. The Principles for Responsible Banking are similar in many respects to the well-established UN-supported Principles for Responsible Investment (see Chapter 3) that have encouraged and supported many institutions in embedding green and sustainable finance principles into their investment and related activities.

This whole-organization approach to green finance is rooted in an understanding that the financial system both serves and relies on the economy, which itself serves society and is embedded in the environment. Such an embedded approach means that business decisions take into account not only the financial implications of the decision, but also the implications for the wider economy, society and the environment. This mindset can influence every area of the business, from operations and staff recruitment and development to investment strategy, product design and pricing, risk management, marketing and financial management. We explore green finance as a strategic approach further in later chapters.

Figure 1.1 The embedded approach to green finance

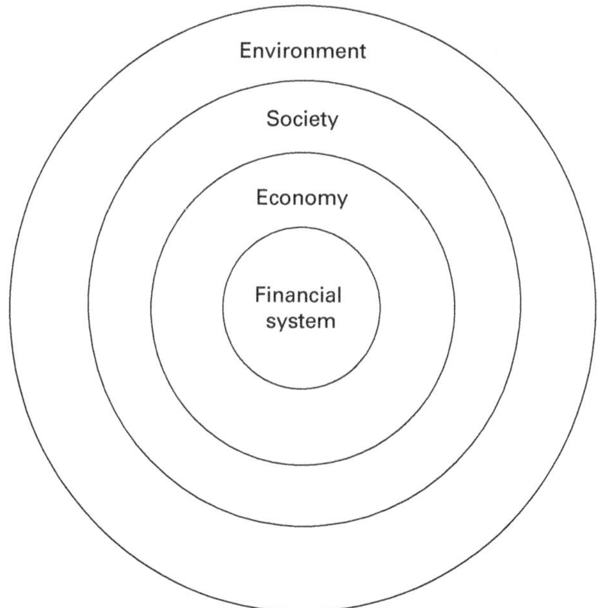

CASE STUDY

Ecology Building Society[11]

Ecology Building Society is dedicated to building a greener society by providing mortgages for properties and projects that respect the environment. It was established in 1981 by a group of pioneering founder members who wanted to help finance environmental building renovations and support sustainable development. By the end of 2018, its assets had reached nearly £180 million and net profit was just over £1 million. As a mutual, any surpluses are used for the benefit of the Society's members, which number nearly 10,000.

The Society's Memorandum states that its purpose is 'making loans which are secured on residential property and are funded substantially by its members… To promote, in carrying on any business or other activity, ecological policies designed to protect or enhance the environment in accordance with the principles of sustainable development.'

Ecology's mortgages incentivize lower-carbon lifestyles through a series of C-Change mortgage discounts linked to the energy efficiency of each property. Mortgage decisions are made on an individual basis, with careful consideration of the potential environmental benefits and impacts of each project.

Ecology's HQ building is designed to have an airtight structure, high levels of insulation and low energy requirements. Wherever possible, materials used in the building are from renewable sources, recycled or low toxicity. All of Ecology's electricity is sourced from renewables and it has offset the carbon emissions generated since it began in 1981.

Green industry sectors

QUICK QUESTION

Which industry (ie non-finance) sectors would you currently associate with green finance?

Most definitions of green finance focus on its role in directing investment towards green sectors – those that protect or enhance the environment. Some sectors are more universally accepted as green than others, as shown in Figure 1.2.

Figure 1.2 Commonly included green technologies

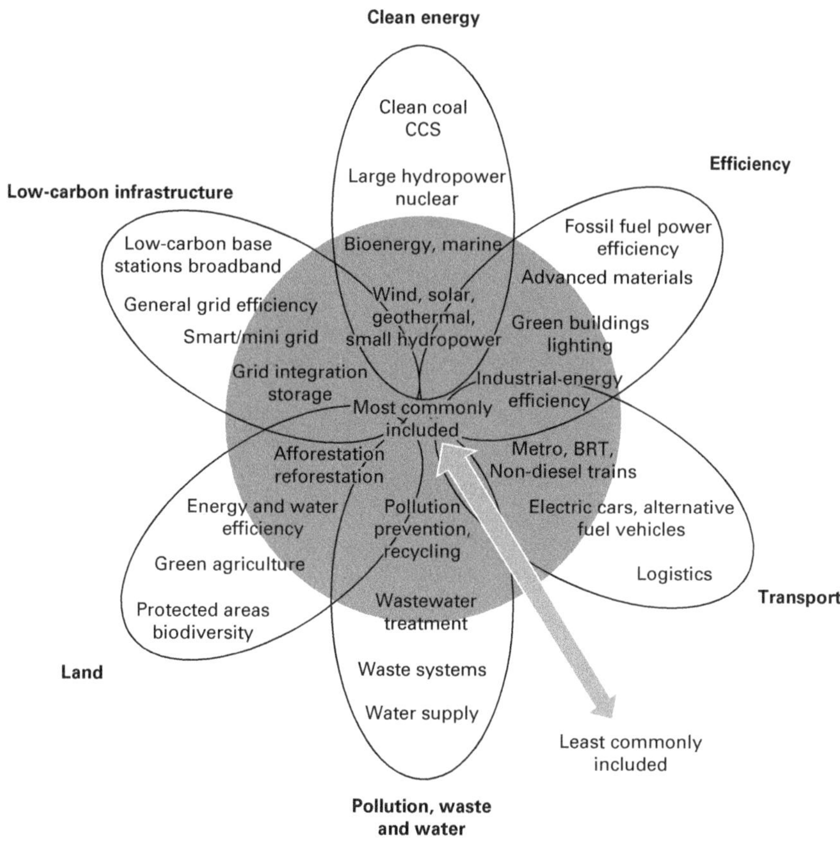

SOURCE UNEP Inquiry into the Design of a Sustainable Financial System. https://unepinquiry.org/

Areas that are usually accepted as green with little controversy include renewable energy production, distribution and storage, energy efficiency in domestic and industrial buildings, green transport, recycling, pollution prevention, water conservation and forestation. Areas that are more contested or infrequently cited include carbon capture and storage (CCS), nuclear energy and fossil fuel efficiency.

Finance can support green areas in a number of ways, for example by providing green bond financing or long-term loans for new renewable energy projects; by providing green mortgages that link repayments to home energy efficiency improvements; or by providing venture capital for innovative new storage technologies. Sometimes projects may have competing environmental and social impacts, and this can often lead to controversial financing decisions. New battery storage technologies, for example, may support the growth of solar or wind energy by providing the means to store and deliver power when weather conditions would not normally allow this, but may require the mining of rare minerals, causing significant environmental damage and social harm.

Finance can also play a role in encouraging and incentivizing firms or industry sectors to decarbonize by divesting, or threatening to divest, from firms or sectors perceived as damaging the environment. One of the better-known examples is Climate Action 100+, a group of investors that seeks to engage systemically important greenhouse gas emitters in order to encourage them to shift resources to clean and/or cleaner energy, thus supporting the goals of the Paris Climate Agreement.[12] In 2018, Royal Dutch Shell agreed to set short- and long-term carbon emissions targets linked to executive remuneration – the first of the large oil companies to do so. Shell aims to reduce its Net Carbon Footprint by approximately 50 per cent by 2050 and by approximately 20 per cent by 2035 as an interim step.[13] Earlier that year, Shell announced that divestment should be considered a material risk to its business. The divestment movement, and the decarbonization of investment portfolios, is covered in more detail in Chapter 9.

The challenges and opportunities for green finance

In later chapters, we will see how a range of man-made environmental issues affects our world, including climate change, habitat and biodiversity loss, air and water pollution, deforestation, soil erosion and water shortages. Overcoming these challenges, and supporting the transition to a sustainable, low-carbon world, requires very substantial capital. Estimates of the investment needed to achieve different (and sometimes overlapping) green objectives vary, and are presented in Table 1.1.

Table 1.1 Financing needs to achieve sustainability goals

Finance need*	Global investment required	Source of finance
To implement 'sustainable growth'	\$0.5–1.5 trillion a year by 2020 \$3–10 trillion a year by 2050	World Business Council for Sustainable Development (2010)
To achieve the Sustainable Development Goals (SDGs)	Incremental financing needs of \$1.4 trillion in low- and lower-middle-income countries by 2030	United Nations Association – UK (2016)

(continued)

Table 1.1 (Continued)

Finance need*	Global investment required	Source of finance
To achieve global sustainable development and climate objectives	$90 trillion in the next 15 years	G20
To meet the below 2°C target of the Paris Agreement	$65 trillion by 2035	International Energy Agency (IEA) (2014)
To transform global energy generation and simultaneously meet emission targets	$79 trillion by 2050 or $1.6 trillion per year	UN World Economic and Social Survey (2011) and Global Energy Assessment, World Economic Forum (2013)
To fully fund nations' green infrastructure requirements between now and 2030	$6 trillion per year	New Climate Economy (Sept 2016)
To deliver new renewable electric power generation to 2025	$6.9 trillion for business-as-usual scenario $12.1 trillion for 2°C or below scenario requirements	Bloomberg New Energy Finance (2016)
To complete developed to developing country flows for climate change adaptation and mitigation	$100 billion per year by 2020	UNFCCC (2010) Cancún decisions

SOURCE UK Green Finance Initiative
* These are different scopes of action and not an additive list

Whichever figures are chosen (and for the purposes of this book we use the $6 trillion per year figure used by the G20 and New Climate Economy[14]), these are very substantial amounts. The scale of investment required means that public funds alone will not be sufficient. The financial services sector therefore has a key role to play in mobilizing and directing private capital to support the necessary transition to a low-carbon world; it is estimated that up to 80 per cent of the funds required will need to come from private sources.

At the moment, however, finance often contributes to environmental problems, such as climate change and habitat destruction, rather than financing environmental solutions. For example:[15]

- Between 2014 and 2016, 37 of the biggest global banks provided a total of $57.92 billion for coal mining and $74.71 billion for coal power.

- From 2010 to 2015, large producers and traders of tropical agricultural products accused of significant deforestation received nearly $50 billion in loans and more than $20 billion through share and bond issues.

> **QUICK QUESTION**
>
> Why might financial decision-making not take environmental goals into account?

Our current financial system has three key characteristics that can contribute to environmental problems, rather than offer solutions:

- a bias towards short-termism in decision-making;
- a narrow focus on profit and shareholders;
- a failure to address externalities.

Short-termism

The time horizons in which financial institutions make decisions are often too short to consider the longer-term environmental effects of an investment or activity. This short-termism is intensified by the pressure to deliver positive, often quarterly results for shareholders. Short-termism can discourage financial institutions from investing in sectors that offer long-term value rather than short-term gain, and encourage them to discount the long-term risks of their activities, which often include environmental risks. Regulatory pressures to enhance liquidity can also dissuade financial institutions from offering products designed to build value over the long term.

The impacts of short-termism demonstrate the link between time horizons and different types of risk and reward. What might in the short term look productive, because of its immediate revenue potential, can in the long term be unproductive and unprofitable, because of its negative environmental impacts.

> What constitutes **productive** cannot be independent of a project's environmental and socio-economic impact because there are often trade-offs between short-term profits and long-term impact. What might appear to be a profitable project over a given time period could have negative impacts that might only become apparent in the longer term.[16]

Short-termism has particularly significant implications for responding to the climate challenge. While the worst impacts of climate change will most likely be felt by future generations, the measures needed to avoid catastrophic climate change and its impact on individuals, communities and the financial system are required urgently. This has been recognized by the Bank of England as an issue that may have significant effects on financial stability.

MARK CARNEY ON 'THE TRAGEDY OF THE HORIZON'[17]

The challenges currently posed by climate change pale in significance compared with what might come... So why isn't more being done to address it?

Climate change is the **Tragedy of the Horizon**.

We don't need an army of actuaries to tell us that the catastrophic impacts of climate change will be felt beyond the traditional horizons of most actors – imposing a cost on future generations that the current generation has no direct incentive to fix.

That means beyond:

- the **business cycle**;
- the **political cycle**; and
- the **horizon of technocratic authorities**, like central banks, who are bound by their mandates.

The horizon for monetary policy extends out to 2–3 years. For financial stability it is a bit longer, but typically only to the outer boundaries of the credit cycle – about a decade.

In other words, once climate change becomes a defining issue for financial stability, it may already be too late.

Narrow focus

Since the 1960s and the growth of the Chicago School of economics, the main purpose and role of business has been viewed by many as being to maximize returns to its shareholders. This idea has had a powerful effect on the conduct of business and approaches to the regulation of firms and to the economy as a whole. It is also a key assumption in many economic models used to inform policy.

This view of the role of business does not have a strict basis in company law, however. Like many powerful ideas, the focus on maximizing shareholder value is based on a certain subjective worldview. Others argue that the purpose of business should be much broader than simply maximizing shareholder return. As the economist Julie Nelson states:

> Case law has established that directors and managers of corporations have a fiduciary duty (duty of loyalty of care) to the corporation. This is often interpreted as requiring them to maximize returns to shareholders. Yet, if you look at the actual descriptions of the duties of directors, what you find is a requirement that they must act 'in a manner… reasonably believed to be in the best interests of the corporation'… [I]t does not specify that the corporation is the shareholders only, nor that serving the 'interests of the corporation' means maximizing profit…
>
> It is my tribe, economists, who are the source of this fixation with *maximization*… While legislators and judges have… generally been rather vague about the purpose(s) of business, mainstream economists have been vociferous in popularizing the idea that firms have a single, simple, and (conveniently!) quantifiable goal.[18]

If financial institutions make decisions based on maximizing shareholder returns as the sole motivation, there is a high risk that such decisions may lead to unintended consequences, including damage to the environment. This may happen in three ways:

- Only financial risk and reward is considered, and so environmental damage is not considered relevant to the decision.
- Those who are affected by the environmental consequences of an investment are not shareholders, and so are not counted as relevant to the decision.
- A focus on profit maximization combines with short-termism, and so the impact of environmental damage on future profits is not considered relevant to the decision.

The implications of a profit maximization approach are not always apparent, because they are cumulative (eg pollution of water caused by the release of industrial chemicals) or not immediately visible (eg climate change caused by the burning of fossil fuels). Industrial accidents and environmental disasters, such as a major oil spillage, however, can bring the dangers of profit maximization to the fore.

More recently, there have been calls for businesses (including financial institutions) to move to a stakeholder value approach. The stakeholder value approach sees the role of business as generating value for all of the stakeholders it serves, including its customers, employees, suppliers, shareholders and the wider community. Some even argue that future generations should be considered as a key stakeholder group, and this has particularly important implications for longer-term environmental issues such as climate change.

A stakeholder value approach has parallels with the embedded model of the financial system we saw in Figure 1.1, in that a financial institution is embedded in society and serves not only its shareholders, but also a wide range of different actors within and beyond the financial system (Figure 1.3).

QUICK QUESTION

Who are the key stakeholders for your organization? Be as specific as possible.

Figure 1.3 The stakeholder value approach

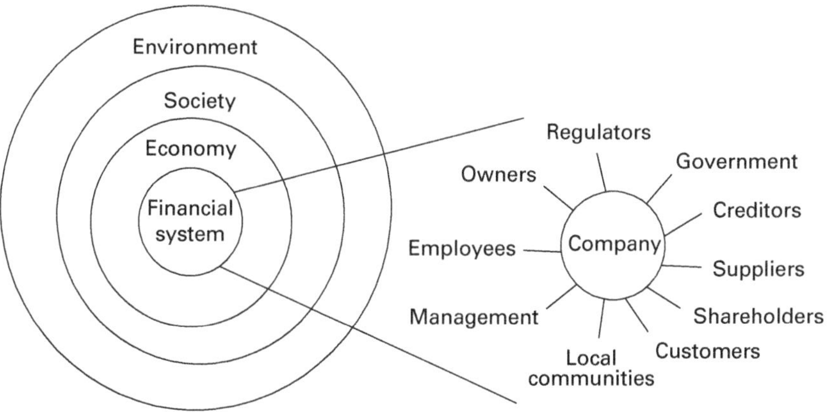

Externalities

> Externalities is the term economists use when they talk about the side effects – or in the positive case, the spillover effects – of a business's operations. They're the impacts that a business has on its broader milieu, either directly or indirectly, but is not obliged to pay for or otherwise take into account in its decision-making.[19]

Imagine a factory produces waste chemicals that slowly drain into a local stream. Downstream, the water gradually becomes unfit for consumption and uninhabitable for aquatic life. Yet the cost of cleaning up the river does not, in many cases, fall to the factory. This is because the factory treats the pollution as an externality – something that is external to its decision-making because the costs are hidden or borne by someone else (in this case, probably, the local community or environment agency).

Externalities are not necessarily negative, however: investing in green public transport systems, for example, can enhance the health of the local community by encouraging them to walk or cycle more.

Externalities mean that when financial institutions assess the risks and rewards of a decision using criteria rooted in maximizing shareholder returns, other factors, including environmental costs, are often not considered. This leads to investment in sectors and projects that generate pollution, carbon emissions, habitat destruction, and other environmental damage. Externalities are linked to a short-term focus (since many environmental effects are not apparent in the short term) and profit maximization (since damage that does not directly affect profits is discounted). Failure to consider externalities may also contribute to the risk of investing in assets that may subsequently become substantially impaired or stranded, as we shall see in later chapters.

Negative externalities may be addressed through enhanced measurement and quantification of climate-related and other environmental impacts, regulation to prevent the most harmful activities, taxes to fund environmental protection and restoration, and public pressure for companies to internalize the cost of their externalities. The identification, measurement and disclosure of climate-related financial risks is a major focus for global regulators. The work and impact of the global Task Force on Climate-related Financial Disclosures (TCFD) in this regard is discussed in Chapter 5.

Opportunities for financial services organizations of a green approach

A green approach to finance can help financial institutions, and the financial system overall, to overcome the challenges of short-termism, narrow focus and externalities, potentially leading to a range of positive outcomes for the organization, its customers, staff, supply chain and other partners – and for our planet as a whole. As we shall see throughout this book, there is a wide range of benefits for institutions adopting a green finance approach, including:

- Reputation and relationships:
  - Enhanced reputation and credibility – helping to demonstrate finance's social purpose and reconnecting banks and society.
  - Stronger, values-based relationships with governments, communities, customers, investors, partners and suppliers.
- Markets:
  - Access to new markets – including new partnerships with governments and communities.
  - Opportunity to improve competitive position and attract new customers through differentiation.
  - Opportunity to develop and market innovative green products and services.
  - Greater resilience to market disruption caused by climate change.
- Operations:
  - Opportunity to decrease risk across portfolios, by avoiding concentration in areas of high environmental risk (such as fossil fuels).
  - Greater resilience to the operational impact of climate change.
  - Increased valuation through resilience planning.
  - More efficient operations, including energy efficiency, resource minimization and reuse, reduced water usage, and adoption of new technologies.
- Regulatory:
  - Potentially lower capital weightings for green assets and higher weightings for 'brown' assets.
  - Preparedness for regulatory and policy changes (eg increased disclosure, stress testing, including climate change scenarios).

- Customers:
  - Managing changing customer preferences, leading to new product and service opportunities.
  - Longer-term, less transactional relationships with customers based on values rather than price.
  - Greater satisfaction – the feel-good factor.
- Staff:
  - Greater ability to attract and retain younger generations who see sustainable values as an important part of their personal and working lives.
  - Greater staff satisfaction and employee engagement from enhanced sense of purpose.
  - Enhanced working environments.
- Partners and supply chains:
  - Increased resilience of the supply chain (less affected by environmental issues).
  - Incentives for partners to enhance the sustainability of their own operations and supply chains.
  - Longer-term relationships with suppliers based on shared purpose and values.

The UN Sustainable Development Goals

As we discussed earlier in this chapter, a broader approach to sustainable finance and development encompasses, but goes beyond green finance to include issues of economic and social equality and justice. Some argue that economic, social and environmental issues are inextricably linked, and that genuine sustainable development (ie meeting the needs of the present without compromising the ability of future generations to meet their own needs) is impossible without considering these wider aspects.

The UN Sustainable Development Goals (SDGs) were defined and adopted by 193 countries in 2015 to encourage governments, business and civil society to tackle these wider issues of sustainability. The 17 Goals are shown in Table 1.2. They set out what the UN perceives as the major economic, environmental and social challenges faced by our world. As can be seen, these go beyond the challenges of climate change mitigation and adaptation, and support of the transition to a low-carbon world addressed by green finance, in that green finance principles and practice are wholly aligned to the holistic approach to sustainability promoted by the SDGs. As we shall see throughout this book, there are many overlaps, for example a Sustainability Bond may support a range of project outcomes aligned to the SDGs, including a range of climate change adaptation and mitigation measures.

Table 1.2 The 17 United Nations Sustainable Development Goals

Goal 1	End poverty in all its forms everywhere
Goal 2	End hunger, achieve food security and improved nutrition and promote sustainable agriculture
Goal 3	Ensure healthy lives and promote well-being for all at all ages
Goal 4	Ensure inclusive and equitable quality education and promote lifelong learning opportunities for all
Goal 5	Achieve gender equality and empower all women and girls
Goal 6	Ensure availability and sustainable management of water and sanitation for all
Goal 7	Ensure access to affordable, reliable, sustainable and modern energy for all
Goal 8	Promote sustained, inclusive and sustainable economic growth, full and productive employment and decent work for all
Goal 9	Build resilient infrastructure, promote inclusive and sustainable industrialization and foster innovation
Goal 10	Reduce inequality within and among countries
Goal 11	Make cities and human settlements inclusive, safe, resilient and sustainable
Goal 12	Ensure sustainable consumption and production patterns
Goal 13	Take urgent action to combat climate change and its impacts
Goal 14	Conserve and sustainably use the oceans, seas and marine resources for sustainable development
Goal 15	Protect, restore and promote sustainable use of terrestrial ecosystems, sustainably manage forests, combat desertification, halt and reverse land degradation, and halt biodiversity loss
Goal 16	Promote peaceful and inclusive societies for sustainable development, provide access to justice for all and build effective, accountable and inclusive institutions at all levels
Goal 17	Strengthen the means of implementation and revitalize the global partnership for sustainable development

The 17 SDGs, with a deadline of 2030, are not legally binding, but countries, business and others are expected to take ownership of the goals and establish national or other frameworks for achieving them. For example:

- In Scotland, the new National Performance Framework, published by the Scottish Government in 2018, incorporates the SDGs in a 'vision for national well-being' in Scotland.
- Carlsberg's 'Together Towards ZERO' programme seeks to significantly improve the organization's sustainability to enhance business performance and reduce impact on the environment and society. Carlsberg focuses its efforts on seven SDGs where it believes it can have the greatest impact: 3, 6, 7, 8, 12, 13 and 17.
- ANZ (Australia and New Zealand Banking Group Limited) has developed an SDG Bond Framework and will issue bonds where proceeds will contribute to SDGs 3, 4, 6, 7, 9, 11 and 12.

QUICK QUESTION

Which of the SDGs are most relevant, in your view, for the finance sector?

As with supporting the transition to a low-carbon world, substantial investment will be required to achieve the SDGs in full, most of which will need to come from the private rather than the public sector. A key challenge cited by the UN is how to mobilize capital to achieve these goals.

Achieving and financing the SDGs will require a shift in business models, both in financial services institutions and business more broadly, including a deeper recognition of the investment chain connecting the finance sector with broad issues of sustainability.

Financial institutions can support the achievement of the SDGs in a number of ways:

1. Ensuring investment decisions incorporate, as a minimum, environmental, social and governance factors, or, more preferably, linking desired investment outcomes with the SDGs.
2. Explicitly aligning definitions of fiduciary duty with sustainable development.
3. Engaging with companies they hold a stake in, either individually or as part of a coalition.
4. Providing debt finance for SDG solutions.

5 Promoting access to finance for individual entrepreneurs and small enterprises seeking to support the SDGs.

6 Developing innovative financial products and processes that allow people to invest in line with the SDGs, reduce the costs of doing so, and strengthen governance where needed.

7 Ensuring that their operations and wider business activities support, rather than detract from, the achievement of the SDGs.

CASE STUDY

Triodos and the triple bottom line[20]

Triodos Bank is a global pioneer in sustainable banking, using the power of finance to support projects that benefit people and the planet. Its approach is based on the fundamental belief that economic activity can and should have a positive impact on society, the environment and culture. Triodos values people, planet and profit – the triple bottom line – and takes all three into account in its strategy, structure, lending and culture.

Founded in 1980, Triodos is overseen by a supervisory board and its shares are administered by a separate Foundation, both of which aim to balance the needs of all of Triodos' stakeholders. It has branches in the Netherlands, UK, Germany, Spain and Belgium, and in 2018 had assets under management of €15.5 billion.

Triodos only lends to organizations that create real social, environmental and cultural value – charities, social businesses, community projects and environmental initiatives. As part of the application review process, Triodos applies its own strict social and environmental lending criteria, and publishes a full list of all the organizations it lends to.

Forty per cent of its loans are in the environmental sector; by the end of 2018 it was financing 513 projects, contributing to a generating capacity of 3,800 MW of energy – enough to avoid 2.9 million tonnes of CO_2 emissions. It also financed 35,000 hectares of organic farmland and 30,000 hectares of nature and conservation land across Europe.

Green finance today

Green finance is a fast-growing sector that will continue to grow rapidly and will in time become part of the mainstream of finance.

As we saw above, there is a wide range of estimates for the costs of the transition to a low-carbon world, requiring very substantial investment for many years, until at least 2050. Using the figures from the G20 and New Climate Economy quoted above, approximately $6 trillion per year will be required, with some two-thirds of this needing to be deployed in developing countries. According to the Climate Policy Initiative, however, approximately $500 billion of investment in climate change mitigation and adaptation was deployed in 2017. There is, therefore, a very substantial investment gap, and the major part of investment opportunity (estimated at some 80 per cent of the total) will need to come from the private sector in the coming years. It is unsurprising, therefore, that the green finance market is growing quickly, and the pace of policy and regulatory development advances at a similar pace.

Recent market developments

- The World Economic Forum's *Global Risks Report 2020* ranked climate change – and specifically the risk of failing to take action on climate change – as the key risk faced by business, finance and society over the next decade.[21]
- The green bond market grew to approximately $230 billion in 2019, a substantial (36 per cent) increase on the previous year, according to data from the Climate Bonds Initiative, with issuers including sovereign states, multilateral development banks, municipalities and corporates.
- Countries are beginning to issue sovereign green bonds, with the first issued by Poland in 2016 and subsequently followed by France (with the largest issue of $7 billion), Fiji, Nigeria, Indonesia and Belgium.
- The US was the largest issuer of green bonds globally in 2018 ($34.1 billion) with China the second largest ($30.9 billion).
- Indonesia issued the first sovereign green sukuk in US dollars in March 2018, raising $1.25 billion, following the launch of the first green sukuk by Malaysia the previous year.
- The European Investment Bank provided more than €19.6 billion to green finance projects in 2017, nearly 30 per cent of its total financing.
- The Asian Development Bank announced that it will invest $80 billion from 2019 to 2030 to combat climate change.
- Green mortgages are now available in countries including the US, UK, Sweden and Australia, with National Australia Bank issuing the world's first Residential Mortgage-Backed Securitization, including a certified

green tranche of AUD 300 million, meeting criteria for low-carbon residential buildings.

- Climate Action 100+ investors manage over $47 trillion of assets.
- Sustainable, responsible or ethical investing now accounts for approximately 26 per cent of assets under management globally (almost $23 trillion) according to the Global Sustainable Investment Alliance (GSIA).
- Assets under management in ESG funds worldwide rose in 2018 to $1.05 trillion, increasing from $655 billion in 2012. BlackRock, the world's largest asset manager, launched a range of exchange-traded funds (ETFs) that invest based on ESG criteria in October 2018.
- 59 green finance centres (2018) are identified in the Global Green Finance Index survey, rising from 47 the previous year.
- 92 per cent of the world's largest banks are members of the UNEP Finance Initiative.

Recent regulatory and policy developments

- The UN launched the Principles for Responsible Banking in September 2019, supported by 130 banks representing more than $47 trillion in assets.
- In March 2018 the EU published the Action Plan: Financing Sustainable Growth, which saw the development of the EU Taxonomy for Sustainable Activities.
- As of September 2018, 513 organizations had expressed their support for the Task Force on Climate-related Financial Disclosures (TCFD) recommendations for consistent, climate-related financial risk disclosures for use by companies in providing information to investors, lenders, insurers and other stakeholders.
- In December 2018, the US Alliance for Sustainable Finance (USASF) was launched by 15 large banks and asset managers, aiming to identify and streamline existing climate-finance initiatives, encourage greater transparency across climate-related financial risks and opportunities, and encourage more capital for sustainable investments.
- 400 global asset managers representing $32 trillion in assets launched the Investor Agenda in September 2018 to support investors as they scale up investments tackling climate change, and to showcase the actions some investors are already taking to improve their climate-related decision-making and risk reporting.

- The development of a national green finance system for China has been publicly endorsed by President Xi and the State Council, supported by 220 of China's largest financial institutions, representing nearly 75 per cent of China's assets under management.
- The People's Bank of China has incorporated green bonds and green loans into Macro-Prudential Assessments, and in June 2018 announced an expansion of the Medium-term Lending Facility to include green loans and green bonds.
- The Bank of England has announced that it is considering the inclusion of the impact of climate change in its UK bank stress tests 'exploratory scenario' in 2019.

As can be seen, green finance is growing rapidly, and there are very significant commercial opportunities for banks, investment funds, insurers and other financial services organizations to support the transition to a low-carbon world. Despite rapid growth in recent years, however, there is still a very substantial investment gap. The scale of the challenge is beyond that of public finances alone, and, given the commitments made by the majority of national governments, a significant increase in support from the financial services sector is required to achieve the objectives set. The scale of the challenge and speed of response required has grown since the announcement of the 2015 Paris Agreement target of limiting global warming to less than 2 degrees, which would require reducing emissions to net zero by 2070, along with the October 2018 Intergovernmental Panel on Climate Change (IPCC) report recommending limiting global temperature rises to 1.5 degrees.

This is not only a commercial opportunity for the financial services sector, however. Importantly, it is also an opportunity for the sector to demonstrate its social purpose, by playing a key role in the transition to a low-carbon economy and a more sustainable world. By supporting activities, organizations and industries that can mitigate climate change and help individuals and communities adapt to the effects of climate change, financial services organizations can help solve some of the world's, and local communities', greatest challenges.

International and national institutions, and financial services firms large and small, have key roles to play in addressing these challenges and supporting the transition to a low-carbon world. Individual finance professionals also have a vital role. As we will explore in Chapter 12, change is ultimately led by individuals, and the changes needed to embed and mainstream green finance principles and practice within financial services requires finance professionals with the relevant knowledge and skills to be able to develop and deploy products, services and tools that can mobilize capital to support the transition. Enhancing the role of the individual Green and Sustainable Finance Professional, and developing a global network of Green and Sustainable Finance Professionals, is key to mainstreaming green finance.

There is a long way to go before green finance achieves the mainstream scale and effectiveness necessary to address our biggest environmental challenges. Banks and investors still provide significant amounts of funding to environmentally destructive activities, including the burning of fossil fuels, that are contributing to potentially catastrophic climate change. In the next chapter we will explore the scale of such environmental challenges, the science underpinning climate change and the connections between these and the financial sector.

QUICK QUESTION

What might be the key barriers to green finance becoming more widespread?

Key concepts

In this chapter we considered:

- the various definitions of green finance, and the difference between green finance and related terms;
- some of the typical characteristics of green finance approaches;
- the challenges and opportunities for green finance;
- the UN Sustainable Development Goals (SDGs), and their links with green finance;
- some indicators of the development of the green finance sector globally.

Now go back through this chapter and make sure you fully understand each point.

Review

There is no fixed definition of green finance, but most definitions focus on the role of the financial system in supporting the environment, preventing environmental damage and managing environmental risks.

Green finance is one of a number of terms that are used to label the broad area of finance that aims to protect or enhance the environment. There is an important difference between the scope of the terms: for example, sustainable finance considers not just environmental but also social, economic and governance issues. Advocates for a sustainable finance approach argue that it is not possible to separate the environment from society.

For the purpose of this book, we define green finance as 'any financial initiative, process, product or service that is designed to protect the natural environment and support the transition to a sustainable, low-carbon world; and/or manage climate-related and other environmental risks impacting finance and investment'. This is a broad definition that focuses on enhancing and sustaining the natural environment, and managing current and future environmental risks.

Green finance products and services include those that channel capital to those green industry sectors that design products and services in order to reward environmentally friendly activity, and that support the effective management of physical and transition risks. The most commonly cited green industry sectors include renewable energy production, distribution and storage, energy efficiency in domestic and industrial buildings, green transport, recycling, pollution prevention, water conservation, agriculture, aquaculture and forestry.

Green finance supports both climate change mitigation and adaptation projects and activities. The former seek to address the causes of climate change, for example by funding renewable energy systems, while climate change adaptation activities address the impacts of climate change, for example measures to reduce coastal community flooding caused by rising sea levels.

Green finance can also be a whole-organization approach, driving strategy, culture and business processes throughout a financial services firm. This is often tied to an environmentally focused corporate mission and an understanding of the financial sector as embedded in the economy, society and the environment. At present, however, the financial sector as a whole is not green. Institutions still provide significant amounts of funding to environmentally destructive activities, including the burning of fossil fuels. Our current financial system has three key characteristics that tend to contribute to environmental problems:

- a bias towards short-termism in decision-making;
- a narrow focus on profit and shareholders;
- a failure to address externalities.

Supporting the transition to a sustainable, low-carbon world requires very substantial capital. Estimates of the investment needed vary, but a figure of $6 trillion per year has been suggested by the G20 and New Climate Economy. The scale of investment required means that public funds alone will not be sufficient. The financial services sector has a key role to play in mobilizing and directing private capital to support the transition; it is estimated that up to 80 per cent of the funds required will need to come from private sources.

The UN Sustainable Development Goals (SDGs) set out the major environmental, social and economic challenges faced by our world. These go beyond the challenges of climate change mitigation and adaptation, and supporting the transition to a low-carbon world in that green finance principles and practice are wholly aligned to the holistic approach to sustainability promoted by the SDGs.

Green finance is a growing global phenomenon and represents a very significant opportunity for the financial services sector. This is not only a commercial opportunity, but also an opportunity for the sector to demonstrate its social purpose, by playing a key role in the transition to a low-carbon, more sustainable world.

Glossary

Afforestation/reforestation: Afforestation means the establishment of forests where previously they did not exist, while reforestation means the re-establishment of forests where they previously existed, either through direct planting or natural growth.

Biodiversity: The full range of ecosystems, species and gene pools in the environment – the full variety of plant and animal life on Earth.

Biodiversity and habitat protection: Biodiversity protection aims to preserve the full range of ecosystems, species and gene pools in the environment – the full variety of life on Earth. Habitat protection aims to conserve, protect and restore the natural environments that sustain these plants and animals.

Climate change adaptation: Projects and activities that aim to improve resilience to the effects of climate change.

Climate change mitigation: Projects and activities that aim to reduce greenhouse gas emissions and the rate of climate change.

De-carbonization: Reducing the amount of carbon (eg carbon dioxide or methane) emitted from an agricultural, industrial or other process.

Divestment: The opposite of an investment, eg selling rather than buying an asset such as shares in a firm.

Embedded approach: An approach that sees the financial system as embedded in the economy, society and the environment.

Emissions reduction and capture: Emission reduction technologies aim to reduce the CO_2 produced by energy generation, transport and industrial processes. Emissions capture tends to refer to carbon capture and storage (CCS) – technology to capture CO_2 emissions produced in electricity generation and industrial processes.

Energy distribution: Most energy is distributed through a grid (an interconnected network for transmitting power). Green energy distribution tends to focus on the integration of renewable energy into the main grid, distributed generation, microgrids (running separately from the main grid), and smart grids that detect and react to changes in energy usage.

Energy efficiency: Energy efficiency means reducing the amount of energy that is required to provide a product or service, and is often applied to buildings (domestic, commercial and industrial), appliances and vehicles.

Energy storage: Renewable energy storage is key to enabling an increase in the take-up and efficiency of renewables, and can include mechanical storage (eg pumped water), batteries and thermal energy storage.

Fossil fuels: Fuel that is formed from the decayed remains of plants or animals, such as coal and oil.

Green buildings: Green buildings are designed, built and used in a way that is energy efficient, minimizes the use of resources and water, encourages biodiversity and provides a healthy indoor environment.

Green finance: Any financial initiative, process, product or service that is designed to protect the natural environment and support the transition to a sustainable, low-carbon world; and/or manage climate-related and other environmental risks impacting finance and investment.

Green transport: Green transport minimizes CO_2 and other harmful emissions, uses renewable energy, is energy efficient and supports sustainable communities. The term can refer to public transport systems and infrastructure and private vehicles.

Greenwashing: Making false, misleading or unsubstantiated claims about the positive environmental impact of a product, service or activity.

Intergovernmental Panel on Climate Change (IPCC): The United Nations body that assesses the science related to climate change. The IPCC provides regular assessments of the scientific basis of climate change, its impacts and future risks, and options for adaptation and mitigation.

Net Carbon Footprint: Total greenhouse gas emissions associated with the production, processing and consumption of products and services, offset by activities to mitigate emissions, such as carbon capture and storage.

Paris Climate Agreement: In December 2015 countries agreed to combat climate change and to accelerate and intensify the actions and investments needed to support the transition to a low-carbon world. The Agreement's central aim is to strengthen the global response to the threat of climate change by keeping a global temperature rise in the 21st century below 2°C above pre-industrial levels and to pursue greater efforts to limit the temperature increase to 1.5°C. The Agreement entered into force in November 2016, after countries accounting in total for at least 55% of total global greenhouse gas emissions ratified the Agreement.

Pollution control: Pollution control aims to reduce or avoid the release of harmful substances into the environment, including the air, water and soil. Pollution can also be defined by the type of pollutant, including plastic pollution and thermal pollution.

Renewable energy: Energy that comes from a source that is not depleted when it is used, or is naturally replenished within a human timescale. This includes solar, wind, geothermal, tidal, wave, hydroelectric and biomass power.

Stakeholder value approach: An approach that sees the role of business as generating value for all the stakeholders it serves.

Tragedy of the horizon: The mismatch between business, political and regulatory cycles, and the timescale needed to prevent climate change impacting on financial stability.

UN Sustainable Development Goals: 17 objectives agreed by 193 countries in 2015 to address the major environmental, social and economic challenges of our time.

Waste reduction and management: Waste reduction aims to minimize the amount of waste produced by individuals, households and organizations, including through resource efficiency and reuse. Waste management involves the collection, treatment, recycling, reprocessing and disposal of waste.

Water conservation: Water conservation aims to sustainably manage freshwater resources and prevent water pollution in nearby lakes, rivers and local watersheds.

Notes

1 Green Finance Initiative (2016) *Globalising Green Finance*, City of London Corporation Research Report [Online] https://www.cbd.int/financial/gcf/uk-hubgreenfinance.pdf (archived at https://perma.cc/4FBA-GXMV)

2 M Forstater and N N Zhang (2016) *Definitions and Concepts: Background note*, Inquiry: Design of a Sustainable Financial System, Working Paper 16/13, UNEP [Online] http://wedocs.unep.org/bitstream/handle/20.500.11822/10603/definitions_concept.pdf?sequence=1&isAllowed=y (archived at https://perma.cc/6AKS-5G4T)

3 UNEP (2015) *The Financial System We Need*, Inquiry: Design of a Sustainable Financial System, UNEP [Online] http://unepinquiry.org/wp-content/uploads/2015/11/The_Financial_System_We_Need_Policy_Summary_EN.pdf (archived at https://perma.cc/4Q48-CFLN)

4 G20 Green Finance Study Group (2016) *G20 Green Finance Synthesis Report*, UNEP [Online] http://unepinquiry.org/wp-content/uploads/2016/09/Synthesis_Report_Full_EN.pdf (archived at https://perma.cc/UBS8-NH2N)

5 OECD (nd) *Green Finance and Investment*, OECD iLibrary [Online] https://www.oecd-ilibrary.org/fr/environment/green-finance-and-investment_24090344#:~:text=Green%20growth%20means%20achieving%20economic,term%20investment%20and%20sustained%20financing (archived at https://perma.cc/84AG-3ERW)

6 European Banking Federation (2017) *Towards a Green Finance Framework*, European Banking Federation [Online] https://www.ebf.eu/wp-content/uploads/2017/09/Geen-finance-complete.pdf (archived at https://perma.cc/T9AD-P9MR)

7 The People's Bank of China (2016) Guidelines for establishing the green financial system [Online] http://enrccef.cufe.edu.cn/info/1002/1171.htm (archived at https://perma.cc/42HG-NSMG)

8 Deutsche Gesellschaft für Internationale Zusammenarbeit (GIZ) (2011) *Green Finance: An innovative approach to fostering sustainable economic development and adaptation to climate change* [Online] https://www.greengrowthknowledge.org/sites/default/files/downloads/resource/Green_finance_GIZ.pdf (archived at https://perma.cc/ZT8Q-4FJS)

9 W Kahlenborn *et al* (2017) Defining green in the context of green finance, Publications Office of the European Union [Online] https://publications.europa.eu/en/publication-detail/-/publication/0d44530d-d972-11e7-a506-01aa75ed71a1/language-en (archived at https://perma.cc/9TPU-ECN5)

10 P Oliver, A Clark and C Meattle (2018) *Global Climate Finance: An updated view 2018*, Climate Policy Initiative [Online] https://climatepolicyinitiative.org/wp-content/uploads/2018/11/Global-Climate-Finance-An-Updated-View-2018.pdf (archived at https://perma.cc/UZN2-PX36)

11 Ecology Building Society (nd) [Online] https://www.ecology.co.uk/ (archived at https://perma.cc/V8PT-VEAB)

12 Climate Action 100 (nd) [Online] http://www.climateaction100.org/ (archived at https://perma.cc/L96P-VUHY)

13 Shell (nd) Our climate ambition [Online] https://www.shell.com/energy-and-innovation/the-energy-future/shells-ambition-to-be-a-net-zero-emissions-energy-business.html (archived at https://perma.cc/92VL-RBNB)

14 Green Finance Initiative (2016) Globalising green finance, City of London Corporation Research Report [Online] https://www.cbd.int/financial/gcf/uk-hubgreenfinance.pdf (archived at https://perma.cc/4FBA-GXMV)

15 Green Finance Initiative (2016) Globalising green finance, City of London Corporation Research Report [Online] https://www.cbd.int/financial/gcf/uk-hubgreenfinance.pdf (archived at https://perma.cc/4FBA-GXMV)

16 D Schoenmaker (2017) *Investing for the Common Good*, Bruegel Essay and Lecture Series [Online] http://bruegel.org/wp-content/uploads/2017/07/From-traditional-to-sustainable-finance_ONLINE.pdf (archived at https://perma.cc/C7DN-P5FG)

17 Bank of England (2015) Breaking the tragedy of the horizon: Climate change and financial stability, Speech by Mark Carney [Online] https://www.bankofengland.co.uk/speech/2015/breaking-the-tragedy-of-the-horizon-climate-change-and-financial-stability (archived at https://perma.cc/EKF6-6Z6V)

18 J Nelson (2018) *Economics for Humans*, University of Chicago Press, Chicago, p123

19 C Meyer and J Kirby (2010) The big idea: Leadership in the age of transparency, *Harvard Business Review*, April

20 Triodos Bank (nd) [Online] https://www.triodos.co.uk (archived at https://perma.cc/BRF9-2K7Z)

21 World Economic Forum (2020) *The Global Risks Report 2020* [Online] www3.weforum.org/docs/WEF_Global_Risk_Report_2020.pdf (archived at https://perma.cc/A6N9-U4QJ)

02

Green finance in our changing world

LEARNING OBJECTIVES

On completion of this chapter you should be able to:

- Describe the major factors in the science of climate change and global warming, and outline current IPCC assessments of future scenarios.
- Describe our changing environment and the risks and opportunities for the finance sector arising from these.
- Explain the nature of stranded assets and the carbon bubble, and describe the challenges these present.
- Outline how the finance sector can support the transition to a green economy.

In this chapter, written with the generous help and assistance of climate science experts from the UK Met Office, we examine the science of climate change and its impact on our planet. Green and Sustainable Finance Professionals need to understand this in order to design, develop, implement and monitor investments to support climate change mitigation, adaptation and the transition to a sustainable, low-carbon world.

Science shows that human activities are having unprecedented effects on the environment, including the global climate. The finance sector has a substantial impact on the environment, both directly and indirectly, through investment choices, and is also affected significantly by climate change. While climate change may have a negative impact on investment, particularly due to the risks of asset impairment and stranding, there are also opportunities for investment, as well as for new products and services designed to support the transition to a sustainable, low-carbon world.

Our changing planet

Our planet – and the people, animals and plants forming life on our planet – is impacted by a wide and interlinked range of environmental factors, caused and/or accelerated by human activity, including:

- Climate change: Large-scale, long-term shifts in the planet's weather patterns and average temperatures.
- Habitat loss: Destruction or damage to habitats, which means that they are no longer able to support the species previously sustained.
- Biodiversity loss: Extinction of species at local or global level, leading to reduction in the variety of plant and animal life.
- Poor air quality: Increasing natural or man-made pollution, making the air unhealthy or toxic for humans, plants and animals.
- Poor water quality: Deterioration in the extent to which water is clean and healthy for human, plant and animal life.
- Scarcity of fresh water: Lack of available water to meet the needs of a particular locality or region.
- Deforestation: Destruction of trees to create clear land for other uses (eg agriculture).
- Soil erosion: Wearing away of topsoil (the upper layer of soil, which contains the most nutrient-rich materials).
- Contaminated land: Land containing substances that are hazardous to human, plant and animal life.
- Contaminated seas: The presence of waste, industrial chemicals, sewage and other materials that harm sea life.

As we will see in this chapter, and throughout this book, the finance sector has a substantial impact on the environment, both directly and indirectly, through investment choices; for example, by financing companies and projects that are heavy users of fossil fuels in production processes, or that create significant environmental damage through deforestation or harmful waste. The finance sector is also affected significantly, both directly and indirectly, by environmental factors, particularly climate change.

Many environmental factors are interconnected. An increase in global temperature, for instance, leads to marginal desert habitats becoming uninhabitable, which may then lead to a significant fall in the numbers, or complete extinction of, one or more species. This process could then have further effects on the food chain.

Humans have always had an impact on the environment – cutting down trees for agricultural land and firewood, for example – but since the Industrial Revolution, and particularly since the mid-20th century, such effects have increased dramatically. The concept of 'planetary boundaries', pioneered by the Stockholm Resilience Centre, attempts to define the 'safe operating space for humanity' and suggests that we may already be exceeding this in some key areas, including climate change.

The effects of climate change are already visible, and include:

- Higher temperatures: Scientific research shows that the average temperature of the planet's surface has risen over the last century. Compared with temperature fluctuations throughout Earth's history, the rate of temperature increase since the Industrial Revolution is extremely high.
- Changing rainfall: There have been observed changes in precipitation, although not all areas have data over long periods. Rainfall has increased in the mid-latitudes of the northern hemisphere since the beginning of the 20th century. There are also changes between seasons in different regions; for example, the UK's summer rainfall is decreasing on average, while winter rainfall is increasing. There is also evidence that heavy rainfall events have become more intensive, especially over North America.
- Changes in nature: Changes in the seasons are bringing changes in the behaviour of species, such as butterflies appearing earlier in the year and birds shifting their migration patterns.
- Sea level rises: Since 1900, sea levels have risen by about 19 cm globally, on average. The rate of sea-level rise has increased in recent decades.
- Retreating glaciers: Glaciers all over the world (in the Alps, Rockies, Andes, Himalayas, Africa and Alaska) are melting and the rate of shrinkage has increased in recent decades.
- Sea ice: Arctic sea ice has been declining since the late 1970s, reducing by about 4 per cent, or 0.6 million square kilometres (an area about the size of Madagascar) per decade.
- Ice sheets: The Greenland and Antarctic ice sheets, which between them store the majority of the world's fresh water, are both shrinking at an accelerating rate.

> **QUICK QUESTION**
>
> Reflecting on the visible effects of climate change outlined above, in what ways do you think the finance sector may have directly or indirectly contributed to them?

The climate system and anthropogenic climate change

Before we begin to understand the science of climate change, we must first be able to differentiate between weather and climate. Weather is the term to describe the daily fluctuations in the state of the atmosphere, characterized by changes in temperature, wind and precipitation, among other weather elements. Changes can occur rapidly, hour by hour or over a period of several days to a week. Climate refers to the average weather conditions for a particular area over a period of time, usually over many years and defined by the World Meteorological Organization as 30 years.[1]

There is natural variability in both weather and climate. In this chapter, and in general use, climate change refers to systematic changes across the climate system in response to a forcing agent, which can be natural (eg solar cycle, volcanic eruption) or a result of human activities (eg emissions of greenhouse gases from industry or changes in land use). The latter is referred to as anthropogenic climate change; that is, caused by humans and human activities.

The Intergovernmental Panel on Climate Change (IPCC) defines climate change as:

> a change in the state of the climate that can be identified (eg, by using statistical tests) by changes in the mean and/or the variability of its properties and that persists for an extended period, typically decades or longer.[2]

Understanding the climate system

Global climate is influenced by many interacting factors that make up the climate system, which is itself highly complex and interactive, and comprises five major components:

1 **Atmosphere:** A layer of mixed gases that circles the globe. This is the most rapidly changing part of the climate system where everyday weather

takes place. Global atmospheric circulation consists of three main cells: the Hadley, Ferrel and Polar cells that provide a natural air-conditioning system, transporting heat from the equator to the poles.

2. **Ocean:** All the liquid surface and underground water, both fresh and saline, which includes rivers, oceans, lakes, aquifers and seas. Approximately 70 per cent of the Earth's surface is covered by oceans, which are important for the transport and storage of energy.
3. **Cryosphere:** Those parts of Earth's surface predominantly covered by snow and ice that play an important role in the climate system due to high reflectivity (*albedo*) of incoming solar radiation. The cryosphere consists of ice sheets, glaciers, sea ice and permafrost.
4. **Biosphere:** The component in which life occurs (terrestrial and marine), and which plays an essential role in the global carbon cycle, mainly through photosynthetic processes in plants.
5. **Lithosphere (land surface):** Includes surface vegetation and soils which play important roles in the flow of air over it, the absorption of solar energy and the water cycle.

The Sun is the most important natural forcing agent, and the primary driver of Earth's climate. In order to maintain a stable global climate, a balance must exist between incoming solar radiation (shortwave radiation) and outgoing radiation (longwave radiation) emitted from and reflected back out to space. This is known as the Earth's energy balance, and is represented in Figure 2.1.

Over the long term, the amount of incoming solar radiation absorbed by the Earth and atmosphere is balanced by the Earth and atmosphere releasing the same amount of outgoing longwave radiation. About half of the incoming solar radiation is absorbed by the Earth's surface. This energy is transferred to the atmosphere by warming the air in contact with the surface (thermals), by evapotranspiration and by longwave radiation that is absorbed by clouds and greenhouse gases. The atmosphere in turn radiates longwave energy back to Earth as well as out to space.

A number of other drivers can lead to variations in the mean state and other elements (eg extremes) of the climate, such as the El Niño event described below. These may occur over a range of timescales from weeks and months, to decades, centuries and millennia.

Figure 2.1 The Earth's energy balance

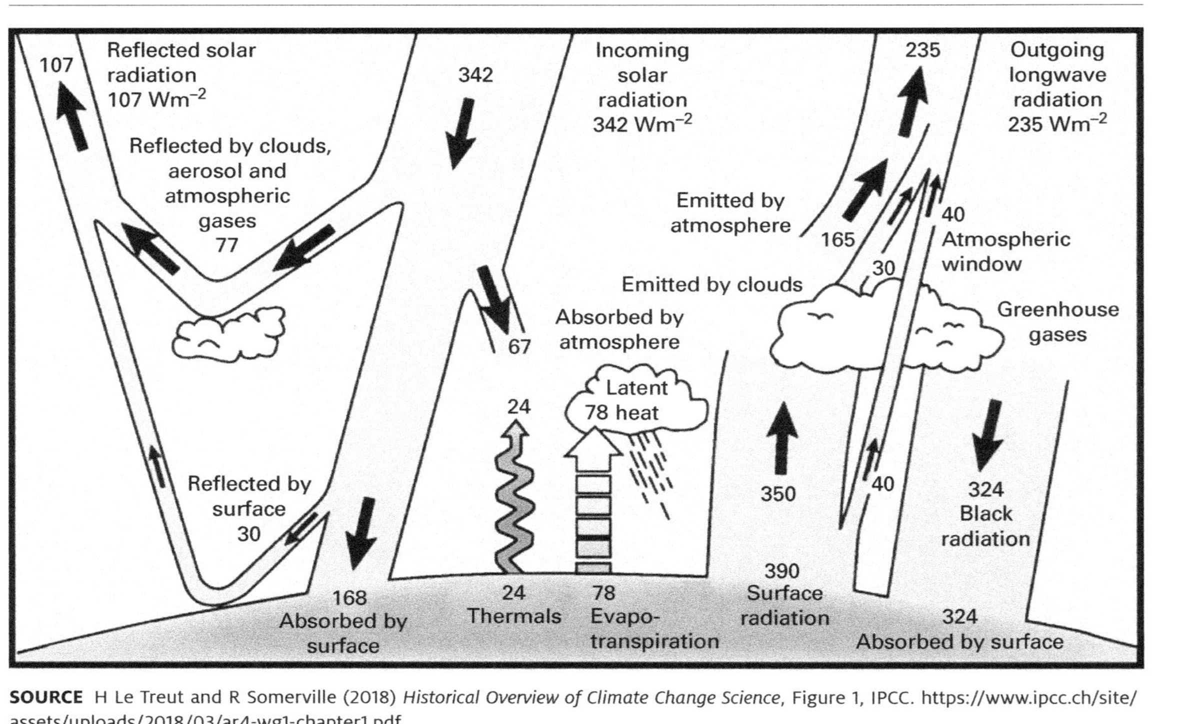

SOURCE H Le Treut and R Somerville (2018) *Historical Overview of Climate Change Science*, Figure 1, IPCC. https://www.ipcc.ch/site/assets/uploads/2018/03/ar4-wg1-chapter1.pdf

CASE STUDY

Natural variability: El Niño Southern Oscillation[3]

What is El Niño?

'El Niño' refers to a change in sea surface temperatures across the Tropical Pacific Ocean, linked to a weakening of the usual easterly trade winds. In a non-El Niño year, strong trade winds blowing from east to west maintain a temperature gradient across the Pacific Ocean, with warmer surface water in the West Pacific (near Indonesia) than in the east (near the coast of South America). This warm surface water provides an ample moisture source for cloud formation and precipitation across the Western Tropical Pacific. During an El Niño event, the trade winds slow, and the warm water in the West Pacific extends east, reducing the temperature gradient. El Niño events are sporadic, taking place every two to seven years, and often peak during December.

The El Niño and La Niña cycle causes a redistribution of energy that changes weather patterns across the entire globe, triggering floods in Ecuador, droughts in Indonesia, and a migration of fish away from the coast of Peru. El Niño even causes an increase in global average temperature. These events are associated with widespread changes in the climate system that last several months, and can lead to significant human impacts, affecting things such as infrastructure, agriculture, health and energy sectors.

El Niño Southern Oscillation: An atmosphere-ocean interaction

These episodes alternate in an irregular inter-annual cycle called the 'ENSO cycle'. ENSO stands for El Niño Southern Oscillation, where Southern Oscillation is the term for atmospheric pressure changes between the east and west tropical Pacific that accompany both El Niño and La Niña episodes in the ocean.

The name ENSO is a reminder that close interaction between the atmosphere and ocean is an essential part of the process. While the global climate system contains many processes, ENSO is by far the dominant feature of climate variability on inter-annual timescales.

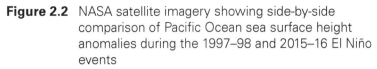

Figure 2.2 NASA satellite imagery showing side-by-side comparison of Pacific Ocean sea surface height anomalies during the 1997–98 and 2015–16 El Niño events

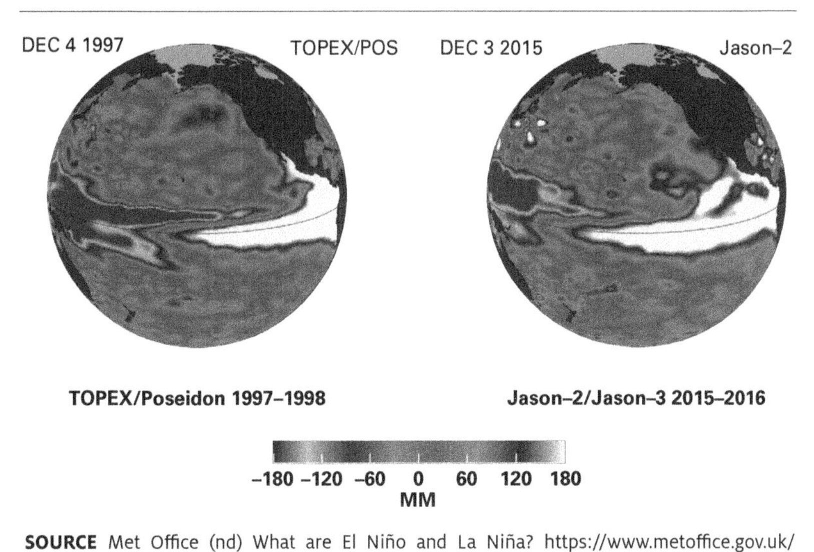

SOURCE Met Office (nd) What are El Niño and La Niña? https://www.metoffice.gov.uk/weather/learn-about/weather/oceans/el-nino

A question often asked about climate change is whether the observed changes in the Earth's climate are due to human influence, or if they can be explained by natural causes. The answer is that both natural causes and human activities ('anthropogenic factors') drive climate change, but the strong scientific consensus is that the latter has had, and continues to have, a significant impact.

The IPCC's 2018 *Special Report: Global Warming of 1.5°C* (see below) contains the most up-to-date assessment of the science relating to global warming. It states that:

> Human activities are estimated to have caused approximately 1.0°C of global warming above pre-industrial levels, with a likely range of 0.8°C to 1.2°C. Global warming is likely to reach 1.5°C between 2030 and 2052 if it continues to increase at the current rate.[4]

Anthropogenic factors may increase the scale, speed and impact of global warming, as the two short case studies on Peru and South-Eastern China demonstrate.

CASE STUDY

The extremely wet March of 2017 in Peru[5]

Peru's rainy, or so-called landslide, season of 2017 was unprecedented. The rains of March 2017 affected 1.7 million people, killed 177, caused $3.1 billion worth of damage, and left half of the country in a state of emergency. The March 2017 rain was distinct from other similarly catastrophic events due to the intensity of heavy rain over short, sharp periods. At the time, sea surface temperatures (SSTs) in the region were much warmer than would be expected, especially given that the El Niño – normally the cause of this increase – had already ended, and the SST was, in fact, warmer than during the previous strong global El Niño. Conditions were partly triggered by a local or coastal El Niño, which increases the likelihood of extreme rainfall in the region, but anthropogenically induced long-term warming of the ocean is likely to have further contributed to the scale and intensification. By examining the effects of man-made climate change on the extreme rainfall events in Peru, such as this one, it was found that the likelihood of similar, or more extreme 1 in 100 year, events were up to three times more likely due to the influence of human activities.

CASE STUDY

Anthropogenic influence on the heaviest June precipitation in South-Eastern China since 1961[6]

In June 2017 many of the provinces in south-eastern China experienced their heaviest and most prolonged rainfall in almost 60 years. In Hunan and Jiangxi provinces alone, over 10 million people were affected; 38 people died, 800,000 people were displaced, 15,000 houses collapsed, and 21,000 homes were severely damaged. A total of 75.6 thousand hectares of cropland became unharvestable and in total China incurred an overall economic loss of CNY19.29 billion (£2.1 billion). Model simulations to ascertain the key influences of this, and similar extreme events, indicated that they were twice as likely in scenarios where anthropogenic inputs were included. Interestingly, models revealed that this probability reduced in scenarios where mitigation efforts were introduced; however, it also progressively increased in line with future human-induced warming.

The greenhouse gas effect

As we saw above, the primary driver of the Earth's climate is energy from the Sun. Most of the Sun's energy that reaches the Earth is reflected back into space, but some is trapped by gases in the atmosphere as it radiates back from the Earth's surface. This is the greenhouse effect, and it warms the Earth like a blanket, making life on Earth possible by elevating the global mean temperature to about 14°C, which is about 30°C warmer than it otherwise would be. Human activity (such as burning fossil fuels and changing land use) since the Industrial Revolution is changing the natural balance of these greenhouse gases, pushing up their concentrations in the atmosphere and increasing the greenhouse effect – leading to increasing global temperature and other changes to our climate.

The main, naturally occurring greenhouse gases are:

- **Carbon dioxide (CO_2):** Atmospheric levels of CO_2 have increased by about 45 per cent since before the Industrial Revolution. CO_2 is the main greenhouse gas responsible for global warming, with an atmospheric lifetime of 50 to 200 or more years. Evidence from ice-cores, which give an insight into CO_2 levels going back hundreds of thousands of years, shows that concentrations are higher now than at any point in the last 800,000 years. CO_2 enters the atmosphere largely through the burning of fossil fuels (coal, natural gas, oil).
- **Methane (CH_4):** Methane is another naturally occurring greenhouse gas with an atmospheric lifetime, on average, of 12 years. Concentrations in the atmosphere now exceed pre-industrial levels by approximately 150 per cent. Man-made methane emissions mainly come from natural gas extraction, with other key sources including wetlands, landfill, livestock and agricultural practices. Methane is 25 times more effective at trapping heat than CO_2, making it a very potent greenhouse gas.
- **Nitrous oxide (N_2O):** Atmospheric concentrations of nitrous oxides have increased by around 20 per cent since 1750 levels. N_2O emissions are largely from agriculture, soil sources and fossil-fuel activities. The photolysis of N_2O in the atmosphere can lead to the depletion of stratospheric ozone and has a lifetime, on average, of 120 years.

Only about 0.1 per cent of the atmosphere is made up of these greenhouse gases. The rest mainly consists of nitrogen (approximately 78 per cent), oxygen (approximately 21 per cent) and argon (approximately 0.9 per cent). Although relatively scarce in our atmosphere, greenhouse gases have a significant effect on the climate system and the Earth's energy balance by trapping heat within the atmosphere, as Figure 2.3 illustrates.

Figure 2.3 The effect of greenhouse gases on the Earth's climate system and energy balance

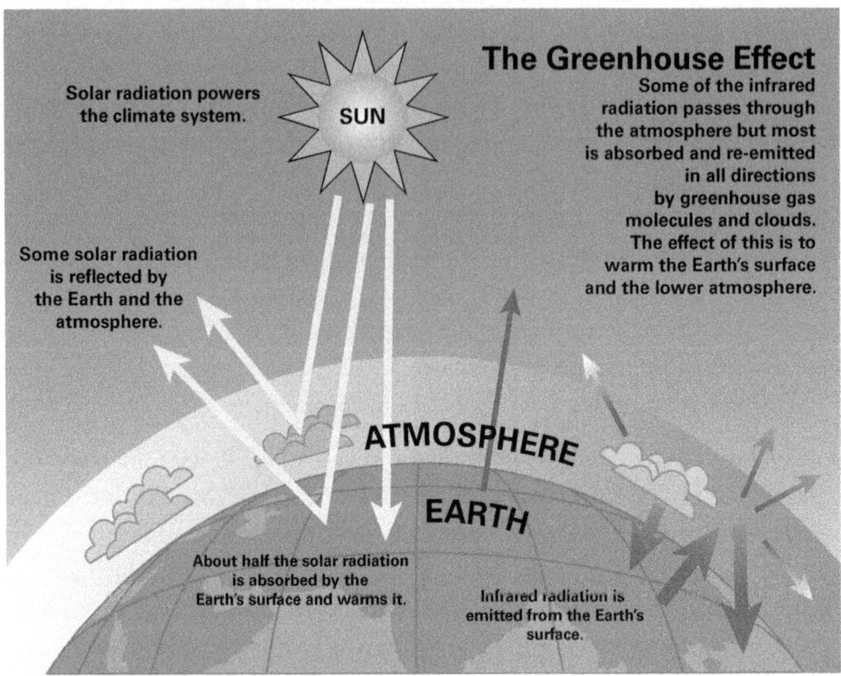

SOURCE H Le Treut, R Somerville, U Cubash, Y Ding, C Mauritzen, A Mokssit, T Peterson and M Prather (2007) *Historical Overview of Climate Change: The physical science basis. Contribution of Working Group I to the Fourth Assessment Report of the Intergovernmental Panel on Climate Change* [S Solomon *et al* (eds)], IPCC FAQ 1.3, Figure 1, Cambridge University Press, Cambridge, UK and New York

QUICK QUESTION

Thinking about the organization you work for, or an organization you are familiar with, what (if anything) has it done/is it doing to reduce its direct or indirect emissions of greenhouse gases?

Observed and projected changes in the climate system

Intergovernmental Panel on Climate Change (IPCC)

Created in 1988 by the World Meteorological Organization (WMO) and the United Nations Environment Programme (UNEP), the Intergovernmental Panel on Climate Change (IPCC) provides regular assessments of the scientific basis of climate change. The IPCC's work includes looking at the causes and consequences of climate change, as well as assessing options for mitigating climate change and the potential for adapting to its consequences.

The IPCC currently has 195 member countries, with thousands of scientists and other experts from member countries contributing to the IPCC's reports. World leading scientists assess the thousands of research papers published each year to bring together a synthesis of current understanding on key topics associated with climate change. This consensus approach, which takes in a wide range of views and expertise, leads to the IPCC's reports being widely viewed as highly authoritative.

The IPCC's reports are intended to provide the scientific information global governments and others need to develop evidence-based climate policies, as well as to underpin international climate negotiations. Outputs include Assessment Reports (published at intervals of around five to eight years), as well as Special Reports on specific subjects around climate change. Since its formation, the IPCC has completed five assessment cycles and is currently in the process of the sixth (expected 2021–22).

IPCC 5th Assessment Report and Special Report on Global Warming

The IPCC's *5th Assessment Report* (AR5), published in 2014, presented several climate projections based on Representative Concentration Pathways (RCPs). Alternative future scenarios up to 2100 were proposed, including:[7]

- A low emissions scenario, called RCP2.6, featuring significant emissions reductions that aim to limit warming and assuming that average greenhouse gas emissions peak between 2010–20 and decline substantially thereafter.
- A high emissions scenario, called RCP8.5, which does not include any explicit efforts to reduce output of greenhouse gases from human activity. In this scenario, emissions continue to rise throughout the 21st century.

Two other scenarios, RCP4.6 and RCP6, provide intermediate views of the future in terms of greenhouse gas emissions and the corresponding response of the climate system. Greenhouse gas emissions in the former peak around 2040 before declining; in the latter they peak around 2080. Given that it is extremely likely that greenhouse gas emissions will continue to rise after 2020, and for some time thereafter, scenarios RCP 4.6, 6 and 8.5 seem more probable, therefore.

The most-up-to-date climate projections from the IPCC's AR5 and the *Special Report: Global Warming of 1.5°C*, published in 2018, conclude that climate change poses a serious risk on a global scale.[8] According to the *Special*

Report, limiting global warming to 1.5°C would require reducing CO_2 emissions by 45 per cent from 2010 levels by 2030, which seems to be highly unlikely – global emissions are currently increasing, not decreasing. Global warming has already had, and will continue to have, a significant impact on the major components of our ecosystem. If global warming exceeds 2°C, there is a fear that factors such as melting sea ice and release of methane currently captured in permafrost could lead to a tipping point of more rapid and irreversible climate change, sometimes referred to as Hothouse Earth.

Observed and future projected changes in the atmosphere

Since the late 19th century (1850–1900), human activities are estimated to have caused around 1°C of global warming, with warming generally greater over the land than over the ocean. More recently, each of the last three decades has been warmer than the preceding one, with the years 2015 to 2018 having been the four warmest years on record globally.

- The rate of human-induced warming is currently increasing at 0.2°C per decade due to past and ongoing emissions.
- If warming continues at the current rate, global average temperatures are likely to rise by 1.5°C between 2030 and 2050 and will continue to rise over the 21st century.

Global surface temperature change by the end of the 21st century (2081–2100) is projected to exceed 1.5°C for all the RCP scenarios apart from RCP 2.6, and to exceed 2°C for RCP 6.0 and RCP 8.5 (and more likely than not to exceed 2°C for RCP 4.5). Extremes of temperature over land are likely to be higher than global mean temperature changes. These could rise by more than 3°C above pre-industrial levels at 1.5°C of global warming and by about 4°C at 2°C of overall warming – meaning that some areas of the planet may become uninhabitable. In addition, risks from heavy precipitation events are projected to become more frequent and intense, with 2°C of global warming, particularly in the mid-latitudes of the northern hemisphere.

Observed and future projected changes in the oceans

AR5 noted that observations taken between 1971 and 2010 from the upper layers of global oceans and the sea surface had shown an overall rise in temperature. The most recent IPCC report (2018) observed ocean surface warming of three ocean basins over the period 1950–2016 (by 0.11°C, 0.07°C and 0.05°C per decade for the Indian, Atlantic and Pacific Oceans respectively), with the greatest changes occurring at higher latitudes.

Ocean warming is projected to increase during the 21st century, with the strongest projected warming in tropical and northern hemisphere subtropical regions. The extent to which oceans will continue to warm in the future depends to a great extent on greenhouse gas emissions. In the top 100 metres of the ocean, current best estimates of future warming project a possible rise by as much as 2°C by 2100 under a high emissions scenario (RCP 8.5). Warming oceans cause sea level to rise as a result of thermal expansion, in which warmer water occupies a greater volume. Combined with the additional input of fresh water from polar ice caps and mountain glaciers, global average sea level is projected to rise by between 0.26–0.98 metres by the end of the 21st century, depending on which RCP scenario is used.

Observed and future projected changes in the cryosphere

Global observations of the cryosphere over the last three decades show an overall decline in the total amount of ice over land and sea. Reductions in sea ice can lead to further warming, as the ice – which reflects much of the incoming radiation from the sun back into space – melts to reveal the less-reflective ocean underneath.

The melting of land ice has similar effects, but also contributes to rising sea levels. The Greenland and Antarctica ice sheets have been losing mass, glaciers worldwide have continued to shrink and the extent of Arctic sea ice has decreased. The IPCC has high confidence that the rate of ice loss from the Greenland ice sheet has accelerated since 1992, from around 34 billion tonnes per year over the period 1992–2001 (sea level equivalent, 0.09 mm per year) to 215 billion tonnes per year over the period 2002–2011 (sea level equivalent, 0.59 mm per year).

The rate of mass loss from glaciers around the world (excluding Antarctica and Greenland) has increased in recent years, from an average of around 224 billion tonnes per year over the period 1971–2009, to 275 billion tonnes per year between 1993 and 2009. The IPCC estimates that the contribution of global glacier mass loss (excluding Antarctica and Greenland) to sea level was 0.25 to 0.99 mm per year sea level equivalent during the period 1971–2010.

Arctic sea ice coverage fluctuates with the seasons, with the maximum extent reached in the winter (February/March) and minimum in the summer (September, at the end of the summer melt). Over the period 1979–2010, Arctic sea ice extent decreased at a rate estimated to be in the range of 3.5–4.1 per cent per decade (0.45–0.51 million km^2 per decade).

Future climate model projections suggest that Arctic sea ice cover will continue to shrink and thin over the next century under all greenhouse gas emissions scenarios. With global average surface temperatures projected to rise, glacier ice mass is also projected to continue to decline. Under a high emissions scenario, climate model simulations suggest that the Arctic Ocean could see nearly ice-free conditions in September during the second half of the 21st century. By the end of the 21st century, global glacier volume (excluding the periphery of Antarctica) is projected to decrease by up to 85 per cent under a high emissions scenario.

QUICK QUESTION

What might be the impact of these observed and projected future changes on the city/country/region where you live and work?

The impacts of climate change on society

The impacts of climate change have been observed across both natural and human systems in recent decades. In terms of the former, these include shifts in species' geographical range, migration patterns and seasonal activities, changes in hydrological and chemical cycles, as well as changes to the components of the climate system (such as the atmosphere, ocean and cryosphere). The IPCC estimates that a 1.5°C average rise in global temperatures may place 20–30 per cent of species at risk of extinction, for example.

Climate change also impacts on human systems and society, both directly and by its impact on natural systems that help support and sustain human life. Although climate change will affect everyone, many of its effects may be felt disproportionately in the developing world, with those perhaps most affected by climate change being the least responsible for it. Oxfam's *Extreme Carbon Inequality* report (2015) estimates that the wealthiest 10 per cent of the global population are responsible for approximately 51 per cent of greenhouse gas emissions.[9] By contrast, the poorest half of the global population are responsible for some 10 per cent of emissions, but are the most threatened by extreme weather events and other impacts of climate change.

These impacts include, but are not limited to the following.

Agriculture

Agriculture is an important sector in many countries, particularly in the developing world, with many individuals, families and regions heavily reliant on the sector for food and economic growth. Global warming scenarios of 1.5°C or above, particularly higher emissions scenarios, predict increasing frequency and impact of extreme weather events and increased frequency of drought and heat waves, leading to soil and water degradation, reduced crop and livestock yields and effects on irrigation systems. Production of major crops such as wheat, rice and maize in both tropical and temperate regions is projected to be significantly impacted, although some individual locations may in fact benefit.

Aquaculture

Aquaculture is another important sector in the developing world. According to the Worldwide Fund for Nature, oceans and marine life are already experiencing large-scale changes at a warming of 1°C, with critical thresholds expected to be reached at 1.5°C and above. Coral reefs, which are already in substantial decline, are projected to decline by a further 70–90 per cent at this level. With global warming of 2°C, virtually all coral reefs will be lost. It is estimated that approximately half a billion people rely on fish from coral reefs as their main source of protein.

Access to water

It is estimated that nearly 2 billion people currently live in regions of the world where clean, fresh water is scarce, and it is expected that this number will increase to nearly 3 billion by 2025. Climate change may significantly reduce access to fresh water due to the increased frequency of droughts, and the drying up/silting up of lakes and other bodies of fresh water.

In addition, in some parts of the world, such as the Himalayas, melting glaciers may have a significant impact not just on the availability of fresh water, but more widely. Himalayan glaciers supply water to 10 of the world's most important river systems, including the Ganges, Indus, Yellow, Mekong and Irrawaddy, and directly or indirectly supply nearly 2 billion people with water, food and hydroelectric energy, clean air and incomes. In the short term, the increased frequency of extreme weather events could lead to severe flooding, and disruption of agriculture, homes and livelihoods. In the longer term, if the glaciers were to continue to reduce in size or even disappear, an important source for these major river systems would be disrupted, reducing access to water for drinking, agriculture and power downstream.

Displacement and migration

The IPCC estimates that, by 2050, up to 150 million individuals may seek to migrate due to the effects of climate change on the areas, countries and regions where they currently live. This will be caused by a combination of extreme weather events, such as flooding and drought, plus longer-term climate change effects including rising sea levels (in the developing and developed world, large numbers of people live close to the coast) and increasing land temperatures causing some parts of the world to become uninhabitable.

Some low-lying island nations, including the Maldives and the Seychelles, are particularly at risk from climate change. Rising sea levels may cause significant, long-term flooding and contaminate fresh water aquifers, potentially making the islands uninhabitable.

Health

Global warming can have both a direct impact (eg due to heatwaves and other extreme weather events) and an indirect impact on health and mortality rates. In terms of the latter, this may include reductions in crop and livestock yields, and reduced access to clean water, as well as increases in the rates of transmission of infectious diseases (eg malaria, spread by insects such as mosquitoes), which may become more prevalent and widespread as global temperatures increase.

Property and infrastructure

Rising sea levels will have a very significant impact on coastal communities in both the developing and developed world, affecting poor smallholders in the former and wealthy property owners, investors and tenants in the latter. In Florida alone, for example, it is estimated, in high emissions scenarios, that more than 10 per cent of homes might be uninhabitable by 2100 due to flooding, creating an economic loss of more than $400 billion. The US National Oceanic and Atmospheric Administration predicts that Miami, a very low-lying city, will flood every year by 2070. This will affect not only homes, but also airports, businesses, logistics hubs, power stations, transport networks and many other aspects of critical infrastructure.

The increased frequency and severity of extreme weather events will impact property and infrastructure in other ways; for example, buildings will need to be constructed, retrofitted or repaired to withstand higher impact storms, heavier rainfall and other types of extreme weather.

Security

Climate change can have a significant impact on many important aspects of human systems and society, including access to food and water, health and property. When such fundamental features and necessities of modern human society are threatened, and communities are in competition for scarce resources, conflict can arise or be exacerbated within or between nations and regions. This may be particularly significant when climate change also leads to substantial displacement and migration within or between countries and regions.

Vulnerability to food insecurity increases in many countries as our world warms. The IPCC estimates that nearly 75 per cent of countries will become more vulnerable when global warming increases by 2°C than at 1.5°C.

Many of the impacts of climate change on human systems and society are interlinked, as illustrated by the case study 'Food security and climate change in Sudan'.

CASE STUDY

Food security and climate change in Sudan[10]

Food security is closely linked to climate. In Sudan, agriculture accounts for around one-third of the country's gross domestic product and employs around 80 per cent of the labour force. Climate change could have a large impact on agricultural production and livelihoods in Sudan, and the World Food Programme and the Met Office undertook a study on the relationship between long-term climate change and future food security.

Sudan lies at the northern-most extent of the band of tropical rains known as the Inter-tropical Convergence Zone. This means it has a strong gradient of rainfall, ranging from extremely dry conditions in the north, to relatively wet conditions in the south. The climate is hot throughout the year but with seasonal rains, which can vary from year to year.

The large differences in rainfall across the country mean there is a wide variety of livelihoods and agricultural production systems, corresponding to the climatological suitability of different regions. Pastoral farming dominates in the north, where rainfall totals are low and the onset of the rains is unreliable; cropping systems are more prevalent in the south, where the rainy season is reliably longer and heavier. However, agriculture is mostly rain-fed in Sudan and is therefore sensitive to rainfall amounts and timings everywhere. This means that climate variability and change are key factors in the future of Sudan's economy, livelihoods and food security.

The study analysed climate model projections for the 2040s. The climate change projections for Sudan indicate a substantial warming trend across the country. In contrast, rainfall projections are mixed, with most models projecting small increases in annual rainfall and some projecting small decreases. However, increased evaporation as a result of higher temperatures will have a negative impact on water availability.

Three scenarios that span the range of available plausible future climates for Sudan were studied. All scenarios showed varying extents of increased heat and water stress, and year-to-year variability in timings and amounts of rainfall. This will make food production more challenging and increase stresses on livelihoods and food security. The study recommends that adaptation measures should focus on reducing sensitivity, improving resilience to variability and extremes, and improving heat tolerance and water efficiency in agricultural production.

Responding to climate change

As we saw in Chapter 1, responses to climate change take two main forms:

- adaptation (responding to the impacts of climate change);
- mitigation (preventing or reducing the harm caused by climate change).

Climate adaptation

Climate adaptation aims to reduce vulnerability to actual or expected climate change and its effects. According to the IPCC: 'In human systems, adaptation seeks to moderate or avoid harm or exploit beneficial opportunities. In natural systems, human intervention may help to facilitate the adjustment to change.'[11]

A very wide range of potential adaptation measures exist, including improving coastal and flood defences, building more climate-resilient infrastructure and property, developing crops and livestock better able to cope with higher temperatures, and more generally enhancing communities' resilience to the impacts of climate change.

As we will see in later chapters, green finance can play an important role in climate adaptation in a number of ways. At macro level, major adaptation projects (eg flood defences) may be funded via green bonds or other green investment tools. Loans and other forms of finance may support adaptation enhancements for existing buildings and infrastructure. At micro level, climate insurance can help increase the resilience of communities and businesses to the effects of climate change. To date, however, the focus of green finance has tended to be more on climate change mitigation than adaptation, although this is now beginning to change.

> **QUICK QUESTION**
>
> How might the community you live in, or a community you are familiar with, need to adapt to climate change?

Climate mitigation

Climate mitigation refers to the active efforts made to reduce or prevent the emission of greenhouse gases, which may be achieved either by reducing the sources of these emissions (eg by reducing the burning of fossil fuels such as coal, gas and oil) or by increasing the carbon sinks that can trap and store greenhouse gases (eg forests). Mitigation covers a very wide range of activities, from efforts as simple as walking or cycling to work instead of driving, using new clean technologies and renewable energy, to comprehensive planning for a new, carbon-neutral city.

There are many international, regional, national and local climate mitigation initiatives, some examples of which we will explore in the next chapter. Key global initiatives to reduce greenhouse gas emissions and mitigate the effects of climate change include:

- The United Nations Framework Convention on Climate Change (UNFCCC): An international environmental treaty, which came into force in 1994 with the aim of stabilizing greenhouse gas concentrations in the atmosphere. The parties to the convention (which has a near-universal membership of nation states) have met annually since 1995 at the Conference of the Parties (COP) to assess progress in meeting the UNFCCC's objectives. Two landmark achievements of the UNFCCC are the 1997 Kyoto Protocol and the 2015 Paris Agreement.
- The Kyoto Protocol: The 1997 Kyoto Protocol commits developed country parties to binding emissions reduction targets. This recognizes that developed countries are principally responsible for the current high levels of greenhouse gas emissions in the atmosphere, as a result of more than 150 years of industrial activity. The Kyoto Protocol is explored further in the next chapter.
- The Paris Agreement: Adopted at COP21 in Paris in December 2015, the Agreement is the first-ever universal, legally binding global climate

agreement. This includes agreement on a long-term goal of keeping the increase in global average temperature to well below 2°C above pre-industrial levels, and to strive to limit the increase to 1.5°C. The Paris Agreement is explored further in the next chapter.

In order to successfully mitigate the effects of climate change, significant reductions in emissions need to be made immediately in order to stay within the IPCC's 1.5°C global temperature rise scenario. The longer countries, businesses and individuals delay in reducing emissions, the more rapidly we will need to reduce emissions in the future to limit global warming. Some nations are already implementing rapid reductions, such as the UK, which has, as of 2017, reduced total greenhouse gas emissions by about 43 per cent since 1993. Overall, however, global annual emissions of CO_2 are at best stabilizing, rather than falling, and may have increased by 2.7 per cent in 2018, according to preliminary data from the Global Carbon Project.

Given the need for rapid cuts in greenhouse gas emissions to meet the 1.5°C target, it will be challenging, if not impossible, to achieve this by seeking to reduce CO_2 emissions alone. Additional mitigation strategies therefore also need to be considered, including:

- Negative emissions: Many pathways to meet 1.5°C or 2°C global temperature rise scenarios suggest we may need to actively remove carbon from the atmosphere to enable us to reduce greenhouse gas emissions at a slower pace than would otherwise be necessary. One way of doing this is to utilize Bio-Energy Carbon Capture and Storage (BECCS). In brief, this includes the mass planting of trees and other crops that extract CO_2 from the atmosphere, and using this biomass to replace fossil fuels for power generation and other industrial processes. In addition, CO_2 will be captured, injected and stored in geological formations, for example in former subsea oil and gas reservoirs.

  Very large amounts of land would be required to operate BECCS on the scale needed to make a significant impact, however, and the short-term impact of land-use change could result in vegetation loss, adding more carbon to the atmosphere rather than reducing it, which means it could take decades for BECCS to become carbon negative. This and other research suggests that negative emissions methods such as BECCS need to be carefully considered alongside other potential strategies.
- Natural climate solutions: Conservation, restoration and management of natural resources such as forests could help limit warming by storing carbon. Research shows, however, that the effectiveness of forests and other natural carbon sinks (processes that absorb and store carbon

dioxide) depends on our future global emissions. In negative emissions scenarios, natural carbon sinks become less effective because there is less CO_2 available in the atmosphere to absorb. This could partially offset the intended outcomes of negative emission strategies. While natural climate solutions have a positive effect and are cost efficient, as with BECCS, very large amounts of land would be needed to make a significant impact.

Methane mitigation

Methane comes from the fossil fuel industry and agriculture, as well as other man-made sources. It has a much shorter lifespan in the atmosphere than CO_2 but is a much more potent greenhouse gas. Methane's atmospheric chemistry also leads to more tropospheric ozone, which contributes further to global warming as it reduces the uptake of CO_2 by plants, and is also harmful to human health.

Methane emissions may be reduced by a variety of means, including improving agricultural practices, reducing methane leaks and flaring from oil and gas production and processing, and reducing the combustion of urban waste. Reducing methane emissions significantly would increase the feasibility of limiting global warming to 1.5°C, while also having additional benefits for human and ecosystem health.

QUICK QUESTIONS

What active steps could you take, as an individual, to mitigate the impact of climate change? What active steps could the organization you work for, or another organization you are familiar with, take?

Climate change and the finance sector

An introduction to climate-related financial risks

The finance sector has a substantial impact on the environment, both directly through the operations of banks, investment firms, insurers and other financial services firms, and indirectly through investment choices.

Both high-carbon activities, such as the extraction of hydrocarbons, and low-carbon activities, such as renewable energy and clean transport, can be financed.

The sector can also experience environmental impacts, particularly from climate change, which can create not only significant risks but also substantial opportunities. Key risks include those of asset impairment and stranded assets, while opportunities can arise from supporting the transition to a sustainable, low-carbon world, such as investing in climate-resilient assets.

We will explore the nature of, and the finance sector's response to, a range of climate-related risks in detail in Chapter 5, but an understanding of and focus on such risks is important at this stage to shape our discussion of green finance more broadly.

QUICK QUESTION

How might a climate-driven natural disaster impact on your organization? Think about the full range of stakeholders.

The risks posed by a changing climate impact both directly and indirectly on the financial system. A climate-related natural disaster, for example, may lead directly to losses for insurers, which may result either in more individuals and businesses taking out such insurance to protect against future events, or a reduction in insurance in affected areas (if premiums become more expensive), potentially affecting property values. Many losses from natural disasters may not be insured, especially in developing countries, and this could have a significant negative impact on the local economy. More widely, changing social norms on the environment and/or a disorderly market response may trigger further economic impacts.

In 2006, the economist Nicholas Stern released a 700-page review assessing the economic risks of climate change on the UK. Stern estimated that taking a business as usual approach (without taking further action to mitigate climate change) would lead to a reduction of at least 5 per cent in gross domestic product (GDP), which could increase to 20 per cent or more. Stern argued that the costs of early action on climate change were far outweighed by these potential negative impacts, which he compared to the effect of 20th century world wars:

> The evidence shows that ignoring climate change will eventually damage economic growth. Our actions over the coming few decades could create risks of major disruption to economic and social activity, later in this century and in the next, on a scale similar to those associated with the great wars and the economic depression of the first half of the 20th century. And it will be difficult or impossible to reverse these changes. Tackling climate change is the pro-growth strategy for the longer term, and it can be done in a way that does not cap the aspirations for growth of rich or poor countries. The earlier effective action is taken, the less costly it will be.[12]

The risks posed to the financial sector – and to all economic sectors and society as a whole – by climate change can be classified in three ways:

- Physical risks arising from the direct impacts of climate-related hazards to human and natural systems, such as droughts, floods and storms.
- Transition risks arising from the transition to a lower-carbon economy, such as developments in climate policy, new disruptive technology or shifting investor sentiment – these can lead to significant losses in economic value due to stranded assets.
- Liability risks arising from parties who have suffered loss or damage from the effects of climate change and who seek compensation from those they hold responsible.

QUICK QUESTION

What might be some of the physical, transition and liability risks for the finance sector?

The Task Force on Climate-related Financial Disclosures (TCFD) identified a number of different types of risk within the physical and transition risk categories (the TCFD groups liability risks as a sub-set of transition risks). We look at these, and at the TCFD overall, in more detail in Chapter 5, but a basic understanding of these at this point is helpful (Tables 2.1 and 2.2).

Table 2.1 Physical risks

Risk type	Example of risks	Example of possible financial impacts
Acute	Increased severity of extreme weather events such as cyclones and floods	Reduced revenue from decreased production capacity (eg transport difficulties, supply chain interruptions)
Chronic	Changes in precipitation patterns and extreme variability in weather patterns	Increased capital costs (eg damage to facilities)
	Rising sea levels	Cost of replacing assets in high-risk locations and/or increased insurance premiums and potential for reduced availability of insurance

Table 2.2 Transition risks

Risk type	Example of risks	Example of possible financial impacts
Policy and legal	Increased pricing of greenhouse gas emissions	Increased operating costs
	Exposure to litigation	Increased costs and/or reduced demand for products and services resulting from fines and judgements (in extremis, certain products and services may be banned)
Technology	Substitution of existing products and services with lower emissions options	Write-offs and early retirement of existing assets
	Costs to transition to lower-emissions technology	Costs to adopt/deploy new practices and processes
Market	Changing customer behaviour	Reduced demand for goods and services due to shift in consumer preferences
	Changing market valuations	Re-pricing of assets (eg fossil fuel reserves, land valuations, securities valuations)

(*continued*)

Table 2.2 (Continued)

Risk type	Example of risks	Example of possible financial impacts
Reputation	Stigmatization of high-carbon sectors	Lower revenues and higher costs from combination of reduced customer demand and negative impacts on workforce management and planning (eg employee attraction and retention)
	Increased shareholder concern of investing in high-carbon sectors	Reduction in capital availability

While the risks from climate change can be categorized, and such risks can be predicted and priced at least to some extent, it is important to note that climate risks are complex, inter-related, dynamic and uncertain, which means that the impacts of climate change can crystallize in surprising ways and at larger scales than expected, as the case study 'Global food shock' demonstrates.

CASE STUDY

Global food shock[13]

In 2015, Lloyd's published a scenario of an acute but plausible disruption to global food production and its consequences to explore the implications for insurance and risk. The scenario – developed by experts in food security and sustainable development economics – was peer-reviewed by a diverse group of leading academics.

The scenario is not a prediction; it is an exploration of what might happen based on past events and scientific, social and economic theory. It raises the question of whether other financial institutions and their regulators should be using such scenario-based approaches in their own stress-testing activities. To summarize the scenario:

- A combination of just three catastrophic weather events could undermine food production across the globe.
- These could lead to a 10 per cent drop in global maize production, an 11 per cent fall in soybean production, a 7 per cent fall in wheat production and a 7 per cent fall in rice production.

- Wheat, maize and soybean prices could increase to quadruple the average levels experienced during the 20 years prior to the global food price shock of 2007/8. Rice prices could increase by 500 per cent.
- The scenario indicates this series of events has the potential to lead to food riots breaking out in urban areas across the Middle East, North Africa and Latin America, leading to wider political instability and having knock-on effects for a wide range of businesses.
- While agriculture commodity stocks might benefit, the overall economic impact of high food prices, combined with rising political instability, could severely impact financial markets. The scenario indicates that the main European stock markets might lose 10 per cent of their value and US stock markets 5 per cent.

Stranded assets and the carbon bubble

As mentioned earlier, if global warming is to be restricted to 1.5°C or below, there will be strict limits on the amount of fossil fuels we can continue using for power generation and in other production processes, and fossil fuels will need to be replaced by alternative, clean and renewable energy sources and raw materials. Although the transition to a more sustainable, low-carbon world may be slower than required to limit global warming to the extent required, the direction of international and national policy is clear, and we should anticipate the substantial substitution of alternatives for coal, oil, gas and similar, high-carbon fuel sources.

This means that many fossil fuel assets may become impaired or **stranded assets**, that is assets that have suffered from unanticipated or premature write-downs, devaluations or conversion to liabilities. Oil and gas companies, and their investors, for example, currently place high valuations, linked to the current market prices, on their key asset – their oil and gas reserves. If – and when – customer demand for oil and gas falls due to the availability of clean and renewable alternatives, and/or the introduction of realistic carbon pricing and other regulatory changes significantly increases the cost of fossil fuels, it may cost more to extract, refine and distribute oil and gas reserves than can be recouped from their sale. Assets will have become impaired, or possibly stranded.

This concept of stranded assets has become prominent in green finance, and debates on climate change more generally, as policymakers, regulators, asset owners and investors consider how and at what speed the transition to a more sustainable, low-carbon world may strand assets in different sectors. This could have a very significant impact across financial markets; financial services firms are major investors in, and lenders to, a wide range of sectors with a heavy dependency on fossil fuels – not just in oil and gas, but other sectors such as vehicle manufacturers, airlines and petrochemicals, for example. Retail investors are highly exposed too, through pension and other investments. As we will see in Chapter 5, financial regulators see a rapid transition to a low-carbon world having the potential to disrupt financial stability, and so are at the forefront of efforts (such as the TCFD) to identify, disclose and mitigate the effects of stranded assets, as well as climate-related financial risks more widely.

The carbon bubble

The carbon bubble is one popular example of the implications of stranded assets and refers to a current, hypothesized overvaluation of fossil fuel companies as the current valuation of their assets does not reflect the risk of them becoming stranded.

A 2015 study in *Nature* estimated that a third of oil reserves, half of gas reserves and more than 80 per cent of coal reserves are at risk of becoming stranded assets. In 2017, Mark Carney, the Chair of the Financial Stability Board, stated that a carbon budget consistent with the Paris Agreement's original 2°C target would leave the 'vast majority' of oil, gas and coal stranded. Although it is difficult to estimate precisely the value of the losses investors could incur, it has been estimated that the exposure of the European financial sector alone is more than €1 trillion.

As set out in Figure 2.4, current fossil fuel reserves, and those anticipated to be added from future exploration and discovery, are significantly greater than those required to remain within global warming scenarios – in this case, 2°C and 3°C scenarios. Reserves would need to remain unexploited – stranding the assets – and the future valuations of asset owners (the oil and gas companies) would need to reflect this.

There is, therefore, not just an environmental case for divesting from the fossil fuel sector, but also an economic one too, based on current overvaluation and significant stranded asset risk. The Fossil Free campaign estimates that, to date (2019), 1,118 institutions with total assets of over $11.4 trillion have committed to divest from some form of fossil fuels (either coal, oil, gas or all together),[14] as well as more than 58,000 individuals

Figure 2.4 The carbon bubble

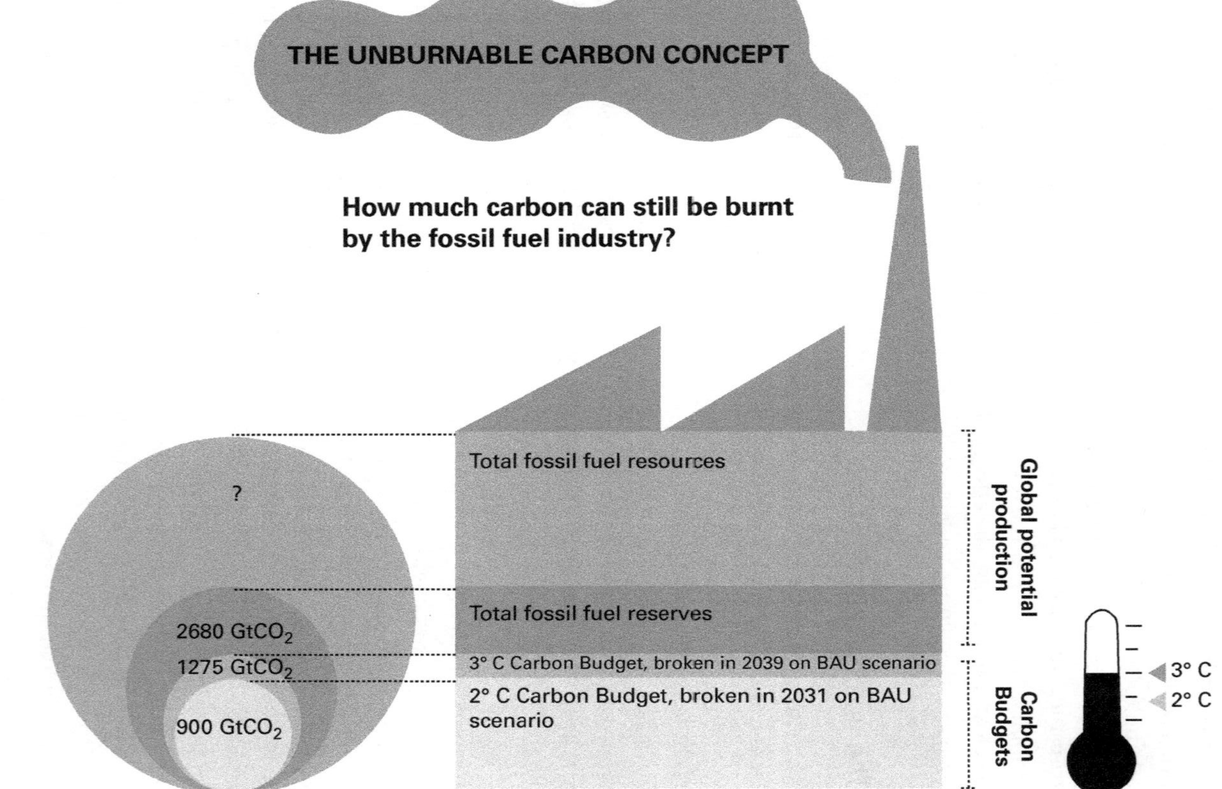

SOURCE Carbon tracker image originally designed by the Carbon Tracker Initiative. Data source: Carbon Tracker and the Grantham Research Institute, LSE (2013) *Unburnable Carbon 2013: Wasted capital and stranded assets*. http://carbontracker.live.kiln.digital/Unburnable-Carbon-2-Web-Version.pdf

with total assets of more than $2 billion. To date, the majority of institutions divesting have been public, faith-based or philanthropic. This is now changing, however. As we will see in Chapter 9, major institutional investors, led by bodies including the Portfolio Decarbonization Coalition and Climate Action 100+, are engaging with the sector and with large oil and gas companies to recognize, quantify and disclose environmental and stranded asset risks, and to encourage them to shift resources to clean and renewable energy on moral and economic grounds.

QUICK QUESTIONS

How much of your pension and other investments are invested in fossil fuels and other high-carbon assets? Do you know? Is it easy to find out?

Supporting the transition to a green economy

Financial institutions, and the finance sector overall, can take advantage of the opportunities provided to support the transition to a more sustainable, low-carbon world – to a green economy – defined by the United Nations Environment Programme as 'one that results in improved human well-being and social equity, while significantly reducing environmental risks and ecological scarcities. It is low-carbon, resource-efficient, and socially inclusive'.[15]

Just as with green finance itself, there is no single, universal definition of a green economy. Most definitions share some similar features: economic growth linked to a reduction in carbon emissions, resource use and pollution; protection of biodiversity and ecosystems; a financial system that values natural resources. As we saw in Chapter 1, the cost of the transition is estimated at $6 trillion per year, with some 80 per cent of investment required from the private sector. It will also require significant regulatory change, changes in social attitudes, and, potentially, the development of new criteria for measuring sustainable economic growth that go beyond current measures of GDP to incorporate wider environmental and social criteria. The UN Sustainable Development Goals, introduced in the previous chapter, provide one such framework.

CASE STUDY

A vision of Europe in 2050: 1. Fast forward[16]

The following scenario was developed by members of the One Planet Economy Network to support policymakers in thinking about the policy effort needed to transform Europe into a One Planet Economy by 2050. This is one of four scenarios that provide an alternative, not necessarily ideal, vision of our future economy.

European demand for green goods and services during the first half of the century resulted in strong competition among trading partners for access to the European market. Consequently, countries producing goods and services with the lowest impact are favoured trading partners. The most successful firms – many of which are European – are those offering eco-innovations, which enable consumption and drive the economy, but which result in minimal environmental impact. Indeed, Europe's technologies often out-innovate the competition, resulting in significant in-house reductions and a green tech revolution.

Competition has catalysed a transformation of the global economy into one centred on low-impact growth and development. Industrial collaboration in the area of environmental and resource management is rising, as firms seek to maximize their economic performance by saving resources. As a by-product, the negative environmental impacts of production are minimized and zero-waste production processes, recycling and reuse have been optimized in many industrial clusters. Waste products from one industry are used as inputs in neighbouring industries as often as possible. The production motive is still largely shaped by shareholder profits, but regulations require businesses to measure changes in their social and environmental performance.

About 70–80 per cent of Europeans live in high-tech accommodations located in close proximity to work and personal, social and community services. The education system reflects the global mindset of Europe and is highly internationalized, focusing on technology and adaptability.

Consumers value products and services based on their resource efficiency, as social status is now linked to sustainable living. They also demand high-quality products; as a result, high-quality, longer-lasting products are more profitable and dominate the market. By producing and selling higher-quality products than today, companies are able to add more value while not increasing their resource inputs, and this value is shared with workers in the form of higher wages. Economic growth is hence achieved without a growth in resource use and its related environmental impacts.

Government policy is required to drive further changes in behaviour. Policies involve price signals such as the taxation of consumption of environmentally harmful products and services rather than direct regulation. Consumers have provided early adopter markets for the new, developing technologies and consumer products. Ultimately this mix of regulation, taxation and advances in technology has delivered a net reduction in consumption for society overall.

Improvements in energy efficiency have continued to contribute to a relative decoupling of energy use from economic growth in Europe between 2011 and 2050, although overall energy demand has increased. Smart metering was rolled out across the EU by 2020, enabling remote load control, but only with the customer's consent.

On the supply side, emissions reductions are achieved via numerous cost-effective low-carbon technologies such as large-scale offshore wind and solar parks, widespread heat recuperation, and utilization of local smart grids. Ultimately, ambitious trans-continental projects are needed to enable the full decarbonization of Europe's energy supply to keep emissions in check.

Mobility is revolutionized, using fewer resources and less energy. During the first quarter of the century, as oil and gas became very expensive and shortages in supply a regular phenomenon, motor and alternative fuel technologies quickly advanced. From 2030, bans are enforced on conventional road vehicles. Most aeroplanes have been redesigned to become lighter, experience less drag and therefore need smaller engines that burn less fuel. Cars run with electricity made from renewable energy sources. Long-distance travel, overall, is less necessary due to the maximum use of videoconferencing technologies.

With a large global population and ongoing focus on income growth and consumption, there is intense pressure on land for food production and human inhabitation. Advances in agriculture have relieved some of this pressure with new technologies, such as multi-storey greenhouses, which substantially contributed to increased global agricultural yields. Significant advances and efficiency improvements in industrial agriculture have also resulted in highly efficient use of land, which enabled a conversion of former agricultural land back to resilient and diverse areas which increased biodiversity and enhanced ecosystem services. Efficiencies gained through industrial agriculture have also enabled an increase in organic agriculture in the EU to 75 per cent by 2050, compared to 4.1 per cent in 2010.

The circular economy and circular economy finance

One approach to developing a green and sustainable economy is the circular economy. In contrast to a traditional linear economy (make – use – dispose), in a circular economy, the value of products and materials is maintained for as long as possible. Waste and resource use are minimized. Resources are kept in use for as long as possible, reused, repaired or recycled, then brought back into use. A 'product as a service' approach is a common feature of many circular economies. Rather than replacing mobile phones every two years, for example, a circular economy approach would focus on repairing, restoring and upgrading mobile phones (as set out in the Fairphone case study below).

Figure 2.5 The circular economy

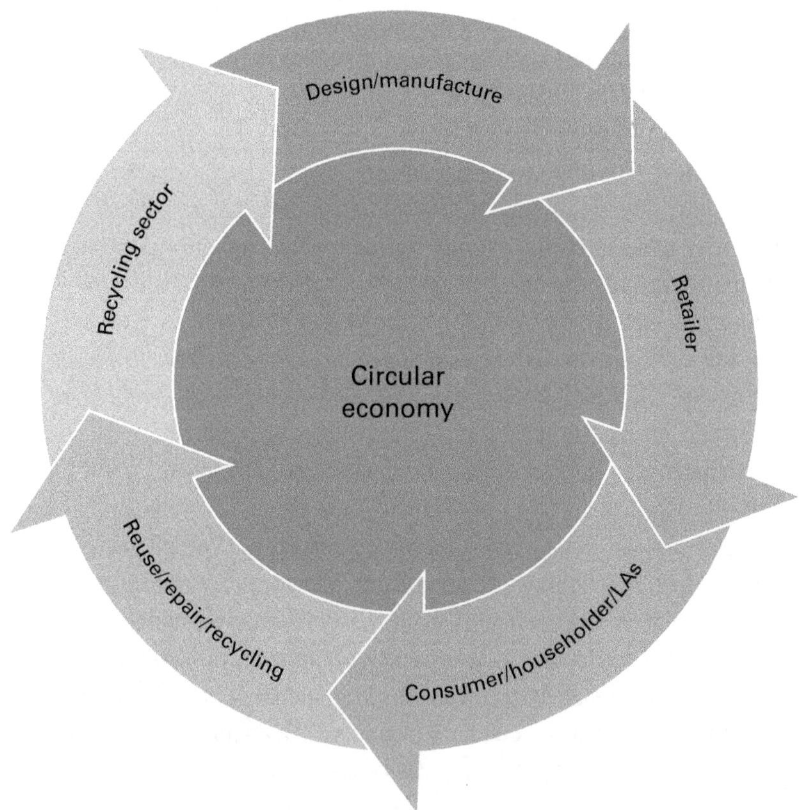

SOURCE Courtesy of the Waste and Resources Action Programme (nd) WRAP and the circular economy. http://www.wrap.org.uk/about-us/about/wrap-and-circular-economy

Friends of the Earth Europe identify four key principles of a circular economy that aims to achieve high resource efficiency, zero waste and zero emissions:

- Material management from extraction to waste: Reduce resource use through product design requirements (to improve performance, phase out hazardous materials, incentivize the repair and reuse of products, and ensure the use of recycled and recyclable materials) and a credible waste policy (with zero landfill and zero incineration).
- Toxic substances: Regulate to ensure that toxic chemicals are avoided at the design stage and do not hinder recycling and reuse.
- Energy efficiency: Preserve the energy embedded in products and materials and prevent them from becoming waste.
- Economic incentives: Ensure that maximizing resource efficiency and keeping materials circulating in the economy is cheaper and simpler than using new resources, through policy, regulation and taxation.

According to a McKinsey/Ellen MacArthur Foundation study (2017), adopting a circular economy approach could create net economic benefit to Europe of €1.8 trillion by 2030, and increase Europe's resource productivity by 3 per cent.[17]

CASE STUDY

Fairphone[18]

Fairphone aims to create positive social and environmental impact from the beginning to the end of a phone's life cycle. Consumer electronics are often viewed as semi-disposable objects, to be upgraded or discarded as soon as something better comes along. As technology advances rapidly, consumers are losing the ability to modify, repair and truly understand how they can keep their devices longer.

The Fairphone 2 first entered the market in December 2015 and is clearly distinctive from other smartphones. In addition to supporting social improvements throughout the supply chain, it is the world's first modular phone, offering easy repair for long-lasting use. All six modules are available in the Fairphone shop. Affordable spare parts and helpful tutorials make it easy for anyone to fix the most commonly broken parts: the screen can be replaced in under one minute. The phone's software is open source and available for anyone to use, review and modify.

Fairphone's take-back programme supports the reuse and recycling of old phones, and Fairphone's designers are researching the best way to make the phone easy to dismantle for recycling purpose. They are also working with partners to improve local collection efforts in countries struggling with electronic waste.

Fairphone owners have already completed hundreds of successful DIY repairs to keep their phones in good working order. Independent research has found that a repair scenario based on five years of use would reduce CO_2 emissions by about 30 per cent.

QUICK QUESTION

What might be the challenges for Fairphone's business model?

In 2014 a group of financial services firms, supported by the Ellen MacArthur Foundation, established the FinanCE Working Group to investigate the circular economy model, and its implications and opportunities for financial services firms and the sector overall. They have developed a definition of circular economy finance:

> Circular economy finance is any type of instrument where the investments will be exclusively applied to finance or re-finance, in part or in full, new and/or existing eligible companies or projects in the circular economy.

In their view, financial institutions have major roles to play in supporting the transition from the linear to the circular economy. The latter requires the development of many innovative business models that will require different types of traditional and non-traditional finance. In 2016 FinanCE published *Money Makes the World go Round*, exploring the role of finance in supporting the circular economy, and highlighting the need for financial institutions to better identify and price risk from linear economy models (in a similar manner, in some respects, to the TCFD model set out above), and for the development of new forms of subscription revenue securitization, reverse factoring and collaborative supply chain financing to support circular business models. It included a set of voluntary process guidelines with the aim of promoting circular economy finance, bringing consistency to approaches, and enhancing integrity in the circular economy finance market.[19] The Circular Economy Finance Guidelines apply both to debt and equity products, and are similar in approach to the more established Green Bond and Green Loan Principles, with four core principles covering:[20]

1 the use of investments;
2 the process for project evaluation and selection;
3 the management of investments;
4 reporting.

Green growth or no growth?

The visions for a green economy explored above either implicitly or explicitly accept the idea that the economy must continue to grow, as measured by GDP. Major organizations such as the OECD and World Bank also see the green economy in terms of growth:

OECD: 'Green Growth means fostering economic growth and development, while ensuring that natural assets continue to provide the resources and environmental services on which our well-being relies.'[21]

United Nations Economic and Social Commission for Asia and the Pacific (UN ESCAP): 'Growth that emphasizes environmentally sustainable economic progress to foster low-carbon, socially inclusive development.'[22]

World Bank: 'Growth that is efficient in its use of natural resources, clean in that it minimizes pollution and environmental impacts, and resilient in that it accounts for natural hazards and the role of environmental management and natural capital in preventing physical disasters.'[23]

Supporters of green growth tend to rely on the concept of decoupling. This is the idea that we can increase wealth without using more resources or increasing negative environmental impacts. Those who advocate decoupling suggest that it can be achieved by means of technology, process and resource innovation and efficiency; for example, by the widespread adoption of renewable energy, or improved approaches to water use and conservation.

This is not a universally accepted perspective, however. Some economists and environmentalists argue that we cannot grow infinitely on a finite planet and there are limits to economic growth. Their arguments take a number of forms:

- Relative vs absolute decoupling: Even if we can reduce the resources used per unit of economic output (relative decoupling), increasing levels of output may still require increases in the overall levels of resources used. What is needed is absolute decoupling – an overall decline in resources used. For this to happen, resource use must decrease as least as fast as overall output increases, and must continue to do so as the economy grows.
- Cost-shifting: What appears to be decoupling may actually be the shifting of costs onto developing nations, for example by moving intensive production overseas.
- Limits to efficiency: We cannot improve the efficiency of specific technologies (eg solar or wind power) infinitely.
- Rebound effect: When a new resource-saving technology is introduced, people have a tendency to change the way they use that technology, which may offset or even outweigh efficiency savings (similar to eating double the amount of a half-fat chocolate bar).
- Consumption paradigm: Technology innovation is not sufficient by itself to change our consumption-based culture; we need to shift our whole economic paradigm away from a resource-intensive accumulation and consumption approach.

Instead, it is argued, nations need to move to steady-state or post-growth economies, in which production and consumption do not continue to grow, but remain within safe limits. Moreover, because we are already overstretching the Earth's resources to sustain our current level of economic output, some argue that we first need to enter a phase of de-growth: planned and fair economic contraction to bring us back within our planetary boundaries. Advocates for de-growth argue that a simpler, less consumerist way of life would bring greater well-being and equality. They may advocate a shorter working week and an emphasis on non-material pursuits.

Steady state or no-growth approaches, if implemented, would have very significant impacts on financial services firms and the finance sector, as these imply that, overall, future asset and investment values would fall (although some values within this would rise). In a similar manner to the carbon bubble example discussed above, but on a system-wide basis, assets would be impaired and/or stranded with significant impacts on investments and loan portfolios, and on financial stability overall.

CASE STUDY

A vision of EUROPE in 2050: 2. Slow motion[24]

The following scenario was developed by members of the One Planet Economy Network to support policymakers in thinking about the policy effort needed to transform Europe into a One Planet Economy by 2050. This is one of four scenarios that provide an alternative, not necessarily ideal, vision of our future economy.

Europeans have embraced frugality, simplicity and sustainability as key elements of their lifestyle. Most Europeans live in cities in socially innovative modes of housing such as co-housing communities, urban co-ops and communes. Urban sprawl has thus declined. Some self-sufficient communities have moved back to the countryside, and many people have developed the green areas of the cities for cultivation. In general, social status across society is gained from immaterial goods such as education, culture and social networks. The education system takes an holistic approach to learning, in which self-awareness, environmental awareness, spiritual and community values play a key part.

The EU's economy is reflective of its values and has become famous for its Beyond GDP approach, which is also being promoted in the rest of the world. When people do make purchases, prices for goods and services are comparatively higher than 40 years ago, as they now reflect the true costs of social and environmental externalities. Most people prefer to share or lease many durable goods that were previously individually owned. Further, roughly half of Europe's population shuns consumerism altogether and has adopted the more extreme lifestyle of voluntary simplicity. These large groups form strong local communities and are often completely self-sufficient. Due to these communities, energy and resource use has declined dramatically over the past 40 years despite lagging technological advancements.

Average wage-based working hours are roughly half as long as they were in 2011, since a large segment of the population has significantly reduced its demand for goods and services. In terms of social values, work and money are less important, whilst building social relations and participating in community activities are high priorities. The reduction in working hours has also contributed to a significant reduction in resource use, as Europeans earn, produce and consume less. Income disparity is also smaller than in 2011, with much less deviation between the wealthiest and the poorest. Every EU citizen spends at least two years of life (not necessarily consecutively) in compulsory paid community service (in hospitals, kindergartens, retirement homes, etc). This fosters the strength of communities and the non-profit and non-governmental sector.

Cooperation and knowledge sharing are more important than competition in business strategies. Firms are expected to maximize community values by their shareholders, who come from a broader societal base than in 2011, are more risk averse, and do not expect very high return on investments. Moreover, there is an increasing number of employee-owned companies.

Using technologies that were available in 2011, networks of industries help to decarbonize the economy. Different firms work together by exchanging materials and energy for mutual benefit, on the basis that by-products from one business can be used as low-cost inputs to the others (the zero-waste production loop). The use of best available technologies is being maximized, largely driven by the high prices for all kinds of materials, including energy. Over the course of a product's lifetime, it is likely to be transferred from the original purchaser to numerous owners or hirers through shared ownership, reuse schemes and hire or lease shops. Products are designed to use fewer scarce resources, to last longer, and – if they cannot be reused – are easily recyclable.

The average European walks, rides a bike or uses excellent public transport. Getting around in Europe, especially in the cities, is easy, thanks to well-connected networks of light rail lines and buses powered by renewable energy sources, bicycle lanes as well as safe and well-designed footpaths. Cars are very expensive to use and individual ownership is shunned by most people, while public transport is strongly subsidized. Car sharing is widespread, but in general there are far fewer cars on the road in Europe compared to 2011.

Electricity is largely generated from renewable technologies. Significant reductions in consumption result from lifestyle changes, the removal of inefficient products from the market and industrial remodelling. This strong demand side effect, combined with the increased utilization of decentralized energy production, make it possible to shut down most centralized power generation facilities by 2050. The utilization of local renewable energy resources for small-scale production of electricity, heat and cooling is widespread (be this via wind, solar, bioenergy, geothermal etc).

Even though the land area used for agriculture has steadily increased over the past 40 years, overall environmental impact is low due to the substantial decline in resource inputs for farming and the dramatic decrease in meat and animal product consumption. There has been a gradual move from conventional agriculture and (industrial) livestock operation towards plant-based, labour-intensive and organic agriculture. The share of organic farming is nearly 95 per cent. Thanks to the spread of permaculture systems, wastes are turned into resources, productivity and yields are high, and natural environments have been restored.

At the international level, global, peaceful agreements ensure convergence of emissions and sustainable and equitable use of resources. A new international consensus was reached to ensure that international trade would contribute to a global One Planet Economy. The regime is built on three guiding principles: (1) trade based on environmental competitive advantage; (2) fair trade; (3) localization. No trade barriers exist for best available technologies in terms of resource and energy efficiency. As a result of large-scale dematerialization, the EU was able to diminish its overall dependence on imports of goods and services to become more self-contained.

QUICK QUESTION

Of the two scenarios presented in this section, which would you prefer to live and work in: 1. Fast forward, or 2. Slow motion? Why?

Key concepts

In this chapter we considered:

- the science of climate change and global warming, and current IPCC assessments of future scenarios;
- our changing environment and the risks and opportunities for the finance sector arising from these;
- the nature of stranded assets and the carbon bubble, and the challenges these present;
- how the finance sector can support the transition to a green economy.

Now go back through this chapter and make sure you fully understand each point.

Review

Our planet is impacted by a wide and interlinked range of environmental factors, caused and/or accelerated by human activity, including climate change, habitat loss, biodiversity loss, poor air and water quality, water shortage, deforestation, soil erosion and contamination of the land and seas. Many of these are interconnected.

Humans have always had an impact on the environment, but since the Industrial Revolution, and particularly since the mid-20th century, this has increased dramatically. An assessment of our planetary boundaries – the safe limits for human life – shows that we are already exceeding the safe limits in some key areas, including climate change.

Both natural causes and human activities ('anthropogenic factors') drive climate change, but the strong scientific consensus is that the latter has had, and continues to have, a significant impact. The IPCC's *Special Report: Global Warming of 1.5°C*, published in 2018, contains the most up-to-date assessment of the science relating to global warming, and states that:

> Human activities are estimated to have caused approximately 1.0°C of global warming above pre-industrial levels, with a likely range of 0.8°C to 1.2°C. Global warming is likely to reach 1.5°C between 2030 and 2052 if it continues to increase at the current rate.[25]

Global climate is influenced by five major, interacting components: atmosphere, ocean, cryosphere, biosphere and lithosphere. The Sun is the most important natural forcing agent, and the primary driver of Earth's climate. Most of the Sun's energy that reaches the Earth is reflected back into space, but some is trapped by gases in the atmosphere as it radiates back from the Earth's surface – this is known as the greenhouse effect, and it warms the Earth like a blanket. Human activity, such as burning fossil fuels, increases the concentration of greenhouse gases including carbon dioxide, methane and nitrous oxide, leading to increasing global temperatures.

The IPCC has published a range of potential scenarios offering visions of the future depending on levels of greenhouse gas emissions and action that might be taken to tackle climate change. Limiting global warming to 1.5°C would require reducing CO_2 emissions by 45 per cent from 2010 levels by 2030, which seems to be highly unlikely. If global warming exceeds 2°C, however, factors such as melting sea ice and the release of methane currently captured in permafrost could lead to a tipping point of rapid and irreversible climate changes, with significant environmental and societal consequences.

Climate change adaptation aims to reduce vulnerability to the effects of climate change on the environment and society. Mitigation aims to reduce or prevent the emission of greenhouse gases, and thereby limit global warming. Key global initiatives to reduce greenhouse gas emissions and mitigate the effects of climate change include: the United Nations Framework Convention on Climate Change (1992), the Kyoto Protocol (1997) and the Paris Agreement (2015). Green finance has a major role to play in supporting both climate adaptation and mitigation activities.

The finance sector has a substantial impact on the environment, both directly through the operations of banks, investment firms, insurers and other financial services firms, and indirectly through investment choices. The sector is also impacted by the environment, particularly by climate change, creating significant risks and substantial opportunities. Key risks include the risks of asset impairment and stranded assets; opportunities flow from supporting the transition to a sustainable, low-carbon world, such as investing in climate-resilient assets.

Climate-related financial risks are often divided into physical risks (direct impacts) and transition risks (arising from the transition to a lower-carbon economy). One of the most significant transition risks is stranded asset risk – the risk of a significant loss of economic value in an asset (eg an investment in an oil company) due to an abrupt change to a low-carbon world. The potential impacts are so significant that regulators consider an abrupt transition as a systemic threat to the stability of the financial sector.

The finance sector can take advantage of opportunities to support the transition to a more sustainable, low-carbon world, sometimes referred to as a green economy. One approach is that of a circular economy, in which resources are kept in use for as long as possible, and waste and resource use are minimized. Supporting the transition from a linear to a circular economy requires the development of innovative business models that will require different types of finance.

While many definitions of a green economy assume continuing economic growth, as measured by GDP, some economists and environmentalists do not believe that this is possible if we are to remain within our planetary boundaries. They argue that we need to move to a steady-state or post-growth economy, in which GDP stays within safe limits. This would have a very significant impact on financial services and financial stability overall.

Glossary

Anthropogenic climate change: Climate change caused by humans and human activities.

Carbon bubble: Hypothesized over-valuation of fossil fuel companies based on the thesis that the current valuation of their assets does not reflect the risk of them becoming stranded.

Circular economy: Economic approach in which the value of products and materials is maintained for as long as possible, with waste and resource use minimized.

Climate change: A change in the state of the climate that can be identified by changes in the mean and/or the variability of its properties and that persists for an extended period, typically decades or longer (IPCC). This may be caused by natural forcing agents or by humans and human activities.

Climate: The average and spread in weather conditions for a particular area over a period of time, defined by the World Meteorological Organization as 30 years.

Decoupling: Concept that economic growth can be separated from growth in resource use and resulting environmental impact.

De-growth: A planned economic contraction to bring us within our planetary boundaries.

Externalities: Effects of one party's activities and operations that are not factored into its assessment of costs, risks and reward.

Green economy: Economic approach that balances economic progress with environmental and social sustainability.

Greenhouse effect: Process by which greenhouse gases absorb heat and raise the temperature of the atmosphere.

Greenhouse gases: Primarily carbon dioxide (CO_2), methane (CH_4) and nitrous oxide (N_2O). Although relatively scarce in our atmosphere (0.1%), they have a potent effect on the climate system.

Planetary boundaries: Environmental limits within which we must stay to ensure the safety of human life.

Representative Concentration Pathways (RCPs): Four potential scenarios, developed by the IPCC, setting out alternative views of the future to 2100 based upon action taken to tackle climate change.

Steady-state economy: An economy that is not based on increasing levels of production and consumption.

Stranded assets: Assets that have suffered from unanticipated or premature write-downs, devaluations or conversion to liabilities.

Notes

1 World Meteorological Organization (nd) Our mandate: Climate [Online] https://public.wmo.int/en/our-mandate/climate (archived at https://perma.cc/KP6E-ETG7)

2 J B Robin (ed) (2018) Glossary, *Special Report: Global warming of 1.5°C*, IPCC [Online] https://www.ipcc.ch/sr15/chapter/glossary/ (archived at https://perma.cc/NM7N-5CPM)

3 Met Office (nd) What are El Niño and La Niña? https://www.metoffice.gov.uk/weather/learn-about/weather/oceans/el-nino (archived at https://perma.cc/EH8X-N58J)

4 IPCC (2013) *Summary for Policymakers* [Online] https://www.ipcc.ch/site/assets/uploads/2018/02/WG1AR5_SPM_FINAL.pdf (archived at https://perma.cc/C3N2-F985)

5 N Christidis, R A Betts and P A Stott (2018) *The Extremely Wet March of 2017 in Peru*, American Meteorological Society [Online] http://www.ametsoc.net/eee/2017a/ch8_EEEof2017_Christidis.pdf (archived at https://perma.cc/FWC9-T54T)

6 Y Sun, S Dong, X Zhang, P Stott and T Hu (2018) *Anthropogenic Influence on the Heaviest June Precipitation in Southeastern China Since 1961*, American Meteorological Society [Online] http://www.ametsoc.net/eee/2017a/ch16_EEEof2017_Sun.pdf (archived at https://perma.cc/8EXB-HDGD)

7 IPCC (2014) AR5 synthesis report: Climate change 2014 [Online] https://www.ipcc.ch/report/ar5/syr/ (archived at https://perma.cc/367S-AHZY)

8 IPCC (2013) *Summary for Policymakers* [Online] https://www.ipcc.ch/site/assets/uploads/2018/02/WG1AR5_SPM_FINAL.pdf (archived at https://perma.cc/C3N2-F985)

9 T Gore (2015) *Extreme Carbon Inequality*, Oxfam, Oxford

10 Met Office (nd) Assessment of food security and climate change in Sudan [Online] https://www.metoffice.gov.uk/climate-guide/food-security-climate-sudan (archived at https://perma.cc/3QD8-6WR8)

11 IPCC (nd) Definition of terms used within the DDC pages [Online] https://www.ipcc-data.org/guidelines/pages/glossary/glossary_a.html (archived at https://perma.cc/FE26-E6ME)

12 N Stern (2006) *Stern Review: The economics of climate change*, Government of the United Kingdom [Online] http://mudancasclimaticas.cptec.inpe.br/~rmclima/pdfs/destaques/sternreview_report_complete.pdf (archived at https://perma.cc/3THA-CTEL)

13 UNEP (2015) *Banking and Sustainability: Time for convergence* [Online] https://www.unepfi.org/fileadmin/documents/BankingSustainability_TimeForConvergence.pdf (archived at https://perma.cc/G6ZX-Y89F)

14 Fossil Free (nd) 1000+ divestment commitments [Online] https://gofossilfree.org/commitments/ (archived at https://perma.cc/5F29-JRNJ)

15 UN Environment (nd) Green economy [Online] https://www.unenvironment.org/pt-br/node/23750 (archived at https://perma.cc/75C4-44JD)

16 One Planet Economy Network (nd) WP6: OPEN:EU scenario storylines report: Scenarios for a one planet economy in Europe [Online] http://www.oneplaneteconomynetwork.org/resources/work-package-6.html (archived at https://perma.cc/4X8Y-XZGR)

17 A Bove and S Swartz (2017) Mapping the benefits of a circular economy, *McKinsey Quarterly* [Online] https://www.mckinsey.com/business-functions/sustainability/our-insights/mapping-the-benefits-of-a-circular-economy (archived at https://perma.cc/2NYW-GKPS)

18 Fairphone (nd) [Online] www.fairphone.com (archived at https://perma.cc/JGF9-FTLT)

19 Working Group Finance (2016) *Money Makes the World Go Round*, Ellen Macarthur Foundation [Online] https://www.ellenmacarthurfoundation.org/assets/downloads/ce100/FinanCE.pdf (archived at https://perma.cc/Q6RB-VLUY)

20 ING (2018) ABN AMRO, ING and Rabobank launch finance guidelines for circular economy [Online] https://www.ing.com/Newsroom/All-news/ABN-AMRO-ING-and-Rabobank-launch-finance-guidelines-for-circular-economy.htm (archived at https://perma.cc/HGC3-5V76)

21 OECD (2011) Fostering innovation for green growth [Online] https://www.oecd.org/sti/inno/fosteringinnovationforgreengrowth.htm (archived at https://perma.cc/3263-6BRC)

22 United Nations Economic and Social Commission for Asia and the Pacific (2013) *Green Growth Indicators: A practical approach for Asia and the Pacific* [Online] https://www.unescap.org/sites/default/files/publications/GGI_2014.pdf (archived at https://perma.cc/2DXH-RH27)

23 World Bank (2012) *Inclusive Green Growth: The pathway to sustainable development* [Online] https://openknowledge.worldbank.org/handle/10986/6058 (archived at https://perma.cc/S6TW-D4RA)

24 One Planet Economy Network (nd) WP6: OPEN:EU scenario storylines report: Scenarios for a one planet economy in Europe [Online] http://www.oneplaneteconomynetwork.org/resources/work-package-6.html (archived at https://perma.cc/4X8Y-XZGR)

25 IPCC (2019) *Global Warming of 1.5°C: Headline statements from the summary for policymakers* [Online] https://www.ipcc.ch/site/assets/uploads/sites/2/2019/06/SR15_Headline-statements.pdf (archived at https://perma.cc/ZN26-WQ6Y)

03

Building a sustainable financial system

International, national, industry and institutional responses

LEARNING OBJECTIVES

On completion of this chapter you should be able to:

- Identify many of the primary actors involved in building a sustainable financial system.
- Identify the key policy and regulatory frameworks supporting green and sustainable finance.
- Explain how intergovernmental bodies, governments and other organizations support the development of green and sustainable finance.
- Describe some key industry initiatives on green and sustainable finance.
- Understand how sustainability may be embedded in organizational strategies.

There are many different actors involved in building a sustainable financial system, including intergovernmental organizations, national governments, central banks, regulatory authorities, banks, institutional investors, international financial institutions (IFIs), multilateral development banks (MDBs) and financial services firms, acting individually and collectively. Intergovernmental bodies, national governments and regulatory authorities have a particularly important impact on the speed at which green and sustainable finance develops, through legal and regulatory regimes, and other policy tools, and can also influence how green and sustainable finance principles are embedded in organizational strategies. This chapter provides an overview of many of the key institutions and policy, regulatory and market initiatives in green and sustainable finance, some of which are explored in greater detail elsewhere in this book.

International and national policy responses

The transition to a sustainable, low-carbon economy requires cooperation and interaction between intergovernmental organizations, governments, regulatory authorities and private sector actors. Climate change is a global problem and action by all is necessary to avoid potentially catastrophic and irreversible changes to our planet.

In recent years there has been an acceleration in the number of policy and regulatory measures designed to promote green and sustainable finance, particularly in emerging and developing countries. The UNEP and the Green Growth Knowledge Partnership (GGKP) identified at least 391 national and sub-national policy and regulatory measures on green finance in 2019 – more than doubling the number identified in 2015.[1] Most of these are at the national level, along with an increasing number of international policy initiatives. The acceleration of policy and regulatory measures has been prompted in large part by the development and publication of net zero legislation by countries including France, Norway, Sweden and the UK; and similar targets (although not yet enshrined in law) by many more countries and bodies, including the EU's European Green Deal.

READING
Net zero, zero carbon and negative emissions

With more countries (and regions such as California, and supranational bodies such as the European Union) setting net zero targets for greenhouse gas emissions, increasingly enshrined in legislation, some clarity is needed around the terminology used. Net zero, carbon neutral, climate neutral, zero carbon and negative emissions are sometimes used interchangeably. There are similarities, but also important differences too:

- **Net zero:** Balances carbon dioxide and other greenhouse gas emissions from production and other activities released into the atmosphere with equivalent amounts captured and stored, and/or offset (eg through buying carbon credits).
- **Carbon neutral:** Similar to net zero in concept, but focuses on carbon dioxide emissions only.
- **Climate neutral:** A close synonym for net zero.
- **Zero carbon:** No carbon is emitted through production or other activities; therefore, no carbon needs to be captured or offset.
- **Negative emissions:** The activity of removing carbon dioxide from the atmosphere. Technologies used include afforestation and reforestation, soil carbon sequestration and direct air capture.

To date, the great majority of climate change mitigation plans developed and adopted by countries and firms tend to set targets for achieving carbon neutrality, or net zero, with 2050 a common deadline. Plans assume that emissions will be very significantly reduced, but that new technologies including carbon capture and storage, and yet-to-be-developed techniques to remove carbon dioxide from the atmosphere at the scale required will also play important roles.

QUICK QUESTION

How might governments around the world collaborate to support green and sustainable finance?

International agreements on climate change

Three major international agreements have focused on limiting average global temperature increases and combatting climate change:

United Nations Framework Convention on Climate Change

Agreed in 1992, and ratified by 197 parties to the Convention, the United Nations Framework Convention on Climate Change (UNFCCC) is the main international treaty to tackle climate change, with the objective of preventing dangerous man-made interference with the global climate system. The **Conference of the Parties**, generally known as the **COP**, is the governing body of the UNFCCC. The COP meets annually to review the implementation of the Convention and agreed climate change instruments, and to provide a forum for the negotiation of new climate change agreements and policies. At COP21, held in Paris in 2015, the Paris Agreement (see below) was finalized and announced.

Kyoto Protocol

Prior to the Paris Agreement, the world's only binding instrument for cutting greenhouse gas emissions is the 1997 Kyoto Protocol. This Protocol has been ratified by 192 of the UNFCCC Parties, but some major emitters of greenhouse gases either failed to ratify (in the case of the United States) or were considered developing countries that had no legal obligations to reduce emissions (in the case of China and India, although India subsequently joined in 2017). This meant that the Kyoto Protocol covered, in its first period, only about 12 per cent of global emissions. Two commitment periods were agreed:

- 1st period (2008–12): Industrialized countries committed to reduce emissions by an average of 5 per cent below 1990 levels.
- 2nd period (2013–20): Parties who joined in this period (including India) committed to reduce emissions by at least 18 per cent below 1990 levels.

Paris Agreement

The Paris Agreement of December 2015 is the first universal, legally binding global climate agreement. By July 2018, 179 of the 197 UNFCCC countries had ratified the Agreement. Article 9 states that developed countries 'should continue to take the lead in mobilizing climate finance from a wide variety of sources'.

The Agreement provides a pathway to limit global temperature rises to below 2°C and seeks to limit such increases to 1.5°C. It is for each country, however, to determine the action they will take on climate change mitigation and adaptation. As a result, some national governments have transcribed their own targets into law through national legislation. Whilst this is encouraged by the Paris Agreement, it is not a requirement, and the Agreement explicitly recognizes countries' 'differing situations and circumstances', resulting in criticism from some environmental activists. Parties to the Agreement are expected to submit their national plans, and there is a binding requirement for countries to assess and review progress against these plans – this is the legally binding part of the Agreement. The intention is that this will encourage governments to continue to raise their targets for mitigation and adaptation measures, collectively limiting global temperature rises.

One of three objectives set out in Article 2 of the Paris Agreement – Article 2.1(c) – commits signatories to making financial flows consistent with a pathway towards low greenhouse gas emissions and climate-resilient development. The recognition of the key role of finance in tackling climate change has been a major influence on the growth of green finance.

Intergovernmental Panel on Climate Change

Supporting the United Nations, and other bodies concerned with climate change, the Intergovernmental Panel on Climate Change (IPCC) was established by the World Meteorological Organization (WMO) and the United Nations Environment Programme in 1988, with a remit to assess and report on the science related to climate change. The IPCC analyses a wide range of scientific papers published each year to provide a comprehensive, annual summary of climate change science, its impacts and future risks, and how adaptation and mitigation can reduce those risks. The IPCC plays a key role in ensuring that international agreements on climate change, and national policies and legislation aligned to these, are based on strong scientific foundations. As we saw in Chapter 2, the October 2018 IPCC report recommended urgent action to limit global temperature rises to below 1.5 degrees, rather than the previous consensus of below 2 degrees.

International agreements such as those outlined above are typically not legally binding at the national level, as in the case of the Paris Agreement. Many national governments, therefore, have aligned their plans and measures on climate change mitigation and adaptation into national legislation, as the case study 'Climate change legislation and policy in the UK' exemplifies.

CASE STUDY

Climate change legislation and policy in the UK

The Climate Change Act 2008 is the basis for the UK's approach to tackling and responding to climate change, stipulating that emissions of carbon dioxide and other greenhouse gases are reduced and climate change risks prepared for. The Act also established the framework for delivering on these requirements. The Act came into law on 26 November 2008, which meant that the UK became the first country in the world to have a long-term, legally binding target for reducing greenhouse gas emissions. The Act incorporates:

- a target to reduce emissions by 80 per cent by 2050 (on 1990 levels) and a requirement to set legally binding, five-yearly carbon budgets (the first five have been put into legislation and run to 2032);
- the establishment of a Committee on Climate Change to advise the Government on emissions targets, and report to Parliament on progress;
- a Government commitment to carry out national climate change risk assessments and develop a National Adaptation Plan, both to be reviewed every five years.

As well as being covered by the Climate Change Act, Scotland, Wales and Northern Ireland have separate climate change policies. For example:

- The Climate Change (Scotland) Act 2009 committed Scotland to a 42 per cent reduction in emissions by 2020 and annual reductions between 2010 and 2050. The Scottish Government has committed to introduce a new, more ambitious Climate Change Bill. In September

2019, the Scottish Government published legislation setting targets to reduce emissions by 75 per cent by 2030, and to becoming net zero by 2045. A Citizens' Assembly on Climate Change is to be established to make recommendations to Ministers on how to achieve the transition to net zero.

- The Environment (Wales) Act 2016 provides for the setting of emission reduction targets to 2050, including at least an 80 per cent reduction (compared with 1990 levels) in 2050, and five-yearly carbon budgets. The first two carbon budgets (2016–20 and 2021–25) were set in 2018.
- The Northern Ireland Executive, in its Programme for Government (2011–15), has set a target of continuing to work towards reducing greenhouse gas emissions by at least 35 per cent (compared with 1990 levels) by 2025.

In July 2019, the UK became the first major economy to agree legislation to enshrine a net zero target for greenhouse emissions, by 2050. The Climate Change Act will be amended to reflect this, with the previous target of reducing emissions by 80 per cent replaced by a target of net zero.

International policy responses

United Nations

The United Nations (UN) is an intergovernmental organization established in 1945 to promote international cooperation and to create and maintain international order. As of 2020, there are currently 193 UN member states, with equal representation in the UN General Assembly, plus two non-member observer states. As outlined above, the UN plays the leading global role in tackling climate change, through the UNFCCC. The UN has also established a wide range of initiatives to mobilize the business and finance communities to promote green and sustainable finance, and to contribute to mitigating global temperature rises, some of which are introduced below.

United Nations Environment Programme Finance Initiative

The United Nations Environment Programme Finance Initiative (UNEP FI) is a partnership between UNEP and the global financial services sector, created in the context of the 1992 Earth Summit, with a mission to promote sustainable finance. Over 200 financial institutions, including banks, insurers and investors, work with UNEP to understand environmental challenges, why they matter to finance, and how to actively participate in addressing them. The backbone of the initiative is the UNEP Statement of Commitment by Financial Institutions on Sustainable Development. By signing up to the Statement, financial institutions recognize the role of the financial services sector in promoting sustainable development, and commit to the integration of environmental and social considerations into all aspects of their operations. UNEP FI's work also includes a strong focus on policy, both nationally and at international level, by promoting finance sector involvement in processes such as the Paris Agreement. For more information, see www.unepfi.org.

UNEP Inquiry into the Design of a Sustainable Financial System

Established in early 2014, the Inquiry is the leading international platform dedicated to advancing national and international efforts to green the financial system. To date, it has published more than 100 reports examining international and national policy options to improve the financial system's effectiveness in mobilizing capital towards a green and inclusive economy. In 2017 it launched the Financial Centres for Sustainability (FC4S) network, which now has 30 members including most of the world's leading financial hubs, comprising $61.3 trillion in equity market capitalization and representing 80 per cent of global equity markets. For more information, see https://unepinquiry.org/

United Nations-supported Principles for Responsible Investment

In early 2005, the United Nations Secretary-General invited a group of the world's largest institutional investors to join a process to develop the United Nations-supported Principles for Responsible Investment (PRI). Launched in 2006, these are a voluntary and aspirational set of investment principles that offer a menu of possible actions for incorporating environmental, social and governance issues into investment practice. By 2019, the Principles had more than 1,750 signatories, from over 50 countries, representing approximately $70 trillion. The PRI are explored in more detail in Chapter 9. For more information, see https://www.unpri.org/

Principles for Sustainable Insurance

Launched at the 2012 UN Conference on Sustainable Development, the Principles for Sustainable Insurance (PSI) serve as a global framework for the insurance industry to address environmental, social and governance risks and opportunities. Endorsed by the UN Secretary General, the Principles have led to the largest collaborative initiative between the UN and the insurance industry. As of July 2017, 83 organizations had adopted the Principles, including insurers representing approximately 20 per cent of world premium volume and $14 trillion in assets under management. The PSI are explored in more detail in Chapter 10. For more information, see https://www.unepfi.org/psi/

Principles for Responsible Banking

The draft Principles for Responsible Banking (PRB), developed by a group of 28 banks, were published in November 2018, with the aim of encouraging financial institutions to incorporate green and sustainable finance principles into their strategies and activities and link their business plans to societal goals, as expressed in the UN Sustainable Development Goals and the Paris Agreement. In September 2019, the final Principles were launched during the UN General Assembly, with 130 banks from 49 countries, representing more than $47 trillion in assets, as the founding signatories. The PRB are explored in more detail in Chapter 6. For more information, see https://www.unepfi.org/banking/bankingprinciples/

Green Climate Fund

Established in 2010 by the parties to the United Nations Framework Convention on Climate Change (UNFCCC), the Green Climate Fund aims to support the efforts of developing countries to respond to the challenges of climate change. Following the 2015 Paris Agreement, the Fund was given an important role in leading climate change mitigation and adaptation efforts, using public finance to stimulate private investment, and aiming to:

- catalyse the flow of climate finance into low-emission and climate-resilient development, driving a paradigm shift in the global response to climate change; and
- support climate adaptation and resilience in areas that are highly vulnerable to the effects of climate change, in particular least developed countries (LDCs), small island developing states (SIDS), and African states.

As of 2019, $5.6 billion had been pledged to the Green Climate Fund, supporting (to date) 124 projects, reducing greenhouse gas emissions by 1.6 billion tonnes of CO_2 equivalent, and helping an estimated 348 million individuals improve their climate resilience.[2] The Fund's investments can be in the form of grants, loans, equity or guarantees, with approximately 40 per cent focused on mitigation, 25 per cent on adaptation and the remainder on a combination of these.

The G20

The G20 (Group of Twenty) is an international forum for finance ministers and central bank governors from 20 major economies. Currently, these are Argentina, Australia, Brazil, Canada, China, France, Germany, India, Indonesia, Italy, Japan, Mexico, Russia, Saudi Arabia, South Africa, South Korea, Turkey, United Kingdom, United States and the European Union. Founded in 1999, the G20 aims to discuss and coordinate policy relating to strengthening the global economy, including improving international financial stability.

On 15 December 2015, the **G20 Sustainable Finance Study Group (SFSG)** was established (originally as the Green Finance Study Group), co-chaired by the central banks of China and the United Kingdom. Recognizing the need to scale up green and sustainable finance over the coming decade, the Study Group's mandate is to 'identify institutional and market barriers to green finance and, based on country experiences, develop options on how to enhance the ability of the financial system to mobilize private capital for green investment'. The Study Group's Synthesis Report was published at China's G20 Summit in September 2016, and recommended work in seven key areas:

1. Provide strategic policy signals and frameworks.
2. Promote voluntary principles for green finance.
3. Expand learning networks for capacity building.
4. Support the development of local green bond markets.
5. Promote international collaboration to facilitate cross-border investment in green bonds.
6. Encourage and facilitate knowledge-sharing on environmental and financial risk.
7. Improve the measurement of green finance activities and their impacts.

The SFSG's most recent (2018) report identifies three priorities for developing sustainable finance through the private sector:[3]

1. Create a wider range of, and encourage investment in, sustainable assets.
2. Develop and scale up sustainable private equity and venture capital.
3. Utilize digital technologies to advance the practice and uptake of sustainable finance.

The Financial Stability Board

Established by the G20, the Financial Stability Board (FSB) brings together major central banks and financial regulators to promote international financial stability. In 2015, the G20 asked the FSB to consider the risks of rapid transition to a low-carbon world, which it viewed as having the potential to be a serious systemic threat to the stability of the financial sector, as discussed in Chapter 2. In response, the FSB launched the **Task Force on Climate-related Financial Disclosures** (**TCFD**) to develop recommendations in this area. The Task Force published its final recommendations in June 2017 (see: https://www.fsb-tcfd.org) and these have been strongly supported and endorsed by a wide range of national and international regulators and policymakers. As of June 2019, nearly 800 organizations had expressed their support for the TCFD's recommendations.

The role of the FSB in coordinating central banks and regulatory responses to climate change, and the report and recommendations of the TCFD, are covered in detail in Chapter 5.

The Organisation for Economic Co-operation and Development

The Organisation for Economic Co-operation and Development (OECD) is an intergovernmental economic organization with 34 member countries, founded in 1960 to stimulate economic progress and world trade. It is a forum of countries describing themselves as committed to democracy and the market economy, providing a platform to compare approaches to policy, seek answers to common problems, identify good practices and coordinate the domestic and international policies of its members. Most OECD members are high-income economies and are regarded as developed countries.

In 2016, the OECD **Centre on Green Finance and Investment** was established. Its mission is to 'help catalyse and support the transition to a green, low-emissions and climate-resilient economy through the development of effective policies, institutions and instruments for green finance and investment'. The Centre publishes analyses, makes recommendations, organizes events and engages in wider policy debates. For more information, see www.oecd.org/cgfi/

European Union Action Plan and European Green Deal

In March 2018, the EU published its Action Plan: Financing Sustainable Growth, based on the recommendations of a High-Level Expert Group on Sustainable Finance, established the previous year.[4] The EU Action Plan forms part of wider EU policies and activities, including the European Capital Markets Union, the EU's Agenda for Sustainable Development, and implementing the Paris Agreement. Key elements of the EU Action Plan include:

- establishing an EU Taxonomy for Sustainable Activities, published in June 2019 and approved by the European Commission, Council and Parliament in December 2019;
- creating EU labels for green financial products to help investors to easily identify investments that comply with agreed criteria, based on the EU Taxonomy;
- clarifying the duty of asset managers and institutional investors to take sustainability into account in their investment processes;
- requiring insurance and investment firms, and other financial advisers, to provide advice, taking into account clients' preferences on green and sustainable outcomes;
- incorporating sustainability in prudential requirements for banks and insurers, including considering a green supporting factor that might reduce capital requirements for green and/or sustainable investments; and
- enhancing transparency in corporate disclosure and reporting to align them with the recommendations of the Task Force on Climate-related Financial Disclosures (TCFD).

Building on the Action Plan, in December 2019, the European Commission published the European Green Deal, which sets out plans for a net zero target for the European Union by 2050, including an intermediate step of reducing emissions by 2030 by 50 to 55 per cent from 1990 levels.[5] The European Commission estimates that an additional €175 billion to €290 billion per year of investment will be needed to achieve these targets. The approval of the EU Taxonomy, and the development and approval of new, green financial products and services are seen as key enabling steps to unlock the substantial private sector investment required.

National policy responses

Given the diversity of countries in terms of climate, geography, level of economic development, legal system and the size and expertise of the finance sector, measures to promote green and sustainable finance need to be tailored to the specific circumstances and requirements of each. This is why international agreements such as the Paris Agreement often call for signatories to develop and report on national policies and plans, rather than seek to implement a single, global approach or model.

QUICK QUESTION

What national policies could governments introduce to support green and sustainable finance?

Many countries have already taken a number of steps to address risks related to climate change, and to encourage the alignment of their financial systems with sustainable development more generally. These include promoting the standardization of green and sustainable finance practices, clarifying the responsibilities of financial institutions, enhancing the transparency of information by promoting disclosure standards for carbon and environmental risks, supporting market development for green investments, and developing and implementing national sustainable finance roadmaps. Examples of green and sustainable finance measures adopted by G20 countries include:[6]

- **Brazil:** The BOVESPA Stock Exchange set up a Corporate Sustainability Index as early as 2005. The Banco Central do Brasil has introduced requirements for banks to monitor environmental risks, building on a voluntary Green Protocol from the banking sector. Brazil's banking association

(Federação Brasileira das Associações de Bancos, FEBRABAN) is developing a standardized assessment methodology and automated data collection system to monitor flows of finance for green economy sectors.

- **China:** Chinese President Xi Jinping and the State Council have made developing and implementing a green finance system for China a national priority. This includes, since 2016, the introduction of green bond standards and a wider series of policy measures to promote green finance, including the planned introduction of climate disclosure requirements for listed companies as well as a requirement for companies to hold pollution (emissions) insurance.
- **France:** In 2015, the French government introduced a law on Energy Transition and Green Growth. Article 173 requires major institutional investors, from 2017 onwards, to report how they take ESG factors into account in their investment decision-making (see the case study 'France: Article 173' for more details).
- **Indonesia:** The Indonesian financial regulatory authority (Otoritas Jasa Keuangan, OJK) published a Green Finance Roadmap in 2014.
- **South Africa:** Environmental, social and governance (ESG) disclosure indicators were introduced in 2010 by the Johannesburg Stock Exchange.
- **Germany:** The German National Development Bank (Kreditanstalt für Wiederaufbau, KfW) devotes 43 per cent (€76.5 billion) of its annual lending to climate change mitigation and adaptation. It plays a major role, working with private sector banks, in financing renewable energy and other low-carbon projects. About half of all wind farms and solar energy projects in Germany involve KfW loans.
- **Malaysia:** The Malaysian Securities Commission published the 'Sustainable and Responsible Investment Roadmap for the Malaysian Capital Market' in November 2019, in addition to a new Energy Efficiency and Conservation Act and updating the National Energy Efficiency Action Plan 2016–25.
- **UK:** The UK published its first Green Finance Strategy in July 2019, bringing together activities and initiatives from across government, regulators and the private sector. It seeks to highlight and accelerate current work to green finance and finance green, and established the new Green Finance Institute to coordinate the delivery of the Green Finance Strategy.

CASE STUDY

France: Article 173

Article 173 of the Energy Transition and Green Growth Act (passed in August 2015) requires major institutional investors to report, from 2017 onwards, how they take ESG factors into account in their investment policies and decision-making, particularly environmental and climate-related factors, following a comply-and-explain approach. This applies to a wide range of public companies, banks, insurers, investment managers and other asset managers.

Investors are required to report on a wide range of areas including:

- investment strategies and policies – both the impact of investments on the environment and the impact of climate change on investments;
- climate-related financial transition risks (in line with the TCFD framework and recommendations);
- exposure to climate-related physical risks;
- carbon footprint of investment portfolios;
- green and brown share of portfolios;
- exposure to fossil fuels;
- alignment to a 2 degree climate goal.

The comply-and-explain approach means that it is possible for institutions not to publish an Article 173 report, if the organization can demonstrate that climate change is not a material risk. A survey of 50 large French institutional investors, conducted by FourTwentySeven, found that 14 did not appear to have published a report for 2017, the first year this was required.[7] The majority of those organizations that did report had not necessarily reported on all the areas envisaged by Article 173, in particular on exposure to physical risks. As 2017 was the first year of reporting, however, it is reasonable to expect to see improvements in future years.

CASE STUDY

UK policies to support green finance

A range of policies has been enacted in recent years that directly or indirectly support green finance in the UK:

- The Pensions Act 2000: Requires investment funds to disclose their policies on ethical (incorporating green) investment. In July 2016 the Pensions Regulator strengthened guidance on the consideration of environmental, social and governance risks in pension fund investments issues. The new code of practice states that trustees must bear in mind longer-term financial risks, including those stemming from climate change.
- UK Stewardship Code 2010 and 2012: Provides principles and guidance on stewardship activities, including interventions resulting from concerns on environmental matters.
- Companies Act 2013 Amendment (Strategic and Directors' Reports): Requires quoted companies to report their annual global greenhouse gas emissions and environmental matters affecting performance (including the impact of the company's business on the environment) and any related policies and their effectiveness.
- The International Climate Fund (ICF): Established by the UK Government in 2011 to help developing countries address the challenges presented by climate change, the ICF has invested £3.87 billion in a broad range of activities across the globe to support sustainable economic growth, build resilience to the impacts of climate change and help sustainably manage natural resources such as forests. The ICF currently funds over 230 programmes focused on adaptation, mitigation and forestry in low- and middle-income countries throughout Africa, Asia, Latin America and the Caribbean, as part of the UK's obligations under the UNFCCC.
- Green Investment Bank (GIB): The first of its kind worldwide was set up in 2012 to support green projects on commercial terms and mobilize private sector capital into the UK's green economy. By 2016 the GIB had directly invested £2.8 billion and mobilized a further £8 billion in private capital, mainly in energy efficiency, waste and bioenergy, offshore wind and onshore renewables. In 2017 the GIB was sold

to Macquarie, an Australian bank, and is now known as the Green Investment Group.

- Green Finance Initiative: Established in 2016 by the City of London Corporation in partnership with the UK Government, the Initiative brings together international expertise from across the financial and professional services sector. The Green Finance Initiative's strategy is to:

  a. Set a clear path: Environmental objectives will only be met if government and industry work together to set a holistic green finance strategy. This could include giving powers to a new or existing independent body to set a long-term path for a greener UK economy; developing open-access green corporate benchmarks; and completing the work undertaken to develop green infrastructure as an asset class.

  b. Strengthen data and transparency: Engage in regulatory green forward guidance, extend the analysis and understanding of climate-related risks, and work to implement the findings of the Task Force on Climate-related Financial Disclosure.

  c. Promote voluntary principles: Maintain the market's integrity whilst removing barriers and permitting it room to grow; work with industry, government, regulators and other financial centres to establish guidelines and consistency, and build upon the success of the green bond market in other areas, such as green tagging for loans.

  d. Enable connection and collaboration: Work to globalize green finance through international best practice, learning and cooperation. Facilitators could include dedicated bilateral or multilateral green financial discussions; a network for the world's leading green financial centres; and public–private, cross-border secondee programmes.

  e. Embed change: Ensure that money managers, analysts, consultants and the financial leaders of the future can address climate-related risk and explore green financial opportunities. This will require the inclusion of environmental awareness right across the financial sector, from fiduciary duty, stewardship and governance guidelines to relevant professional and university qualifications.

f. Provide public sector leadership: Provide certainty that ratification of the Paris Agreement represents the first step of persistent government support for a low-carbon transition. The UK could lead in this area by building green objectives and metrics into its industrial strategy; for example: making clear the frameworks under which the UK's path to a greener future will be implemented and financed; including environmental risk analysis and green mandates into public sector funds; and further building upon the successes of the International Climate Fund.

- Green Finance Taskforce: Established by the UK Government in 2017 to build on the UK's global leadership in the green finance sector, and the initial work of the Green Finance Initiative, the Taskforce brings together senior leaders from the financial sector and works with industry to accelerate the growth of green finance and deliver the investment required to meet the UK's carbon reduction targets. In 2018, it was announced that the UK would establish a new Green Finance Institute to continue and extend this work.

Financial regulation

Financial regulation defines the rules for banks, financial institutions and insurance firms at both individual firm level (microprudential regulation, sometimes referred to as supervision) and at systemic level (macroprudential regulation). Financial regulation may have a number of aims (eg to promote competition, to ensure fair treatment of customers) and these may differ between jurisdictions, but one of the most important and generally agreed upon is to safeguard the stability of the financial system. This can include rules around the amount and type of capital institutions must hold relative to their assets in case of defaults, and also specific restrictions on certain types of activity.

Banking regulation

International banking regulation is overseen by the Basel Committee on Banking Supervision (BCBS), based in Basel, Switzerland. The BCBS sets the framework for calculating the minimum level of capital that banks must hold as a proportion of their assets, and includes setting risk weights for each asset class, which are applied to determine a bank's exposure to potential losses. The BCBS also sets rules and standards for bank supervision and risk management.

The latest Basel III framework is based on three pillars:

- Pillar 1: Defines eligible capital and methods for calculating capital adequacy requirements for credit, market and operational risks.
- Pillar 2: Covers the supervisory review process which ensures that banks have sufficient capital to back all risks and also requires appropriate management of these risks.
- Pillar 3: Defines transparency and minimum disclosure requirements for banks.

Most developed countries have adopted the Basel III framework. In the European Union, it has been implemented through the Capital Requirements Directive IV.

The Basel III framework has been criticized for not explicitly addressing the financial stability risks associated with systemic environmental risks. According to the University of Cambridge Institute for Sustainability Leadership (CISL) and UNEP, while the framework does require banks to assess the impact of specific environmental risks on their credit and operational risk exposures, these are mainly transaction-specific risks that affect a borrower's ability to repay a loan. There is no requirement under Basel III for banks to identify and disclose the risks of climate change overall, consider portfolio-wide risks, or for supervisory regimes to monitor potential macroprudential risks to financial stability.

> The Basel Committee should explicitly acknowledge environmental risks and their increasing impact on the stability and sustainability of the economy as an emerging source of systemic risk for banks and banking stability. On this basis, it should encourage and support bank regulators to work with banks to adopt current best practice in the management of environmental issues, and to collect the necessary data and conduct analysis to refine the banking sector's understanding of, and ability to address, systemic environmental risk in the future.[8]

Despite the limitations of Basel III, the identification and disclosure of climate risk and the potential for climate-related financial risks to impact financial stability have attracted significant international and national regulatory attention. Examples of this, which we will examine in more detail in later chapters, include:

- the creation, by the Financial Stability Board in 2015, of the TCFD;
- the establishment, in 2017, of the Network of Central Banks and Supervisors for Greening the Financial System, with more than 20 members by 2019;
- emerging regulatory approaches to the identification and disclosure of climate risk, including as a factor in bank stress tests and other supervisory programmes in countries including Brazil, China, the UK and the EU.

CASE STUDY

China Banking Regulatory Commission[9]

According to its 2012 Green Credit Guidelines, the China Banking Regulatory Commission (CBRC) works towards promoting bank lending to environmentally sustainable economic activities such as the manufacturing of renewable energy infrastructure and companies that have developed lower-carbon production processes.

China has multiple long-term environmental sustainability goals, including a number that focus on transportation and buildings. Banks are requested to collect data from these projects and turn them over to the CBRC, which in turn is strongly interconnected with other ministries, including the Environment Ministry, which can use the information to initiate an investigation of environmental regulation violations.

In 2012, the CBRC began requiring banks to monitor borrowers' compliance with environmental regulations and to begin implementing loan contract changes that either allow the bank to accelerate loan repayments of a customer in violation of environmental laws or else to demonstrate compliance within a certain timeframe. If compliance cannot be shown, the bank could suspend further lending and trigger accelerated loan repayment.

Insurance regulation

In 2016 the European Union introduced a new, Europe-wide system for insurance regulation called Solvency II. Its main objective is the adequate protection of policyholders and beneficiaries. Solvency II sets out a new, risk-based and harmonized EU-wide approach to the assessment of capital adequacy, risk management and reporting for insurers. It follows a similar three-pillar approach to Basel III:

- Pillar 1: Defines the quantitative requirements around the amount of capital that insurers must hold.
- Pillar 2: Covers the supervisory review process that ensures that insurers have in place appropriate governance and risk management procedures to manage risks.
- Pillar 3: Defines transparency and minimum disclosure obligations for insurers.

The Solvency II regime requires insurers to be sufficiently capitalized to withstand the losses of a 1 in 200-year event, over a one-year time horizon. A new UN initiative called 'The 1-in-100 Initiative' is exploring how to extend this approach through new requirements to report financial exposure to a 1 in 100-year event, in order to reflect the growing risk of extreme climate-related events. Reweighting capital by introducing a green supporting factor, or a brown penalty factor for Pillar 1 would tip insurers towards lower carbon investments and portfolios.

The **Sustainable Insurance Forum** was launched in 2016 to promote cooperation on critical sustainable insurance challenges, such as climate change. It comprises an international network of insurance regulators and supervisors and includes insurance supervisors and regulators from more than 20 countries including Australia, Brazil, France, Germany, Ghana, Jamaica, Morocco, the Netherlands, Singapore, the UK and the US, as well as the International Association of Insurance Supervisors.

Industry responses

As outlined in Chapter 1, while estimates of the total cost of financing the transition to a sustainable, low-carbon world vary, a figure of $6 trillion per year is plausible. It is widely agreed that public funds will be insufficient to finance the transformation, and that substantial amounts of private capital are needed, estimated at up to 80 per cent of the total.

QUICK QUESTIONS

What should industry bodies do to support green and sustainable finance? What examples can you identify from your country?

In response to policy signals, regulatory pressures, growing appreciation of the true costs of climate change and changing customer, client and investor demands, financial institutions are already beginning to provide a wide variety of green and sustainable finance products and services. These are discussed in more detail in Chapters 6 to 11. This is being supported – and in many cases led – by a number of industry initiatives to promote international cooperation on different aspects of green and sustainable finance. UNEP, through the United Nations-supported Principles for Responsible Investment, Responsible Banking and Sustainable Insurance, has played a key role. In addition, there is a growing range of finance sector initiatives to develop and inculcate green and sustainable finance principles – fundamental norms that direct policies and procedures that can be used to guide behaviour and decision-making, and to shape strategies for green and sustainable finance that can then be put into practice. Some of the key principles Green and Sustainable Finance Professionals should be aware of are outlined below, together with other important initiatives to help embed green and sustainable finance practices.

QUICK QUESTION

What principles are you aware of that you would associate with green and sustainable finance?

Banking and financial services

Equator Principles

The Equator Principles comprise a voluntary code of conduct and a risk management framework for determining, assessing, managing and reporting on environmental and social risks in major projects, such as in energy or infrastructure. Established in 2003, as of 2019, 101 financial institutions in 38 countries have officially adopted the Equator Principles, covering over 70 per cent of international project finance debt in emerging markets. For more information, see www.equator-principles.com

Global Alliance for Banking on Values

The Global Alliance for Banking on Values (GABV) is a network of banking leaders from around the world, committed to advancing positive change in the banking sector. The goal is to change the banking system so that it is more transparent, supports economic, social and environmental sustainability, and is composed of a diverse range of banking institutions serving the real economy. Founded in 2009, it is a growing network of banks, banking cooperatives and credit unions, microfinance institutions and community development banks. For more information, see www.gabv.org

Sustainable Banking Network

The Sustainable Banking Network (SBN) is a community of more than 50 financial sector regulatory agencies and banking associations from emerging markets, committed to advancing sustainable finance in line with international good practice. The SBN facilitates the collective learning of members and supports them in policy development and related initiatives to create drivers for sustainable finance in their home countries. To date, 15 countries, including Bangladesh, Brazil, China, Colombia, Indonesia, Kenya, Mexico, Mongolia, Nigeria, Peru, Turkey and Vietnam, have launched national policies, guidelines, principles or roadmaps, focusing on environmental sustainability.

Green Bond Principles

The Green Bond Principles (GBP) are voluntary process guidelines that recommend transparency and disclosure and promote integrity in the development of the Green Bond market. Established by the International Capital

Market Association (ICMA), they provide guidance for issuers on the key components involved in launching a credible Green Bond; aid investors by ensuring availability of information necessary to evaluate the environmental impact of their Green Bond investments; and assist underwriters by moving the market towards standard disclosures to facilitate transactions.[10]

Green Loan Principles

Launched in March 2018, the Green Loan Principles (GLP) provide a framework and standards for green lending by institutions, designed to promote global consistency in the application and reporting of green loans. In particular, their aim is to ensure consistency in the use of the term green loan in order to maintain the integrity of the green loan market and avoid instances and accusations of greenwashing. The GLP have been developed primarily for the syndicated loan market, but have broad applicability across most, if not all types of corporate lending.[11]

Climate Bonds Initiative

The Climate Bonds Initiative (CBI) is an international, not-for-profit organization working to mobilize the global bond market for climate change solutions, with the aim of promoting investment in projects and assets necessary for a rapid transition to a low-carbon and climate-resilient economy. The Climate Bonds Standard has been developed to bring consistency to bond issues, including clarity over green project outcomes and use of proceeds. The CBI's further objectives are to develop a large and liquid Green and Climate Bonds Market that will help drive down the cost of capital for climate projects in developed and emerging markets; to grow aggregation mechanisms for fragmented sectors; and to support governments seeking to tap debt capital markets. For more information, see https://www.climatebonds.net

The Green Bond and Green Loan Principles, and Climate Bonds Initiative and Standard are covered in more detail in Chapters 6 and 7, in the context of banking and the development of the green bond market, and the characteristics of green and other types of bonds and loans linked to green and sustainable project outcomes.

Investor initiatives

Global Sustainable Investment Alliance

The Global Sustainable Investment Alliance (GSIA) is a collaboration of membership-based sustainable investment organizations around the world. The GSIA's mission is to increase the impact and visibility of sustainable investment organizations at global level. Members of the GSIA include the UK Sustainable Investment and Finance Association (UKSIF), European Sustainable Investment Forum (Eurosif), Responsible Investment Association Canada (RIA Canada), the US Forum for Sustainable & Responsible Investment (US SIF), Responsible Investment Association Australasia (RIAA) and the Dutch Association of Investors for Sustainable Development (VBDO). For more information, see www.gsi-alliance.org

Institutional Investors Group on Climate Change

The Institutional Investors Group on Climate Change (IIGCC) is a forum for large investors to collaborate on climate change, providing investors with a collaborative platform to encourage public policies, investment practices and corporate behaviour that address long-term risks and opportunities associated with climate change. As of 2019, IIGCC had more than 190 members, from 15 countries, representing over €28 trillion in assets. For more information, see https://www.iigcc.org/

Investment Leaders Group

The Investment Leaders Group (ILG) is a global network of pension funds, insurers and asset managers committed to advancing the practice of responsible investment. The ILG's vision is an investment chain in which economic, social and environmental sustainability are delivered as an outcome of the investment process as investors go about generating robust, long-term returns. Like ClimateWise (see below), the ILG is facilitated by the University of Cambridge Institute for Sustainability Leadership (CISL). For more information, see https://www.cisl.cam.ac.uk/business-action/sustainable-finance/investment-leaders-group

Portfolio Decarbonization Coalition (PDC)

The Portfolio Decarbonization Coalition (PDC) was established in 2014 as a multi-stakeholder initiative that seeks to mobilize institutional investors to decarbonize their investment portfolios. As at October 2019, it had 32 members representing over $3 trillion in assets under management, with $800 billion in decarbonization commitments. The PDC aims to provide a platform to drive action by investors and send strong signals to policymakers and companies about investors' commitment to the transition to a low-carbon economy. For more information, see https://unepfi.org/pdc/

Climate Action 100+

Climate Action 100+ is a five-year initiative led by institutional investors to engage systemically important greenhouse gas emitters that have significant opportunities to drive the clean energy transition and help achieve the goals of the Paris Agreement. This requires investors to engage with companies to improve governance on climate change, curb emissions and strengthen climate-related financial disclosures. By 2019, more than 300 investors with $35 trillion in assets under management had agreed to support the initiative. For more information, see http://www.climateaction100.org/

The PDC and Climate Action 100+ in particular are covered in more detail in Chapter 9, as part of an examination of the role of equity markets and institutional investors in green finance.

Insurance initiatives

As major institutional investors and asset owners, insurers play significant roles in many of the investor initiatives introduced above. In addition, a number of networks and initiatives have been created for insurers and reinsurers, including the following:

ClimateWise

ClimateWise is a global network of leading insurance industry organizations established to support the insurance industry to better communicate, disclose and respond to the risks and opportunities associated with climate change. It runs the Societal Resilience Programme, which publishes research to help insurers proactively respond to the widening climate risk protection gap. ClimateWise is convened by CISL, which also facilitates the Investment Leaders Group described above. For more information, see: https://www.cisl.cam.ac.uk/business-action/sustainable-finance/climatewise

InsuResilience Global Partnership

The InsuResilience Global Partnership, launched at COP23 in 2017, aims to increase the resilience of 400 million poor and vulnerable people around the world by 2020 by providing direct insurance (where individuals or small businesses insure themselves) or indirect insurance (where governments insure themselves) against climate risks, including extreme weather events. To date, more than 60 governmental, civil society and insurance industry organizations have joined the initiative. For more information, see https://www.insuresilience.org/

Sustainable Insurance Forum

The Sustainable Insurance Forum, introduced above, is an international network of insurance regulators and supervisors. For more information, see https://www.sustainableinsuranceforum.org/

Institutional responses: Embedding sustainability into strategy

We have already discussed many of the key intergovernmental and governmental policy and regulatory measures, and industry initiatives that have been instigated to tackle climate change and accelerate the growth of green and sustainable finance. Some of the key principles and frameworks in this area, for example the United Nations-supported Principles for Responsible Investment, Principles for Sustainable Insurance, Principles for Responsible Banking, and the Green Bond and Green Loan Principles, have also been highlighted. To be truly effective in developing and mainstreaming green and sustainable finance, international, national and industry frameworks, principles and initiatives need to be translated into meaningful action by the finance sector. This will require banks, insurers and investors to embed green and sustainable finance principles and practice that guide their short-, medium- and long-term planning into their own organizational strategies, while also using these same principles to assess the strategies of companies they invest in, or lend to.

While every competent organization has a strategy, green and/or sustainability factors may not always be incorporated in the development and implementation of the strategy, in terms of:

- how climate change will impact on the demand for the organization's products and services, creating both challenges and opportunities;
- how climate change will affect the organization's operations, including impacts throughout the supply chain;
- the impact of the organization's chosen strategy, as expressed through its products, services and operations, on the environment, and on society more broadly;
- the long-term impact on desired financial and other returns to owners, investors, employees and other stakeholders.

Light green strategies and greenwashing

Light green strategies are those in which green and sustainability factors are not central to an organization's strategy and operations, but rather additions to a strategy that does not have a green and sustainable vision and purpose at its core. Whilst organizations may display genuine and well-intentioned commitments to avoiding harmful activities and supporting the transition to a low-carbon world, in practice such commitments may not always be embedded within their purpose and strategy. In some cases, commitments may prove to be little more than marketing-led activities that make organizations appear greener than is the reality.

The following examples illustrate what might be considered as light green strategies:

- An energy company creates a new green strategy focusing on their administrative processes, such as encouraging greater energy efficiency and recycling in company offices, and increasing their use of videoconferencing rather than flying to internal and client meetings. Their central business operations are untouched and rely on fossil fuel CO_2 intensive extraction.
- An investment fund announces that they will invest £10 million in renewable technologies. The rest of their investment portfolio remains untouched, which means that less than 0.5 per cent is considered to be green, with the remaining 99.5 per cent of their investments including a significant proportion of high-carbon investments.
- A no-frills airline enables passengers to pay for a voluntary carbon-offsetting scheme whilst increasing its expenditure on fuel to serve expanding flight operations.

- A fossil fuel company issues a green bond to demonstrate its green credentials and the steps it is taking to support the transition to a low-carbon economy.
- An oil company highlights its investments in carbon capture and storage research to imply that this makes oil consumption compatible with meeting climate change commitments.

Light green strategies, particularly those that are marketing-led and designed to give a misleading impression of an organization's commitment to green and sustainable operations, can lead to charges of **greenwashing**, a term introduced in Chapter 1 and defined as making false, misleading or unsubstantiated claims about the positive environmental impact of a product, service or activity. In the context of strategy, greenwashing indicates that organizations are giving the illusion of supporting green and sustainable principles whilst not fundamentally adapting or changing their behaviour.

In the organizational context, there are two general types of greenwashing:

1 When the efforts of a company to be green make a small, positive difference, but that contribution is insignificant relative to the harm or damage caused by the company's core activities, as exemplified by the energy company above.
2 When the efforts of a company to be green are not green at all, and make no difference to (or may actively harm) the environment, for example when a green bond is used to finance slightly cleaner coal power.

Central to understanding whether or not an activity is really green involves considering whether it has a genuinely positive and additional impact on the environment and/or mitigating the effects of climate change, and whether that impact would have occurred anyway without that activity taking place.

Greenwashing is a real risk to the long-term viability of green and sustainable finance, and to the development of green products and services in finance, and more widely. If investors, lenders and consumers lack confidence in the integrity of organizations, activities, products and services labelled as green, then organizational and individual behaviour will not shift to accelerate the transition to a more sustainable, low-carbon world. One high-profile example of greenwashing was the Volkswagen diesel emissions-testing scandal, when software embedded in engine management systems was used to detect and cheat emissions tests in order to make Volkswagen's cars appear more environmentally friendly than was, in fact, the case. In this example, it appears that greenwashing was intentional; in other cases, it may occur unintentionally but the long-term impact remains the same.

QUICK QUESTIONS

Have you come across examples of greenwashing in the products and services you consume, or have read about? How did/does this make you feel?

As we have already seen, intergovernmental bodies such as the UN and EU, national governments and finance industry initiatives can play an important role in identifying green and sustainable products, services and activities by developing classifications (eg in the Green Bond Principles and Climate Bonds Standard), taxonomies and labelling systems (such as that proposed in the EU for green financial products). These can bring consistency to the market and enhance investor and consumer confidence but are, in many cases, still in development.

Financial regulators are also beginning to consider their role in avoiding greenwashing. In the UK, the Financial Conduct Authority published a Feedback Statement: *Climate Change and Green Finance: Summary of responses and next steps* in October 2019.[12] This sets out that firms:

- should clearly communicate to investors if they pursue environmental, social or other non-financial objectives and, if they do, how they do this;
- should communicate this in ways that are fair, clear and not misleading, and ensure that relevant updates are timely and transparent;
- need to minimize the conduct risks of greenwashing by reviewing green products and services against market standards and benchmarks; and
- must disclose material climate-related risks and prepare for mandatory TCFD disclosure.

At present, civil society organizations, particularly environmental non-governmental organizations (NGOs), play a key role in maintaining market integrity by identifying organizations, activities, products and services that could be accused of greenwashing. Green and Sustainable Finance Professionals, as we shall see in Chapter 12, also have an important role to play today, and will continue to play an important role in ensuring market integrity, with a moral and professional duty to be honest with themselves, with customers and with colleagues about the genuine or other nature of products and services labelled as green and/or sustainable. Green and

Sustainable Finance Professionals must actively avoid being involved in greenwashing, whether intentional or inadvertent, take active steps to be assured about the genuine green and sustainable credentials of organizations, activities, products and services, and must not overstate the benefits of, or avoid disclosing harm caused by these.

We will return in the next chapter to monitoring and evaluation practices in green and sustainable finance to see how these can help prevent greenwashing, provide greater certainty to investors and consumers and ensure the integrity of the green and sustainable finance market. In turn, this will encourage and accelerate the further development of green and sustainable finance.

Deep green strategies

In contrast to light green strategies, such as those described above, deep green strategies are those in which green and sustainable principles and practices are fully embedded in, and direct the strategy and operations of, an organization. An organization with a deep green strategy aligns its vision and purpose with mitigating the effects of climate change, and supporting the transition to a more sustainable, low-carbon world. These may be the main drivers of an organization's strategy, or form an important part of a wider strategic purpose, for example one aligned to several of the UN Sustainable Development Goals. Once agreed, a deep green strategy can be embedded throughout an organization's activities, operations, supply chain, policies, procedures, products and services, thus becoming part of, and supporting, an organization's culture.

There are many organizations with a genuine, deep green approach to strategy; see for example the case study of Ecology Building Society in Chapter 1. It is worth revisiting it, to see how the Society embedded green principles into their strategy, stating that their purpose is:

> making loans which are secured on residential property and are funded substantially by its members... To promote, in carrying on any business or other activity, ecological policies designed to protect or enhance the environment in accordance with the principles of sustainable development.

Another example of a genuine deep green strategy is found in the commercial flooring company Interface. The company was founded by Ray Anderson in 1973, making carpet and other flooring products; by the mid 1990s the business had grown to an annual turnover of nearly $1 billion. In 1994, after reading *The Ecology of Commerce* by Paul Hawken, the founder became appalled at the environmental damage and waste of resources his company was responsible for.[13] Anderson set a new vision for the organization: to transform production from a take–make–waste to a circular model, in which they would not take more from the Earth than they put back in. Changes included creating a new product – carpet tiles – that would allow damaged carpet to be replaced in small sections only, removing the need to throw away whole carpets. Additionally, Interface substantially increased the proportion of recycled materials used for production from 1 per cent in the 1990s to 49 per cent in 2014, inventing new flooring products produced from recycled materials to help achieve this. As a global business, Interface worked with their supply chain to ensure that the proportion of recycled materials continued to increase. The organization expected to achieve its goal of eliminating any negative impact on the environment by 2020.

For Ray Anderson, and his successors at Interface, 'going green' was not something that could simply be 'added on' to the business – it meant fundamentally reshaping the company's approach, leading to new inventions and new ways of actively interacting with suppliers in order to achieve the organization's goal of a fully circular model of production.

QUICK QUESTION

Can you think of other examples of organizations with genuine deep green strategies?

Products and services can – and in a genuine deep green strategy will – be designed to support the implementation of a green finance strategy. In Chapters 6 to 11 we will look at the growing range of products and services developed by the finance sector to support sustainable banking, investment and insurance activities. As with organizations themselves, products and services can be light or deep green. Understanding how to assess and evaluate the green credentials of products and services – and the activities and projects that underpin these, working with suitably qualified experts able to verify environmental impact – is discussed in the following chapter and is a core part of the Green and Sustainable Finance Professional's work.

As we will see in Chapter 12, in order to maintain confidence in the integrity of green and sustainable finance, Green and Sustainable Finance

Professionals should take active steps to ensure that their activities and, as far as possible, those of their organizations, are aligned with and support the transition to, a low-carbon, sustainable world – that is, adopt a deep green approach. This involves, at a minimum, ensuring that products, services, and advice offered are consistent with promoting this transition and that financial activities that may damage the environment are identified and disclosed. Green Finance and Sustainable Professionals have a particular responsibility to avoid greenwashing, and should take active steps to ensure their advice and activities do not in any way damage the integrity of their profession.

The importance of organizational culture in driving sustainability

Organizational culture is a system of beliefs, assumptions, values and principles shared by members of an organization that derive from a common understanding of a shared vision and purpose. As individuals generally find it very difficult, if not impossible, to constantly refer to complex and often lengthy sets of principles and corporate strategy documents, it is culture that shapes the delivery of strategy and the decisions that employees make on a day-to-day basis. As we have seen in financial services in recent years, when organizational cultures do not support an ethos of customer-focused, ethical professionalism, this results in detrimental outcomes for customers, communities and usually (over the longer term) for the organization itself. On a more positive note, where an organization has adopted and successfully communicated a vision for green and sustainable finance and embedded this in a clear, deep green purpose supported by well-defined principles and policies, and where these are themselves supported by an organizational culture driven by tone from the top, successful genuine green strategies can lead to positive, sustainable outcomes for customers, the organization and society as a whole.

To support tone from the top and to develop and maintain a green and sustainable organizational culture, many financial institutions now have a sustainability team or similar who seek to influence, formulate, drive, support, monitor and improve the organization's strategic green and sustainable goals. Such teams are necessary as change agents and require a depth of knowledge that enables them to balance environmental and social impacts with revenue generation, cost savings, and other business objectives.

Ideally, these teams should come from across different areas of the business to contribute the necessary in-depth and practical knowledge of different departments and functions. Figure 3.1 illustrates how a sustainability team in banking can work.

Banking sustainability team

Practically, how can organizational culture be developed and maintained to support green and sustainable finance values? Recruiting and retaining staff based on shared organizational values is a fundamental element. Staff training and development, in particular ensuring that all colleagues develop knowledge of green and sustainable finance principles and practice, rather than being contained only within smaller, specialist teams, is also important. Training and development will not suffice by itself, however. Organizations must also encourage, celebrate and incentivize green and sustainable finance activities by employees, so that knowledge and skills developed through training and development are put into practice.

Figure 3.1 Synergies of sustainability in banking

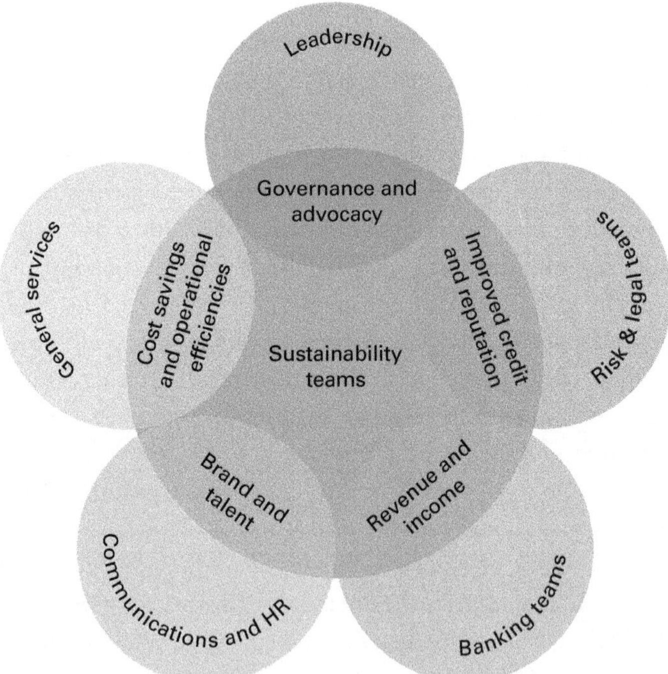

SOURCE Reproduced with permission. UNEP (2016) *Guide to Banking and Sustainability*. https://www.unepfi.org/wordpress/wp-content/uploads/2017/06/CONSOLIDATED-BANKING-GUIDE-MAY-17-WEB.pdf

Triodos Bank, for example, has two approaches to staff development and training which impact on the skills and competencies needed:

- **Experience:** Staff are given time and space to interact with environmental entrepreneurs so that they can learn about and experience first-hand the challenges they face.
- **Evaluation:** Reflective spaces are created where staff can work together to understand challenging questions and problems, and come up with strategies to try to move forward. Learning from within the organization and from colleagues can be a great way to bring everyone together around an issue (such as the challenges of mainstreaming green finance within an organization).

QUICK QUESTION

How could you use your learning from this course to train and encourage colleagues?

Key concepts

In this chapter we considered:

- the primary actors involved in building a sustainable financial system;
- the key policy and regulatory frameworks supporting green and sustainable finance;
- how intergovernmental bodies, governments and other organizations are supporting green and sustainable finance;
- some key industry initiatives on green and sustainable finance;
- how sustainability may be embedded in organizational strategies.

Now go back through this chapter and make sure you fully understand each point.

Review

In recent years there has been significant growth in the number of policy, regulatory and industry measures to accelerate the growth of green and sustainable finance, led by intergovernmental organizations, national governments, regulatory authorities, industry bodies and others. In 2019, the UNEP identified 391 policy and regulatory measures supporting green and sustainable finance, covering more than 60 countries. An overview of the key institutions and policy, regulatory and market initiatives in green and sustainable finance was provided in this chapter.

The UN Framework Convention on Climate Change (UNFCCC) is the main international treaty to combat climate change. Prior to the Paris Agreement, the 1997 Kyoto Protocol was the main global framework for cutting greenhouse gas emissions, but this has had limited impact as some major emitters and developing countries did not ratify or were not included. At COP21 in 2015, 197 countries concluded the Paris Agreement – the first, universal, legally binding global climate agreement providing a pathway to limit global temperature rises to below 2°C.

The UNEP Finance Initiative (UNEP FI) is a partnership between the UN Environment Programme and the global financial sector, with a mission to promote sustainable finance. In 2014, UNEP established the Inquiry into the Design of a Sustainable Financial System, the leading international platform dedicated to advancing efforts to green the global financial system.

A wide range of international initiatives exist to support green and sustainable finance, including, but not limited to, the United Nations-supported Principles for Responsible Investment, Principles for Sustainable Insurance, Principles for Responsible Banking, the Green Climate Fund, the EU Sustainable Finance Action Plan, the G20 Green Finance Study Group, Green Bond and Green Loan Principles, Climate Bonds Standard and the Task Force on Climate-related Financial Disclosures.

International regulators also play important roles in promoting green and sustainable finance, but could do more. In banking, Basel III requires banks to assess the impact of specific environmental risks, but does not explicitly address the wider financial stability risks associated with systemic environmental risks. In insurance, Solvency II requires insurers to be sufficiently capitalized to withstand the losses of a 1 in 200-year event, but the growing risk of extreme climate-related events may expose insurers to losses of a 1 in 100-year event.

At national level, there is a wide diversity of green and sustainable finance initiatives, reflecting the individual circumstances of different countries, with examples ranging from green bond standards in China to the Indonesian Sustainable Finance Roadmap. There is also a wide and growing range of finance industry initiatives to promote and embed green and sustainable finance, covering banking, investment and insurance. Examples include the Global Alliance for Banking on Values, the Portfolio Decarbonization Coalition and the InsuResilience Global Partnership.

Green and sustainable principles and practice may be embedded in organizational strategies to guide short-, medium- and long-term planning and, ultimately, deliver a growing range of green and sustainable products and services. Light green strategies are those in which green and sustainability factors are not central to an organization's strategy; deep green strategies have green and sustainable vision and purpose at their core.

Strategies designed to give a misleading impression of an organization's commitment to green and sustainable operations may amount to greenwashing. If greenwashing is not identified, and prevented, it may become a real risk to the long-term viability of green and sustainable finance, and to the development of green products and services in finance, and more widely, by undermining market integrity. Green and Sustainable Finance Professionals have an important role to play in ensuring that greenwashing – whether intentional or inadvertent – is identified and avoided.

To support the development of deep green strategies, and ensure that they are embedded throughout an organization's activities and operations, developing and maintaining an appropriate organizational culture is key.

Glossary

Basel III: The current framework for international banking regulation, developed by the Basel Committee on Banking Supervision.

Carbon zero: No carbon is emitted through production or other activities, therefore – in contrast with 'net zero' – no carbon needs to be captured or offset.

Conference of the Parties (COP): The governing body of the UNFCCC, which meets annually to review the implementation of the Convention and agreed climate change instruments, and provides a forum for the negotiation of new climate change agreements and policies. Annual COP meetings are numbered sequentially, with the most recent meeting being COP25 in Madrid, Spain (2019).

Deep green strategies: Strategies in which green and sustainable principles and practices are fully embedded and direct the strategy and operations of an organization.

FSB: Financial Stability Board

Kyoto Protocol: Prior to the Paris Agreement coming into effect in 2020, the 1997 Kyoto Protocol was the main global framework for cutting greenhouse gas emissions. In its first phase (2008–12) the Protocol covered only 12% of global emissions, as some major emitters (eg the USA) and developing countries did not ratify or were not included in the agreement.

Light green strategies: Strategies in which green and sustainability factors are not central to an organization's strategy and operations.

Negative emissions: Removing carbon dioxide from the atmosphere. Techniques have not yet been developed successfully at the scale required to make a substantial contribution towards net zero targets.

Net zero: Balancing carbon dioxide emissions released into the atmosphere with equivalent amounts captured and stored, and/or offset (eg through buying carbon credits).

OECD: Organisation for Economic Co-operation and Development

Paris Agreement: See Chapter 1's key terms, page 000.

Physical risks: Risks linked to the direct impact of climate-related events, such as floods and storms.

Solvency II: EU framework for insurance regulation.

TCFD: Task Force on Climate-related Financial Disclosures, set up by the Financial Stability Board to develop recommendations on disclosure of climate risks.

Transition risks: Risks from the process of adjustment towards a lower-carbon economy.

UNEP FI: United Nations Environment Programme Finance Initiative. A partnership between the UN Environment Programme (UNEP) and the global financial sector to promote sustainable finance.

UNFCCC: United Nations Framework Convention on Climate Change. Agreed in 1992, and ratified by 197 parties to the Convention, the UNFCCC is the key international treaty providing a global framework for combatting climate change.

Notes

1 UNEP (2019) Measures backing green finance more than doubled since 2015, UN figures show [Online] https://www.unenvironment.org/news-and-stories/press-release/measures-backing-green-finance-more-doubled-2015-un-figures-show (archived at https://perma.cc/2T47-4HJP)

2 Green Climate Fund (nd) Portfolio dashboard [Online] https://www.greenclimate.fund/projects/dashboard (archived at https://perma.cc/E8J2-DC9R)

3 G20 Sustainable Finance Study Group (2018) *Sustainable Finance Synthesis Report* [Online] http://unepinquiry.org/wp-content/uploads/2018/11/G20_Sustainable_Finance_Synthesis_Report_2018.pdf (archived at https://perma.cc/GZ9C-JXQF)

4 European Commission (2018) Action Plan: Financing Sustainable Growth [Online] https://eur-lex.europa.eu/legal-content/EN/TXT/?uri=CELEX:52018DC0097 (archived at https://perma.cc/2LDP-PWFN)

5 European Commission (nd) A European green deal [Online] https://ec.europa.eu/info/strategy/priorities-2019-2024/european-green-deal_en (archived at https://perma.cc/Y3TJ-W4N8)

6 Berensmann, *et al* (2018) Fostering sustainable global growth through green finance: What role for the G20? *G20 Insights* [Online] http://www.g20-insights.org/wp-content/uploads/2017/04/Climate_Green-Finance_V2.pdf (archived at https://perma.cc/G5F9-ZH7Q)

7 L Chatain (2018) Art 173: Lessons learned from climate risk disclosures in France, FourTwentySeven, 21 March [Online] http://427mt.com/2018/03/21/art-173-lessons-learned-climate-risk-disclosures-france/ (archived at https://perma.cc/J8YH-FCQW)

8 University of Cambridge Institute for Sustainability Leadership (CISL) and UNEP FI (2014) *Stability and Sustainability in Banking Reform: Are environmental risks missing in Basel III?* [Online] http://www.unepfi.org/fileadmin/documents/StabilitySustainability.pdf (archived at https://perma.cc/7FP8-GMXC)

9 University of Cambridge Institute for Sustainability Leadership (CISL) and UNEP FI (2014) *Stability and Sustainability in Banking Reform: Are environmental risks missing in Basel III?* [Online] http://www.unepfi.org/fileadmin/documents/StabilitySustainability.pdf (archived at https://perma.cc/7FP8-GMXC)

10 ICMA (2018) Green Bond Principles: Voluntary process guidelines for issuing Green Bonds [Online] https://www.icmagroup.org/green-social-and-sustainability-bonds/green-bond-principles-gbp/ (archived at https://perma.cc/4X7X-XUTU)

11 LMA (2018) The LMA publishes Green Loan Principles, 21 March [Online] https://www.lma.eu.com/news-publications/press-releases?id=146 (archived at https://perma.cc/XH93-57XK)

12 FCA (2019) *Climate Change and Green Finance: Summary of responses and next steps – Feedback to DP18/8* [Online] https://www.fca.org.uk/publication/feedback/fs19-6.pdf (archived at https://perma.cc/E575-MRZE)

13 Interface (nd) Our sustainability journey [Online] https://www.interface.com/EU/en-GB/sustainability/our-journey-en_GB (archived at https://perma.cc/LG5M-8MLT)

04

Monitoring flows of finance and environmental performance

LEARNING OBJECTIVES

On completion of this chapter you should be able to:

- Explain the importance and challenges of monitoring, measuring and reporting the flow of investment to support the transition to a sustainable, low-carbon world.
- Outline different ways in which green and sustainable investment impacts and outcomes may be monitored and verified.
- Explain the importance of independent, external review in green and sustainable finance.
- Describe how advances in data availability and analysis can support the development of green and sustainable finance.

In this chapter, we consider the importance of monitoring, measuring and reporting the flow of public and private sector investment to support climate change mitigation and adaptation activities, in order to track progress towards the Paris Agreement's objectives of making these consistent with the transition to a sustainable, low-carbon world. We also look at the challenges of identifying, monitoring and reporting these on a consistent basis. We examine how impacts and outcomes of green and sustainable investments may be measured and monitored, stressing the importance of ensuring independent external review, and transparent reporting. Finally, we consider advances in the gathering and analysis of environmental performance and asset-level data using advances in technology, including remote sensing and big data analysis, and how these may support the development of green and sustainable finance.

Monitoring, measuring and reporting in green and sustainable finance: Tracking flows of climate finance

In the context of green and sustainable finance, monitoring, measuring and reporting can refer to:

- tracking and reporting flows of investment to green and sustainable assets, activities and projects with the aim of meeting the Paris Agreement and other climate targets;
- measuring and reporting the environmental impact and outcomes of green and sustainable finance investments.

In this section, we consider how flows of public and private finance are monitored, measured and reported. This is critical for the transition to a sustainable, low-carbon world as the overwhelming majority of global activities at both macro and micro level (whether government, industrial, business, agricultural, household or individual) involve and require investment from, or the facilitation of, the financial services sector in one or more ways.

The Paris Agreement has three main goals:

- **Article 2.1a:** Holding the increase in the global average temperature to well below 2°C above pre-industrial levels and pursuing efforts to limit the temperature increase to 1.5°C above pre-industrial levels, recognizing that this would significantly reduce the risks and impacts of climate change.
- **Article 2.1b:** Increasing the ability to adapt to the adverse impacts of climate change and foster climate resilience and low greenhouse gas emissions development, in a manner that does not threaten food production.

- **Article 2.1c:** Making finance flows consistent with a pathway towards low greenhouse gas emissions and climate-resilient development.

It is highly significant that finance is given such prominence in the Paris Agreement. This sends a powerful signal to governments, central banks and regulators, the financial services sector and society as a whole that both green finance and financial services overall play a central role in addressing climate change mitigation and adaptation, and supporting the transition to a sustainable, low-carbon world.

QUICK QUESTION

What, in your view, is required to ensure that finance flows are consistent with the Paris Agreement targets?

Implementing the Paris Agreement and measuring its progress therefore requires not just measuring and monitoring environmental factors such as global temperatures and greenhouse gas emissions, but also monitoring, measuring and reporting on flows of public and private finance, in which there are two key aspects:

1. **Tracking flows of investment to identified climate change mitigation and adaptation projects and activities:** According to the Climate Policy Initiative (see Chapter 1), more than $500 billion of investment in climate change mitigation and adaptation was identified in 2017 – much less than the estimated $6 trillion per year required to meet the Paris Agreement objectives. Despite the lack of standard definitions for climate finance (and despite many initiatives to improve this), it is relatively straightforward to identify labelled financial activities, such as green bonds and green loans, directly targeted at climate change mitigation and adaptation projects and activities. The publication of the EU Taxonomy, and the development of market standards such as the Green Bond and Green Loan Principles, and the Climate Bonds Standard, make the identification and tracking of green and sustainable investments easier, and easier to compare and contrast.
2. **Tracking flows of investment that detract from change mitigation and adaptation projects and activities:** Achieving the objective of Article 2.1c also requires monitoring and measuring investment and other financial activities that are financing activities and projects that detract from the

achievement of the Paris Agreement objectives; for example, the financing of high-carbon power generation, or cement production. Such monitoring and measuring is more difficult and complex. While the flows of finance to some sectors can be measured directly – for example, between 2014 and 2016, global banks provided approximately $58 billion for coal mining and $75 billion for coal power activities – most large financial institutions are unable at present to accurately measure greenhouse gas emissions and carbon footprints across their entire investment portfolios and loan books, and the supply chains and end users associated with these. Given the size and complexity of portfolios and supply chains, this is not surprising, but with the emergence of bank and insurer stress tests incorporating climate change scenarios, the potential introduction of mandatory TCFD reporting and a greater awareness of climate-related risks in general there are many efforts at global, national, sectoral and institutional level to track investment flows through portfolios.

Measuring and monitoring in this context refers to the identification and quantification of investments either supporting or detracting from climate change mitigation and adaptation. **Verification** refers to a level of assurance that, if investment claims to support mitigation and/or adaptation, it actually does so. This usually requires some form of independent, expert review that the finance provided has been used for the intended activities, and that these have had the environmental impacts intended, rather than simple self-declaration. **Reporting** refers to financial institutions making available data on green investments and loans, and, more broadly, reporting on emissions and carbon footprints across institutional portfolios, although, as already noted, very few large financial institutions are actually able to do this at present.

Monitoring, measuring and reporting investment flows: UNFCCC Standing Committee on Finance

At global level, the leading role in monitoring, measuring and reporting flows of climate finance (as opposed to green and sustainable finance more broadly) is played by the UNFCCC Standing Committee on Finance. Members of the OECD – known as the Annex II Parties – are thereby committed to providing $100 billion per year by 2020 to developing countries for climate change mitigation and adaptation projects and activities, a target that encompasses both public and private investment.

The Standing Committee publishes biennial assessments (BA) of climate finance flows, most recently in 2018. These are based on biennial reports (BR) submitted in a common format by Annex II Parties. In addition, the

Standing Committee reports investment through Multilateral Climate Funds and Multilateral Development Banks (MDBs) and seeks also to identify and report flows of private and domestic climate finance, while noting that data on private and domestic climate finance flows are harder to obtain and of poorer quality and consistency.

Acknowledging these difficulties in obtaining accurate, complete data on global climate finance, the 2018 BA estimates that overall climate finance grew from $584 billion in 2014 to $680 billion in 2015 and to $681 billion in 2016, on a comparable basis.[1] The significant increase in investment in 2015 was driven mainly, according to the Standing Committee, by high levels of private sector investment in renewable energy. This decreased the following year, but was offset by an increase in investment in energy efficiency technologies in the building, industry and transport sectors.

More specifically, according to the 2018 BA:

- Flows from Annex II Parties to developing countries increased by 24 per cent from 2014 to 2015 (to $33 billion) and by 14 per cent from 2015 to 2016 (to $38 billion). This is still well below the 2020 target of $100 billion.
- Funds channelled through Multilateral Climate Funds, in particular the Green Climate Fund, increased from $1.4 billion in 2015 to $2.4 billion in 2016, although this represents a decrease of 13 per cent on the previous two-year period.
- MDBs provided $23.4 billion in 2015 and $25.5 billion in 2016, a 3.4 per cent increase on the previous two-year period (many MDBs have subsequently significantly increased their levels of, and/or commitments to, climate finance).

The overall picture of global climate finance in 2015–16 (including estimates of private and domestic climate finance), according to the 2018 BA, is set out in Figure 4.1.

The 2018 BA was the first to include information on tracking flows of finance to meet the objectives of Article 2.1c of the Paris Agreement. The Standing Committee notes that:

- the reporting of data on flows of finance to climate change mitigation and adaptation is at an early stage, with green bond markets the most advanced in terms of data availability and quality;
- other market segments lack comparable data and/or data quality is less consistent;
- there are emerging reporting initiatives, but many are at an early stage.

Figure 4.1 Climate finance flows in the period 2015–16

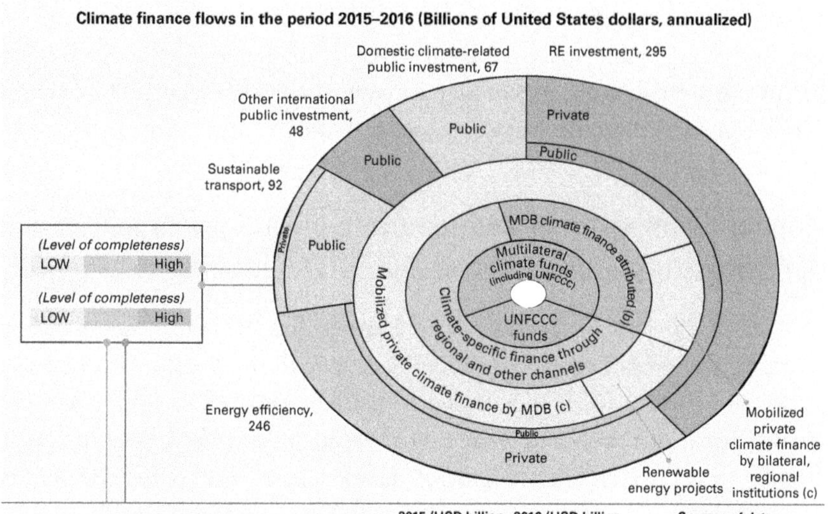

		2015 (USD billion face value)	2016 (USD billion face value)	Sources of data and relevant chapter
Global total flows	Renewable energy investments	320.9	269.5	Chapter 2.2.1
	Public investment	61.7	52.3	CPI based on multiple sources
	Private investment	259.2	217.1	
	Energy efficiency investments	233.9	257.8	Chapter 2.2.2
	Public investment	25.7	32.9	IEA Energy Efficiency Market Reports/CPI
	Private investment (a)	208.2	224.9	
	Sustainable transport	78.0	105.8	Chapter 2.2.3
	Public investment	69.7	92.5	IEA World Energy Investment Report/CPI
	Private investment	8.3	13.3	
	Other sectors public investment	47.3	47.5	Chapter 2.2.2 – 2.2.5 CPI based on multiple sources
	Domestic climate-related public investment	67.0	67.0	Chapter 2.3 BURs, CPEIRs (UNDP), I4CE
Flows to non-Annex I Parties	UNFCCC funds	0.6	1.6	Chapter 2.5.2 Fund financial reports, CFU
	Multilateral climate funds (including UNFCCC)	1.4	2.4	Chapter 2.5.2 Fund financial reports, CFU
	Climate-specific finance through bilateral, regional and other channels	29.9	33.6	Chapter 2.5.1 Annex II Party Biennial Reports
	MDB climate finance attributed (b)	17.4	19.7	Chapter 2.5.2
	Renewable energy projects	2.4	1.5	Chapter 2.5.4 CPI based on multiple sources
	Mobilized private climate finance by MDB (c)	10.9	15.7	Chapter 2.5.4 MDB Joint Reports
	Mobilized private climate finance by bilateral, regional institutions (c)	2.3		Chapter 2.5.4 OECD

Abbreviations: BEV = battery electric vehicle, BUR = beinnial update reports, CPEIR = climate public expenditure and institutional reviews, CPI = Climate Policy Initiative, IEA = International Energy Agency, I4CE = Institute for Climate Economics, MDB = multilateral development bank, OECD = Organisation for Economic Co-operation and Development, UNDP = United Nations Development Programme.

[a] Value discounts transport energy efficiency estimates by 8.5 per cent to account for overlap with electric vehicle estimates.
[b] From members of the OECD Development Assistance Committee (DAC), minus the Republic of Korea, to OECD-DAC recipients eligible for official development assistance. Refer to chapter 2.5.2 of the 2018 Biennial Assessment and Overview of Climate Finance Flows technical report for further explanation.
[c] Estimates include private co-financing with MDB finance.

SOURCE United Nations Framework Convention on Climate Change (2018) *UNFCCC Standing Committee on Finance: 2018 biennial assessment and overview of climate finance flows – Technical report.* https://unfccc.int/sites/default/files/resource/2018%20BA%20Technical%20Report%20Final.pdf

Green and Sustainable Finance Professionals and their institutions can play key roles, therefore, in supporting the development of reporting initiatives designed to bring consistency and comparability to the identification and labelling of green and sustainable finance, including climate finance. In turn, and over time, this will support increasing flows of finance to climate change mitigation and adaptation projects and activities.

Monitoring, measuring and reporting private investment flows: OECD Research Collaborative and ISO standards

We saw in Chapter 1 that the private sector has a major role to play in financing the transition to a sustainable, low-carbon world, with approximately 80 per cent of the investment required estimated to come from that sector. Private sector climate finance, and green and sustainable finance more broadly, is also required to help the Annex II Parties meet their $100 billion commitment to climate change mitigation and adaptation in developing countries.

Monitoring and reporting on flows of private sector finance is vitally important, therefore, in measuring progress towards this target as well as to the broader objective of meeting the requirements of Article 2.1c of the Paris Agreement. As already noted, however, obtaining good quality, consistent and comparable data on the flow of private sector finance is particularly challenging. This is not surprising given the enormous variety of financial institutions, financial instruments and approaches to/definitions of green, sustainable and climate finance in the private sector. The publication of the EU Taxonomy, similar national initiatives (eg in China) and developing global market standards such as the Green Bond and Green Loan Principles, and Climate Bonds Standard can bring consistency, support market integrity and, over time, will help the tracking of private climate finance flows. An EU Green Bond Standard is in development, aligned with the EU Taxonomy, which will bring further consistency at the European level.

At global level, two key initiatives seeking to improve the monitoring and reporting of private finance flows are the OECD Research Collaborative and the International Organization for Standardization's (ISO) forthcoming Climate Finance Standard (ISO 14097), currently in development.

Formed in 2013, the OECD Research Collaborative is formed of governments, research institutions and international finance institutions, and aims to:

- identify, develop and evaluate possible methodologies for measuring overall private climate finance flows to, between and in developing countries;
- identify, develop and evaluate possible methodologies to determine private climate flows mobilized by developed-country public sector interventions;
- conduct the measurement (tracking) of private climate finance and flows mobilized by public sector intervention.

The Research Collaboration has published a series of papers exploring approaches to tracking private climate finance, most recently in March 2019.[2] The researchers highlight a number of key weaknesses in the data currently available for tracking private climate finance flows:

- Existing finance tracking efforts typically focus on specific financial asset classes (eg bonds or equities), actors (eg development finance institutions), and/or geographies – but often do not combine these to build up a whole picture.
- While there is an increasing amount of data available in relation to international and multilateral climate finance flows, there is lack of data relating to domestic finance flows, such as commercial bank loans and other forms of domestic corporate finance.
- Most current initiatives focus on tracking finance for climate change mitigation and adaptation activities only, whereas assessing progress towards Article 2.1c of the Paris Agreement requires tracking all investments, and including those that undermine climate change objectives.

To overcome such data challenges, the researchers propose to monitor and measure investment in new infrastructure and equipment, and in refurbishment of same. This will complement existing efforts to track climate finance, focusing on publicly traded financial assets such as bonds, loans and equities, which are hard to monitor consistently because of definitional issues, as well as the other issues set out above. The researchers believe that tracking infrastructure and equipment investment will help improve monitoring and measurement of private climate flows as production and use accounts for a very large proportion of future greenhouse gas emissions.

Improving the consistency and quality of climate finance data is also the objective of the ISO, a global network comprising a wide range of international and national organizations and associations and including more than

100,000 experts from over 160 countries. The ISO oversees thousands of technical committees developing and maintaining standards across business, industry, science, technology and many other areas. Over the past 10 years, ISO has developed and published a wide range of standards relating to the environment in general, and to climate change more specifically, eg ISO 14064 for monitoring and reporting greenhouse gas emissions, ISO 14065 for accrediting verifiers of emissions, and ISO 14031 on environmental performance evaluation.

More recently (from 2017 onwards), ISO has established working groups to develop international standards relating to climate finance, one of which is **ISO 14097 – Framework and principles for assessing and reporting investments and financing activities related to climate change**, currently in development.[3] The aim of ISO 14097 is to set a global framework for assessing and reporting investments and financing activities related to climate change, thereby (over time, as it will take many years for the standard to be adopted by financial services institutions globally, and will require significant regulatory endorsement) improving the availability, consistency, comparability and quality of data on climate finance. This should help governments and the financial services sector to better track, and report against, progress towards meeting the objectives of Article 2.1c of the Paris Agreement.

Monitoring, measuring and reporting in green and sustainable finance: Environmental impact

> Investors understand their returns in far greater detail than their so-called non-financial performance. As a result they have very little to say to beneficiaries about the wider impacts of their investments on society. It is not an exaggeration to say that in the main investors do not actually know whether the flows of capital they are responsible for do good or harm in society. And of course, if they were to make claims in this area they may be contested: [what is] good for one stakeholder may very well be regarded as harm by another.
>
> *Hervé Guez, Director, Responsible Investment Research, Mirova*[4]

As already noted, in the context of green and sustainable finance, monitoring, measuring and reporting can refer to:

- tracking and reporting flows of investment to green and sustainable finance assets, activities and projects with the aim of meeting the Paris Agreement and other climate targets;

- measuring and reporting the environmental impact and outcomes of green and sustainable investments.

In this section, we examine ways in which green and sustainable investment impacts and outcomes may be monitored, measured and reported, rather than tracking overall flows of finance. Developing, implementing and embedding consistent approaches to monitoring and reporting impact and outcomes is important as, if green and sustainable finance is to be mainstreamed, such monitoring and reporting will need to become business-as-usual for organizations and Green and Sustainable Finance Professionals, so that genuinely green and sustainable investments can be tracked and reported.

Identification of green and sustainable investments is often known as green tagging. Being able to consistently identify and classify investments as green, brown or neutral is a key step in supporting the transition to a sustainable, low-carbon world. Data on individual assets and investments can be combined to (eventually) give a whole-organization portfolio view. Data from organizations can then be further aggregated at sectoral, industry, national or global levels, thus helping to track progress towards achieving the objectives of Article 2.1c of the Paris Agreement.

QUICK QUESTION

In what ways (if any) are green and sustainable investments and activities monitored and reported in your organization, or in an organization with which you are familiar?

The identification and monitoring of green, brown and neutral investments is also key for investors and asset owners in recognizing investments and assets that might be impaired or stranded due to the transition to a sustainable, low-carbon world – especially if the transition is more abrupt than had been anticipated.

In addition, monitoring, verifying and reporting the environmental impacts and outcomes of investments is important to help prevent greenwashing – inadvertently or deliberately misleading customers or investors about environmental benefits. Avoiding greenwashing and maintaining the integrity of the green finance market is essential if it is to grow to the scale needed to support the transition to a sustainable, low-carbon world.

What are we measuring?

Monitoring systems may seek to measure processes intended to lead to positive green and sustainable outcomes, and/or to measure the impacts and outcomes directly. To ensure the delivery of positive environmental outcomes and to avoid greenwashing, the monitoring and measuring of impacts, including review by suitably qualified, independent third parties, is essential to maintain the integrity of green and sustainable finance.

Processes

Process monitoring describes the assessment and evaluation, by independent third parties, of an organization's principles, policies, procedures and practices. In the context of green and sustainable finance, these would be intended to shape an organization's decision-making to lead to positive environmental outcomes from investments or other activities. The main focus may be on environmental or broader sustainability due diligence on financial investments, to ensure that approval is given only to those investments meeting the desired criteria.

It is worth looking at the implementation of the Equator Principles (introduced briefly in Chapter 3) to illustrate and understand the advantages and disadvantages of this approach. The Equator Principles are a risk management framework which financial institutions, especially banks involved in project financing and commercial loans to infrastructure, have adopted for assessing and managing environmental and social risks in projects. They provide a framework to which financial institutions' own policies, procedures and practices can be aligned and benchmarked.

The UNEP Inquiry (2016) found that the impact of the Equator Principles has been mixed.[5] Supporters argue they are visionary principles that have helped to redefine and enhance environmental and social practices, by promoting convergence around common environmental and social standards. Critics argue that the Principles are process-orientated and do not set criteria on desired environmental and sustainable outcomes, nor give guidance on conditions that would result in the rejection of project finance because of environmental or social issues. There are also concerns regarding the validity of CO_2 emissions calculations, and about the willingness of financial institutions to disclose data voluntarily. In addition, the UNEP Inquiry found that organizations' main motivations for adopting and using the Equator Principles were centred on regulatory compliance, managing project risks and seeking reputational benefits rather than on positive environmental outcomes.

Although adopting positive green and sustainable finance principles and practices, such as those included in the Equator Principles, is desirable in the sense that it may reflect a changing culture and approach within an organization, they do not by themselves ensure that green and sustainable finance outcomes are actually achieved. Process monitoring can confirm that principles, policies and procedures are in place; independent assurance and verification can be sought to validate this, but this does not by itself necessarily lead to changes in investment flows consistent with achieving the objectives of Article 2.1c of the Paris Agreement.

Impacts and outcomes

We therefore need to monitor and measure the impacts and outcomes of investment decisions, rather than the principles, policies and procedures that guide decision-making. In the context of green and sustainable finance, this means identifying the desired environmental outcomes before making an investment, and then monitoring and measuring the environmental impact during the life of the investment, and often beyond. For financial institutions, this implies moving from traditional accounting measures of financial performance to measuring, monitoring and reporting non-financial performance, including a wide variety of environmental impacts relating to climate change mitigation and adaptation, such as reducing greenhouse gas emissions, supporting reforestation, or improving biodiversity. A key challenge in measuring impacts and outcomes is the availability and quality of relevant data.

A useful methodology for monitoring the impact and outcomes of green and sustainable investments is the assess–monitor–report approach, as used by the UK's Green Investment Bank (now Green Investment Group) and others, set out in the next case study, and which suggests that there is a considerable amount of work required at the pre-investment stage.

CASE STUDY

Green Investment Bank's assess-monitor-report approach[6]

Assess

1 Develop and make publicly available a set of policy requirements, investment criteria, and/or stated objectives against which potential projects can be assessed for alignment.
2 Assess the potential investment's management team's capability, capacity and commitment to meet stated objectives against policy requirements.

3. Request performance data from investee management, including the project's forecast renewable electricity and/or heat generation or demand reduction, and project life. The forecast carbon savings associated with the project can then be considered.
4. Scope of works for consultant – in addition to assessing the potential green impact, where appropriate, environmental and social experts can be appointed to support due diligence.
5. Green risks that the project may not deliver the forecast green and other intended impacts should be considered. Material green risks identified during this process should be mitigated in an action plan and/or included in any post-financial close monitoring.
6. Where the due diligence process identifies gaps or non-alignment to policy requirements, an action plan should be agreed with investee management to close these.
7. Green covenants should be integrated into financing/loan documentation, which must have equal legal status and recourse to enforcement measures as other financial covenants.
8. Investment decision – due diligence, forecast green performance and green risk assessment should be considered as part of investment decision-making. Once a financial commitment is made, projects should be subject to monitoring.

Monitor

1. Annual green reporting – the investee should complete an annual report detailing the forecast and/or actual performance of the project, including all relevant source data and references required for audit purposes. The report might be prepared or verified by a suitable, independent third party.
2. Investees should also report material environmental and social events and accidents to the investor as soon as possible (with associated details of any mitigation and/or actions taken to address the issue). The investor should consider these and, in consultation with investee management, assess if there is a requirement for remediation or mitigation action.
3. Independent monitoring – as part of the covenants agreed, investors should retain an independent environmental and social expert to conduct periodic monitoring and verification of green risks, action plans, forecast and actual green performance and ongoing compliance with wider environmental and social covenants.

4 Once the data from an investment has been collected and verified by an independent third party as appropriate, it can be aggregated for external reporting to stakeholders.

Report

1 It is critical that performance is reported to stakeholders on a periodic basis, utilizing global standards and established reporting processes. In brief, the environmental benefits arising are estimated by comparing the impact of the investment against an alternative outcome (scenario) if the project in question had not taken place. This alternative outcome is referred to as the counterfactual. Green impact is calculated by subtracting the project footprint from the counterfactual footprint and can be applied to greenhouse gas savings (tonnes CO_2 [equivalent] [CO_2e) and energy demand reduction (MWh). Renewable energy generated (GWh) is reported as the project's net power generated.

2 In calculating the green impact, the Greenhouse Gas Protocol for Project Accounting Guidelines should be used for reference. For energy efficiency projects, the guidance set out in the International Performance Measurement and Verification Protocol (or other such defined energy efficiency protocol as applicable) should be referred to.

The Green Investment Bank approach is broadly similar to that taken by many green and sustainable finance institutions and codified in developing market standards and guidelines such as the Green Bond and Green Loan Principles, as well as the Climate Bonds Standard and the proposed EU Green Bond Standard (see later chapters). All place significant emphasis on identifying intended green and sustainable outcomes pre-investment, then monitoring, measuring, external review – usually requiring suitably qualified, independent third parties – and reporting on impact. The four core components of the Green Bond Principles, for instance, are:

- **Use of proceeds:** Green bonds should be used to finance projects with green outcomes, such as an offshore wind farm or clean transport.
- **External review:** Issuers of green bonds should evaluate the intended green outcomes of projects with the help of a suitably qualified external reviewer.

- **Disclosure and management of proceeds:** The allocation of funds raised from a green bond should be independently audited and made easily available to investors and others.
- **Reporting:** Issuers should report on the environmental impacts of green bonds.

Measuring, monitoring, external review and reporting on the climate change mitigation and adaptation impact and outcomes of green and sustainable investments, therefore, is much more likely to lead to flows of finance consistent with achieving the objectives of Article 2.1c of the Paris Agreement. With ongoing monitoring and independent review of impacts against intended outcomes, investors can have greater confidence that their investment decisions are achieving their desired objectives, from both a financial and environmental and/or broader sustainability perspective. With transparent reporting, investors, customers, policymakers, regulators and others can be confident in tracking flows of finance to climate change mitigation and adaptation projects, and that investments promoted as green and sustainable are, in fact, just that.

To avoid accusations of greenwashing, however, and to maintain the integrity of the growing green finance market, independent third-party review is key in measuring and reporting on impacts and outcomes, as advocated by the Green Investment Bank's assess–monitor–report approach, the Green Bond Principles and other market standards and guidance.

QUICK QUESTION

Why, in your view, is independent external review of impacts and outcomes so important?

External review

As we have seen, independent external review is key in monitoring, measuring and reporting in green finance. Green and Sustainable Finance Professionals and their organizations will need to work with independent verifiers, either as part of their investment decision-making and monitoring processes (as investors), or as potential investees preparing green and sustainable projects for investment. It is important, therefore, for Green and Sustainable Finance Professionals to understand different approaches to external review and the advantages and disadvantages of each.

In green and sustainable finance, the term external review is generally used as a catch-all to cover similar terms such as audit, assurance, attestation, certification, validation, verification and second- or third-party review. Although there are differences between these, which we explore below, the intended outcomes are the same – to verify the environmental or broader sustainability impacts of investments with the aims of bringing certainty to investors, avoiding greenwashing, maintaining confidence in the green and sustainable finance market and helping track progress towards the objectives of Article 2.1c of the Paris Agreement. External reviews may be conducted at different levels, for instance at individual investment or project level, at investment programme level, or at organizational level, encompassing an institution's entire portfolio, although this is in its infancy given the scope and complexity involved.

Importantly, as in the Green Investment Bank's assess–monitor–report approach and the Green Bond Principles, external review does not only occur in respect of monitoring and measuring impact and outcomes once an investment has been made. In order to ensure positive environmental outcomes, it is recommended that expert, independent review of potential investments and projects is undertaken at an early stage of the investment decision-making process. This would usually seek to ensure that investments and intended project outcomes are:

- supported by organizational strategy, policies and procedures aligned with green finance principles and practices;
- likely to contribute to environmental objectives such as climate change mitigation or adaptation, and related areas such as improving biodiversity, reforestation and/or sustainability more broadly (depending on the investor's desired outcomes);
- unlikely to harm other environmental and/or social objectives;
- aligned with recognized investment and project categories, such as renewable energy, biodiversity conservation and clean transportation (as set out, for example, in the Green Bond Principles, Climate Bonds Standard and the EU Taxonomy); and
- supported by a realistic assessment of material green risks, ie that may prevent the investment or project achieving the desired impacts.

There are various types and levels of external review, identified by the Green Bond Principles and others:

- **Self-certification:** Self-certification, also known as a first party review, refers to the self-review of green investments and projects by the organization.

There is clear scope for conflicts of interest, or the perception of these to arise. Some green and sustainable finance market standards and frameworks do allow self-certification, eg the Green Loan Principles, but this is not recommended. By definition, self-certification is not a form of external review, but is included here for completeness.

- **Second/third party review and opinion:** In general, this refers to a review by a suitably qualified expert or institution (depending on the scope and size of the investments or projects under consideration) of the areas set out above. A second party review is when there is a degree of independence between the investment/project managers and the reviewer, but where there may be a conflict of interest, or a perception of one; for example, when the costs of the review are paid for by the organization seeking investment. A third-party review, for example a review paid for by the potential investor rather than the investee, is fully independent and therefore provides a greater level of confidence in the integrity of the review and its outcomes.
- **Verification:** Verification is when an investor obtains independent third-party assurance against designated criteria identified in advance, often including reference to market standards and guidance such as the Green Bond or Green Loan Principles, the Climate Bonds Standard, and/or standards such as those published by the ISO relating to environmental performance. Criteria may relate to processes to be followed (eg a verifier might report that an organization has benchmarked its internal policies and procedures to the Equator Principles) but, in green and sustainable finance, verification of impacts and outcomes is of greater importance.
- **Certification:** Certification refers to a process by which investments are measured against recognized external standards and criteria, ie the criteria are not defined by the investor, as is the case with verification. Certification, therefore, provides a more independent and higher level of assurance than verification. One of the best-known certification schemes in green finance is the Climate Bonds Standard, which seeks to ensure that certified bonds meet a range of criteria so that the projects they support will achieve climate change mitigation and adaptation outcomes consistent with the objectives of the Paris Agreement. For a bond to be certified as a Climate Bond, prospective issuers must appoint an approved verifier (as illustrated in the case study 'Become a Climate Bonds Standard Approved Verifier'). The Climate Bonds Standard is considered in more detail in Chapter 7.

CASE STUDY

Become a Climate Bonds Standard Approved Verifier[7]

What is an Approved Verifier?

Under the Climate Bonds Standard and Certification Scheme, an Approved Verifier will check a bond issuer's upcoming bond against our Standard and sector-based technical criteria (eg solar energy).

If the bond complies with our Standard and Criteria, the Verifier will write a report to verify that the bond can be marketed to investors as a Climate Bonds Certified Bond and join the growing list of Certified Bonds.

This is a rapidly growing market and more companies around the world are joining us to become an Approved Verifier, in order to help us Certify the increasing number of green bonds.

Training, support and oversight of Approved Verifiers are provided by the Climate Bonds Secretariat.

Requirements to become an Approved Verifier

In order to become an Approved Verifier, the company must demonstrate that they have competence and experience in the following three areas:

- issuance of debt instruments in the capital markets and management of funds within issuing organizations;
- technical characteristics and performance of low-carbon projects and assets in the areas covered by the specific criteria available under the Climate Bonds Standard;
- provision of Assurance Services in line with the International Standards on Assurance Engagements ISAE 3000.

Verifiers are expected to use teams of professional staff and/or insured contractors who meet all of these requirements for each engagement.

In addition to the three criteria laid out above, approval of Verifiers is also based on their geographic coverage and areas of technical competence:

- Geographic coverage of the approval is aligned with the coverage provided by the Verifier's insurance policies for professional indemnity/professional liability.
- Technical scope of the approval is determined by the Verifier's levels of experience and expertise in the different technical sectors covered by the Climate Bonds Standard.

In addition to the Climate Bonds Standard, other global market frameworks and standards supporting the external review, verification and certification of environmental and broader sustainability impacts and outcomes (and that support the measurement of these more generally) include:

Impact Reporting and Investment Standards

Developed by the Global Impact Investment Network (GIIN), the Impact Reporting and Investment Standards (IRIS) provide a catalogue of standardized social and environmental metrics for users to assess the environmental or broader sustainability impacts of investments. Environmental metrics include biodiversity, land and water, conservation, energy and fuel efficiency and natural resources conservation. There are also metrics for organizations' general operational impacts (eg of their day-to-day business activities, and on employees and the environment).

Global Impact Investing Rating System

The Global Impact Investing Rating System (GIIRS), established by the B-Lab organization (which oversees the certification of B-Corps, among other activities) is a third-party analysis, verification and certification system that measures the social and environmental performance of investments, providing a basis for comparison between them.[8] For example, an investment that scores very highly for impact may receive a platinum certificate, which may increase its attractiveness to investors. GIIRS can be seen as a social and environmental equivalent to credit ratings systems (such as Moodys, Fitch) commonly used to assess financial instruments. It is worth noting, however, that, using GIIRS, it is possible for an investment to achieve a highly positive environmental impact score but a negative social impact score (or the reverse), which may call into question its overall sustainability.

ISO 14031

In 2013 the ISO published ISO 14031, which provides guidance on the design and use of environmental performance evaluation, and on the identification and selection of appropriate environmental performance indicators.[9] There are three types of such indicators:

- **Management performance indicators:** Information on a management team's influence on overall environmental performance.
- **Operational performance indicators:** Information about the environmental performance of operations (eg greenhouse gas emissions, waste products).

- **Environmental condition indicators:** Information about the state of the environment where the organization operates, or where its products and services have an impact.

At the time of writing, ISO 14031 is under review.

IFC Performance Standards on Environmental and Social Sustainability

Launched in 2012, the International Finance Corporation's (IFC) Environmental and Social Sustainability Performance Standards apply to all investment and advisory clients whose projects go through the IFC's credit review process.[10] The Standards apply to eight areas: risk management, labour, resource efficiency, community, land resettlement, biodiversity, indigenous people and cultural heritage. The IFC Standards do not require, but do recommend, the use of external review to verify impacts and outcomes, and encourage including representatives of communities impacted by investments and projects in such reviews.

Measuring environmental and sustainable impact

We have discussed the importance of monitoring, measuring, external review of and reporting on climate change mitigation and adaptation impacts and outcomes. However, we have not yet considered what actually needs to be measured in terms of environmental and broader sustainability outcomes. In many cases, this requires the monitoring, measurement and reporting of environmental metrics based on scientific analysis of, for example, greenhouse gas emissions. Green and Sustainable Finance Professionals would be unlikely to be qualified to measure and report on these, which is why obtaining independent third-party review, verification and certification is so important. Investors, customers, regulators, policymakers and others need to have confidence in the environmental data reported so that progress towards the objectives of Article 2.1c of the Paris Agreement can be accurately tracked, and to avoid accusations of greenwashing.

> **QUICK QUESTION**
>
> What indicators are you aware of that relate to environmental performance or other areas of sustainability, and/or are in use in your organization or in an organization with which you are familiar?

Common metrics used in reporting environmental impacts in some key sectors include:

Energy efficiency:

- Annual energy savings, usually expressed in annual megawatt or gigawatt hours (MWh/(GWh), or equivalents.
- Reduction in greenhouse gas emissions, usually expressed in annual tonnes of CO_2 equivalent (CO_2e).
- Greenhouse gas emissions avoided (annual CO_2e).

Clean/renewable energy:

- Reduction in greenhouse gas emissions (annual CO_2e).
- Greenhouse gas emissions avoided (annual CO_2e).
- Renewable energy generation (annual MWh/(GWh), or equivalents).
- Total capacity of renewable energy plants in megawatts or gigawatts (MW/GW).

Sustainable land use:

- Capture of greenhouse gas emissions (estimated annual CO_2e), eg via reforestation.
- Surface area under conservation/reforestation (verified by appropriate certification scheme).
- Impact on biodiversity (number of species, distribution of species).

Water conservation:

- Annual water savings/reductions in leakages.
- Waste water discharged per unit of product.
- Water quality indicators (eg chemical pollutant content, fitness for human consumption).
- Impact on biodiversity and aquaculture (number of species, distribution of species, contaminant concentrations).

Clean transport:

- Reduction or avoidance of greenhouse gas emissions (annual CO_2e, and other gases emitted by vehicles, for example NO_2) in comparison with existing transportation methods.

- Quantity of new clean transport infrastructure/assets provided (eg number of electric vehicles, length and capacity of new railway lines).
- Estimated reduction in non-clean transport use (ie substitution effect).

READING
Carbon dioxide equivalent (CO_2e)

The most commonly used measure of greenhouse gas emissions is carbon dioxide equivalent, abbreviated to CO_2e, with reductions in emissions often reported using **annual CO_2e**. While carbon dioxide is the most common greenhouse gas responsible for global warming, other greenhouse gases including methane (CH_4), nitrous oxide (N_2O) and hydrofluorocarbons (HFCs) also have a significant impact. Methane, for instance, is 28 times more effective at trapping heat than carbon dioxide, and nitrous oxide 265 times more effective, making them important contributors to the greenhouse effect.

This value for the effectiveness of other greenhouse gases is known as the **global warming potential** (GWP), measured over a 100-year timescale, with carbon dioxide given a GWP of 1. Different sources offer different values for the GWP of other greenhouse gases, but the IPCC's Assessment Reports provide a generally accepted benchmark. In the IPCC Fifth Assessment Report (AR5), methane is attributed a GWP of 28, and nitrous oxide a GWP of 265.

In measuring and reporting greenhouse gas emissions, and the impact of activities designed to reduce these, CO_2e is used as a common unit of measurement. A given quantity of greenhouse gas emissions can be reported as CO_2e by multiplying it by its GWP. For example, if an oil and gas company can reduce leakage in its methane pipeline by 10 tonnes per year, this could be expressed as 280 tonnes annual CO_2e (ie 10 tonnes CH_4 x 28).

With annual CO_2e being one of the most widely quoted metrics for reporting environmental impacts, due to the extent of investment in energy efficiency and clean/renewable energy projects, there are many different approaches used for estimating and reporting greenhouse gas emissions avoided and/or reduced. These mainly differ according to the assumptions used in models (eg in estimating emissions avoided, assumptions have to be made regarding the future efficiency of, and emissions from, fossil fuel power stations and other industrial units). It is good practice, therefore, for Green and Sustainable Finance Professionals and their organizations to publish the methodologies they use to estimate emissions, and where possible to keep methodologies consistent to facilitate comparison between investments and environmental impacts over time.

As with many other areas in green finance, standardized approaches and methodologies are likely to emerge, either through regulatory interventions or the development and adoption of market standards and guidelines. In particular, ISO 14604 (revised and republished in 2018) provides a basis for such standardization, and aligning approaches and methodologies with the ISO standard is strongly encouraged. ISO 14031 provides guidance on the design and use of environmental performance evaluation, and its adoption can help the standardization of environmental measurement and reporting in a wide range of areas beyond greenhouse gas emissions.

QUICK QUESTION

What, in your view, might be some of the challenges of monitoring and measuring broader sustainability impacts beyond environmental performance?

Measuring the broader sustainability impact

While environmental performance metrics are not necessarily easy to monitor, in the sense that capturing accurate data for greenhouse gas emissions or other indicators at the individual asset or investment level can be difficult, at least the metrics themselves are generally quantitative, well-understood, credible and mostly comparable. When seeking to assess broader sustainability impacts, however, this can be more challenging, as qualitative judgements may have to be made alongside monitoring and measuring quantitative metrics. There is, therefore, no single right approach, and investors will need to determine their own methodologies for measuring impact. As with measuring environmental performance, though, it is important that:

- desired outcomes and impacts are identified at the pre-investment stage (and, ideally, examined by suitably qualified, independent experts);
- there is regular, ongoing monitoring and reporting through the life of the investment;
- measurement and monitoring of impact and outcomes are verified by independent review;
- impact and outcomes are publicly reported.

One approach to measuring sustainability impact (including environmental impact) is the Impact Reporting and Investment Standards (IRIS), described above. Another approach, based on the UN Sustainable Development Goals introduced in Chapter 1, has been developed by the Investment Leaders Group, and is presented in the case study 'Investment Leaders Group'.

CASE STUDY

Investment Leaders Group[11]

The Investment Leaders Group (ILG) is a global network of pension funds, insurers and asset managers committed to advancing responsible investment, and supported by the University of Cambridge Institute for Sustainability Leadership (CISL). It envisions an investment chain whereby economic, social and environmental sustainability is delivered as an outcome of the investment process, while also delivering robust, long-term financial returns.

The ILG found that, unlike financial performance, social and environmental impact remains largely opaque to both investors and their clients and customers. To tackle this problem the ILG developed a framework to support the quantification and communication of investment impact.

The framework distils the UN's Sustainable Development Goals into six key impact themes relevant to investors. The ILG argues that, unlike other initiatives which propose numerous technical metrics aimed at investment professionals and covering both financial risk and sustainability impact, the proposed proxy for each theme is simple, outcomes-based and communicable to retail investors and pension plan beneficiaries, empowering them to drive demand for sustainable investments.

The framework has three defining characteristics:

1. It focuses on non-financial outcomes rather than intentions or policies. In a world of volatile environmental risks, scarcities and increasing income inequality, it is not enough to know simply that a company is improving its social and environmental performance. It has become essential to understand the impact a firm has on society.
2. It focuses on impact on the environment and society, not financial materiality. Many frameworks assess the materiality of environmental, social and governance (ESG) issues to financial performance, and the ILG does not wish to add to this list. What is lacking is a simple way to

understand non-financial impacts that is standard across the industry. It is worth noting that sustainability and (long-term) financial performances are correlated, but that is not the lens taken by this framework.

3 The information derived from the framework is transparent, simple and relevant to help beneficiaries make practical choices about how they allocate their money. All the evidence points to clients and beneficiaries having a low appetite for (and tolerance of) complexity.

Impact themes in relation to the SDGs

A three-step approach to quantitative measurement is proposed for each of the six themes:

1. **Base:** A quantitative measure of the impact on an asset (or fund) across its life cycle.
2. **Stretch:** An enhanced measure to be implemented when the required data becomes available.
3. **Ideal:** An enhanced measure allowing comparison of performance with the level required by the relevant Sustainable Development Goal(s).

A set of six metrics is proposed in Table 4.1. Given the themes are broad and high level, it is impossible to capture their full extent in a single number or judgement. Simple proxies of each theme are therefore captured to convey their main essence. Being quantitative in nature, the base metrics provide objective, comparable, consistent and reproducible results. However, it is well recognized that the current level of disclosure by companies across the six themes is limited at present, with much of the information being anecdotal.

Once the impact has been quantified, for example for GHG emissions, it can then be expressed clearly, for the benefit of consumers and investors, by placing it in categories representing the impact on the relevant SDG as:

- highly positive contribution;
- positive contribution;
- limited to no contribution;
- negative contribution;
- highly negative contribution.

Figure 4.2 Impact themes and their relationship to the UN Sustainable Development Goals

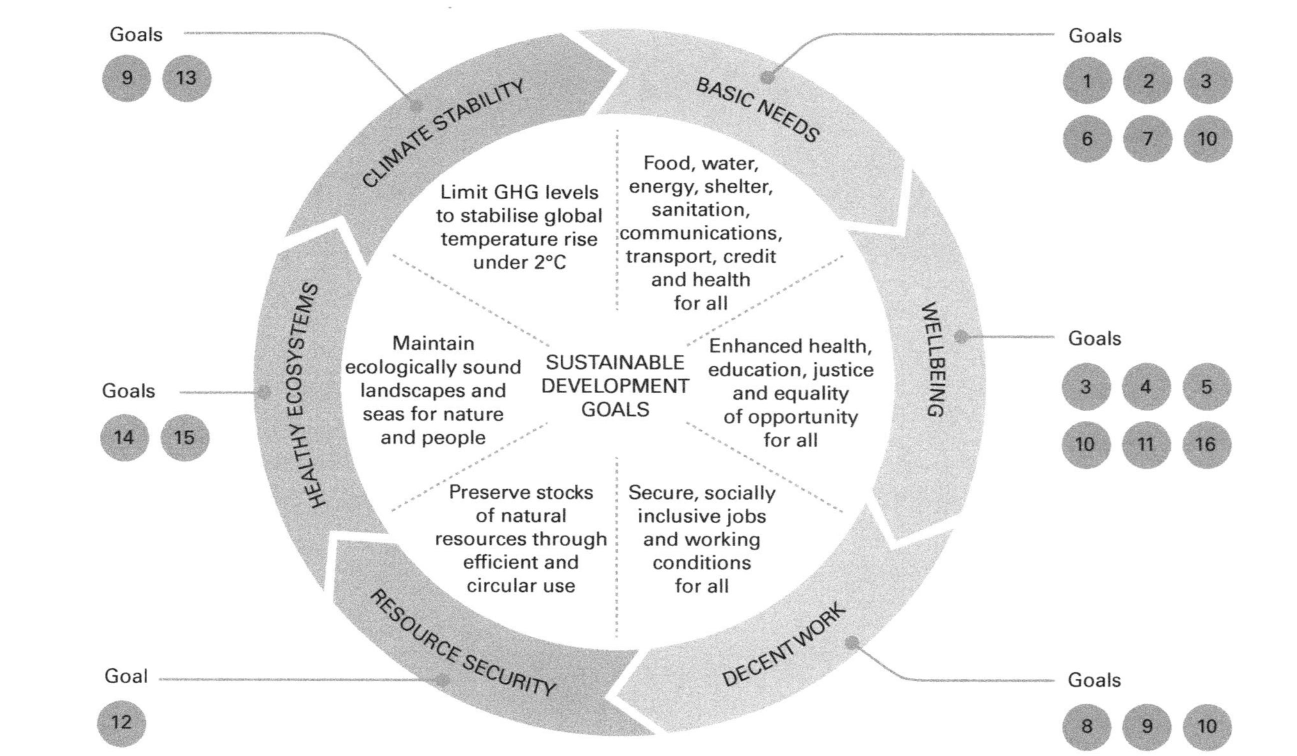

SOURCE University of Cambridge Institute for Sustainability Leadership (2016) *In Search of Impact: Measuring the full value of capital*. https://www.cisl.cam.ac.uk/resources/publication-pdfs/impact-report.pdf

Table 4.1 Description of ILG metrics

Theme	Metric	Rationale	Refinements
Basic needs	Revenue from products serving low-income groups ($)*	Proxy for addressing needs of low-income groups	• Purchasing power • Restriction to 'basic needs' products • Fair dealing • Product ethics
Well-being	Total tax burden ($)*	Proxy for public value contribution	• Corruption record of government • Negative externalities (alcohol, air pollution, tobacco, sugar) • Revenue from healthcare, education, justice and environmental protection
Decent work	Number of jobs	Proxy for livelihoods supported in operations and supply chain	• National level of unemployed and vulnerable workers • Living wage • Stable (open-ended) contracts • Labour conditions • Indirect job creation
Resource security	Consumption of virgin material (tonnes)*	Proxy for resource burden and waste of operations and supply chain	• Scarcity of hard commodity • Regeneration of soft commodity • Toxicity
Healthy ecosystems	Land footprint (hectares)*	Proxy for ecosystem burden of operations and supply chain	• Level and trend of national ecological deficit • Full ecological footprint • Restoration of ecosystem services
Climate stability	Scope 1–3 GHG emissions (tCo_2e)	Proxy for climate burden of operations + supply chain + product use	• Avoided emissions from product use • Sector-specific targets and contributions • Alignment with 2°C scenario

SOURCE University of Cambridge Institute for Sustainability Leadership (2016) *In Search of Impact: Measuring the full value of capital*. https://www.cisl.cam.ac.uk/resources/publication-pdfs/impact-report.pdf

* Proposals only, subject to further definition.

Qualitative assessments of impact can also be presented in colour-coded schemes, based on research into, for example, an asset's forward strategy, capital investment, operating standards, past track record, and so on. Clearly these assessments can supplement historic quantitative results with a fuller analysis of the asset's likely future impact. The categorization method proposed for the stretch and the ideal metrics reflects this, combining quantitative and qualitative results to produce a judgement on an asset's contribution to the SDGs.

When quantitative data are absent, sparse or of insufficient quality or consistency to be used meaningfully, qualitative assessment may be the only usable method of analysis. The development of a uniform approach to quantitative and qualitative impact measurement, sharing the consistency of financial performance reporting and credit ratings, will undoubtedly increase investors' confidence in the use of impact information.

The data challenge

In this chapter we have learned that meeting the objectives of (and tracking progress towards) Article 2.1c of the Paris Agreement requires the development and implementation of consistent, ideally standardized, approaches to measuring, monitoring, review and reporting on flows of climate finance, and on the wider environmental and broader sustainability impacts and outcomes of investments. As many bodies and experts such as the UNFCCC Standing Committee on Finance have commented, issues of data availability, comparability and quality create challenges for investors, regulators, policymakers and others seeking to monitor and report on both environmental impact and flows of climate finance.

Environmental performance data, however, are becoming ever more widely available – and the quality (including the granularity) of data is improving, including data from satellites, meteorological flights, weather balloons and other climate/weather monitoring platforms, as well as data gathered by drones, remote sensors linked via the internet, and smartphones – the latter particularly helpful in gathering data from parts of the world where use of the highly expensive, bespoke monitoring systems required is unlikely to be feasible. Remote sensing also improves accessibility to data at more granular levels; for example, emissions from a particular factory or power station, or pollutants emitted into a local stream, which may not be possible using satellite or airborne monitoring. In addition, climate model data – once the preserve of national research centres – are now much more widely available, with the falling cost of computing power and the use of advanced data analytics, employing artificial intelligence and machine learning techniques, and facilitating the analysis and use of such data by investors, analysts and others.

QUICK QUESTION

What, in your view, are the advantages of the increasing availability and quality of environmental performance and climate data?

The combination of improved data availability and quality, and the ability to analyse this supports the growth of green and sustainable finance in a number of key ways:

- improving the accuracy, consistency, credibility and rigour of reporting on environmental and other (eg social) impacts, giving greater confidence to investors and helping to avoid greenwashing;
- improving the granularity of reporting (eg through the use of remote sensors attached to/tracking single assets or investments);
- supporting the standardization of data on environmental performance and sustainability, allowing different potential investments to be more easily and effectively compared;
- improving transparency of reporting, and availability/communicability of reporting (eg using data visualization techniques) to make this meaningful to retail investors and customers;
- reducing the costs and time of making investment decisions, thereby reducing the additional costs (compared with vanilla financial investments) of environmental impact assessments and similar;
- enabling real-time monitoring and verification of investment performance in terms of desired environmental and other outcomes, for instance monitoring emissions data or power usage, helping investors manage investments more dynamically.

Perhaps most importantly in the context of tracking progress towards the objectives of Article 2.1c, developments in data availability, quality and analysis enable investors, analysts and management to combine data from hundreds or thousands of data sources in order to gain a more comprehensive overview of the environmental performance and sustainability impacts of investments across whole portfolios, organizations, sectors, countries or regions. The Spatial Finance Initiative launched in 2019 by the Alan Turing Institute, UK Green Finance Institute, Satellite Applications Catapult and the University of Oxford, seeks through the availability of much cheaper, internet-enabled sensors able to transmit real time data, new satellite monitoring capabilities and significant improvements in AI-enabled data analysis and modelling to include environmental performance data in financial institutions' decision-making and risk management.

A number of technology-driven, environmental analytics and ratings firms have been established in recent years, including Sustainalytics (see Chapter 9) and Arabesque (see Chapter 11). Arabesque S-Ray®, for example, is a proprietary tool that uses machine learning to combine over 200 ESG metrics with news signals from over 50,000 sources across 20 languages to allow investors and others to easily monitor the sustainability of over 7,000 of the world's largest corporations via simple reporting dashboards.

Developments in data availability, quality and analysis driven by the growth of internet-enabled sensors, satellite monitoring and AI-powered big data analysis may also help investors and asset owners to more easily recognize investments and assets that might be impaired or stranded due to the transition to a sustainable, low-carbon world, and then to take prompt action to reduce exposure to, or divest from, high-carbon assets.

Some believe the development of a global catalogue of every physical asset in the world is already within the reach of technical feasibility. The process of identifying and tagging assets (eg power stations and coal mines) and asset-level features (eg cooling technologies, air pollution control technologies) can be automated through the use of AI and machine learning. Greenhouse gas or other environmental metrics can be recorded from each asset, with satellites, drones and the increasing use of remote sensing, generating more accurate and more frequently refreshed metrics. These can then be tied to asset ownership, ultimately enabling investors and others to aggregate data at company, sector, regional or global level. This opens up the possibility of embedding environmental performance data within financial institutions and the financial sector overall. It also enables tracking progress towards the objectives of Article 2.1c with much greater accuracy, allowing measurement of the transition to a sustainable, low-carbon world in a way that is not possible at present.

Key concepts

In this chapter we considered:

- the importance and challenges of monitoring, measuring and reporting the flow of investment to support the transition to a sustainable, low-carbon world;
- different ways in which green and sustainable investment impacts and outcomes may be monitored and verified;
- the importance of independent, external review in green and sustainable finance;
- how advances in data availability and analysis can support the development of green and sustainable finance.

Now go back through this chapter and make sure you fully understand each point.

Review

In the context of green and sustainable finance, monitoring, measuring and reporting can refer to:

- tracking and reporting flows of investment to green and sustainable finance assets, activities and projects with the aim of meeting the Paris Agreement and other climate targets;
- measuring and reporting the environmental impact and outcomes of green and sustainable investments.

Tracking and reporting flows of public and private climate, green and sustainable finance is critical for the transition to a sustainable, low-carbon world. The overwhelming majority of global activities at both macro and micro level involves and requires investment from, or the facilitation of, the financial services sector in one or more ways. Article 2.1c of the Paris Agreement requires parties to make flows of finance consistent with a pathway towards low greenhouse gas emissions and climate-resilient development. This necessitates tracking flows of investment to identified climate change mitigation and adaptation projects and activities as well as flows of investment that detract from these.

At global level, the leading role in monitoring, measuring and reporting flows of climate finance is played by the UNFCCC Standing Committee on Finance, which publishes biennial assessments (BA) of climate finance flows, most recently in 2018. The 2018 BA estimates that overall climate finance grew from $584 billion in 2014 to $680 billion in 2015 and to $681 billion in 2016, on a comparable basis.

Although the UNFCCC and others have made good progress in identifying and measuring flows of public climate finance, obtaining good quality, consistent and comparable data on the flow of private climate finance, and green and sustainable finance more broadly, is more challenging. Two key initiatives seeking to improve the monitoring and reporting of private climate flows are the OECD Research Collaborative and the ISO's forthcoming Climate Finance Standard, ISO 14097.

The environmental and sustainable performance of investments also needs to be monitored and measured. Monitoring systems seek to measure processes intended to lead to positive green and sustainable outcomes, and/or to measure the impacts and outcomes directly. Measuring, monitoring, verifying and reporting the climate change mitigation and adaptation impact and outcomes of green and sustainable investments is much more likely to lead to flows of finance consistent with achieving the objectives of Article 2.1c.

Independent third-party review is key in monitoring, measuring and reporting in green finance, both pre-investment and during investment. A number of approaches to review exist, with verification and certification the most credible and robust methods. This is particularly important as, in many cases, assessing the environmental performance of investments requires the monitoring, measurement and reporting of environmental metrics based on scientific analysis of, for example, greenhouse gas emissions. Green and Sustainable Finance Professionals would be unlikely to be qualified to measure and report on these, and so obtaining independent third-party verification or certification is crucial.

Issues of data availability, comparability and quality create challenges for investors, regulators, policymakers and others seeking to monitor and report on environmental and sustainability impacts and flows of climate finance. Environmental performance data, however, are becoming ever more widely available, and the quality of data is improving, driven by advances in technology, data analysis and the application of artificial intelligence and machine learning.

The availability of much cheaper, internet-enabled sensors able to transmit real time data, new satellite monitoring capabilities and significant improvements in AI-enabled data analysis and modelling can help financial institutions incorporate and embed environmental performance data in decision-making, modelling and risk management.

Glossary

Annex II Parties: Members of the OECD required to provide financial ($100 billion per year by 2020) and technical support to economies in transition and developing countries to assist them in reducing their greenhouse gas emissions and manage the impacts of climate change.

Article 2.1c: The Paris Agreement has three main goals, set out in Article 2. Article 2.1c requires Parties to the Agreement to make finance flows consistent with a pathway towards low greenhouse gas emissions and climate-resilient development.

Asset-Level Data Initiative (ADI): A non-commercial, research-based initiative that aims to collect, verify and distribute asset-level data on all companies in key sectors globally.

Carbon dioxide equivalent (CO_2e): The most commonly used measure of greenhouse gas emissions, often expressed in annual CO_2e.

Certification: Process by which investments are measured against recognized external standards and criteria.

External review: Catch-all term covering similar terms such as audit, assurance, attestation, certification, validation, verification and second- or third-party review.

Impact monitoring: Assessment and evaluation of the impacts and outcomes of investments or operations.

ISO 14097: A forthcoming international standard for assessing and reporting investments and financing activities relating to climate change, currently (2020) under development.

Process monitoring: Assessment and evaluation of an organization's principles, policies, procedures and practices.

UNFCCC Standing Committee on Finance: The UN body responsible for monitoring, measuring and reporting flows of climate finance.

Verification: Obtaining independent third-party assurance against designated criteria, often including reference to international or market standards and guidance.

Notes

1 United Nations Framework Convention on Climate Change (2018) *UNFCCC Standing Committee on Finance: 2018 biennial assessment and overview of climate finance flows – Technical report* [Online] https://unfccc.int/sites/default/files/resource/2018%20BA%20Technical%20Report%20Final.pdf (archived at https://perma.cc/N63T-W52L)

2 R Jachnik, M Mirabile and A Dobrinevski (2019) Tracking finance flows towards assessing their consistency with climate objectives, OECD Environment Working Papers, No 146 [Online] https://doi.org/10.1787/82cc3a4c-en (archived at https://perma.cc/8WFG-K7CP)

3 ISO (nd) ISO/DIS 14097: Framework including principles and requirements for assessing and reporting investments and financing activities related to climate change [Online] https://www.iso.org/standard/72433.html (archived at https://perma.cc/ZPK3-LCYL)

4 University of Cambridge Institute for Sustainability Leadership (CISL) (2016) *In Search of Impact: Measuring the full value of capital* [Online] https://www.cisl.cam.ac.uk/resources/publication-pdfs/impact-report.pdf (archived at https://perma.cc/54NW-W35R)

5 UNEP Inquiry (2016) The Equator Principles: Do they make banks more sustainable? [Online] http://unepinquiry.org/wp-content/uploads/2016/02/The_Equator_Principles_Do_They_Make_Banks_More_Sustainable.pdf (archived at https://perma.cc/D65W-YPH8)

6 UK Green Investment Bank plc (2017) *Green Investment Handbook: A guide to assessing, monitoring and reporting green impact* [Online] https://www.greeninvestmentgroup.com/assets/gig/news/green-investment-handbook-india.pdf (archived at https://perma.cc/6QWB-CFAN)

7 Climate Bonds Initiative (nd) How to become an Approved Verifier [Online] https://www.climatebonds.net/certification/become-a-verifier (archived at https://perma.cc/GT48-SMHM)

8 B Analytics (nd) Demonstrate your leadership with a GIIRS rating [Online] https://b-analytics.net/giirs-funds (archived at https://perma.cc/EK99-YGAH)

9 ISO (nd) ISO 14031:2013: Environmental management — environmental performance evaluation — guidelines [Online] https://www.iso.org/standard/52297.html (archived at https://perma.cc/7XHJ-U7YU)

10 IFC (2012) *IFC Performance Standards on Environmental and Social Sustainability* [Online] https://www.ifc.org/wps/wcm/connect/topics_ext_content/ifc_external_corporate_site/sustainability-at-ifc/publications/publications_handbook_pps (archived at https://perma.cc/P9HR-QK4L)

11 University of Cambridge Institute for Sustainability Leadership (CISL) (2016) *In Search of Impact: Measuring the full value of capital* [Online] https://www.cisl.cam.ac.uk/resources/publication-pdfs/impact-report.pdf (archived at https://perma.cc/54NW-W35R)

05

Risk management

LEARNING OBJECTIVES

On completion of this chapter you should be able to:

- Describe the nature and importance of key climate-related and environmental risks.
- Explain the different types of climate-related risk (physical, transition, liability) and their impact on the finance sector.
- Describe the nature and importance of stranded asset risk, and its potential impact on the finance sector.
- Examine approaches to identifying, disclosing, managing and pricing climate-related risks, the use of scenario analysis, and the developing regulatory agenda in this area.

The effects of environmental change and the transition to a sustainable, low-carbon economy are already having a significant impact on key sectors of the global economy. In this chapter, we explore key climate-related and environmental risks, and consider how risks may be matched, in some cases, with opportunities. We also examine emerging approaches to identifying and managing climate-related risks, including the use of scenario analysis, and the development of regulation in this area. Many green and sustainable finance norms, standards and practices aim to take account of, identify, assess and effectively manage climate-related risks that can impair or strand assets.

Climate-related and environmental risks, and stranded assets

In 2015, BlackRock, the world's largest asset manager, noted that momentum towards mitigating climate risk in investment portfolios appeared to be growing and that more asset owners were beginning to consider the risks of climate change and stranded assets.[1] That momentum has significantly increased in recent years, and in January 2020 Larry Fink, the BlackRock Chief Executive, wrote in his annual letter to clients that climate change presented a substantial, systemic risk to firms and markets. BlackRock would, henceforth, use its position as the world's largest asset manager to compel firms to disclose their climate-related and other environmental risks in line with the Task Force on Climate-related Financial Disclosure (TCFD) and other standards. BlackRock would also rebalance its own funds to reduce exposure to some high-carbon sectors, such as thermal coal.

Also in January 2020, the World Economic Forum Global Risks Report ranked climate change – and specifically the risk of failing to take action on climate change – as the key risk faced by business, finance and society over the next 10 years.[2] Climate action failure – not taking action on climate change mitigation and adaptation to the extent required – was identified by business leaders, academics and NGOs as the number one risk by impact, and the number two risk by likelihood. Even more striking was that all of the top five risks identified were environment and climate related. In addition to climate action failure, extreme weather, natural disasters, biodiversity loss and man-made environmental disasters were also recognized as key concerns.

As we will see in this chapter, a large and increasing number of regulators and institutions have identified climate-related risks and other environmental risks as a significant sources of risk to customers, institutions and the economy overall in the short, medium and long term, including as a significant potential threat to global financial stability. Where there are risks, however, there are also opportunities for asset managers, investors and lenders in areas such as green infrastructure and energy, energy efficiency and more generally in climate mitigation and adaptation technologies. With an estimated $6 trillion of investment per year required to support the transition to a sustainable, low-carbon world (see Chapter 1), there are significant opportunities as well as significant risks.

A very wide range of risk factors exist that can have an impact on asset values. Environmental factors, particularly climate change, are increasingly driving assessments of financial risk, including potential asset impairment and stranding, at both institutional and financial system levels. Many of these risks are currently poorly understood and mispriced, and their probability and/or impact underestimated, resulting in over-exposure to climate-related environmental risks throughout the world. This situation represents a potential opportunity for institutions and Green and Sustainable Finance Professionals to help clients and communities by pricing such risks accurately, and offering products and services specifically designed to mitigate them.

QUICK QUESTION

What might be some of the key climate-related and environmental risks faced by businesses?

At an organizational level, environmental risks can have impacts across an organization (see Table 5.1).

Ultimately, environmental risks can damage not only institutions, but also the stability of the whole financial system. This is a particular concern in the case of climate change, which we explore further below. Such risks have already materialized across a wide range of sectors and geographies, and this trend appears to be accelerating. Multiple risk factors can develop in a specific sector or geography simultaneously, and can demonstrate correlation with one another; for example, the deployment of renewables, worsening air pollution and decreasing water availability caused by climate change, coupled with widespread social pressure to reduce China's demand for thermal coal, has negatively impacted affected coal mine assets in Australia.

Alternatively, one specific risk can materialize that can affect multiple sectors and markets in similar or different ways. For example, a once-in-a-century drought in China (2010–11) contributed to global wheat shortages and skyrocketing bread prices in Egypt, the world's largest wheat importer. The unrest generated by these high prices is thought to have subsequently contributed to the 2011 Arab Spring and its political and social impacts.

Research by Caldecott and McDaniels (2014) for UNEP shows that the speed at which environmental risks materialize is often proportional to the difficulties of adapting to them, with fast-moving risks often being harder to

Table 5.1 Environmental and social risk impact areas

Environmental and social risk impact areas				
Financial/credit	**Market**	**Operational**	**Reputational**	**Compliance/legal**
• Loss of collateral/ asset value • Borrower's inability to repay loans • Access to capital • Liquidity	• Reduced competitiveness • Production obsolescence • Missed market share	• Higher costs • Process inefficiencies • Irresponsible product stewardship • Equipment end-of-life obligation	• Damage throughout financed clients • Licence to operate • Talent acquisition and retention	• Regulations and regulatory actions • 3rd party civil actions • Lender liability

SOURCE Reproduced with permission from UNEP Finance Initiative (2016) *Guide to Banking and Sustainability, Edition 2*. https://www.unepfi.org/publications/banking-publications/guide-to-banking-and-sustainability-2/

manage than those that emerge at a slower pace.[3] For example, in the case of slow but constant water depletion, investors and asset owners of a bottling plant would have enough time to redirect new investments to geographical areas with higher water security, while continuing to use the existing facility until the end of its useful life. On the other hand, if the introduction of new regulations restricted water-access rights for commercial users, the production facility could rapidly become stranded. In both cases, the underlying environmental driver is the same but the potential loss of proportional value would be much higher in the second case, where societal response to environmental factors accelerates the speed at which such risks materialize. However, slow-moving risks can still pose challenges to companies and entire sectors. Climate change is a process that happens over many decades, with its impact becoming evident only gradually, which slows down the imperative to take action.

Environmental and climate-related risks are not new or emerging risks; we saw earlier that the effects of climate change and the transition to a low-carbon economy are already having an impact on the finance sector, as evidenced in the direct costs of climate-related events, such as the cost to insurers following extreme weather events like hurricanes. These are explored in more detail in Chapter 10, and represent losses that have already occurred, and can be quantified.

We introduced the concept of **stranded assets** in Chapter 2 – assets that have suffered from unanticipated or premature write-downs, devaluations or conversion to liabilities. Although asset stranding is part of the creative destruction that can occur in any market economy, the stranding of assets in the environmental context is more significant in that the transition from a high- to low-carbon economy could lead to higher rates of stranding, and much greater financial impacts. Physical environmental change and the transition to a sustainable, low-carbon world (particularly if this were abrupt, eg if coal production in one or more regions was stopped within a decade) could strand entire regions and global industries within a very short timeframe, with direct and indirect impacts on financial services institutions and potentially on financial stability, too. Whether this is the case, and to what extent it might be different from business-as-usual levels of asset stranding is an important and growing area of research.

Potential losses from stranded assets induced by climate-related risks are difficult to estimate because they depend on different scenarios regarding the speed of transition, legal liabilities and how asset owners might respond. One estimate, however, has put the exposure of the European financial sector alone at more than €1 trillion.

The scale of the risks associated with climate change and transition to a low-carbon economy is potentially so significant that financial stability could be threatened, which is why central banks and regulators are playing an increasing role in seeking to understand, define, promote disclosure of and manage such risks. In 2017 eight central banks and regulators established the Network for Greening the Financial System (NGFS). By 2019 it had already grown to 36 members, highlighting how climate risk identification and management has become a priority for central banks and other supervisors of the financial system.

CASE STUDY

Transition risks as financial risk[4]

One specific example of transition risk relevant to the fossil fuel extractive sector is the concept of unburnable carbon – the idea that a large share of fossil fuel reserves will need to stay unburned for climate targets to be achieved.

As noted in the PRA's 2015 report, the assets that could be impacted are not just limited to sectors involving the production of fossil fuels, such as coal, oil and gas, but could also include utilities, heavy industry, and the transportation sector, among others, whose business models rely upon using fossil fuels or are energy intensive. While some sectors may be more affected than others, the shift towards a lower-carbon, ultimately net zero emission economy is likely to have meaningful implications across multiple sectors of the economy.

There is evidence to suggest that the modelling of medium- and long-term factors (beyond five years) by financial firms can be limited, and that environmental factors are not fully integrated into financial and corporate decision-making.

There are already examples of how disruptive changes, linked to policy, technology and other economic factors, can indeed cause sharp changes in valuations. For instance, the combined market capitalization of the top four US coal producers has fallen by 95 per cent since the end of 2010, and three of the top five US firms have recently filed for bankruptcy. There has also been a similar, albeit less severe, valuation shift for German utilities, which were seen as slow in responding to changes in domestic energy policy (towards renewables and away from nuclear).

As part of a highly globalized financial centre, UK financial institutions are exposed to a wide range of sectors across the world, many of which may be affected. Shifts in valuation could, for example, reduce the value of insurance firms' investment portfolios. Similarly they could impact on the balance sheets of UK banks through reduced collateral values or by affecting business models of borrowers. As the United Kingdom implements its targets to reduce emissions from sectors ranging from power to industry to transport, there could also be domestic exposures to transition risk.

While the risk of a sudden and significant system-wide adjustment may not be immediate, the financial risk from an abrupt transition to a lower-carbon economy can increase if, over the coming years, portfolios are not aligned with climate targets. If governments push ahead with climate policies but investors do not adapt their investment strategies accordingly, misallocation will grow.

This could ultimately lead to a 'climate Minsky moment' – a rapid system-wide adjustment that threatens financial stability, as discussed by Governor Carney in 2015. A sudden, abrupt re-pricing of carbon-intense assets could also have systemic implications that go beyond direct financial losses. The allocation of capital and labour to projects not aligned with climate policies and technological changes could be a drag on productivity and economic growth. Conversely, allocating capital and labour to green technologies can be growth enhancing.

All this means that risks to financial stability will be minimized if the transition begins early and follows a predictable path, thereby helping the market anticipate the transition to a 2°C world.

QUICK QUESTION

What environmental risks is your organization (or an organization you know well) most exposed to?

Classification of climate-related risks

Risks posed to the financial sector – and to all economic sectors and society as a whole by climate change – can be classified in three ways:

- **physical risks** arising from the direct impacts of climate-related hazards with human and natural systems, such as droughts, floods and storms;

- **transition risks** arising from the transition to a low-carbon economy, such as developments in climate policy, new disruptive technology or shifting investor sentiment – these can lead to significant losses in economic value due to impaired or stranded assets;
- **liability risks** arising from parties who have suffered loss or damage from the effects of climate change and who seek compensation from those they hold responsible.

Physical risks

Physical risks relate to the material effects of climate change, some of which we are already experiencing. As we saw in Chapter 2, climate change is increasing the frequency of severe weather events, and the impact of these, in many cases, is greater than before because of the distribution of the growing global population. Hurricanes, cyclones, floods and other weather events can have especially devastating impacts on coastal populations and other low-lying areas. In the longer term, rising temperatures and sea levels may make parts of our planet uninhabitable.

There are quantifiable direct costs associated with physical risks. A severe flood will damage property and infrastructure, disrupt supply chains and trade, and leave communities facing substantial costs for clean-up and redevelopment. Insurers may cover some or all of the direct costs, but economic disruption may continue for months or years, and the value of assets may fall (eg if a significant business decides to move production out of an area due to an increase in the perceived risk of flooding, commercial real estate values in an area may decrease). There may be consequent impact on financial firms that own, lend to or invest in that area. Insurance premiums may well rise, and in some cases assets may become uninsurable, unless there is public sector intervention to share some of the risk with insurers.

According to the US National Centers for Environmental Information (NCEI), in the US in 2019 there were at least 10 extreme weather and climate-related events leading to losses exceeding $1 billion each. 2019 was the fifth consecutive year in which losses at this scale were experienced. Also in 2019, the European Environment Agency estimated that floods, droughts, heatwaves and other extreme weather events led to economic losses of €13 billion per year in the European Economic Area (33 countries). Looking ahead, a 2019 Economist Intelligence Unit study predicted that extreme weather events, with impacts including increased drought, flooding and crop failures, could cost the global economy nearly $8 trillion per year (approximately 3 per cent of global GDP). The costs of physical risks caused by climate change, particularly the increased frequency and severity of extreme weather events, are therefore significant both to individuals, firms and communities directly affected, and to the economy and society overall.

Mark Carney, former Governor of the Bank of England, and Chairman of the Financial Stability Board discusses the physical risks of climate change in relation to the insurance industry in the reading below.

READING
Breaking the Tragedy of the Horizon

Excerpt from speech by Mark Carney on climate change risk[5]

Mark Carney introduces one important way in which climate change can affect financial stability.

The insurance response to climate change

It stands to reason that general insurers are the most directly exposed to such losses. Potential increases in the frequency or severity of extreme weather events driven by climate change could mean longer and stronger heatwaves; the intensification of droughts; and a greater number of severe storms.

Despite winter 2014 being England's wettest since the time of King George III, forecasts suggest we can expect at least a further 10 per cent increase in rainfall during future winters – a prospect guaranteed to dampen the spirits and shoes of those who equate climate change with global warming. While the attribution of increases in claims to specific factors is complex, the direct costs of climate change are already affecting insurers' underwriting strategies and accounts.

For example, work done here at Lloyd's of London estimated that the 20 cm rise in sea level at the tip of Manhattan since the 1950s, when all other factors are held constant, increased insured losses from Superstorm Sandy by 30 per cent in New York alone.

Beyond these direct costs, there is an upward trend in losses that arise indirectly through second-order events like the disruption of global supply chains. Insurers are therefore amongst those with the greatest incentives to understand and tackle climate change in the short term. Your motives are sharpened by commercial concern as capitalists and by moral considerations as global citizens. And your response is at the cutting edge of the understanding and management of risks arising from climate change.

Lloyd's underwriters were the first to use storm records to mesh natural science with finance in order to analyse changing weather patterns. Events like Hurricanes Andrew, Katrina and Ike have helped advance catastrophe risk modelling and provisioning. Today Lloyd's underwriters are required to consider climate change explicitly in their business plans and underwriting models. Your genius has been to recognize that past is not prologue and that the catastrophic norms of the future can be seen in the tail risks of today.

For example, by holding capital at a one in 200-year risk appetite, UK insurers withstood the events of 2011, one of the worst years on record for insurance losses. Your models were validated, claims were paid, and solvency was maintained. The combination of your forecasting models, a forward-looking capital regime and business models built around short-term policies mean general insurers are well placed to manage physical risks in the near term.

But further ahead, increasing levels of physical risk due to climate change could present significant challenges to general insurance business models. Improvements in risk modelling must be unrelenting as loss frequency and severity shifts with:

- insurance extending into new markets not covered by existing models;
- previously unanticipated risks coming to the fore;
- increasingly volatile weather trends and hydrological cycles making the future ever harder to predict.

For example, the extent to which European windstorms occur in clusters could increase the frequency of catastrophes and reduce diversification benefits.

Indeed, there are some estimates that currently modelled losses could be undervalued by as much as 50 per cent if recent weather trends were to prove representative of the new normal. In addition, climate change could prompt increased morbidity and mortality from disease or pandemics. Such developments have the potential to shift the balance between premiums and claims significantly, and render currently lucrative business non-viable.

Absent actions to mitigate climate change, policyholders will also feel the impact as pricing adjusts and cover is withdrawn. Insurers' rational responses to physical risks can have very real consequences and pose acute public policy problems.

In some extreme cases, householders in the Caribbean have found storm patterns render them unable to get private cover, prompting mortgage lending to dry up, values to collapse and neighbourhoods to become abandoned. Thankfully these cases are rare. But the recognition of the potential impact of such risks has prompted a publicly-backed scheme in the UK – Flood Re – to ensure access to affordable flood insurance for half a million homes now considered to be at the highest risk of devastating flooding.

This example underlines a wider point. While the insurance industry is well placed to adapt to a changing climate in the short term, their response could pose wider issues for society, including whether to nationalize risk. The passage of time may also reveal risks that even the most advanced models are not able to predict, such as third party liability risks. Participants in the Lloyd's market know all too well that what appear to be low probability risks can evolve into large and unforeseen costs over a longer timescale.

The TCFD divides physical risks into **acute risks** (severe, short-term impact such as a flood or hurricane) and **chronic risks** (more gradual longer-term impacts such as rising sea levels).

The former, as evident in the aftermath of many extreme weather events, can lead to significant short- and medium-term costs for clean-up and redevelopment, many of which may be borne by insurers. The latter may be hard to quantify today, but rising temperatures and sea levels may be on such a scale as to make parts of our planet uninhabitable. In worst-case scenarios, major cities such as Amsterdam, Miami, Osaka and Shanghai, and including financial centres such as London and New York, could be significantly affected. Even less dramatic scenarios will see coastal communities, industrial areas and sea ports affected, stranding assets and requiring relocation/redevelopment of existing facilities, although not all regions or areas will necessarily suffer the same net effects of climate change.

Although the 2015 Paris Agreement provides some measure of risk management through inter-governmental collaboration, investors want to understand what and when further action will be taken to meet the climate change goals of the Agreement – to hold temperatures to 'well below 2 degrees' and pursue efforts to achieve a 1.5°C threshold. This issue has become more pressing given the IPCC's October 2018 report prioritizing the latter.

The long-term goals agreed imply that our economies must substantively decarbonize globally, if not move towards negative emissions, by mid-century, well within the lifetime of infrastructure invested in today. Green and Sustainable Finance Professionals and investors will need to take a view on how effectively such goals are being translated into action, and therefore to what extent physical risks such as those discussed above will crystallize.

Uncertainty caused by differences in the development and implementation of national climate, economic and energy policies creates additional risks. Uncertainty is compounded by the complex, systemic nature of climate change. As discussed above and in earlier chapters, it is a dynamic and interrelated process, as changes in one part of the system have an effect elsewhere. This means that the precise impacts of climate change are extremely difficult to predict, and no one can say with certainty what the future will hold.

QUICK QUESTIONS

Which physical risks are highest for your organization? What strategies could you put in place to minimize and/or mitigate these risks?

Transition risks

Transition risks are those risks that arise from the transition to a low-carbon economy. The TCFD divides these into four categories:

1. Risks from developments in climate policy, legislation and regulation, eg the introduction of carbon pricing may increase a power station's operating costs and profit margin.
2. Risks from new, lower-carbon technologies that substitute for existing products and services, eg renewables replacing fossil fuels, which may lead to impairment or stranding of assets.
3. Risks from changing consumer behaviour and investor sentiment, leading to changes in demand for products and services (eg diesel cars) and in investment demand (eg for assets heavily dependent on fossil fuels).
4. Reputational risks, where organizations (and, potentially, whole sectors) may suffer from association with high-carbon methods of production and distribution, or environmental destruction, leading to falling demand and revenues, and reduced attractiveness to potential employees and investors.

Political and regulatory risks

Political and regulatory risks are closely linked (a change in government may lead to new policy and regulatory priorities) but are distinct. Rapid changes in the political climate, which may be related or unrelated to climate change and the transition to a low-carbon world, bring uncertainty to long-term investments. In the United States, for example, the Trump administration was highly sceptical about climate change, and announced that it would pull out of the Paris Agreement, rolled back some environmental protection regulation, and increased investment in fossil fuels. Such actions may hurt the economic value of some US green and sustainable assets and make them less attractive to investors, at least in the short term. In the longer term, a new US administration may have very different priorities, making greener and sustainable assets more attractive once more.

Other governments have taken a different, more proactive approach to climate change policy. There is a moratorium on fracking in Scotland, for example; a 5p charge for plastic bags was introduced in Scotland ahead of the rest of the UK; and the Scottish Government pledged to ban new petrol and diesel cars by 2032, although the UK government has more recently announced a target of 2030 to end the sale of these. Norway will ban petrol and diesel cars by 2025 and has announced that it will be disinvesting 52 companies linked to coal from its sovereign wealth fund. Again, there is always the potential for a change in government leading to a change in approach and policy. The transition to a low-carbon world requires long-term commitments which many governments can find hard to make, given the relatively short lifespan of administrations.

This is related to market risks such as changing consumer behaviour, as campaigning often seeks to influence political views (and hence policy and regulation) as well as to encourage individuals to change their behaviour and use consumer/financial pressure to promote change too. An emerging political risk for the finance sector is that, as the physical effects of climate change become increasingly apparent, support for alternative and more radical political approaches may increase, which could target the financial services sector as being part of the problem, rather than part of the solution.

Regulatory risks are a subset of political risk, encompassing changes to legislation and regulation that could have a direct effect on the viability of a project or the value of investments. This might include government ministries (eg agriculture, energy, transport), central banks, environmental regulators, financial regulators proposing or making changes to carbon pricing, taxation regimes, energy efficiency incentives, permitted activities (eg allowing or banning wind farms), etc. Regulatory developments designed to encourage sustainability and/or disclosure of climate-related risks may also offer opportunities for financial institutions and Green and Sustainable Finance Professionals, eg by offering capital relief for green and sustainable lending, or by stimulating the growth of new markets and low-carbon industries.

In many cases, regulation designed to mitigate the effects of climate change and support the transition to a low-carbon economy is based on the internalizing of externalities related to climate change and environmental degradation. A good example of this is carbon pricing, which we consider below.

Technology risks

Technology risks occur when new, lower-carbon (or other) technologies replace existing products and services, which may lead to the impairment or stranding of assets. This is by no means unique to green finance; the introduction of music streaming services has led to sharp declines in the sale of CDs and in the value of record companies, for example. What is perhaps unique to the green and sustainable finance sector is the potential scale of substitution and asset impairment and stranding, as a result of the transition to a low-carbon world. As we saw earlier, one estimate puts the potential scale of stranded assets as €1 trillion in relation to Europe alone.

A successful transition from a high-carbon to a low-carbon world will mean the substitution of a wide range of products and services built using existing technologies including, but not limited to, energy, transport, petrochemicals, construction, agriculture and food, clothing and consumer appliances. This will not only have a substantial impact on the producers of high-carbon goods, but also throughout their supply chains. Whilst we might perceive that the transition to a sustainable, low-carbon world is proceeding slowly overall, in individual cases the effects of that transition may be dramatic, especially when prompted by changes in regulation (eg to reduce or remove non-recyclable food packaging).

QUICK QUESTIONS

How vulnerable are some products and services you use to substitution by low-carbon alternatives? What would cause you to switch?

Risks from changing behaviour and social norms

Risks from changing consumer behaviour and social norms, leading to changes in demand for products and services (eg diesel cars) and in investment demand (eg for assets heavily dependent on fossil fuels) are closely linked to the physical and substitution risks discussed above, and also to reputational risks discussed below. The distinction comes in the fact that changing consumer behaviour (eg buying fewer avocados to try to prevent further deforestation) and investor sentiment (eg reducing investments in all car manufacturers because of problems with one) may depend less on the observable impacts of climate change and the transition to a low-carbon economy, and more on consumer and investor perceptions of potential benefits, costs and impacts of certain behaviours.

If changing perceptions lead to changes in consumer behaviour, this can affect demand (positively or negatively) for particular goods and services, and impact the value of the organization(s) that provide them. If changing investor sentiment leads to a greater or lesser appetite for risk, in this case environmental and climate-related risk, then this may in turn lead to changes in asset allocation, diversification or disinvestment from certain companies or sectors or to greater or lesser decarbonization of portfolios more generally.

Finance itself can play a role in changing behaviour and social norms within the financial services sector, particularly by encouraging and incentivizing firms to decarbonize by divesting, or threatening to divest, from firms or sectors perceived as being major emitters of greenhouse gases.

In 2016, Peabody, then the world's biggest coal company, announced plans for bankruptcy, claiming that the divestment movement, which was making it hard to raise the capital it needed to continue operations, was one of the main challenges it faced in continuing to operate. The coal sector in general, at least in some Western jurisdictions, has become much less attractive to investors in recent years due to changing behaviour and social norms, and the disinvestment/decarbonization movement. The introduction of realistic carbon pricing (see below) will put further pressure on large producers and users of coal.

In 2018 Climate Action 100+, an investor group with approximately $35 trillion assets under management that seeks to engage systemically important greenhouse gas emitters, secured the agreement of Royal Dutch Shell to set short- and long-term carbon emissions targets linked to executive remuneration. Shell aims to reduce its Net Carbon Footprint by approximately 50 per cent by 2050 and by approximately 20 per cent by 2035 as an interim step. Earlier that year, Shell had announced that divestment should be considered a material risk to its business.

Reputational risks

Reputational risks arise where organizations (and, potentially, whole sectors) suffer from association with high-carbon methods of production and distribution, or environmental destruction, leading to falling demand

and revenues, and reduced attractiveness to potential customers, employees and investors. Reputational risks may also arise in relation to a range of broader social and sustainability factors, such as using child or forced labour. Financial services firms can find themselves suffering reputational (and financial) damage if they are seen to be supporting organizations and sectors that contribute to global warming, or causing other environmental or social harm, even if their own operations are, within themselves, highly sustainable – as many financial institutions are.

Reputational risks may also arise when organizations are accused of greenwashing, some examples of which (eg Volkswagen installing 'defeat device' software in diesel vehicles) were given in earlier chapters. This may lead to activist and consumer campaigns and boycotts, reducing revenues and profitability. This is a significant issue in financial services as, despite increases in capital deployed to support green and sustainable finance investments and activities, many financial institutions still provide substantial investment to high-carbon sectors. As we noted in Chapter 1, for example, 33 global banks have provided financing of more than $1.9 trillion to fossil fuel companies since the signing of the Paris Agreement in 2015, according to the *Banking on Climate Change* 2019 report.[6]

Climate activists, NGOs and journalists are increasingly investigating, and disclosing the financing of oil, gas, coal and similar activities, especially where this stands in contrast to financial institutions' public pronouncements on climate change and sustainability. With significant economic value attached to intangible assets such as brands and goodwill, as well as impacting on revenues and profitability, reputational damage can also affect the value of an organization and its attractiveness to investors.

Liability risks

Liability risks include costs that arise from legal claims (**litigation**) prompted by poor environmental management (eg discharging waste chemicals into a river), from claims against emitters of greenhouse gases and also the potential costs that may arise from legal challenges led by activists seeking to pressure companies and governments to do more to prevent climate change and accelerate the transition to a low-carbon world.

The direct costs of legal action can be significant; however, much greater may be the costs arising from changes in legislation, regulation (or sentiment) as a result of such action, for example when a 'polluter pays' principle is established, or upheld. This may lead to a re-pricing of assets and, in some cases, to significant impairment or stranding.

The next reading offers a classification of litigation risks related to climate change and the transition to a low-carbon world (referred to here as the energy transition, or ET) and goes on to consider how litigation can both drive the transition and be a consequence of it. Some observers believe that litigation costs – or the threat of them – will be a major driver of the transition to a low-carbon world in the United States in particular.

READING
Litigation risk as a consequence and driver of the energy transition[7]

The taxonomy by MinterEllison in *The Carbon Boomerang* offers a general classification of litigation risks that may crystalize and/or result from the energy transition.

In Table 5.2, litigation is seen in this work as a driver of the energy transition. Figure 5.1 sets out how litigation may be both a driver and a consequence of the transition.

Perhaps most significantly, litigation can have a far broader impact than the direct financial impost on the claimant(s) and defendant(s): as a **driver of regulatory reform and/or on corporate strategy and governance within the relevant industry**. Claimants may also seek to deploy litigation as a **strategic** tool, recognizing the value of even 'ostensibly unsuccessful' litigation as a mechanism to raise the profile of a particular issue, as a procedural mechanism to obtain the defendant's internal documents or information, to impact on a corporation's social licence to operate, to raise potential defendants' costs, and/or to apply pressure on governments to introduce relevant regulation. And a single successful claim may have significant, broader impacts as a driver and/or consequence of the energy transition.

Table 5.2 Litigation risks

Failure to mitigate (Claims seeking to establish liability for emissions that cause the physical impacts of climate change)	**A: Citizens/states vs emitters/states (including carbon debt claims)** Claims by citizens/states against large emitters (or other states) seeking compensation for damages caused by, or costs incurred due to, climate change.	Causes of action generally include: • **tort (negligence, nuisance, trespass)** • **international law** • **human rights law**
	B: Citizens/states vs states Claims by citizens (or sub-national governments) against their own state for a failure to restrict emissions.	Causes of action may arise under: • **constitutional, human rights or tort (negligence) laws,** • for **breach of statutory obligation,** or • under the **public trust doctrine** (including 'atmospheric trust' claims)
Failure to adapt (including failure to report or disclose) (ie claims deriving from commercial failures to take into account the physical and economic transition risks associated with climate change, and/or to accurately disclose related exposures)	**C: Regulatory investigations and claims against corporations (and/or their directors)** who fail to accurately manage, report or disclose the risks associated with climate change.	Causes of action may arise under: • **securities laws (misleading disclosure/ securities fraud)** and/or (in some jurisdictions) • **corporate governance laws (directors' statutory and fiduciary duties)**
	D: Investor/beneficiary claims against corporations/trustees (and/or their directors) who fail to accurately manage, report or disclose the risks associated with climate change to their business.	Claims may include: • **'stock-drop claims'** under **securities laws (misleading disclosure/securities fraud)** and/or • **derivative actions against directors/fund trustees for breach of fiduciary/statutory duty**

(*continued*)

Table 5.2 (Continued)

	E: Corporation/investor claims against professional advisors (eg accountants, consultants, investment brokers, asset managers or credit ratings agencies) for negligent service provision in failing to adequately account for energy transition risks.	Causes of action may include: • **misrepresentation** • **tort (negligence)** and • **breach of contract**
	F: Contractual disputes: litigation between counterparties seeking to avoid or repudiate contractual obligations under evolving ET market norms, and insured vs insurer disputes over the scope of policy indemnities.	Claims are likely to turn on: • **contract law**
ET-specific regulatory compliance (ie claims relating to compliance with emissions-related laws and standards introduced to implement energy transition policies, and/or misrepresentations to customers)	**G: Regulatory claims for a breach of emissions- (or adaptation-) related regulations introduced to give effect to ET policies** The relevant causes of action include breaches of **transition-related statutes or regulations,** and/or **consumer protection/consumer fraud** laws.	Claims in this category may also give rise to secondary litigation exposures under corporate and securities laws (discussed under C and D above)
	H: Anti-regulatory litigation (emitters as plaintiffs) Companies materially impacted by national and supra-national governments' ET regulations (or related trade associations, sub-national governments or other interest groups) may challenge their validity.	Bringing claims under: • **international trade, administrative** or **constitutional laws**

SOURCE Reproduced with permission from MinterEllison (2017) *The Carbon Boomerang: Litigation risk as a driver and consequence of the energy transition*. https://yoursri.com/media-new/images/2017-09-22_the-carbon-boomerang.pdf

Figure 5.1 Litigation risk: driver and consequence

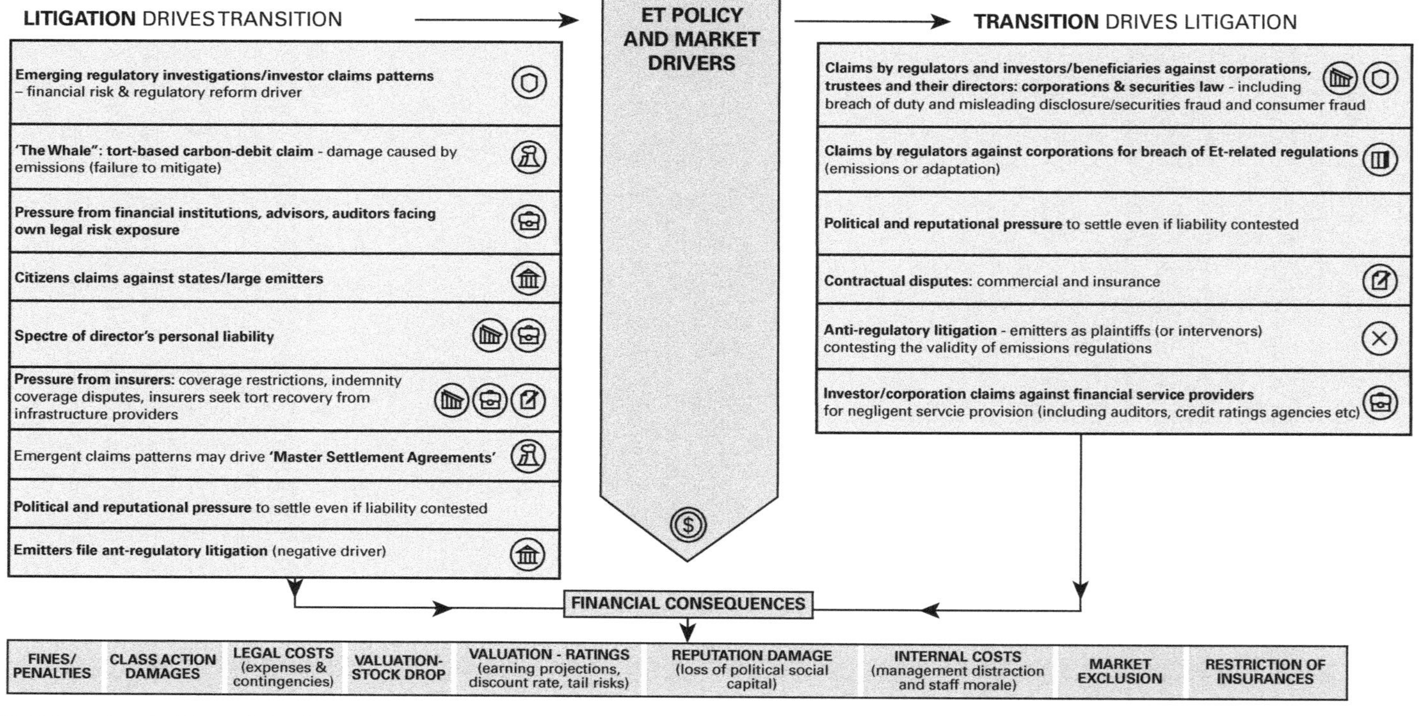

THE LITIGATION BOOMERANG: DRIVER AND CONSEQUENCE OF THE ET
LITIGATION DRIVES TRANSITION
Emerging regulatory investigations/investor claims patterns – financial risk & regulatory reform driver
'The Whale": tort-based carbon-debit claim - damage caused by emissions (failure to mitigate)
Pressure from financial institutions, advisors, auditors facing own legal risk exposure
Citizens claims against states/large emitters
Spectre of director's personal liability
Pressure from insurers: coverage restrictions, indemnity coverage disputes, insurers seek tort recovery from infrastructure providers
Emergent claims patterns may drive 'Master Settlement Agreements'
Political and reputational pressure to settle even if liability contested
Emitters file ant-regulatory litigation (negative driver)
ET POLICY AND MARKET DRIVERS
TRANSITION DRIVES LITIGATION
Claims by regulators and investors/beneficiaries against corporations, trustees and their directors: corporations & securities law - including breach of duty and misleading disclosure/securities fraud and consumer fraud
Claims by regulators against corporations for breach of Et-related regulations (emissions or adaptation)
Political and reputational pressure to settle even if liability contested
Contractual disputes: commercial and insurance
Anti-regulatory litigation - emitters as plaintiffs (or intervenors) contesting the validity of emissions regulations
Investor/corporation claims against financial service providers for negligent servcie provision (including auditors, credit ratings agencies etc)
FINANCIAL CONSEQUENCES
FINES/ PENALTIES
CLASS ACTION DAMAGES
LEGAL COSTS (expenses & contingencies)
VALUATION- STOCK DROP
VALUATION - RATINGS (earning projections, discount rate, tail risks)
REPUTATION DAMAGE (loss of political social capital)
INTERNAL COSTS (management distraction and staff morale)
MARKET EXCLUSION
RESTRICTION OF INSURANCES

SOURCE Reproduced with permission from MinterEllison (2017) *The Carbon Boomerang: Litigation risk as a driver and consequence of the energy transition*. https://yoursri.com/media-new/images/2017-09-22_the-carbon-boomerang.pdf

Risk management in green and sustainable finance

Risk and return are central considerations for finance professionals when considering equity, debt, infrastructure and project finance and other financing opportunities of all sizes and in all sectors. A range of variables will have an impact on expected returns and many variables that will change over the lifespan of the investment need to be identified, assessed, managed and mitigated in the context of the deal structure. Before investing or providing finance, financial institutions will need to undertake detailed due diligence and risk assessment in areas including:

- country, political and regulatory risk;
- financial risks;
- legal risks;
- market risks;
- technical risks;
- environmental risks (including climate-related risks).

In many traditional risk assessments, although climate, environmental and broader sustainability risks may form part of the overall assessment, the focus tends to be on shorter-term, narrower risks such as the potential costs of an unauthorized discharge of pollution. As we have seen in this chapter, however, the risks of climate change – physical, transition and liability – can have very significant short-, medium- and long-term consequences. The potential impairment or stranding of assets, in particular, could have a major impact on the attractiveness or feasibility of a potential investment, by changing the balance of risk and return.

> AXA is a long-term global investor with a duty to act in the best interests of its stakeholders, which means understanding the risks and opportunities related to ESG issues in our portfolios. We believe that these factors have the potential to impact investment portfolios over time, therefore affecting risk and returns. But only collective action can produce meaningful change. This is why we are proud to sign the UN-supported Principles for Responsible Investment.[8]

We have considered in previous chapters how approaches to identifying, disclosing and managing environmental, particularly climate-related, risks are being coordinated and stimulated by international organizations, governments, central bankers, regulators and industries bodies concerned about the risks to overall financial stability. Collaboration and cooperation are key to successful risk management at industry level, as is also a coordinated, systematic approach to climate-related risks, especially disclosure, in order to provide help and advice to boards, investors and other key stakeholders.

At organizational level, each organization faces a different combination of climate-related risks and opportunities. Business impacts related to climate change may vary significantly depending on the industry and economic sector(s)/sub-sector(s) in which an organization operates and may also depend on:

- the geographic location of the organization's value chain (both upstream and downstream);
- the organization's assets and nature of operations;
- the structure and dynamics of the organization's supply and demand markets;
- the organization's customers;
- the organization's other key stakeholders.

QUICK QUESTION

Which of these factors are most significant in terms of your organization's climate risks, or an organization with which you are familiar?

Task Force on Climate-related Financial Disclosures

The Task Force on Climate-related Financial Disclosures (TCFD) was established in December 2015, under the chairmanship of Michael Bloomberg, by the Financial Stability Board. With 32 members drawn from banks, insurance companies, asset managers, pension funds, large non-financial companies, accounting and consulting firms, and credit rating agencies, its remit was to develop voluntary, climate-related financial risk (physical, liability and transition risk) disclosures for use by companies providing information to investors, lenders, insurers and other stakeholders to bring consistency to effective disclosures across industry sectors. By encouraging and promoting greater, more consistent disclosure, climate-related financial risks should become more central to board and investor decision-making, as well as to shareholder engagement with management on climate change issues.

In June 2017 the TCFD published its report, *Recommendations of the Task Force on Climate-related Financial Disclosures*, setting out proposals for consistent, climate-related financial risk disclosures.[9] These are intended to be relevant to preparers and users of financial information in all industry sectors, although the Task Force stresses that financial services firms, such as banks, insurers and asset managers, have a particularly important role to play in influencing the organizations in which they invest in order to provide better climate-related financial disclosures.

The TCFD notes that climate change may affect all parts of an organization's financial performance, including, but not limited to, capital, financing, revenue, expenditure, assets and liabilities. Given that, in the TCFD's view, climate-related financial risk is or could be material for many organizations, and will likely become more so in the future, it recommends that organizations disclose these in their annual and other statutory, public reports. Importantly, the framework for disclosures is intended to be incorporated into existing disclosures, rather than imposing an additional burden onto reporting firms.

The TCFD also sets out four key thematic areas that, in its view, represent core elements of how organizations operate, and recommends that organizations report their approach to identifying and managing climate-related financial risks against these:

1 **Governance:** The organization's governance around climate-related risks and opportunities.
2 **Strategy:** The actual and potential impacts of climate-related risks and opportunities on the organization's businesses, strategy and financial planning.
3 **Risk management:** How the organization identifies, assesses, and manages climate-related risks.
4 **Metrics and targets:** Used to assess and manage relevant climate-related risks and opportunities.

The TCFD also proposes a number of Recommended Disclosures for each, as set out below:

1 **Governance:**
   a. Describe the board's oversight of climate-related risks and opportunities.
   b. Describe management's role in assessing and managing climate-related risks and opportunities.

2 **Strategy:**

   a. Describe the climate-related risks and opportunities the organization has identified over the short, medium and long term.

   b. Describe the impact of climate-related risks and opportunities on the organization's businesses, strategy and financial planning.

   c. Describe the resilience of the organization's strategy, taking into consideration different climate-related scenarios, including a 2°C or lower scenario [scenario analysis is examined in more detail below].

3 **Risk management:**

   a. Describe the organization's processes for identifying and assessing climate-related risks.

   b. Describe the organization's processes for managing climate-related risks.

   c. Describe how processes for identifying, assessing and managing climate-related risks are integrated into the organization's overall risk management.

4 **Metrics and targets:**

   a. Disclose the metrics used by the organization to assess climate-related risks and opportunities in line with its strategy and risk management process.

   b. Disclose Scope 1, Scope 2 and, if appropriate, Scope 3 greenhouse gas emissions, and the related risks.

   c. Describe the targets used by the organization to manage climate-related risks and opportunities and performance against targets.

In addition, for the financial services sector and for some non-financial sectors, supplemental guidance was developed to highlight important sector-specific considerations and provide a fuller picture of potential climate-related financial impacts in those sectors.

The TCFD's proposals have been strongly supported and endorsed by national and international regulators and policymakers, and by June 2019 nearly 800 organizations had expressed their support for the Task Force's recommendations, with increasing encouragement from policymakers, regulators and business groups in many countries promoting alignment. In the UK, for instance, all listed companies and large asset owners will be expected to disclose climate-related financial risks in line with the TCFD's approach by 2022. In France, Article 173 of the Energy Transition Law will be amended to align reporting and disclosure with the TCFD. Signatories to the United Nations-supported Principles for Responsible Investment will be expected to follow the TCFD's recommendations from 2020. At a European level, the updated Non-Financial Reporting Directive, which sets out minimum requirements for climate-related and other environmental risk disclosures for more than 6,000 European companies, has been aligned with the TCFD.

Some experts have criticized the voluntary nature of the TCFD and other disclosure initiatives, as some companies may choose not to disclose information. Despite the rapid growth in support for the TCFD's recommendations, 800 organizations, albeit large and influential global corporations, still only represents a very small minority of firms. Others have questioned whether relying on disclosure will ever be sufficient, given the difficulty of securing accurate and consistent disclosures from all relevant firms in all the key jurisdictions. Some suggest an alternative approach to securing data on company and investor exposure to climate-related risks without the need for disclosure, for example through ultra-transparency enabled by remote sensing from satellites, as discussed in the previous chapter. This is a long way from becoming a reality, however.

As of 2019, given growing organizational, regulatory and policymaker support for the TCFD and its recommendations, it appears probable that these will develop into the accepted, global framework for climate-related financial risk disclosures used by the majority of issuers and investors, at least in the public markets. It seems likely that the current voluntary nature of disclosures will, over time, become mandatory, at least for financial institutions, listed companies and large asset owners, and become part of the regulatory framework in many major markets.

Since the publication of the TCFD's recommendations, other organizations and groups have developed and are developing further guidance to support the recommendations, particularly around appropriate reporting metrics. For example, to support a consistent approach to the disclosure of physical climate risks, opportunities and scenario analysis reporting, the European Bank for Reconstruction and the Development and Global Centre for Excellence on Climate Adaptation have developed guidance and a proposed, standard set of metrics, including:

- **First-order impacts:** Direct hazards to an organization from acute and chronic climate change that can be measured in physical terms (eg degrees of warming, mm of rainfall) that affect specific regions.
- **Second-order impacts:** All impacts of climate change on economic, human and ecosystems beyond the organization (eg changes in availability of natural resources, migration, transport disruption).

Climate Disclosure Standards Board

Predating the TCFD, another framework designed to promote consistency in disclosure and reporting of climate-related risks and natural capital has been developed by the Climate Disclosure Standards Board (CDSB), an international consortium of business and environmental NGOs founded at the World Economic Forum in 2007. The CDSB's Climate Change Reporting Framework, published in 2012, provides detailed standards and guidance for reporting climate-related risks and natural capital aligned with traditional financial reporting standards such as those of the International Accounting Standards Board.[10]

In November 2018, the CDSB, together with a number of international accounting and sustainability reporting standard-setting bodies, launched a project to bring greater consistency to sustainability and climate-related risk reporting. Amongst other intended outcomes, it is proposed that the project will seek to align standards with the TCFD's recommendations, supporting the TCFD's status as the developing global framework for such reporting. CDSB standards, and standards and frameworks developed by other standard-setters and project partners, seem likely to provide useful, detailed guidance for preparers of corporate reports and should help bring greater consistency (and, hence, comparability and usefulness) to such reports.

Scenario analysis

As we have seen in this chapter and elsewhere, it is difficult for organizations and investors to understand, model and quantify climate risks, due to the complexity and inter-related nature of variables and feedback loops involved. It is also difficult to estimate the financial impacts of climate-related risks, as they depend on different scenarios regarding the degree of global warming, speed of transition, changing regulation, cost of legal liabilities and many other variables.

Organizations and investors may use **scenario analysis** (a well-established method for developing strategic plans that are more flexible or robust in a range of future states) to try to understand the impact of different assumptions regarding the speed and impacts of climate change on products, services, organizations and investment portfolios. In its guidance for firms, the UK Prudential Regulation Authority states that it should be used 'to explore the resilience and vulnerabilities of a firm's business model to a range of outcomes, based on different transition paths to a low-carbon economy, as well as a path where no transition occurs'.[11] Scenario analysis is not intended to produce accurate and detailed forecasts of the future, particularly in the longer term, but to provide insight and a potential range of outcomes that can help firms, regulators and investors with their strategic planning, asset allocation, risk management and other decisions.

The use of scenario analysis is encouraged by the TCFD, with one of its key recommended disclosures (as set out in the section above) focusing on the resilience of an organization's strategy, taking into consideration different climate-related scenarios, including a 2°C or lower scenario. At the same time as publishing its Recommendations, the Task Force published a technical supplement, *The Use of Scenario Analysis in Disclosure of Climate-Related Risks and Opportunities*, to help organizations use scenario analysis to model the impact of climate risks, and including publicly available scenarios and resources on scenario analysis to assist with such modelling.

READING
Scenario analysis

TCFD's *The Use of Scenario Analysis in Disclosure of Climate-Related Risks and Opportunities*[12]

The Task Force on Climate-related Financial Disclosures provides an introduction to scenario analysis in respect of climate change. This allows organizations to explore and develop an understanding of how the physical and transition risks and opportunities of climate change might impact the business over time. Scenarios should be plausible, distinctive, consistent, relevant and challenging to the conventional wisdom, seeking to alter the basis for business-as-usual assumptions.

The Task Force believes that organizations should use a range of scenarios that illuminate future exposure to both transition and physical climate-related risks and opportunities, such as business-as-usual, NDC, and 2°C scenarios. In identifying scenarios that might work best, organizations may make use of existing publicly available scenarios and models or organizations may wish to internally develop their own scenarios. The approach taken will depend on an organization's needs, resources and capabilities. Among the range of scenarios used, the Task Force believes it is important that organizations include a 2°C scenario given the agreed international climate change commitments.

Applying scenario analysis, although potentially complex, has a number of significant benefits for organizations faced with the uncertainties of climate change. For organizations just beginning to use scenario analysis, a qualitative approach may be appropriate.

As organizations gain experience with scenario analysis, and for organizations already conducting scenario analysis, greater rigour and sophistication in the use of data sets and quantitative models and analysis may be warranted. Quantitative approaches may be achieved by using existing external scenarios and models (eg those provided by third-party providers) or by organizations developing their own, in-house modelling capabilities.

The choice of approach will depend on an organization's needs, resources and capabilities. Organizations that are likely to be significantly impacted by climate-related transition and/or physical risks should consider some level of quantitative scenario analysis.

Organizations should apply scenario analysis as part of their strategic planning and/or enterprise risk management processes by:

- identifying and defining a range of scenarios, including a 2°C scenario, that reasonably cover the range of future potential exposure to climate-related transition and physical risks (and opportunities);
- evaluating the potential effects on their strategic and financial position under each of the defined scenarios; and
- using the results to identify options for managing the identified risks and opportunities through adjustments to strategic and financial plans.

Over time, organizations can improve disclosure through documenting: the process and transparently disclosing key inputs, assumptions and analytical methods and outputs (including potential business impacts and management responses to them) and the sensitivity of the results to key assumptions.

Considerations for building climate change into scenario analysis

Recognizing the benefits of scenario analysis and the need to minimize implementation costs, organizations undertaking scenario analysis for the first time may want to consider starting with a simple, yet robust, process for incorporating climate-related considerations into their scenarios.

First, an organization needs to understand the nature of the climate-related risks and opportunities it may face. Each individual organization faces a different blend of climate-related risks and opportunities. The business impacts related to climate change may vary significantly depending on the industry and economic sector(s)/sub-sector(s) in which an organization operates. Business impacts may also vary significantly depending on:

- the geographic location of the organization's value chain (both upstream and downstream);
- the organization's assets and nature of operations;
- the structure and dynamics of the organization's supply and demand markets;
- the organization's customers; and
- the organization's other key stakeholders.

Many organizations already disclose their views on climate-related risks and opportunities at a high, qualitative level. The Task Force's Phase I report identified several frameworks for reporting climate-related information, many of which include disclosures around risks and opportunities. Such information provides a starting point for scenario analysis and for further disclosure.

Organizations should carefully consider the key parameters, assumptions and other analytical choices made during scenario analysis as well as the potential impacts or effects that are identified and how those results are considered by management. Organizations should consider disclosing this information where appropriate. In particular, organizations are encouraged to disclose the approach used for selecting scenarios used as well as the underlying assumptions for each scenario regarding how a particular pathway might develop (eg, emergence and deployment of key technologies, policy developments and timing, geopolitical environment around climate policies). This information will be important for an organization to disclose and discuss, including the sensitivity of various assumptions to changes in key parameters such as carbon prices, input prices, customer preferences, etc, so that investors and other stakeholders have a clear understanding of the scenario process – not only the outcomes each scenario describes, but the pathway envisioned by an organization that leads to that outcome (ie the how and why of those outcomes).

Transparency around key parameters, assumptions and analytical choices will help to support comparability of results between different scenarios used by an organization and across organizations. In turn, this will support the evaluation, by analysts and investors, of the potential magnitude and timing of impacts on individual organizations and sectors and the robustness of organizations' strategies across the range of plausible impacts, thereby supporting better risk and capital allocation decisions.

Figure 5.2 A process for applying scenario analysis to climate-related risks and opportunities

1 Ensure governance

Integrate scenario analysis into strategic planning and/or enterprise risk management frameworks. Assign oversight to relevant board committees/sub-committees. Identify which internal (and external) stakeholders to involve, and how.

2 Assess materiality of climate-related risks

- Market and technology shifts
- Reputation
- Policy and legal
- Physical risks

What are the current and anticipated organizational exposures to climate-related risks and opportunities? Do these have the potential to be material in the future? Are organizational stakeholders concerned?

3 Identify and define range of scenarios

- Transition risk scenarios
- Physical risk scenarios

What scenarios (and narratives) are appropriate, given the exposures? Consider input parameters, assumptions, and analytical choices. What reference scenario(s) should be used?

4 Evaluate business impacts

Impact on:

- Input costs
- Operating costs
- Revenues
- Supply chain
- Business interruption
- Timing

Evaluate the potential effects on the organization's strategic and financial position under each of the defined scenarios. Identify key sensitivities.

5 Identify potential responses

Responses might include:

- Changes to business model
- Portfolio mix
- Investments in capabilities and technologies

Use the results to identify applicable, realistic decisions to manage the identified risks and opportunities. What adjustments to strategic/financial plans would be needed?

6 Document and disclose

Document the process; communicate to relevant parties; be prepared to disclose key inputs, assumptions, analytical methods, outputs, and potential management responses.

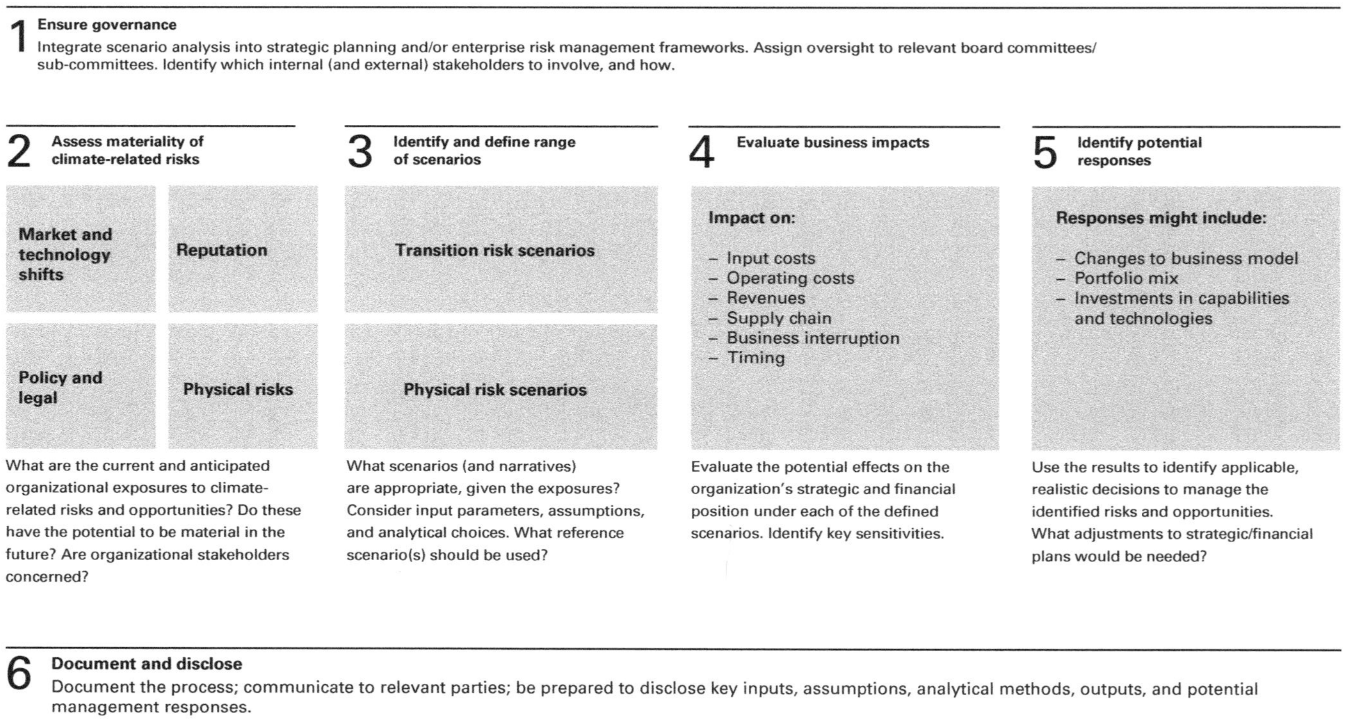

SOURCE Reproduced with permission from Task Force on Climate-related Financial Disclosures (TCFD) (2016) *The Use of Scenario Analysis in Disclosure of Climate-Related Risks and Opportunities: Technical supplement*. https://assets.bbhub.io/company/sites/60/2020/10/FINAL-TCFD-Technical-Supplement-062917.pdf

Given the number of variables and analytical approaches to scenario analysis, there will be a wide range of scenarios used that describe various outcomes. Given this, direct comparability across organizations is likely to be a very real challenge. This underpins the importance of transparency across the three categories of considerations. Keeping in mind that improved disclosure and transparency are important for comparability, organizations should consider disclosing as many of these considerations as possible and endeavour to increase their levels of disclosure over time.

For investors, scenario analysis may be applied in different ways, depending on the nature of the asset(s) being considered; for example, some investors may develop energy transition pathways that they believe to be either optimal and/or likely and use them to model the expected return(s) from investments under different scenarios. Alternatively, investors with different time horizons may conduct their scenario analysis differently. Investors with shorter-term horizons may place more weight on short-term physical risks that may (in some cases) be easier to forecast with greater accuracy); those with longer-term horizons may be more interested in longer-term transition risks and the development of climate policies such as carbon pricing.

Other investors may consider how climate-related scenarios relate to the future performance of particular sectors, regions, or asset classes. The results may show that some portions of a portfolio are set to benefit from a particular scenario, whilst others face losses. Such results, while not conclusive, can be a useful additional factor in determining where to prioritize further risk management activities and in making decisions relating to asset allocation, diversification and decarbonization.

Given that firms, investors and others may choose – for sound reasons – different climate-related scenarios and to focus on different aspects of these it can be difficult to compare results. Central banks and other regulators, therefore, are beginning to try to standardize approaches with the publication of climate scenarios, albeit these are at an early, exploratory stage. In 2019, the UK Prudential Regulation Authority published three climate change scenarios as part of its *Life Insurance Stress Test*, emphasizing that these should be completed on a 'best endeavours' basis.[13]

Pricing climate-related risks

Following a series of major natural disasters in the 1990s and 2000s, the insurance sector has led the way in efforts to accurately identify and price climate-related risks, with particular reference to extreme weather events such as droughts, floods, hurricanes and tropical storms. The Bank of England reports:

> [there is] evidence to suggest that insurance payouts... arising from global natural catastrophes are increasing. The number of registered weather-related natural hazard loss events has tripled since the 1980s and inflation-adjusted insurance losses from these events have increased from an annual average of around $10 billion in the 1980s to around $50 billion over the past decade.[14]

The frequency and impact of extreme weather events are predicted to increase in the coming years.

In response, national and international insurance regulators required insurers to hold sufficient capital to cover losses from extreme weather events of the type predicted to occur once every 200 years, imposing significant costs in terms of the capital held. In addition, advances in and greater availability of weather and climate change data from satellites and other forms of monitoring, combined with improved modelling and data analytics, have enabled more accurate underwriting of climate-risk insurance.

Until recently, asset management and investment sectors are lagging behind insurance, although as we will see in Chapter 9 there is now emerging evidence of a climate change risk premium for equities. This is not, perhaps, surprising given the absence (until recently) of consistent approaches for identifying, disclosing and pricing climate risks and especially the lack of analysis of the true, long-term costs of investing in fossil fuels and other carbon-intensive assets. A more consistent approach to the disclosure of climate-related risks should lead, over time, to a premium for those assets most resilient to such risks. In addition, the greater adoption of realistic carbon pricing should encourage the accurate pricing of climate risks, leading to writedowns in the value of high-carbon investments, and premiums for low-carbon alternatives.

Carbon pricing

Carbon pricing is thought by many academics and policymakers to be one of the most effective ways of encouraging decarbonization and the reduction of greenhouse gases. By assigning an economic value to carbon (usually per tonne), it creates an incentive for firms to invest in low-carbon technologies, as well as reduce their carbon use and emissions where this can be done at a cost that is less than the carbon price. Assigning a price to carbon also helps quantify the impact (and opportunities) arising from climate-related risks, and can assist with climate-related scenario analysis, as set out above.

There are two main approaches to carbon pricing:

- **Carbon taxes:** These may include some energy taxes, eg on petrol and diesel fuel. Countries that have implemented carbon taxes include India, Japan, Denmark, Norway and Sweden. Australia introduced a carbon tax in 2012, but this was repealed in 2014.
- **Cap-and-trade schemes:** Organizations (usually large firms and/or the major emitters of greenhouse gases) purchase permits that allow them to emit greenhouse gases. The cap on emissions usually becomes more onerous over time; organizations can buy and sell (trade) permits, meaning that those firms able to cut emissions and carbon usage can sell permits to others. The market, through the demand and supply for permits, sets the carbon price.

Probably the best-known example of a cap-and-trade scheme is the EU Emissions Trading System (EU ETS), established in 2005, which limits emissions from more than 11,000 major emitters such as airlines, power stations and large industrial plants accounting for approximately 45 per cent of the EU's greenhouse gas emissions. By 2016 it was reported that emissions had fallen by 8 per cent as a result of the scheme, and that by 2020 it was anticipated that emissions covered by the scheme would be 21 per cent lower than in 2005. The EU ETS has been criticized for its generous caps and surplus of permits, meaning the carbon price has been lower than many, particularly environmental NGOs, would have liked – in May 2017 a tonne of carbon cost €4.40. Reforms to the scheme, particularly in reducing the supply of permits, resulted in the carbon price rising to more than €28 per tonne by July 2019.

Other emissions trading schemes operate at national and/or regional level in countries including the USA, Japan, India and New Zealand. In 2017 China announced plans for a 'cap and trade' market, to be fully operational in 2020.

In 2019 the IMF estimated that a global carbon tax of $75 per tonne would be required by 2030 to reduce emissions to a level consistent with 2°C of global warming. The price per tonne of carbon varies considerably worldwide, however, from the equivalent of $2 per tonne in pilot ETS schemes in China, to more than $126 per tonne in Sweden (January 2019).[15]

Wide variations in carbon pricing make using this to quantify climate-related risks challenging, and comparisons between approaches, organizations and jurisdictions difficult. Despite this, the number of organizations using carbon pricing to inform their business strategy and risk management appears to be rising. The Carbon Disclosure Project (CDP) reports that the number of large, international organizations using carbon pricing in this way had grown from 150 in 2014 to over 600 in 2017 and that this number was likely to increase to nearly 1,400 organizations – including more than 100 Fortune Global 500 companies – in 2019.[16]

A major issue with the lack of a global carbon price, and large differences between the carbon price in different countries and regions, is carbon leakage. This occurs when firms responsible for significant levels of greenhouse gas emissions move from jurisdictions with high carbon taxes to ones with much lower taxes. Whilst it might be difficult or impossible for coal-fired power stations to move, given the costs and complexities of power transmission, it is feasible that production of many high-carbon goods (eg petrochemicals) might be moved to low tax jurisdictions, and then imported into the higher tax jurisdiction. The EU and others have therefore proposed **carbon border taxes** which would charge imports on the basis of their carbon footprint to create a level playing field. Detailed proposals that would not conflict with global trade rules are currently being developed, but given the need for agreement between a wide range of national and international governments and bodies, the introduction of carbon border taxes seems some years away.

Despite the challenges of ensuring a consistent approach, carbon pricing is playing an increasingly important role in climate risk quantification and management, enabling boards, investors and lenders to price climate risk more accurately, identify the likelihood of asset impairment and spot opportunities for profitable investment in low-carbon technologies.

Use of data to better assess climate-related risks

By encouraging and enhancing climate-related risk disclosures, the Task Force on Climate-related Financial Disclosures (TCFD) and similar initiatives (such as the Climate Disclosure Standards Board mentioned above) should increase the quantity and quality of climate risk data publicly available. In turn, this should improve risk management and risk decision-making by boards, investors, lenders and others.

For good risk management and decision-making, the availability of accurate, verifiable and timely climate datasets (eg emissions, temperature, water levels, crop production, weather) is key, but until relatively recently these have been difficult and expensive to obtain except for some developed countries. Advances in technologies for gathering data (eg satellite monitoring), data analytics and data modelling, often supported by funds from governments, multilateral development banks and similar, are now making such datasets more widely available, and covering countries and regions for which such data was not previously available. The International Finance Corporation, for example, makes use of data sources, including the National Center for Atmospheric Research, the National Aeronautics and Space Administration's Global Climate Change Directory, the United States Environmental Protection Agency, Columbia's Consortium for International Earth Science Information Network, the Earth Institute, and the National and Oceanic and Atmospheric Administration, and combines this with localized data on weather and other relevant information to develop models for the impact of climate change on specific countries, regions, businesses or potential investments.[17]

The World Bank has developed climate and disaster risk screening tools to provide a structured and systematic way of undertaking due diligence and understanding climate-related risks when considering potential investments and projects, especially those targeted at the developing world.[18] The tools link to climate projections, country adaptation profiles and disaster risk data sources brought together by the World Bank.

There has been significant growth in the number of companies and consultancies using data, and in particular the power of big data analytics and modelling to assess climate-related risks. These may support the boards and managers of organizations seeking to better understand, disclose and price climate risk, and/or investors looking to identify how the value of their investments may be impacted (positively or negatively) by climate change. One example is Carbon Delta (now part of MSCI), which describes itself as an 'environmental FinTech' and provides analysis on 22,000 companies. Carbon Delta's Climate Value-at-Risk methodology assesses the future costs of climate change for organizations over a 15-year horizon, taking into account a range of climate change scenarios, allowing for more accurate pricing of current investments.[19]

The future of risk management

The development of global frameworks, such as the TCFD, for the disclosure of climate-related risks, combined with wider usage of carbon pricing and advances in the collection, analysis and modelling of climate risk data, is improving the consistency of approaches to the identification and management of climate-related risks. It is reasonable to assume that improvement will continue in the coming years as more organizations adopt the TCFD's recommendations (voluntarily, or prompted by regulators), and more jurisdictions implement carbon pricing (eg China) and climate risk data become even more widely available, and the quality and completeness of data improves. Also, greater awareness of asset owners and investors of the risks of impaired or stranded assets as a result of climate change will prompt further action.

In addition, further regulatory encouragement seems likely to increase the focus on climate risk management, at least within the financial services sector. Utilizing the UK's new Senior Manager Regime, the Prudential Regulatory Authority has introduced a requirement that banks and insurance companies nominate a senior executive responsible for managing climate risk, and climate change scenarios (albeit exploratory) are being included in bank and insurer stress tests. As covered elsewhere in this book, the EU's 'Action Plan: Financing sustainable growth' includes guidance to improve corporate disclosure of climate-related information. In China, as well as the development of an Emissions Trading Scheme, the People's Bank of China has incorporated green bonds and green loans into its Macro-Prudential Assessments of banks.

Given ever-growing regulatory and investor pressure, and awareness of the scale and nature of climate-related and other environmental and sustainability risks, it seems undeniable that climate, environmental and sustainability risk management will rapidly become part of the mainstream of risk management.

Key concepts

In this chapter we considered:

- the nature and importance of key climate-related and environmental risks;
- different types of climate-related risk (physical, transition and liability) and their impact on the finance sector;
- stranded asset risk, and its potential impact on financial institutions and financial stability;
- approaches to identifying, disclosing, managing and pricing climate-related risks, and the use of scenario analysis.

Now go back through this chapter and make sure you fully understand each point.

Review

A wide range of environmental risks, particularly climate-related risks, is already having a significant impact on financial institutions, and the economy more generally (which in turn will impact on financial institutions). The scale of the risks associated with climate change and a transition to a sustainable, low-carbon economy is so significant that the entire financial system could be damaged, and overall financial stability severely threatened. Central banks, regulators (and many other organizations) are working to understand and try to manage exposures.

Risks associated with climate change and a transition to a low-carbon economy can be classified as physical, transition and liability risks. The TCFD has established a framework for voluntary, climate-related financial risk disclosures for use by companies, providing information to investors, lenders, insurers and other stakeholders that is designed to encourage consistency in identifying, disclosing and managing such risks.

By encouraging and promoting greater, more consistent disclosure, climate-related financial risks should become more central to board and investor decision-making, and to shareholder engagement with management on climate change issues.

Physical risks are those that arise from the direct impacts of climate change, such as droughts, floods and storms. Such risks may be divided into acute risks (severe, short-term impact such as a flood or hurricane) and chronic risks (more gradual longer-term impacts such as rising sea levels).

Transition risks are those that arise from the move to a low-carbon economy, and may be divided into:

- risks from developments in climate policy, legislation and regulation;
- risks from new, lower-carbon technologies which substitute for existing products and services;
- risks from changing consumer behaviour and investor sentiment;
- reputational risks.

Liability risks include costs that arise from litigation prompted by poor environmental management, and also the potential costs that may arise from legal challenges, seeking to pressure companies and governments to do more to prevent climate change. The direct costs of such legal action can be significant; longer-term costs arising from changes in legislation, regulation (or sentiment) as a result of legal action may be much higher.

Physical, transition and liability risks may result in stranded assets, where assets have suffered from unanticipated or premature write-downs, devaluations or conversion to liabilities.

It is difficult for organizations and investors to understand, model and quantify climate risks, due to the complexity and inter-related nature of variables involved. It is also difficult to estimate the financial impacts of climate risk, as they depend on different scenarios regarding the degree of global warming, speed of transition, changing regulation, cost of legal liabilities and many other variables. Scenario analysis is a useful technique to use in attempting to understand the impact of different assumptions regarding the speed and impacts of climate change on products, services, organizations and investment portfolios. Carbon pricing and the use of big data have the potential to improve accuracy in pricing climate-related risks.

Given ever-growing regulatory and investor pressure, and awareness of the scale and nature of climate-related and other environmental and sustainability risks, it seems undeniable that climate, environmental and sustainability risk management will rapidly become part of the mainstream of risk management.

Glossary

Acute risks: Risks from severe, short-term environmental impacts such as floods or hurricanes.

Cap-and-Trade Scheme: Where organizations (usually large firms and/or the major emitters of greenhouse gases) purchase permits that allow them to emit greenhouse gases, and can buy and sell these to others.

Carbon border tax: Charges imports on the basis of their carbon footprint to prevent cheaper imports from jurisdictions with lower carbon taxes.

Carbon pricing: Assigning an economic value to carbon to create an incentive for firms to invest in low-carbon technologies and reduce carbon use.

Chronic risks: Risks from longer-term environmental impacts such as rising sea levels.

Liability risks: Risks that arise from parties who have suffered loss or damage from the effects of climate change and who seek compensation from those they hold responsible.

Physical risks: Risks that arise from the direct impacts of climate-related hazards inherent in human and natural systems, such as droughts, floods and storms.

Scenario analysis: A well-established method for developing strategic plans that are more flexible or robust in a range of future states.

Stranded asset risk: The risk of assets suffering from unanticipated or premature write-downs, devaluations or conversion to liabilities.

Task Force on Climate-related Financial Disclosures (TCFD): Established in 2015 by the Financial Stability Board, the TCFD has developed a global framework for the voluntary disclosure of climate-related financial risks.

Transition risks: Risks that arise from the transition to a lower-carbon economy such as developments in climate policy, new disruptive technology or shifting investor sentiment.

Notes

1. BlackRock Investment Institute (2015) *The Price of Climate Change: Global warming's impact on portfolios* [Online] https://www.blackrock.com/corporate/literature/whitepaper/bii-pricing-climate-risk-us.pdf (archived at https://perma.cc/WYD3-LWW6)
2. World Economic Forum (2020) *The Global Risks Report 2020* [Online] www3.weforum.org/docs/WEF_Global_Risk_Report_2020.pdf (archived at https://perma.cc/A6N9-U4QJ)
3. B Caldecott and J McDaniels (2014) *Financial Dynamics of the Environment: Risks, impacts, and barriers to resilience.* Working paper for the UNEP Inquiry, July 2014 [Online] https://unepinquiry.org/publication/financial-dynamics/ (archived at https://perma.cc/4VKH-E92R)
4. Bank of England (2017) The Bank of England's response to climate change, *Bank of England Quarterly Bulletin*, Q2 [Online] https://www.bankofengland.co.uk/-/media/boe/files/quarterly-bulletin/2017/the-banks-response-to-climate-change.pdf?la=en&hash=7DF676C781E5FAEE994C2A210A6B9EEE44879387 (archived at https://perma.cc/K4UV-Y4XA)
5. Bank of England (2015) Breaking the tragedy of the horizon: Climate change and financial stability, Speech by Mark Carney [Online] https://www.bankofengland.co.uk/speech/2015/breaking-the-tragedy-of-the-horizon-climate-change-and-financial-stability (archived at https://perma.cc/4757-CD3D)
6. Rainforest Action Network (RAN) *et al* (2019) *Banking on Climate Change: Fossil fuel finance report card 2019* [Online] https://www.ran.org/wp-content/uploads/2019/03/Banking_on_Climate_Change_2019_vFINAL1.pdf (archived at https://perma.cc/XN2X-EVN3)
7. MinterEllison (2017) *The Carbon Boomerang: Litigation risk as a driver and consequence of the energy transition* [Online] https://yoursri.com/media-new/images/2017-09-22_the-carbon-boomerang.pdf (archived at https://perma.cc/Y9LM-T3DC)

8 PRI (2016) Principles for Responsible Investment: An investor initiative in partnership with UNEP Finance Initiative and the UN Global Compact [Online] https://www.sedcocapital.com/sites/default/files/downloads/pri_brochure_2016_0.pdf (archived at https://perma.cc/7HRM-NUZE)

9 Task Force on Climate-related Financial Disclosures (TCFD) (2017) *Recommendations of the Task Force on Climate-related Financial Disclosures: Final report* [Online] https://assets.bbhub.io/company/sites/60/2020/10/FINAL-2017-TCFD-Report-11052018.pdf (archived at https://perma.cc/G9MZ-S59D)

10 Climate Disclosure Standards Board (2012) *Climate Change Reporting Framework: Advancing and aligning disclosure of climate change related information in mainstream reports* [Online] https://www.cdsb.net/sites/cdsbnet/files/cdsb_climate_change_reporting_framework_edition_1.1.pdf (archived at https://perma.cc/G7EW-MK7L)

11 Bank of England Prudential Regulation Authority (2019) Enhancing banks' and insurers' approaches to managing the financial risks from climate change, Supervisory Statement SS3/19 [Online] https://www.bankofengland.co.uk/prudential-regulation/publication/2019/enhancing-banks-and-insurers-approaches-to-managing-the-financial-risks-from-climate-change-ss (archived at https://perma.cc/XC6C-85MW)

12 Task Force on Climate-related Financial Disclosures (TCFD) (2016) *The Use of Scenario Analysis in Disclosure of Climate-Related Risks and Opportunities: Technical supplement* [Online] https://assets.bbhub.io/company/sites/60/2020/10/FINAL-TCFD-Technical-Supplement-062917.pdf (archived at https://perma.cc/2GW9-TMR4)

13 Bank of England (2019) *Life Insurance Stress Test 2019* [Online] https://www.bankofengland.co.uk/-/media/boe/files/prudential-regulation/letter/2019/life-insurance-stress-test-2019-scenario-specification-guidelines-and-instructions.pdf (archived at https://perma.cc/R8JT-NN4Z)

14 Bank of England Prudential Regulation Authority (2015) The impact of climate change on the UK insurance sector [Online] https://www.bankofengland.co.uk/-/media/boe/files/prudential-regulation/publication/impact-of-climate-change-on-the-uk-insurance-sector.pdf (archived at https://perma.cc/ZH8E-6FQL)

15 The World Bank (nd) Carbon pricing dashboard [Online] https://carbonpricingdashboard.worldbank.org/ (archived at https://perma.cc/766U-839U)

16 CDP (nd) Carbon pricing [Online] https://www.cdp.net/en/climate/carbon-pricing (archived at https://perma.cc/DBK8-H5ZM)

17 International Finance Corporation (2016) How new data tools can assess climate risks, *EM Compass*, Note 10 [Online] https://www.ifc.org/wps/wcm/connect/9a31c7b5-4ddf-4d4e-9f37-ea9cdbb32015/Note-10-EMCompass-How-New-Data-Tools-Can-Assess-Climate-Risks.pdf?MOD=AJPERES&CVID=lt8amXR (archived at https://perma.cc/5XTG-9CM9)

18 The World Bank (nd) Climate and disaster risk screening tools [Online] https://climatescreeningtools.worldbank.org/ (archived at https://perma.cc/TRT3-988J)

19 Carbon Delta (nd) Climate Value-at-Risk [Online] https://www.carbon-delta.com/climate-value-at-risk/ (archived at https://perma.cc/N7NH-VYYH)

06

Retail, commercial and corporate banking

LEARNING OBJECTIVES

On completion of this chapter you should be able to:

- Describe the role of banking within the wider financial system.
- Describe how different banking activities can affect the quality and functioning of the natural environment and natural systems.
- Describe how different types of banking products and services can improve the quality and functioning of the natural environment and natural systems.
- Cite examples and case studies of innovative green and sustainable banking products and services.
- Describe the UN Principles for Responsible Banking and the Green Loan Principles.

Banks are well positioned to reallocate credit and mobilize capital away from environmentally harmful activities and towards the green economy. There are four main types of banks, each of which play different roles in the economy and offer different types of products and services: retail banks serving individuals and small businesses; wholesale and investment banks serving corporate clients; national and multilateral development banks; and central banks. This chapter focuses on retail, wholesale and investment banks, and describes a growing range of innovative green finance products and services, together with industry initiatives to improve alignment of strategy and activities with green and sustainable finance principles, promote market consistency and integrity and avoid greenwashing (eg the UN Principles for Responsible Banking and the Green Loan Principles).

The role of banking in the financial system

The banking system plays a number of critical roles in the economy, including taking deposits, creating and allocating credit, managing the payments system, underwriting securities, raising finance in capital markets, offering investment products, providing advisory services and undertaking research. It is the primary source of credit for households and businesses. The term banking can be applied to a large range of financial institutions that cater to a diverse range of clients, regions and sectors, from large global banks that serve huge, multinational corporations to small, mutually owned building societies that serve local households and businesses. Public banks also play important roles in many countries.

In this book we distinguish between the following four types of banks, each of which play different roles in the economy and offer different types of products and services:

- retail banks, primarily offering products and services to individuals and small business customers (the latter is sometimes referred to as commercial banking) – these may include public and private banks, building societies, credit unions and cooperative banks;
- wholesale and investment banks, serving larger, corporate clients and other financial institutions;
- national and multilateral development banks, eg KfW (German Development Bank), Asian Development Bank;
- central banks, eg the Bank of England, the People's Bank of China, acting as financial services regulators and with 'lender of last resort' responsibilities.

In practice, many banks offer products and services across more than one of these functions. Some banks also offer other services such as asset management, wealth management and insurance. Financial regulation also plays an important role in determining how the banking system functions, and how banks are organized and delineated in different countries. In this chapter, we focus on green and sustainable products and services in retail, commercial and corporate banking, while the following chapter considers the corporate banking market for green and sustainable finance, looking at green bonds and other asset-backed securities in more detail. The role of development and central banks is covered separately in Chapter 8.

> **QUICK QUESTIONS**
>
> How might retail and commercial banks be negatively affected by climate change? And what might the opportunities be for green and sustainable banking?

As discussed in Chapter 5, climate change poses **physical risks** that arise from the direct impacts of climate-related hazards, **transition risks** that arise from the transition to a lower-carbon economy and **liability risks** that arise from parties who have suffered loss or damage from the effects of climate change and who seek compensation from those they hold responsible. We also saw, in the previous chapter, that climate-related risks were now identified by many as the key risks faced by business, finance and society over the next decade and that central banks and financial regulators are worried about the threat to financial stability caused by climate change and an abrupt transition to a low-carbon world. Exposure to carbon-intensive companies or sectors is making financial institutions ever more vulnerable to reputational risks, which in turn may have significant financial impacts on institutions through reduced demand from customers and investors.

As banks provide the main source of credit in most economies and play a major role in capital markets too, investment decisions made within banks have material consequences on the environment. They are uniquely positioned to reallocate credit and mobilize capital away from environmentally harmful activities and towards green and sustainable projects and activities. By continuing to finance high-carbon, environmentally damaging activities, banks contribute to the acceleration and impacts of climate change. By supporting green and sustainable finance, banks have a key role to play supporting the transition towards a more sustainable low-carbon economy. As we noted in Chapter 1, however, despite the growth in green and sustainable finance the banking sector still often contributes to increasing greenhouse gas emissions rather than reducing them, with the $1.9 trillion of financing provided by 33 global banks to fossil fuel companies since the signing of the Paris Agreement in 2015 far outweighing their flows of finance to emissions reduction and other sustainable objectives.

Banks with significant exposure to carbon-intensive companies or sectors may be vulnerable to volatility in asset prices and/or increased borrower defaults. As the banking sector is the largest source of finance in most economies, how banks manage the financial risks associated with the transition towards a more sustainable economy and world is crucial for financial stability as well as environmental sustainability.

For the banking sector, climate change need not only mean being exposed to more significant risks, but can also present opportunities, as HSBC has recognized:

> Climate change has the potential to materially affect HSBC's customers and, by extension, HSBC's long-term success, introducing new risks to business activity. However, it also has the potential to stimulate a new era of low carbon growth, innovation and development.[1]

The UN Principles for Responsible Banking

In recent years, moves to incorporate environmental and related sustainability factors into the banking system have gathered pace, driven by a combination of market forces, policy factors and changing customer attitudes, which have led banks to consider a range of environmental, social and governance risks and opportunities in their operations. Most recently, the launch of the UN's Principles for Responsible Banking in 2019, supported by 130 banks from 49 countries as the founding signatories, encourages banks to incorporate green and sustainable finance principles into their strategies and activities and link their business plans to societal goals, as expressed in the UN Sustainable Development Goals and the Paris Agreement.

The six Principles for Responsible Banking are:

Principle 1: Alignment We will align our business strategy to be consistent with and contribute to individuals' needs and society's goals, as expressed in the Sustainable Development Goals (SDGs), the Paris Climate Agreement and relevant national and regional frameworks.

Principle 2: Impact and target setting We will continuously increase our positive impacts while reducing the negative impacts on, and managing the risks to, people and environment resulting from our activities, products and services. To this end, we will set and publish targets where we can have the most significant impacts.

Principle 3: Clients and customers We will work responsibly with our clients and our customers to encourage sustainable practices and enable economic activities that create shared prosperity for current and future generations.

Principle 4: Stakeholders We will proactively and responsibly consult, engage and partner with relevant stakeholders to achieve society's goals.

Principle 5: Governance We will implement our commitment to these Principles through effective governance and a culture of responsible banking.

Principle 6: Transparency and accountability We will periodically review our individual and collective implementation of these Principles and be transparent about and accountable for our positive and negative impacts and our contribution to society's goals.[2]

Within 18 months of becoming a signatory, banks have to publish their first self-assessment of their alignment with the Principles for Responsible Banking. This should take the form of an initial impact analysis to identify their most significant impacts on the economies, environments and societies where they operate, and develop plans to increase the positive and reduce negative impacts.

Signatories should then set and publish a minimum of two (but ideally more) targets that seek to increase the positive and reduce negative impacts, and are aligned with the Sustainable Development Goals. Targets should be measurable, milestones should be agreed and suitable governance and reporting arrangements put in place to oversee the achievement of the targets. Signatories have a four-year period in which to make significant progress towards the targets, including annual progress reporting. Limited external assurance of banks' self-assessment is required.

Banks are not required or expected to produce a separate report, rather to include their annual assessment of alignment with the Principles for Responsible Banking in existing public reporting.

The Principles for Responsible Banking are principles for organizations, but for the Principles to drive and continue to support a culture of responsible, sustainable banking, alignment is needed at industry, institutional and individual levels:

- **Industry level:** Policymakers, regulators and industry trade associations leading a collective approach to endorsing and implementing the Principles.
- **Institutional level:** Founding signatories leading by example and sharing good practice.
- **Individual level:** Professional bodies and educators such as the Chartered Banker Institute bringing the Principles to life for individuals, embedding them in professional standards and qualifications, and setting out how they can be demonstrated by bank staff in day-to-day professional banking practice.

As we will see in Chapter 12, mainstreaming responsible, green and sustainable finance, including the Principles for Responsible Banking, needs to be led, ultimately, by individuals committed to changing their individual professional practice, the practice of others in their organization and, ultimately, the organization itself. To support the implementation of the Principles, therefore, the finance sector requires increasing numbers of Green and Sustainable Finance Professionals with an understanding of the critical role of financial services in supporting the transition to a sustainable, socially just world, and the knowledge and skill to be able to develop and deploy financial products, services and tools that will mobilize capital to support that transition, address climate-related and societal risks, and help customers and communities direct investment to green and sustainable finance opportunities.

QUICK QUESTIONS

Has your organization, or organizations you are familiar with, signed the Principles for Responsible Banking? How might you encourage them to do so if they have not yet endorsed the Principles?

Green and sustainable banking practices are at different stages of evolution across the world, reflecting variation in broader national financial and economic circumstances. While progress has been slower in some countries than others, green banking has grown to encompass a wide range of practice. Emerging green and sustainable banking practices across G20 countries can be grouped into two categories:

- **Mainstreaming** environmental factors across bank strategy and governance, risk management functions, culture and skills. These actions are often part of a wider trend to promote sustainable banking practices, managing both the environmental and social dimensions of financial activity. While the driving objective has been to avoid or mitigate financial losses, reputational risk, and social and environmental harm, leading banks are now working to achieve positive impact across all activities. Some banks are taking steps to monitor their balance sheet exposure to stranding risks, often adapting frameworks supplied by specialists, such as Carbon Tracker.
- **Mobilizing** private capital for green investments, including through loan and credit provision, retail savings products, as well as intermediation and capital markets activities.[3]

Some of the main ways in which banks are incorporating green and sustainable practices are summarized in Table 6.1.

Table 6.1 Incorporating green and sustainable practices in banking

Function	Mainstreaming	Mobilizing
Credit and lending	• Ensuring environmental due diligence in credit decisions • Assessing loan portfolios for emerging environmental risks • Enhancing the positive performance and impact of lending	• Extending green credit to key sectors, such as energy-efficient housing • Extending green credit to a broadening range of commercial sectors, such as clean energy, clean transport, green buildings, water and sanitation
Savings	• Reducing environmental impacts of banking operations	• Offering green savings products to retail customers
Capital markets	• Integrating environmental risks into investment research	• Raising capital through equity placements and IPOs • Raising capital through debt market underwriting of green bonds

SOURCE United Nations Environment Programme (2016) *Greening the Banking System: Taking stock of G20 green banking market practice* [Online] http://unepinquiry.org/wp-content/uploads/2016/09/9_Greening_the_Banking_System.pdf

Retail banking products and services

Retail banking is the provision of products and services by a bank to individual consumers and small and medium-sized businesses (SMEs), rather than to large corporations or other banks. Sometimes referred to as community banking, the term is generally used to distinguish these banking services from corporate, wholesale and investment banking. It may also be used to refer to a division or department of a bank dealing with retail customers. Retail banks play an important role in the financial system, and have three main functions:

- **Deposit taking:** Retail banks are where individuals and SMEs can safely deposit their money. If there were no retail banks, people would have to store and protect their savings themselves, which would involve significant risks.
- **Managing the payments system:** Banks are responsible for the payments systems used to settle electronic financial transactions. Electronic payments are becoming more important as people use less cash, meaning that this function has become increasingly important.
- **Extending credit:** Retail banks extend credit to individuals and SMEs through loan and overdraft products. Without retail banks, it would be difficult for people to buy a home or for businesses to make investments.

Products and services provided by retail banks to individuals include current and savings accounts, mortgages, personal loans, debit and credit cards, and overdrafts. SMEs are offered a range of accounts, payment services and loans. Retail banks can vary widely in scale; for example, some operate globally while others are limited to certain countries or regions, and may take many different corporate forms:

- **Commercial banks:** Owned by shareholders with (for the most part) the main objective of maximizing shareholder value.
- **Cooperative banks:** Owned and controlled by members on the basis of one member one vote, rather than by shareholders in proportion to their shareholdings. Any customer can choose to become a member by investing a small amount of money in the cooperative. Unlike commercial retail banks, however, members of cooperatives cannot sell their stake to a third party and do not have any legal claim on the profits or capital accumulation of the bank. Cumulative profits are owned by the cooperative itself and used to reinvest in the business.

- **Mutuals:** Similar to cooperatives, but customers of mutuals automatically become members without having to buy a share. Building societies in the UK are a type of mutual that traditionally focuses on providing mortgages, although they also provide other retail banking products and services.
- **Credit unions:** A type of non-profit financial cooperative offering a restricted range of financial services to members within a community that shares a common bond such as living or working in a particular geographical area, or working for the same organization. These close relationships help them to assess loans and ensure repayment. In some countries they often focus on the needs of the most financially marginalized, but in others (eg the US) they may compete with other types of retail banks for customers. In many countries they play a significant role in improving financial inclusion.
- **Microfinance institutions:** These specialize in providing banking services, and in particular credit, to individuals and small businesses that might previously have been excluded from financial services. Although often associated with the developing world, microfinance institutions can be found worldwide. Whilst the majority of microfinance institutions are funded or supported, at least in part, by donors seeking to reduce poverty by improving access to financial services, in recent years an increasing number of commercial microfinance institutions have developed to take advantage of growing market opportunities.
- **Public savings banks:** These also have much in common with cooperative banks, but have key differences in ownership and governance. Their ownership structures often reflect a public interest mandate, meaning that they have a dual financial and social mission. Their assets are managed by trustees, often under a stakeholder governance structure. Crucially, however, nobody has ownership rights over profits or capital – the capital is in essence 'unowned'.

QUICK QUESTION

How might the different corporate forms outlined above affect how a bank sees its role in relation to the environment?

Because retail banks tend to have close relationships with individual customers, and in some countries may offer a wide range of financial advice, they play a key role in understanding changing markets and the evolving needs and expectations of customers. Retail banks are well placed to respond to changing attitudes towards the environment, and to help customers shift towards more sustainable modes of consumption and production by offering products and services which enable customers to save, invest and borrow in a sustainable way.

CASE STUDY

YES BANK Green Future Deposits[4]

On World Environment Day in June 2018, India's 4th largest private sector bank launched an innovative Green Future Deposit savings product. The 18-month, fixed-term deposit scheme offers high rates of interest (up to 7.5 per cent pa and up to 8 per cent for senior citizens), and allocates the funds raised to invest in projects and sectors aligned with the UN Sustainable Development Goals.

Speaking about the Green Future Deposit scheme, the CEO of YES BANK, Rana Kapoor, said:

> YES BANK has established itself as India's pre-eminent Green Bank with pioneering initiatives in the sustainable finance domain. YES BANK has been a strong proponent of sustainable banking and has been at the forefront of supporting the Green Good Deeds campaign that was recently launched by the Government of India. The new Green Future: Deposit is an important step in this direction, and the first of many green retail products that will be launched by YES BANK in this financial year.

Recognizing its leadership in India in green and sustainable finance, in November 2019 YES BANK was approved as an accredited entity by the UNFCCC-led Green Climate Fund, established to support developing nations in responding to climate change. As an accredited entity, the bank will develop and implement climate change mitigation and adaptation projects funded by the Green Climate Fund.

Transactional accounts and payment services

A transactional account, also known as a current account, checking account or demand deposit account, is a personal bank account which is available to the account owner on demand with immediate access to withdraw cash, use cheques, or make payments by electronic transfer. Both personal users and businesses need some sort of current account to manage their day-to-day banking.

In recent years, some banks have started to offer green current account products, which enable customers to have influence over how their deposits are used. More recently still, banks such as the Bank of Aland (Finland) and Nordea (Sweden) have launched CO_2 trackers linked to mobile and digital banking apps, helping customers see the impact of their consumption decisions on their carbon footprints.

CASE STUDY

Ekobanken[5]

Ekobanken is a Swedish member-owned bank aimed at those who want to take responsibility for the influence of their money in society, how their money is invested, and the origin of money that is lent.

The bank allows retail clients to choose how their deposits are used. Clients can either decide that their money is used in line with the bank's other investments, which already mainly go to operations that create social, environmental or cultural added value, or they can pick on a sector-level where their money should be invested. In this way, it is possible for clients to, for instance, put their money into sectors that promote climate protection.

Accounts are offered with or without interest return and clients can deliberately refrain from interest and make it possible for loan clients to get loans with a lower interest rate. Customers receive regular information about the loans the bank has granted. A deposit in Ekobanken therefore gives a twofold return: an economic return, and a contribution to making the world more sustainable.

The growth of FinTech, particularly in relatively new banking markets such as Africa and China, has seen traditional current account banking replaced and/or supplemented by online and mobile payments services. Amongst the best known of these are Paypal, MPesa (a mobile phone-based money transfer service operating in several African countries, India and the Balkans), and

Alipay (the world's largest online and mobile payment provider with more than 1 billion users). Alipay is part of the Ant Financial Services Group, now one of the largest financial services firms in the world. The growth of these and similar FinTech institutions offers a significant opportunity to understand and shape consumer behaviour in many respects, including in the area of green and sustainable finance, as the case study below demonstrates. We examine the use of FinTech tools and techniques in green and sustainable finance in more detail in Chapter 11.

CASE STUDY

Ant Forest[6]

Launched in 2016, Ant Forest (China) is a personal carbon account hosted on Alipay, the world's most popular payment app with more than 1 billion users. It is designed to encourage users to reduce their personal carbon footprint, and more generally to consider the impact of their activities and purchases on the environment. It combines behavioural 'nudges' for Alipay's users with gamification and satellite monitoring in a very advanced way to change consumer behaviour, reduce carbon emissions and increase reforestation.

Ant Forest offers 16 different ways in which users can reduce their carbon footprint, including using public transport, paying bills online and cutting the use of paper at home and at work, tracked through Alipay. Users claim carbon points for their activity, and save these to their personal carbon account. Carbon points are converted into virtual green energy which is used to water and grow virtual saplings in the Ant Forest app; gamification encourages users to compete to grow their virtual saplings and share their progress with family, friends and others. When enough green energy has been accrued to grow a virtual tree, this is converted into the planting of a real tree. Some of the planting is monitored via satellite and drone, allowing Ant Forest users to see the progress and results of tree planting in desert regions in Inner Mongolia, for example.

The size and scale of the Alipay payment platform enables Ant Forest to have a significant impact on consumer behaviour and carbon emissions, with some 500 million users of the Ant Forest app by August 2019:

- A total reduction in carbon emissions of 1.22 million tonnes CO_2e were achieved in the first year of Ant Forest's operation.
- More than 100 million real trees had been planted by Ant Forest by August 2019, covering a total area of 112,000 hectares in North West China.

Green savings products

Retail banks typically offer customers a range of savings accounts and products that pay a higher rate of interest than current accounts. Unlike current accounts, customers do not typically have immediate access to money invested in savings products. Savings products include investment accounts, certificates of deposit and bonds. In many countries, retail savings products attract tax benefits to incentivize household saving.

Some banks have started to offer green and sustainable savings products that enable customers to choose to responsibly save and invest. This can involve products that contribute towards the financing of green projects or businesses directly, or products that invest money in investment funds with a green and/or sustainable focus.

CASE STUDY

Green ISAs in the UK

In the UK, an ISA (individual savings account) is a savings account that enables individuals to save or invest money – currently up to £20,000 per year – without paying tax on the interest or on the capital gains received. Some banks and other financial institutions are beginning to offer ISAs that invest in green and environmentally sustainable areas, although these are still niche products rather than mainstream investment options. As with other investments labelled as green or sustainable, care needs to be taken by investors and advisers to ensure that the component stocks of ISA investment portfolios are genuinely sustainable.

Examples of genuinely green and sustainable ISAs in the UK include:

Ecology Building Society Cash ISA

The Ecology Cash ISA enables individuals to save in a straightforward, no notice savings account. The main difference between the Ecology Cash ISA and similar cash ISAs and other savings products offered by mainstream banks is that the deposits received are used to fund mortgages for projects that make a positive environmental and/or social impact. In 2018, the Ecology Building Society lent £38.4 million to support 255 sustainable properties and projects.

Abundance Green ISA

The Abundance Green ISA takes advantage of a new type of Innovative Finance ISA introduced by the UK Government in 2016. Abundance is not a bank, but Innovative Finance ISAs allow individuals to include peer-to-peer lending in their ISA, performing one of the key functions of a bank – the provision of credit. The Abundance Green ISA provides investors with a choice of green energy projects including wind, solar and marine projects, and other projects focused on social sustainability. Investors can choose to invest in the projects that most appeal to them, and so build their own portfolios.

In the first year of the Green ISA's operation (2016–17) Abundance attracted more than 1,400 investors with a total investment of £10.5 million. Many of the investments offer relatively high returns of 10 per cent to 12 per cent; however, this reflects the higher risks involved, and whilst investments are carefully vetted by Abundance the risk of impairment or default is higher than that for many more traditional ISAs.

Triodos Ethical Stocks and Shares ISA

Customers saving with Triodos's Ethical Stocks and Shares ISA can choose to invest in one or both of the Triodos Global Equities Impact Fund and/or the Triodos Pioneer Impact Fund. Both funds seek to provide both financial returns and a positive impact on society and the environment, with seven transition themes used by Triodos to select investments from a sustainability perspective:

- sustainable food and agriculture;
- sustainable mobility and infrastructure;
- renewable resources;
- circular economy;
- prosperous and healthy people;
- innovation for sustainability;
- social inclusion and empowerment.

The Global Equities Impact Fund invests primarily in large listed global equities. The Pioneer Impact Fund mainly invests in small and medium sized companies that are assessed by Triodos as innovators and pioneers in sustainability. In both cases companies are selected for the funds following a comprehensive sustainability assessment by Triodos' investment management arm.

Green mortgages

Residential homes account for between 20 per cent and 25 per cent of all global man-made CO_2 emissions.[7] For many national and region governments, cutting emissions from housing is seen as a key priority to help them meet national and international commitments to reduce emissions, with building codes and other legislation/regulation being updated to reflect this.

Green mortgages, a term used mainly to refer to mortgages on energy-efficient homes, are one way of incentivizing individuals to purchase lower emission homes. Green mortgages are an example of green tagging of loans, whereby the terms of the loan are linked to the underlying asset's energy performance, fuel efficiency or environmental standards. In general, green mortgages provide retail customers with below-market interest rates for purchasing new, energy-efficient homes or invest in green retrofits, energy-efficient appliances or green power. Some banks also offer mortgages that include the cost of switching a conventional home to an energy-efficient one. Recent years have seen the development of green mortgages, in most cases linked to (and limited to) the purchase of new, energy-efficient homes in countries including the US, the UK, Sweden, the Netherlands and Australia.

Whilst the term green mortgage is becoming more popular, and seems to resonate with potential customers, banks may also integrate aspects of a green mortgage into more traditional mortgage lending. A property's current energy efficiency and/or plans to improve energy efficiency might be factored into affordability calculations, for instance, enabling a lender to offer a higher overall sum or loan-to-value ratio.

In some cases, green mortgages are offered at a slightly lower interest rate than conventional mortgages in order to reflect either the lower risk profile of green mortgage customers or the presence of government incentives to support subsidized interest rates. There is some evidence from the US that owners of new, energy-efficient homes are less likely to default on their mortgage payments, justifying a lower rate of interest. This might be because energy efficiency lowers energy use, energy-efficient homes should have lower utility bills and homeowners should have higher levels of disposable income with which to service their mortgages. It might also be that purchasers of energy-efficient homes are more likely to have higher disposable income to begin with, however, and are less likely to default on their mortgage payments overall.

CASE STUDY

Barclays Green Mortgages[8]

In 2018, Barclays launched the UK's first Green Home Mortgage for purchasers of new, energy-efficient homes.

Barclays Green Home Mortgages are available to customers purchasing a new-build home with an Energy Performance Certification (EPC) rating of A or B from an initial group of partner house builders who provide more than half of the new-build homes in the UK between them; there are plans to widen the availability in future years. Green Mortgages are available for up to 90 per cent loan to value.

Homeowners will benefit from preferential interest rates – up to a 0.1 per cent discount compared to standard Barclays' mortgage products – on two- and five-year fixed rate mortgages. At launch, the bank claimed that the discounted interest rate plus the energy savings from a more efficient home could save a typical three-bedroom UK household £1,335 over five years.

Using data on mortgage defaults from the US and the UK showing that owners of energy-efficient homes are less likely to default, the lower credit risk for green mortgages means that Barclays can still make an acceptable return despite the discounted interest rate. In addition, some of the proceeds of Barclays' 2017 €500 million green bond issue are being used to support green mortgages, in addition to refinancing low-carbon residential properties more generally in England and Wales.

CASE STUDY

European Energy Efficiency Mortgage[9]

The European Energy Efficient Mortgage Initiative brings together a consortium led by the European Mortgage Federation (EMF) and funded by the EU's Horizon 2020 Programme to develop a standardized energy-efficient mortgage based on preferential interest rates for energy-efficient homes and renovations resulting in improved energy efficiency. The initiative is premised on the belief that mortgage lenders 'can play a game changing role in providing long-term financing for energy improvements to the existing European housing stock'.

The underlying concept is that mortgage lenders in the EU will offer households the possibility of a preferential interest rate and/or additional funds at the time of origination of the mortgage/re-mortgage in return for making energy-efficient improvements to the property.

A standardized approach to the provision of mortgage financing for energy-efficient investment will also ensure the ultimate pricing-in of the added value triggered by improvement measures. The proposed mechanism rests on two key assumptions regarding market characteristics that will be tested by the initiative:

1 Retrofitting impacts positively on property value, ensuring wealth conservation and loss mitigation by preventing 'brown discount'.
2 Energy efficiency leads to a reduction in the impact of energy costs on income, reducing the borrowers' probability of default.

The consortium includes the World Green Building Council, RICS, E.ON, the University of Ca Foscari (Venice), Goethe University (Frankfurt), and a number of leading banks across Europe that will be piloting the scheme and working to substantiate the correlation between a property's energy rating and the financial performance of the mortgage. The two-year project began in June 2017.

An interesting development in 2018 was the issue by National Australia Bank (NAB) of the world's first Residential Mortgage-Backed Securitization including a certified green tranche of AU$300 million for low-carbon residential buildings. The green tranche comprises mortgages originated by NAB that meet the Climate Bonds Standard Criteria for Australian low-carbon residential buildings. Securitizing green and/or energy-efficient mortgages in this way should help the green mortgage market to grow substantially in the coming years.

Car loans

Operation of the world's 700 million vehicles, together with vehicle manufacturing, contributes around 5–6 per cent of global greenhouse gas emissions.[10] It is expected that global car ownership will triple by 2050, and therefore incentivizing the purchase of environmentally friendly vehicles is crucial for reducing greenhouse gas emissions. One way that the banking sector can help to do this is by offering green car loans.

Green car loans are another example of green tagging, whereby customers are incentivized to purchase cars that demonstrate low greenhouse gas intensity and/or high fuel efficiency ratings with below-market interest rates. As with green mortgages, the lower interest rates reflect either the lower risk profile of green car loans (as borrowers will have lower operating costs and electric or hybrid vehicles have higher resale values) or the presence of government incentives to support subsidized interest rates.

CASE STUDY

Bank Australia[11]

Bank Australia links all car loans to the environmental impact of the vehicle being purchased. The bank calculates the greenhouse gas emissions associated with the vehicle type and uses this to determine the interest rate on the loan.

The bank also commits to offsetting 100 per cent of the car's CO_2 emissions for the term of the customer's loan by purchasing carbon offsets that are eligible under the National Carbon Offset Standard (NCOS) to offset the estimated emissions from each car for each year the loan is active. The bank also waives the establishment fee for cars that have a superior greenhouse rating.

Credit and debit cards

Payments made with credit and debit cards amounted to $23.1 trillion globally in 2016, surpassing the value of payments made with cash for the first time.[12] As such, credit and debit cards have become an increasingly important part of the global banking and payments system.

In recent years, many banks have introduced green debit and credit cards that typically offer a small donation to an environmental charity on every purchase, balance transfer or cash advance made by the card owner. However, the extent to which these cards can be classified as green has been subject to debate – particularly given that their effect may be to incentivize consumption of high-carbon goods and services (eg air travel, petrol and diesel).

QUICK QUESTION

Referring to the definition of green finance outlined in Chapter 1, do you believe that green debit and credit cards should be described as a form of green finance?

Small and micro business lending

Bank (and other, eg peer-to-peer) lending to small and micro businesses is a key driver of economic growth in both developed and developing markets. Definitions of small and micro businesses vary, and differ between countries and regions, but in general we may consider micro businesses as employing fewer than five people, and small businesses to be larger than this. Loans may be used by entrepreneurs and their businesses for a wide variety of purposes, including, but not limited to, providing working capital, buying stock or new equipment, leasing business premises, expanding into new segments and markets, and recruiting additional employees or contractors. Loans may be secured, ie where the borrower pledges assets as collateral, which the lender may sell to recoup some or all of the sum borrowed in the event of default, or unsecured, where there is no such collateral pledged, and loans are therefore riskier and often may incur higher interest rates.

Green lending to small and micro businesses may take a variety of forms, but generally offers more favourable terms (eg lower interest rates, more relaxed collateral requirements) for loans with a clearly defined green purpose, such as investing in more energy-efficient or otherwise more sustainable production equipment or premises. The demand for green loans may be driven, in some cases, by developments in regulation, particularly around energy efficiency, eg where building codes require energy efficiency improvements. There is also substantial demand, particularly in developing markets, for green lending in the agricultural sector where farmers and smallholders may comprise a substantial part of the economy, as well as being key stakeholders in climate change mitigation and adaptation efforts.

In developed markets, banks and other financial institutions may offer a range of green and/or sustainable finance loans, such as Lloyds Banking Group's Clean Growth Finance initiative or Nordea Bank's green lending scheme set out in the case study.

CASE STUDY

Nordea Bank's green lending scheme[13]

Nordea is offering green financing to small and medium-sized corporates in the Nordics – financing that promotes sustainable investments, which means that small and medium-sized corporate customers will be able to level up their sustainability work.

Green bonds have been available for some time, especially for large real estate companies, but Nordea – as the first player in the market – has, since July 2018, also offered green financing to small and medium-sized companies in several different industries.

'We have over half a million small and medium-sized corporations as customers. We are in constant dialogue with our customers and sustainability is a topic that is often raised. This indicates that the demand for products such as green loans is high and will continue to increase,' says Anders Langworth, the bank's Head of Group Sustainable Finance.

The whole value chain is sustainable; the product is based on green market funding and the customer commits to using the financing for a sustainable investment, which requires them to report the positive impact from the investment on power or water consumption, for example. This means that both the investment and financing will be sustainable. Examples of sustainable investments are energy-efficient buildings, wind power, pure water treatment and sun power.

The customers qualifying for the green financing will also get slightly more favourable commercial terms compared to non-sustainable financing.

Positive environmental impact

This type of green loan can have a positive impact on the environment. When it comes to real estate, buildings must be at least 25 per cent more energy efficient than the Swedish building regulations for new buildings. Nordea will also provide financing for investments in renewable energy, which have an even stronger positive effect on reducing emissions.

'We believe that green financing is here to stay and will be established as a market standard in future. We do also believe that our own credit portfolio will grow stronger since the most sustainable companies are the winners of tomorrow – something studies already show,' says Anders Langworth.

First, an internal investigation examines whether the loan can be classified as green. There then follows an external investigation using established environmental certificates approved by Oekom Research, the independent Second Party Opinion provider of Nordea's framework for green bonds.

In developing countries (and in some developed countries too) microfinance lending plays a key role in promoting green and sustainable development. Householders, farmers and microbusinesses in developing countries may often be involved in activities that can damage the environment, such as agriculture and forestry, and/or where significant environmental benefits can be gained from adopting more sustainable practices (eg reducing water consumption, or switching to renewable energy). Microfinance lenders can support green and sustainable practices by providing green loans and other financial services to individuals and microbusinesses, linked to achieving environmentally positive outcomes, as well as additional services, such as education and training, for entrepreneurs and microbusiness owners.

In Kazakhstan, for example, the Asian Credit Fund (ACF) provides small loans for households and small businesses, primarily in rural areas. In 2017, the ACF launched its Green Economy programme, providing microfinance to help 1,100 householders improve the energy efficiency of their homes. In conjunction with the microfinance lending programme, ACF also sought to raise awareness about energy efficiency and responsible use of energy by providing lessons in rural schools.

In many developing countries, green lending, and other lending designed to support a wider range of sustainable goals including financial inclusion and gender equality – by established banks, microfinance institutions and/or other traditional and non-traditional lenders – is often supported by national or multilateral development banks (see Chapter 8), development charities and/or other impact investors, as the capital required and risk/return profile may not be attractive for commercial lenders. This is beginning to change, however, as the introduction of FinTech tools and techniques, especially banking via smartphones (see Chapter 11) makes it easier and more cost effective to provide lending and other financial services to previously unbanked populations.

New approaches are being developed to stimulate the growth of green and sustainable lending. In Kenya, for example, the Climate Smart Lending Platform, developed by F3 Life, is designed to reduce credit default risk and improve lender profitability (and hence lenders' desire and ability to lend) in agricultural lending to smallholders. As well as benefitting microfinance lenders, the scheme is also designed to promote the adoption of more sustainable farming practices that sequester carbon into farm soils, and enhance resilience to climate change and extreme weather events. It is an excellent example of how the combination of traditional banking skills (credit assessment) with FinTech style tools and techniques can support farmers who might otherwise struggle to access affordable credit, providing a commercial return, supporting climate change mitigation and adaptation activities, as well as broader sustainability goals.

CASE STUDY

Climate Smart Lending Platform[14]

The Climate Smart Lending Platform, trialled in Kenya in 2019, integrates with agrilenders' core banking systems and credit scoring processes. Through partners, the Platform reduces the costs and complexity of client onboarding, whilst the F3 Life Systems reduce credit default risk, particularly from extreme weather events, and promote positive environmental outcomes by supporting climate-smart farming practices and land use decisions.

Step 1: Farmer signs a loan and land management agreement
The agrilender issues farmers with credit, on the condition that they adopt climate-smart and sustainable farming practices.

Step 2: Loan repayment and environmental restoration
The farmer repays the loan and implements the required climate-smart and sustainable agricultural and land management practices on their land.

Step 3: Monitoring
F3 systems are used to monitor implementation of climate-smart practices and this data is passed back to Financial Access.

Step 4: Climate-smart credit scoring
When a farmer complies with the climate-smart requirements of their loan agreement, they are provided with a new score that boosts their initial credit score.

Later in this chapter we look at green and sustainable commercial and corporate lending on a larger scale, and introduce the Green Loan Principles.

Government tax incentives

In some countries, the government has introduced tax incentives to encourage the channelling of savings into green and sustainable initiatives via the banking sector. In this approach, individual investors lend their money to banks at a low interest rate, compensated by a tax incentive, and banks then offer cheaper loans to environmental projects. In the Netherlands, for example, this government-led approach has proven to be a successful way of mobilizing household savings towards investment in green and sustainable projects.

Wholesale and investment banking products and services

Wholesale and investment banking (also known as corporate banking) refers to the provision of products and services by a bank to corporate and institutional clients, rather than to individual customers and SMEs. Corporations and large enterprises usually have more complex financing needs than small firms.

Wholesale banks provide banking products to large corporations, including corporate loans to finance investment, project finance for large infrastructure or industrial projects, and trade finance to help companies buy and sell from abroad. Investment banks help companies to raise debt and equity finance through capital markets. When a company wishes to borrow money by issuing a bond, for instance, investment banks can help match the company with investors. Investment banks also underwrite the issuance of shares or bonds, meaning that they guarantee to provide finance at a predetermined price when the shares or bonds are issued. We examine green bonds in the following chapter, and equity markets in Chapter 9. Investment banks also provide advice in relation to mergers and acquisitions and offer research and advisory services. For the most part, investment banks carry out trades on behalf of their clients; however, occasionally they undertake trading on their own account (known as proprietary trading).

QUICK QUESTION

How might corporate and investment banks support the transition towards a more sustainable economy?

Bank loans remain the single biggest source of funding for corporations globally, and firms engaged in environmentally harmful activities rely on wholesale and investment banks to provide their financing needs. As noted in Chapter 1, according to the 2019 *Banking on Climate Change*, 33 of the largest global banks had provided financing of more than $1.9 trillion to fossil fuel companies between 2015 and 2018, greatly outweighing their financing to sustainable, low-carbon alternatives.[15] Wholesale and investment banks therefore have an important role to play – and need to do much more – in mobilizing private capital for green investments through lending and capital markets activities and integrating environmental risks and opportunities into their research and advisory services. Whilst the report showed that many banks maintained or increased financing to fossil fuel companies during the period, some, including Deutsche Bank, RBS and Unicredit, substantially reduced funding to the fossil fuel sector. Overall, however, fossil fuel financing increased from approximately $611 billion in 2016 to $654 billion in 2018.

Corporate loans

The greening of corporate lending (generally speaking, lending to businesses larger than the small and micro businesses described above) is taking a number of different forms. In recent years most major international banks across the G20 have developed methodologies and implemented procedures to integrate environmental and climate-related risk factors into risk management systems. These include ensuring environmental due diligence in credit decisions and assessing loan portfolios for emerging environmental and climate-related risks.

Whilst there is currently no accepted definition of what comprises a green loan, the launch of the Green Loan Principles in 2018 (see below) included the publication of a definition which seems likely to become the market standard, given the degree of institutional support for the Principles:

> Green loans are any type of loan instrument made available exclusively to finance or re-finance, in whole or in part, new and/or existing eligible Green Projects. Green loans must align with the four core components of the Green Loan Principles.[16]

CASE STUDY

Integrating environmental factors in risk assessment[17]

- **Barclays** has embedded environmental risk management within its wholesale credit risk process, obliging all credit risk teams across the group to follow policies on environmental factors. In addition, relationship managers are required to engage with clients on environmental challenges and opportunities.
- **ICBC** imposes an industrial limit on all industries with serious overcapacity to prevent risks, and scales back loans to the fields relating to heavy metal emission and highly hazardous chemicals – with

loans to the steel sector being reduced by approximately $7.45 billion since 2013.

- **Garanti Bankasi** established Environmental and Social Loan Policies and an accompanying assessment process in 2011/12, which act as a screen for loan requests. Projects above $10 million are subject to an Environmental and Social Impact Assessment Model, which is used to calculate a risk rating to guide financing decisions.
- **UniCredit** recently established a Group Economic Environmental and Social Council to oversee all activities relating to environment at Group level, including operations management, risk governance, internal capacity building and monitoring. This includes the implementation of special credit policies for financing and corporate lending for large dams, nuclear energy, mining and coal-fired power generation. Qualitative survey information taken when applying for credit is translated into a rating weight, which may affect decisions.

In addition, some banks have set targets around the provision of corporate financing for companies in sectors that support the low-carbon transition. These green loans are only available for investments that meet certain green and sustainable criteria, and are often offered at preferable interest rates.

CASE STUDY

RBS doubles lending to sustainable energy projects[18]

RBS lent more than £1 billion to support UK customers' sustainable energy projects in 2015, more than doubling lending from 2014 in a third consecutive year of growth for the sector.

The record £1 billion confirms RBS's position as the largest lender to the UK renewable energy sector and comes as the bank ramps up support for all businesses, from SMEs to large corporates, looking to become more energy efficient.

The rise in lending to renewable energy projects was driven by significant increases to both solar and biomass projects, with lending to solar more than trebling to over £450 million compared to 2014. RBS has been at the forefront of the UK solar market since its inception in 2010, and in addition to direct lending over that period it has arranged financing for £550 million worth of solar projects.

The increase in lending to biomass – from less than £50 million in 2014 to more than £150 million in 2015 – was largely driven by Lombard, RBS's specialist asset finance lender. Lombard's focus on renewable energy projects led to a change in policy last year, enabling the lender to use the asset and resulting revenue as security against lending for these projects as an alternative to cash or land, granting greater cash efficiency to customers.

Some smaller banks, such as the Guyana Bank for Trade and Industry (GBTI), offer a wide range of green loans that, while not at present consistent with the Green Loan Principles, nonetheless support business investment in low-carbon assets and climate change mitigation projects. As well as the green loans outlined in the case study below, the bank also supports sustainable development more broadly, via:

- **Rupununi Ventures:** A collaborative partnership between GBTI, Conservation International and the Inter-American Development Bank (IDB), supporting community-based activities in a rural area of Guyana, while preserving natural capital.
- **Small Business Bureau Loans:** Offers credit of up to $30 million for micro and small businesses in low-carbon sectors at a low rate of 6 per cent per annum, supported by the Guyana Ministry of Business and the IDB funding.

CASE STUDY

GBTI Bank green loans[19]

GBTI Bank has launched a range of green loans providing financing for products, businesses, projects and home and office improvements that promote low-carbon emissions. Eligible categories include:

- solar energy products;
- water treatment, water recycling, water filters;

- hybrid motor vehicles;
- energy saving appliances;
- air filters;
- wind-powered projects;
- hand-powered projects;
- low-carbon economic investments, eg high-end fruits and vegetables, aquaculture.

Benefits to clients include:

- competitive interest rates;
- fast approvals;
- 25 per cent discount on lending services;
- 1–6 month moratorium on payment of instalments where applicable;
- no late payment fees or prepayment penalties;
- a low equity contribution of 10 per cent.

This initiative was driven by Guyana's Low Carbon Development Strategy, and GBTI's desire to:

- promote non-pollution to improve the ecological systems;
- promote conservation of energy through the use of energy savings appliances and methodologies;
- facilitate investment and employment in low-carbon sectors and new enterprises;
- contribute to the economic value of the country;
- maintain ecological systems and good business practices;
- help secure a healthy planet for future generations.

Other banks, such as ASN Bank, have gone further in their commitment to environmental sustainability by not lending to certain firms or sectors that are environmentally harmful, and instead focusing lending on activities that improve the functioning of the natural environment.

CASE STUDY

ASN Bank[20]

For Dutch ASN Bank, environmental sustainability is key in every aspect of its operations. The bank orientates its sustainability policy around three pillars: climate change, biodiversity and human rights. ASN Bank has set itself the long-term goal of achieving full net carbon neutrality in all its banking activities by 2030. It reduces the carbon emissions of its banking activities in a number of ways:

- It does not invest in the extraction, production and refining of fossil materials and their use to generate electricity.
- It only finances energy obtained from renewable energy sources, such as wind and solar energy.
- It also finances energy-saving measures, low-energy buildings and energy efficiency.
- It avoids investments in energy-intensive companies, preferring companies that limit their energy consumption.

Syndicated loans

A syndicated loan is one offered by a group of lenders – referred to as a syndicate – that work together to provide funds for a single borrower. The borrower could be a corporation, a large project or a sovereignty, such as a government. Loan syndication most often occurs in situations where a borrower requires a large sum of capital that may be too much for a single lender to provide or outside the scope of a lender's risk exposure levels. Thus, multiple lenders work together to provide the borrower with the capital needed. Recently, syndicated loans have been used to raise large amounts of money to finance major green and sustainable projects.

CASE STUDY

BBVA[21]

In June 2017 the Spanish Bank BBVA arranged a £265 million green syndicated term loan with Tradebe, the Spanish waste reclamation and recycling firm. The transaction was signed by 11 national and foreign financial institutions, and was the world's first green syndicated financing agreement. The loan is Tradebe's main source of corporate funding and provides the company with the ability to comfortably fund general corporate needs, together with its future mid-term growth plan, combining organic growth with selective acquisitions.

The facility was structured as a green instrument in accordance with an assessment by Sustainalytics, an independent global provider of ESG research and ratings. Sustainalytics' review was based on Tradebe's sources of income, which are derived from recycling and energy recovery activities, and considered to have a positive environmental impact.

Green Loan Principles

In March 2018 the Loan Market Association (LMA), a large grouping of banks, investors and professional services firms active in the syndicated loan markets in Europe, the Middle East and Africa, together with the Asia Pacific Loan Market Association (APLMA) and the International Capital Markets Association (ICMA), launched the Green Loan Principles. These are based on a similar approach to the Green Bond Principles (GBP) covered in more detail in Chapter 7, and refer to the GBPs to define what is meant by a Green Project.

The Green Loan Principles provide a framework and standards for green lending by institutions and are designed to promote global consistency in the application and reporting of green loans. In particular, they aim to ensure consistency in the use of the term green loan, to maintain the integrity of the green loan market and avoid instances and accusations of greenwashing. Although voluntary, the Principles are endorsed by a wide range of institutions and seem likely, as has been the case with the Green Bond Principles, to become generally accepted as market standards and encouraged, if not endorsed, by key regulatory and policymaking bodies. The Principles were developed primarily for the syndicated loan market, but have broad applicability across most, if not all, types of corporate lending.

Under the Green Loan Principles, lenders and their advisers are expected to apply the four key components of the Principles on a deal-by-deal basis, with some flexibility allowed to account for the many different types of and uses for loans:

1 **Use of proceeds:** Green loan proceeds should be utilized for green projects – the Green Loan Principles provide a list of eligible categories

(eg renewable energy, clean transport, climate change adaptation), drawn from the Green Bond Principles to ensure consistency across markets. Environmental benefits should be assessed, and where feasible, quantified, measured and reported by the borrower. Recognizing that a green loan may take the form of one or more tranches of a loan facility, green tranches must be clearly designated, with proceeds credited to a separate account or tracked by the borrower in an appropriate manner.

2. **Process for project evaluation and selection:** Borrowers should clearly communicate their eligibility, environmental sustainability objectives and material environmental risks to lenders. Borrowers are encouraged to position this within their general business aims, objectives, strategies, policies and processes.
3. **Management of proceeds:** Proceeds from a green loan should be credited to a dedicated account or otherwise tracked by borrowers in an appropriate way so as to maintain transparency and promote the integrity of the green loan market. Borrowers are encouraged to establish an appropriate internal governance process through which they can track the allocation of funds.
4. **Reporting:** Borrowers should make and keep readily available up-to-date information on the use of proceeds, to be renewed annually until a loan is fully drawn, and as necessary thereafter in the event of material developments. This should include a list of the Green Projects to which the green loan proceeds have been allocated and a description of the projects, the amounts allocated and their expected impact. The use of qualitative and quantitative performance indicators to demonstrate impact is recommended.

Currently, an independent review of green loans is recommended, but not required. Reviews might be carried out by independent consultants or agencies, who may formally certify against external, green assessment standards or verify claims made and/or internal standards. The Green Loan Principles also recognize self-certification by borrowers where, in the opinion of the lender, they have the relevant expertise to do so. Over time, as the Principles become more widely used and embedded, it is likely that third-party assurance, verification and assurance is more likely to become the norm, to better ensure consistency and integrity.

Corporate deposit schemes

Some banks have established ESG deposit schemes in response to growing client demand for products that create positive environmental and social impacts. Much like green current accounts for retail customers, these schemes provide a facility for companies to deposit money with a bank in the knowledge that it will be invested in initiatives that have a positive social or environmental impact. In 2015, for instance, Lloyds Banking Group in the UK launched a new ESG deposit scheme under which deposited funds are used to make loans to finance SMEs and healthcare providers as well as renewable energy and energy efficiency projects in the most economically disadvantaged parts of the UK. Another example is the Westpac Green Tailored Deposit Scheme described in the following case study.

CASE STUDY

Westpac Green Tailored Deposit Scheme[22]

In November 2018 Westpac (Australia) launched a Green Tailored Deposit (GTD) scheme for corporate customers seeking to support climate change mitigation and adaptation projects.

A minimum of AU$ 1 million can be deposited for between one and five years. Deposits will be allocated to a pool of eligible assets or projects supporting renewable energy, low-carbon buildings, cleaner transport and improving water infrastructure. The scheme is the first such deposit scheme to be certified by the Climate Bonds Initiative.

Commenting on the launch, Westpac Institutional Bank CEO Lyn Cobley said: 'This is a great example of Westpac's customer driven innovation. The new green tailored deposit delivers an innovative solution for customers seeking an independently certified green investment product.'

The launch of the GTD scheme was supported by two Australian public institutions that agreed to be among the first investors – the City of Sydney Council (with AU$ 30 million in GTDs, at rates between 2.65 per cent and 3 per cent, and maturities of up to 5 years) and the South Wales Central Coast Council. Other Australian local government institutions were expected to follow suit.

Commercial real estate loans

An estimated 47 per cent of commercial real estate investment across Europe is in the form of debt finance.[23] Commercial real estate lenders can therefore play a key role in making the transformation towards a greener built environment. Whilst, historically, environmental considerations for commercial real estate lenders have tended to focus on managing regulatory risk as part of due diligence, in recent years some banks have taken a more proactive approach to environmental sustainability by offering specific green commercial real estate loans. In a similar way to green mortgages, green commercial real estate loans link the terms of the loan to the underlying property's environmental impact. As commercial property building codes and other legislation and regulation have been tightened in many jurisdictions in terms of energy efficiency, emissions and other criteria, bank financing is often linked to the achievement of performance certificates or other standards evidencing these.

CASE STUDY

Lloyds Banking Group[24]

Lloyds Bank is one of the UK's largest commercial real estate lenders, completing £8.6 billion in lending in 2016. Recognizing the scale of its commercial lending activities and the potential impact it could have, Lloyds Bank has taken a market leadership stance and has developed a new product that provides commercial real estate debt at advantageous rates to reward and incentivize better sustainability performance.

Lloyds Bank's Green Lending Initiative was launched in March 2016 with a pledge of £1 billion of commercial mortgage lending, aimed at reducing CO_2 emissions from their real estate assets. This first-of-its-kind fund will be used to incentivize clients' adoption of energy efficiency measures and provide margin improvements of up to 20bps on new borrowing requirements of £10 million and above.

Lloyds Bank expects this initiative could facilitate carbon savings equivalent to approximately 110,000 tonnes, on the basis of the average four-year loan tenor. The comparative energy saving is equivalent to the annual energy usage of more than 22,000 households.

By offering a margin discount on green loans, Lloyds Bank aims to support its clients' sustainability programmes, incentivize improved energy efficiency, data flow, and catalyse a market for green loans to support growing investor demand for green and sustainable fixed income products such as green bonds.

Lloyds Bank has worked with Trucost, an environmental consultancy firm, to create a tool to benchmark sustainability performance. This will be used to assess the initial eligibility for the green loan and to agree appropriate energy/CO_2 saving KPIs that borrowers will have to meet or maintain to benefit from the margin improvement. These KPIs will be structured to align with the Green Bond Principles of which Lloyds Bank is a member, and will demonstrate how each building is outperforming.

Project finance

Project finance – also known as non-recourse finance – refers to loans offered in wholesale banking to fund large infrastructure projects. A project financing structure often involves a number of equity investors, known as sponsors, and a syndicate of banks or other lending institutions that provide loans to the operation. These targeted projects, typically found in sectors such as telecommunications, petrochemicals and natural resources, obtain loans that are repaid to the bank through the project revenue generated rather than the balance sheets of its sponsors. Some banks, such as BBVA in the next case study, have developed specific project finance products for green and sustainable initiatives such as large-scale renewable energy projects.

CASE STUDY

BBVA[25]

In July 2017 BBVA signed a project finance green loan with Italian energy company Terna. The first of its kind in the world, the funding enabled Terna to build a transmission line between cities of Melo and Tacuarembó in Uruguay. The Funding was structured into a $56 million A loan awarded by the Inter-American Development Bank and a $25 million B loan subscribed by BBVA in its entirety. In addition to heading the green structuring of the funding, BBVA acted as the Green Loan Coordinator. In accordance with the Green Bond Principles, the loan was structured as a green instrument based on the certification by Vigeo. Benefits of building the transmission line include:

- connecting projects for the generation of renewable energy to the country's electrical grid;
- contributing to the fight against climate change;
- contributing towards the achievement of the Sustainable Development Goals.

Trade finance

International trade involves buying and selling over extended periods across countries with different legal systems, cultures and business environments. Financing exports, therefore, is often riskier and more complex than financing domestic business. Typically, there is less understanding between suppliers and customers across different countries, a requirement to transact in foreign currencies, and longer lead times for physical trade to take place. Given that few exporters are able to sell to customers that will routinely pay in advance, there is often a cash-flow issue, and thereby an interim financing need.

Because of the risks associated with international trade, the World Trade Organization estimates that between 80 and 90 per cent of world trade relies on some kind of trade finance. Trade finance is a primary driver in enabling the production, trade, shipping and processing of most commodities – including those linked to environmental harm, such as soy, palm oil, timber and beef. Banks therefore have a unique role in working across commodity supply chains to support sustainable production. According to the University of Cambridge Institute for Sustainability Leadership (CISL), banks can help to promote environmentally sustainable production in a number of ways:

- innovation in the products and trade finance solutions available to enable sustainability information to be traced and identified in trade finance processes in the first place;
- incentivizing sustainably produced commodities, by finding ways to reduce the price differential between the trade of sustainable commodities relative to their unsustainable alternatives;
- amplifying the demand signal already set by certain importers, by committing to only financing sustainably produced commodities progressively over time.[26]

CASE STUDY

Sustainable trade finance[27]

The CISL Banking Environment Initiative (BEI) seeks to explore ways to scale up the role that banks can play in supporting the shift towards sustainable commodity supply chains. The BEI has established two key initiatives so far:

Sustainable Shipment Letter of Credit

The Sustainable Shipment Letter of Credit (SSLC) is an approach that enables banks to reduce the cost of exporting certified sustainable palm oil to other emerging markets. This concept addresses a pivotal issue in the palm oil supply chain which is that major emerging market importers do not favour sustainable methods of production, often because of the premium prices expected, leaving producers with mixed demand signals.

The Sustainable Trade Finance Council has been exploring how the SSLC approach can be expanded beyond palm oil to other forest sensitive commodities and beyond the Letter of Credit to other trade finance instruments.

Soft Commodities Compact

The Soft Commodities Compact is an initiative that aims to mobilize the banking industry to help soft commodity supply chains, thereby helping corporate clients to achieve their goal of zero net deforestation by 2020. This commitment to achieve zero net deforestation was made in 2010 by the Board of the Consumer Goods Forum, representing their 400 members with combined procurement power of over $3 trillion.

In recognition of the role that banks can play in transforming to sustainable supply chains, the Soft Commodities Compact was developed in 2013 through collaboration between the BEI and the Consumer Goods Forum, with input from the World Wide Fund for Nature. It calls for banks to help achieve this goal of zero net deforestation by 2020 through their financing of soft commodity supply chains. Twelve banks have so far adopted the Compact, which account for over 50 per cent of global trade finance.

Initial public offerings and underwriting

One of the primary roles of an investment bank is to serve as an intermediary between corporations and investors through initial public offerings (IPOs). Investment banks provide underwriting services for new share issues when a company decides to go public and raise equity funding. Underwriting involves the investment bank purchasing an agreed number of new shares, which it then re-sells through a stock exchange. Typically, there is a bookrunner that syndicates with other investment banks in order to lower its risk. When more than one bookrunner manages an issuance, the parties are referred to as joint bookrunners.

In deciding which firms to support, investment banking activity can have significant positive or negative environmental, social or other consequences. When positive, banks can play a key role in facilitating the transition to a low-carbon economy. For example, some investment banks have played a pivotal role regarding IPOs for companies supporting the green transition, such as those in renewable energy, energy storage, energy efficiency, low-carbon transport and recycling sectors.

Investment banks also help firms raise capital by underwriting securities issuances. As will be discussed in the next chapter, the market for green bonds and green equities has grown rapidly in recent decades. Investment banks play a key role in supporting and mainstreaming these markets by underwriting issuances and stimulating investor demand. The level of engagement with the green bond market by banks is key to adding credibility to an emerging green bond market.

CASE STUDY

Dong Energy initial public offering[28]

Danish utility provider Dong Energy's IPO of its shares on Nasdaq Copenhagen in June 2016 was the largest European stock market listing for five years, raising kr 19.7 billion ($2.6 billion). JP Morgan Securities, Morgan Stanley and Nordea Markets (a division of Nordea Bank) were joint bookrunners. Citigroup Global Markets, Danske Bank and UBS were joint bookrunners, while ABG Sundal Collier, Norge, Rabobank and RBC Capital Markets were co-lead managers.

Dong is one of the leading offshore wind farm developers and operators, having built more than a quarter of the world's offshore deployments. The results of Dong Energy's IPO included a final offer price of kr 235 ($35.72) per share, leading to a market capitalization of kr 98.2 billion. Retail investors in Denmark were allocated approximately 10 per cent of the offer shares, and the remaining 90 per cent were allocated to Danish and international institutional investors.

The listing raised a gross kr 17 billion for the Danish state and a consortium of investors led by Goldman Sachs. The transaction was controversial in Denmark because of the terms of the deal, which included special veto rights for Goldman Sachs over big investment decisions and strategy changes. There was also anger about Goldman Sachs' use of a Luxembourg-based investment vehicle owned by Cayman Islands and Delaware shareholders.

At the time, nearly 200,000 people signed an online petition against the deal. One of the three members of the minority coalition that ruled the country left the government, while the Danish prime minister at the time, Helle Thorning-Schmidt, resisted pressure to resign. The Kingdom of Denmark, the company's majority shareholder, sold part of its shareholding, and maintained a 50.1 per cent shareholding. Goldman Sachs retained a 13.4 per cent stake.

QUICK QUESTION

What might be the wider business benefits of supporting a green IPO?

Research and advisory services

Investment banks offer research and advisory services that can contribute significantly to the greening of the financial system. For example, by questioning and critiquing companies' performance and plans, sell-side research analysts can help to shape the debate on environmental, social and sustainable performance and hold companies to account. Some banks have also established dedicated in-house research teams on climate issues that can influence decisions, both internally and externally, among clients.

Through their advisory services, banks can also help their clients evolve and raise awareness of environmental issues among investors in order to stimulate demand for green and sustainable products and services.

CASE STUDY
HSBC and Natixis

HSBC[29]

In 2007 HSBC established a Climate Change Centre of Excellence, the aim of which was to provide the best analysis of climate change and its implications for economies, industries and sectors. The centre focused its research on three main areas:

- Financing a 2°C world: How to allocate capital to deliver the transition to a low-carbon world and build resilience to the impacts of climate change.

- Climate policy: How to reduce carbon emissions and achieve the decoupling of energy use from economic growth and the decarbonizing of the energy mix.
- Climate impacts: To ensure the wider climate survival, it is vital that we are able to embed resilience to shifting temperature norms and water availability, weather extremes and sea level rise.

Natixis[30]

In September 2017 Natixis established a green and sustainable hub in its corporate and investment banking division that provides clients across the world with a broad spectrum of green and sustainable finance expertise.

The hub has two main missions:

- Design and steer product innovation to generate and develop green revenues.
- Enhance syndication and distribution bases and promote a green 'originate to distribute' business model.

Equipment leasing

Equipment leasing is where banks lend equipment to firms in exchange for regular payments, while retaining ownership of the asset. This enables the borrower to get the benefit of using the equipment without having to pay the upfront capital cost. Leasing can play an important role in promoting the uptake of green equipment and technologies.

Through green leasing, banks provide environmentally friendly technologies, for example, energy-efficient equipment or renewable energy assets, at preferential rates to customers. Some European governments have played a large role in promoting green leasing through public awareness campaigns, business incentive programmes and tax incentives.

CASE STUDY

Rabobank[31]

Rabobank's leasing division, DLL, specializes in the leasing of vehicles, agricultural equipment, construction equipment and office technology. DLL promotes circular business models that focus on reusing and improving the use of products and materials, using raw and other materials for a different purpose each time.

DLL is also encouraging its customers to extend the economic life of the assets it leases by altering or repairing them in order to give them a second life. In 2016 DLL was named the winner of the Alliance Trust Award for Circular Economy Investor at the Global Economic Forum in Davos, Switzerland. Organized by the Forum's Young Global Leaders in conjunction with management consulting services company Accenture, this award is presented to investment companies that provide financial support to help build the circular economy.

On 21 January 2016 Rabobank and two other Dutch banks, ABN Amro and ING Bank, announced a new initiative designed to facilitate the transition to a circular economy. The three banks plan to accelerate the transition to a circular economy by combining insights into circular business models with knowledge of financial products and risk management.

Key concepts

In this chapter we considered:

- the role of banking within the wider financial system;
- how different banking activities can affect the quality and functioning of the natural environment and natural systems;
- how different types of banking products and services can improve the quality and functioning of the natural environment and natural systems;
- examples and case studies of innovative green and sustainable banking products and services;
- the UN Principles for Responsible Banking and the Green Loan Principles.

Now go back through this chapter and make sure you fully understand each point.

Review

There are four main types of banks: retail banks serving individuals and small businesses; wholesale and investment banks serving corporate clients;

national and multilateral development banks; and central banks. This chapter focused on retail and wholesale and investment banks, and described a growing range of innovative green and sustainable finance products and services, together with industry initiatives, to improve market consistency, integrity and avoid greenwashing.

The banking sector is the largest provider of finance in most economies, which means that banks are well positioned to reallocate credit and mobilize capital away from environmentally harmful activities towards the green economy, supporting the transition to a sustainable, low-carbon world. At the same time, how banks manage environmental, particularly climate-related, financial risks associated with the transition is crucial for financial stability as well as for environmental and sustainability reasons.

In recent years, the incorporation of green and sustainable factors into banking activities, products and services has accelerated, driven by a combination of policy and regulatory developments, changing customer attitudes and broader market factors. Many banks now consider a range of environmental, social and governance risks and opportunities when planning their strategies, activities and operations. The UN Principles for Responsible Banking, launched in September 2019, provide the leading global framework for banks to align their strategies and activities with green and sustainable finance principles.

As retail banks tend to have (or, at least, seek) close relationships with individual customers, they play a key role in understanding changing markets and evolving customer needs and expectations. Retail banks are well placed to respond to changing attitudes towards the environment, and to help customers shift towards more sustainable modes of consumption and production by offering products and services which enable them to save, invest and borrow in a green and sustainable way. Green and sustainable retail banking products and services include green current accounts, savings accounts, mortgages, car loans, credit and debit cards, small and micro business lending and government tax schemes.

Wholesale and investment banks provide banking products and services to large corporations, including corporate loans to finance investment, project finance for large infrastructure or industrial projects, and trade finance to help companies buy and sell from abroad. Green and sustainable wholesale and investment banking products and services include corporate loans, corporate deposit schemes, syndicated loans, commercial real estate loans, project finance, trade finance, initial public offerings and underwriting, research and advisory services and equipment leasing.

Green lending plays a key role in reallocating capital to support the transition to a low-carbon world, and to mitigate the effects of climate change.

The Green Loan Principles provide a global framework and standards for green lending. They aim to promote consistency in green, corporate lending to maintain the integrity of the green loan market and avoid instances and accusations of greenwashing. Whilst voluntary, the Principles are endorsed by a wide range of institutions and seem likely over time to become generally accepted as market standards. Developed primarily for the syndicated loan market, the Principles have broad applicability across most, if not all, types of corporate lending.

Glossary

Green Loan Principles: A framework and standards for green lending by institutions designed to promote global consistency in application and reporting of green loans.

Green loan: A loan instrument made available exclusively to finance or re-finance, in whole or in part, new and/or existing eligible green projects. Green loans must align with the four core components of the Green Loan Principles.

Green mortgage: A mortgage on an energy-efficient home, usually (at present) referring to new-build homes.

Green tagging: Linking the terms of a loan to the underlying asset's energy performance, fuel efficiency or environmental standard.

Investment banking: Helping companies raise debt and equity finance through capital markets.

Partial credit guarantee: Partial insurance against non-payment by a borrower for any reason – political, commercial or otherwise.

Project finance: Funding for large infrastructure projects, typically including a combination of equity investors and a syndicate of banks or other lending institutions that provide loans that are repaid through revenue generated by the project.

Retail banking: The provision of products and services by a bank to individual consumers and SMEs.

Syndicated loan: A large loan offered by a group of lenders – referred to as a syndicate – that work together to provide funds for a single borrower to finance a major project.

Trade finance: Products and services offered by banks to help exporters manage cash flow, credit risk, exchange risk and other risks of trading internationally.

UN Principles for Responsible Banking: Launched in September 2019 with 130 banks from 49 countries as the founding signatories, the Principles provide a framework for banks to align their strategies and activities with sustainable finance principles and societal goals, as expressed in the UN Sustainable Development Goals and the Paris Agreement.

Wholesale banking: The provision of products and services by a bank to larger corporations, and to other banks.

Notes

1 HSBC Bank plc (2010) *2010 Annual Report and Accounts* [Online] https://www.hsbc.com/investors/results-and-announcements/all-reporting/group?page=1&take=20 (archived at https://perma.cc/UU4Q-8JNR)

2 UNEP Finance Initiative (nd) Principles for responsible banking [Online] https://www.unepfi.org/banking/bankingprinciples/ (archived at https://perma.cc/GTQ8-DEYH)

3 United Nations Environment Programme (2016) *Greening the Banking System: Taking stock of G20 green banking market practice* [Online] http://unepinquiry.org/wp-content/uploads/2016/09/9_Greening_the_Banking_System.pdf (archived at https://perma.cc/8MZE-GZS3)

4 YES BANK (2018) YES BANK launches green future: Deposit, India's first ever green deposit product [Online] https://www.yesbank.in/media/press-releases/yes-bank-launches-green-future-deposit-indias-first-ever-green-deposit-product (archived at https://perma.cc/6RXN-E4ZJ)

5 Ekobanken (nd) About Ekobanken [Online] https://www.ekobanken.se/en/about-ekobanken/ (archived at https://perma.cc/7JAW-89CL)

6 United Nations Framework Convention on Climate Change (nd) Alipay Ant Forest: Using digital technologies to scale up climate action – China [Online] https://unfccc.int/climate-action/momentum-for-change/planetary-health/alipay-ant-forest (archived at https://perma.cc/4WMC-KJ5B)

7 NHBC Foundation (2009) *Zero Carbon Compendium: Who's doing what in housing worldwide* [Online] http://www.zerocarbonhub.org/sites/default/files/resources/reports/Zero_Carbon_Compendium_Whos_Doing_What_in_Housing_Worldwide.pdf (archived at https://perma.cc/6Y35-G8S8)

8 Barclays (nd) Barclays green home mortgages [Online] https://www.barclays.co.uk/mortgages/green-home-mortgage/ (archived at https://perma.cc/UA39-ZWLS)

9 Better Buildings Partnership (2017) *Beyond Risk Management: How sustainability is driving innovation in commercial real estate finance* [Online] https://www.betterbuildingspartnership.co.uk/sites/default/files/media/attachment/BBP_BeyondRiskManagement_Insight_Final.pdf (archived at https://perma.cc/JR6L-EBAV)

10 Carbon Trust (2011) International carbon flows: Automotive [Online] https://www.carbontrust.com/resources/international-carbon-flows (archived at https://perma.cc/27SL-CWBR)

11 Bank Australia (nd) Car loan [Online] https://www.bankaust.com.au/personal/borrow/car-loans/car-loan (archived at https://perma.cc/UD5T-75T4)

12 Euromonitor International (2016) Consumer card transactions overtake cash payments for the first time in 2016 [Online] https://blog.euromonitor.com/consumer-card-transactions-overtake-cash-payments-first-time-2016/ (archived at https://perma.cc/AV3H-6ATY)

13 Interview with Anders Langworth, Head of Group Sustainable Finance, Nordea Bank.

14 F3 Life (nd) [Online] f3-life.com (archived at https://perma.cc/597Z-2BF6)

15 Rainforest Action Network (RAN) *et al* (2019) *Banking on Climate Change: Fossil fuel finance report card 2019* [Online] https://www.ran.org/wp-content/uploads/2019/03/Banking_on_Climate_Change_2019_vFINAL1.pdf (archived at https://perma.cc/R53G-Z8QS)

16 APLMA, LMA and LSTA (2020) Green Loan Principles: Supporting environmentally sustainable economic activity [Online] https://www.lsta.org/content/green-loan-principles/ (archived at https://perma.cc/NVA2-R83Q)

17 United Nations Environment Programme (UNEP) (2016) Greening the Banking System: Taking stock of G20 green banking market practice [Online] http://unepinquiry.org/wp-content/uploads/2016/09/9_Greening_the_Banking_System.pdf (archived at https://perma.cc/8MZE-GZS3)

18 RBS (2016) RBS doubles lending to sustainable energy projects [Online] https://www.rbs.com/rbs/news/2016/04/rbs-doubles-lending-to-sustainable-energy-projects-.html (archived at https://perma.cc/4CUT-SJGM)

19 GBTI (2020) Spotlight on GBTI and its agricultural loans [Online] https://www.gbtibank.com/media-center/spotlight-on-gbti-and-its-agricultural-loans/?cn-reloaded=1 (archived at https://perma.cc/7CXX-VGHU)

20 UNEP Finance Initiative (2016) *Guide to Banking and Sustainability* [Online] https://www.unepfi.org/fileadmin/documents/guide_banking_statements.pdf (archived at https://perma.cc/TB5J-7Q5Y)

21 BBVA (2017) BBVA leads the world's first green syndicated financing in term loan format [Online] https://www.bbva.com/en/bbva-leads-worlds-first-syndicated-financing-scheme-loan-format/ (archived at https://perma.cc/62B7-KJSP)

22 Westpac (2018) Westpac launches world's first certified Green Tailored Deposit [Online] https://www.westpac.com.au/about-westpac/media/media-releases/2018/26-november2/ (archived at https://perma.cc/VPQ5-FGQT)

23 CBRE (2017) *European Commercial Real Estate Finance: 2017 update* [Online] https://www.cbre.co.uk/-/media/cbre/countryunitedkingdom/documents/8145_cbre%20european%20commercial%20real%20estate%20finance%202017_final.pdf (archived at https://perma.cc/K2EC-ES38)

24 Trucost (2016) Lloyds Bank launches first of its kind £1bn green lending fund for commercial property [Online] https://www.trucost.com/trucost-news/lloyds-bank-launches-first-kind-1bn-green-lending-fund-commercial-property/ (archived at https://perma.cc/BHU4-HNMJ)

25 United Nations Environment Programme (UNEP) (2017) *Green Tagging: Mobilising bank finance for energy efficiency in real estate* [Online] http://unepinquiry.org/wp-content/uploads/2017/12/Green_Tagging_Mobilising_Bank_Finance_for_Energy_Efficiency_in_Real_Estate.pdf (archived at https://perma.cc/RDL6-YMKY)

26 University of Cambridge Institute for Sustainability Leadership (CISL) (nd) *Incentivising the Trade of Sustainably Produced Commodities: A discussion paper prepared for the Banking Environment Initiative's Sustainable Trade Finance Council* [Online] https://www.cisl.cam.ac.uk/publications/publication-pdfs/incentivising-the-trade-of-sustainably-produced.pdf (archived at https://perma.cc/H7AM-P9WM)

27 University of Cambridge Institute for Sustainability Leadership (CISL) (nd) *Incentivising the Trade of Sustainably Produced Commodities: A discussion paper prepared for the Banking Environment Initiative's Sustainable Trade Finance Council* [Online] https://www.cisl.cam.ac.uk/publications/publication-pdfs/incentivising-the-trade-of-sustainably-produced.pdf (archived at https://perma.cc/H7AM-P9WM)

28 Environmental Finance (2017) Initial public offering 2017: Dong Energy [Online] https://www.environmental-finance.com/content/deals-of-the-year/ipo-dong-energy.html (archived at https://perma.cc/94N7-S78P)

29 HSBC (nd) Sustainable financing [Online] https://www.gbm.hsbc.com/solutions/sustainable-financing/climate-research (archived at https://perma.cc/6EPN-YLNV)

30 Natixis (nd) Green and sustainable hub [Online] https://gsh.cib.natixis.com/ (archived at https://perma.cc/2MMY-TS2V)

31 Rabobank (2016) Rabobank brings the circular economy to life [Online] https://www.rabobank.com/en/about-rabobank/in-society/sustainability/articles/2016/rabobank-brings-the-circular-economy-to-life.html (archived at https://perma.cc/2L9W-TEB5)

07

Green bonds and asset-backed securities

LEARNING OBJECTIVES

On completion of this chapter you should be able to:

- Describe the range of debt products available to green finance investors.
- Describe the main types and features of green bonds, including green sukuk.
- Understand the Green Bond Principles, and identify how these and other frameworks, standards and guidelines support the development of the green bond market.
- Describe how asset-backed securities may be used to securitize loans supporting smaller green finance projects, helping these attract capital from institutional investors.

The debt capital markets play a vital role in allocating capital to finance solutions to environmental, climate change and transition challenges. They can also help investors to diversify and manage risk in their portfolio and to integrate responsible and ethical investment approaches. Green bond issuance has grown rapidly in recent years, to $230 billion in 2019, including corporate, municipal and, most recently, sovereign bonds. As the market grows, so does the risk of greenwashing. Clear guidelines for issuers and investors, such as the Green Bond Principles, help to maintain market integrity and transparency.

Debt capital markets

Debt products include a range of bonds, asset-backed securities and similar products, and the term **debt capital markets** is used to describe the business of issuing, managing and trading in these. Institutions wanting to raise long-term finance might issue bonds or securities that allow secure investment without diluting share holdings and without having to repay the principal for a long time, possibly decades. Investors provide capital by buying bonds and securities to generate a return, offset liabilities, and diversify portfolios (geographically, across economic sectors, and in terms of risk profile).

Debt products fall into two main categories:

- **Organization-guaranteed bonds:** These raise money for general purposes and are backed by the issuing organization as a whole. Government (sovereign) bonds and corporate bonds are the main types by issuer (with some other issuers such as multilateral organizations like the World Bank). Use of the money raised (proceeds) of these may be linked to certain qualifying assets or purposes.
- **Asset-backed securities:** Interest payments are tied directly to specified assets such as a solar energy project. Such assets are often placed in a corporate structure called a special purpose entity/vehicle, which is set up with the specific purpose of holding the assets.

There are also a wide variety of hybrid structures where lenders have recourse to the income from assets and from the issuing company; these are less common, and are not relevant to our focus on green finance.

Bonds are the largest single asset class in the financial system, with a current value of around $100 trillion. Their importance has increased as, in the aftermath of the global financial crisis, capital requirements on bank lending have tightened and equity markets are raising less new capital.

The investment characteristics of bonds are based on risk:

- **Issuer risk:** How likely is it that the borrower (eg a company or a government) will pay back the money?
- **Currency risk:** Bonds can be issued in many currencies, and fluctuations in exchange rates may affect their existing and future value to international investors.

- **Coupon:** The rate of interest paid on the original amount, or principal (usually paid annually, semi-annually, or quarterly). The higher the risk of default, the higher the interest or coupon needed to compensate investors for taking on that risk.
- **Maturity:** How long is it before the investor gets their money back? The further into the future the maturity date is (and so the longer the term of the bond is), the greater the risk. Some bonds are issued in perpetuity, with no maturity date.

Unlike equity investors, bond investors do not have voting rights or the opportunity to participate in the growth of a company or asset. Conversely, bond holders are not exposed directly to a fall in the stock market value of a company and have an earlier call on assets if a company does get into trouble and goes into default (in general, bank loans have first call, then bond holders, and finally shareholders).

QUICK QUESTION

Why might a company choose to raise finance for new green projects by issuing bonds, rather than other sources of capital?

Debt capital is particularly suited for financing many green and sustainable projects, particularly those involving renewable energy such as wind or solar, and plays a considerably more important role in financing renewable energy infrastructure projects than equity capital. McKinsey (2016) found that the average debt-to-equity ratio of 3,700 renewable energy projects worldwide, receiving financing between 2000 and 2015, is 70 to 30 debt to equity.[1]

For most renewable energy projects, the majority of project costs are incurred upfront, during construction. Ongoing, marginal costs are low, as the wind blows and the sun shines for free. This contrasts with traditional thermal power generation projects, where marginal costs are high relative to construction costs due to project owners having to pay for continued fossil fuel inputs from volatile commodity markets including oil, gas and coal.

Although risk profiles differ considerably between different clean technologies and geographies, the typical project life cycle is characterized by higher levels of risk in development and construction phases due to technology and construction risks. Risk levels decrease once a project becomes operational and produces predictable and stable cash flows to service debt and generate returns. Renewable energy infrastructure projects therefore face a higher cost of capital in the development and construction phases and a lower cost of capital when operational.

To date, many renewable energy projects have been financed directly by corporations, often power utilities, using balance sheet-financing and general bank loans. Public equity and debt capital markets have played only a minor role in financing projects over the last decade. This looks set to change, however. The scale of investment needed to finance the transition to a sustainable, low-carbon world ($6 trillion per year, as we saw earlier) will exceed both the capabilities of the post-financial crisis banking sector and the constrained balance sheets of utility companies, which is why the debt capital markets will be significant in facilitating the continued operation of existing projects via refinancing, and the development and construction of a wide range of new projects supporting climate change mitigation and adaptation.

Green bonds

The development of the green bond market

The emergence of green bonds has been one of the key developments in recent years, with the aim of improving the ability of debt capital markets to raise capital to finance solutions to environmental and climate challenges, while also offering investors an opportunity to share in financial returns available from the transition to a sustainable, low-carbon world. Green bonds can also help investors to diversify and manage risk in their portfolios and to integrate responsible and ethical investment approaches. There is the further potential advantage of allowing governments and other institutions supporting issuance to support the flow of capital to priority sectors in order to achieve public policy and other goals, such as climate change mitigation and adaptation.

Green bonds are those where the proceeds raised are allocated to environmental projects or uses. They might be used to raise capital for a wide variety of purposes, including renewable energy projects, clean transport infrastructure, sustainable buildings, flood defences or sustainable forestry and agriculture. Green bonds are a relatively new asset class and, as yet, only a small proportion of bonds issued in connection with such projects are labelled as green bonds. There are four, generally agreed aspects to a green bond which differentiate them from normal, vanilla bonds. In brief, these are:

- **Use of proceeds:** Green bonds should be used to finance projects with green outcomes, such as an offshore wind farm or clean transport.
- **External review:** Issuers of green bonds should evaluate the intended green outcomes of projects with the help of a suitably qualified external reviewer.
- **Disclosure and management of proceeds:** The allocation of funds raised from a green bond should be independently audited and made easily available to investors and others.
- **Reporting:** Issuers should report on the environmental impacts of green bonds.

Some green bonds carry a recognized label and/or certification, which enables investors to better understand how the proceeds are used, while others may be marketed as green but not carry a specific label (this may or may not indicate a lesser degree or quality of environmental benefit). As the green bond market grows, there is an increasing risk of greenwashing, where financial instruments are marketed as green but the projects supported by them are not widely recognized as such (eg supporting power generation using cleaner coal). The development of market and regulatory frameworks, standards and guidance for issuers and investors, such as the Climate Bonds Standard, published by the Climate Bonds Initiative, Green Bond Principles and the EU Taxonomy (see earlier chapters) will play an important role in maintaining market integrity and transparency.

The majority of green bonds issued to date are, according to the Climate Bonds Initiative (CBI) which tracks the issue of green bonds, **green use-of-proceeds bonds** where the capital raised is used for specific climate change mitigation and/or adaptation projects, and bonds are backed by the issuer's entire balance sheet.[2] This is known as a recourse-to-the-issuer debt obligation and gives confidence to investors and rating agencies by significantly reducing (in most cases) credit risk and the risk of default. Importantly, this approach encourages *pari passu* pricing of green and conventional vanilla bonds from issuers, where there is no premium charged for the former.

Green project bonds differ in that these are backed not by an issuer's whole balance sheet, but by the green project's or projects' assets and balance sheet(s) only. Generally, there is no recourse to the issuer, which increases the risk profile of the bond, in some cases very significantly, making them less attractive to investors, who will require a higher return to compensate for the higher risk. For this reason, many project bonds are issued, supported by and/or underwritten (in whole or in part) by national and multilateral development banks, with a mandate to operate in areas of the market that commercial issuers and underwriters might find unattractive. A common credit enhancement support tool used by development banks is first loss provision, where a bond's risk–return profile is improved by a guarantee to underwrite losses, up to a certain agreed amount. The role of development banks is covered in more detail in the next chapter.

Green revenue bonds are backed by pledged revenue streams from a project, usually with no recourse to the issuer. Again, these tend to be riskier than use-of-proceeds bonds as revenue streams may be uncertain. In 2016, for example, New York's Metropolitan Transportation Authority (MTA) issued a $500 million revenue bond to finance improvements to public transport, backed by the revenues from the MTA system.[3]

CASE STUDY

The French green bond market[4]

As early as 2012, the Île-de-France regional government issued one of the first large sub-sovereign public green bonds for €350 million, renewed with an issuance of €600 million in 2014. The Agence Française de Développement joined other development banks with a €1 billion climate bond issuance of its own in 2014.

The French green bond market accounted for 21 per cent of the self-labelled green bond global market as of the end of 2015. In 2015, the total issuance on the French market amounted to €4 billion. Issuers (corporate non-financials, financials and public sector), investors and rating agencies alike are represented.

The French market has traditionally been at the forefront of the development of the green bond market. After the first years where supranationals, agencies and government were the most active issuers, 2014 marked a turning point for corporates. Following this worldwide trend, the French market has also recently experienced increased corporate activity. Throughout 2015, French non-financial corporates, financials and public sector agencies issued almost €4 billion in green bonds. As a result of this rapid diversification of issuers, a diversified ecosystem has emerged in France.

In the private sector, the largest issuances came from French corporates. In the energy sector, Électricité De France issued a €1.4 billion green bond in 2013 and Engie (formerly GDF Suez) issued the largest green bond to date at €2.5 billion in 2014. They both pledged not to develop new projects in the coal industry and to build massively in the renewable energy sector. In addition, several French banks (Crédit Agricole, BNP Paribas and Société Générale) have developed the expertise to support corporate companies in their issuance process. French management companies such as Amundi, Natixis and Mirova, among others, have announced the launch of investment funds in projects related to energy transition and are committed to reducing the carbon footprint of their portfolios. In the insurance sector, AXA launched the AXA WF Planet Bond fund to encourage clients to invest in the low-carbon economy. Agencies specialized in ESG analysis and ratings such as Vigéo or Novethic contribute to the dynamism of this ecosystem.

Meanwhile, the French Government has played a proactive role in promoting green investment. It passed an Energy and Green Growth Act into law that aims to reduce final energy consumption by 50 per cent in 2050 compared to 2012 and to reduce fossil fuel consumption by 30 per cent in 2030 compared to 2012. In addition, Article 173 of this law introduces mandatory environmental reporting for institutional investors (asset managers, insurance companies, pension and social security funds). The French Government has also endorsed non-monetary incentives such as the creation of a public label called Transition Energétique Climat, which excludes any support to fossil or nuclear energy and specifies positive investment areas that can be used by funds. The list of positive investment areas was based on the Climate Bonds Initiative Taxonomy.

QUICK QUESTION

Why might a government prioritize the development of green bond markets?

Initially, the development of green bonds was led by international financial institutions such as the World Bank Group's private sector lending arm, the International Finance Corporation (IFC), and multilateral development banks such as the European Investment Bank (EIB) and the European Bank for Reconstruction and Development (EBRD). The former issued the first green bond in 2007; by 2017 the EIB's green bond portfolio had grown to €24.5 billion in seven currencies, supporting 160 projects in 46 countries.

In recent years the green bond market has developed rapidly, with more than $230 billion of issuance in 2019 reported by the CBI, although not all these issues will meet market standards such as the Climate Bond Standard and/or Green Bond Principles.[5] There have been very significant increases in the diversity of issuers, investors and types of green bonds, as well as greater size of issues and longer maturities on the bonds.

According to the CBI, to the end of 2018, 628 corporate, municipal and sovereign issuers from 47 countries had issued a green bond, including six sovereigns. Investor appetite is high, with high levels of oversubscription for many green bond issuances. The CBI maintains a database of current and historic green bond issues at: www.climatebonds.net/cbi/pub/data/bonds.

In 2018, the largest overall issuer of green bonds was the US's Federal National Mortgage Association (Fannie Mae), with nearly $20 billion of green mortgage-backed securities issued in the year. The US was the leading country in the green bond market in 2018, with China in second place. France was the largest sovereign issuer with more than €15 billion in green bonds issued by the end of 2018.

As the green bond market has developed, related products and services have appeared, including green bond indices (eg S&P Green Bond Index) and green bond exchange-traded funds (ETFs).[6] In early 2018, Amundi (Europe's largest asset manager) and the IFC launched a $2 billion emerging market green bond fund, called the Amundi Planet Emerging Green One (Ego) fund, listed on the Luxembourg Stock Exchange. The growth of indices and funds has improved the visibility of green bonds to investors, encourages secondary market trading, and should help the market continue to grow.

Climate bonds are a sub-category of green bonds where proceeds are used to finance projects to mitigate or adapt to the effects of climate change. Green bond proceeds may be used to finance environmental projects more widely, and not just for climate change mitigation and adaptation. In practice, the great majority of green bond proceeds have been used to fund climate change projects.

As already mentioned, the terminology is often used interchangeably. In this book, we use green bond as our preferred terminology, except where the context or examples and case studies require specific reference to climate bonds. The Climate Bonds Initiative (CBI) has developed the **Climate Bonds Standard** (covered in more detail below) to provide assurance to investors (via certification) who want to be able to easily identify and invest in products that are supporting action on climate change.[7]

In October 2018 the Republic of the Seychelles issued the world's first **blue bond,** launching a new sub-category of green bonds designed to support sustainable marine and fisheries projects. Despite the small size of the issue ($15 million), this represents the beginning of an interesting new green bond sector, and reflects issuer and investor interest in using green bonds to finance climate change mitigation and adaptation in more specialist areas.

Social bonds are a type of bond where proceeds are used to fund projects with positive social – as opposed to environmental – outcomes, eg improvements in education or gender equality. The **Social Bond Principles** set out guidelines for use of proceeds for a bond to qualify as a social bond.

Sustainability bonds combine aspects of green and social bonds, with the proceeds funding green as well as a wide range of projects intended to have positive social outcomes, often linked to the UN's Sustainable Development Goals, outlined in Chapter 1. The European Investment Bank issued its first Sustainability Bond (€500 million) in 2018; HSBC issued the first private (ie non public/development bank) sustainability bond linked to the SDGs in the same year, a $1 billion issue designed to support a mixture of green and social projects, including:

- improving access to education, essential healthcare, fresh water and sanitation;
- increasing the share of renewables in the global energy mix;
- building sustainable cities and transport systems;
- helping communities adapt to the effects of climate change.[8]

Some critics, however, have pointed out that the majority of proceeds from HSBC's SDG bond have been used to fund projects that would have been funded via vanilla or green bonds, or other financial instruments, including the construction of HSBC HQ buildings in the UK and Dubai.

Nasdaq launched the first sustainable bond market in 2015, joined more recently by the Luxembourg Stock Exchange's Green Exchange and Sustainability Bond Window. As with the green bond market, the difficulty of agreeing common approaches to defining sustainability bonds and use of proceeds has held back development. In June 2018, the International Capital Markets Association (ICMA) published the **Sustainability Bond Guidelines** to promote consistency, integrity and transparency in this category of bonds, and we may reasonably expect to see the market develop as the guidelines become more widely adopted.

CASE STUDY

The development of national green bond markets[9]

National green bond markets provide an additional source of long-term green finance to bank lending and equity finance. This is especially valuable in countries where demand for green infrastructure investment is high but supply of long-term bank loans is limited. Of the seven options, support for the development of national green bond markets has been very strong. Governments have been playing an active role (including through sovereign and sub-sovereign issuance) and development banks are increasing their support.

Examples include:

Argentina: La Rioja Province issued its first green bond.

Australia: The State of Victoria became the first Australian government to issue a green bond.

Brazil: The Brazilian Federation of Banks (FEBRABAN) and the Brazilian Business Council for Sustainable Development (CEBDS) launched the voluntary 'Guidelines for issuing green bonds in Brazil 2016'.

Canada: The Province of Ontario issued its third and largest green bond to date in January 2017, while the Province of Quebec launched its first green bond issuance in February 2017.

China: Following the issuance of a domestic green bond catalogue and green bond guidelines, green bond issuance (domestically and internationally) reached $34 billion in 2016, up from $1 billion in 2015. The China Security Regulatory Commission released guidelines for green bonds issued by listed corporates in March 2017.

France: In January 2017, France issued a landmark €7 billion long-dated 22-year sovereign green bond, with a view to promoting best market practices (especially in terms of evaluation and impact reporting) and supporting the development of the green bond market.

Germany: The state development bank of North Rhine-Westphalia issued another green bond. The Federal Government extended and expanded KfW's mandate to support the green bond market as an anchor investor. The Association of German Public Banks launched a German Green Bond Initiative in June 2017.

India: The Securities and Exchange Board of India issued disclosure requirements for the issuing and listing of green debt securities.

Indonesia: OJK announced it would launch a framework and introduce regulation for green bond issuance in Indonesia in 2017.

Italy: Borsa Italiana launched a green and social bonding listing in March 2017.

Japan: The Ministry of the Environment released green bond guidelines in March 2017, and the Metropolitan Government of Tokyo announced plans for issuing green bonds.

Mexico: The Mexican development bank, Nacional Financiera, issued the first green bond in local currency.

Russian Federation: The Central Bank of Russia conducted a 'Review of financial market regulation: Green bonds'.

Singapore: The Monetary Authority of Singapore offers a grant fund to offset the costs of corporates issuing sustainability-related bonds.

South Africa: The National Treasury is exploring the possibility of a sovereign green bond.

South Korea: The Ministry of Finance and Strategy is developing Green Bonds Guidelines. The State-owned Korea Development Bank issued its inaugural green bond ($300 million) in June 2017.

Spain: The Comunidad de Madrid has announced it would launch a five-year EUR-denominated sustainability bond adhering to the Green Bond Principles and a number of the SDGs.

Turkey: The country's first green infrastructure bond was issued in November 2016 under a public–private model with development bank credit enhancement. The proceeds will be used for the Government's hospital building programme and the bond has been certified as both a green and social bond.

UK: The LSEG issued a 'Guide to ESG investing', including debt finance, in February 2017.

USA: the California State Treasurer released plans to scale up the green bond market in January 2017.

Figure 7.1 Overview of national green bond markets worldwide (shaded darker grey)

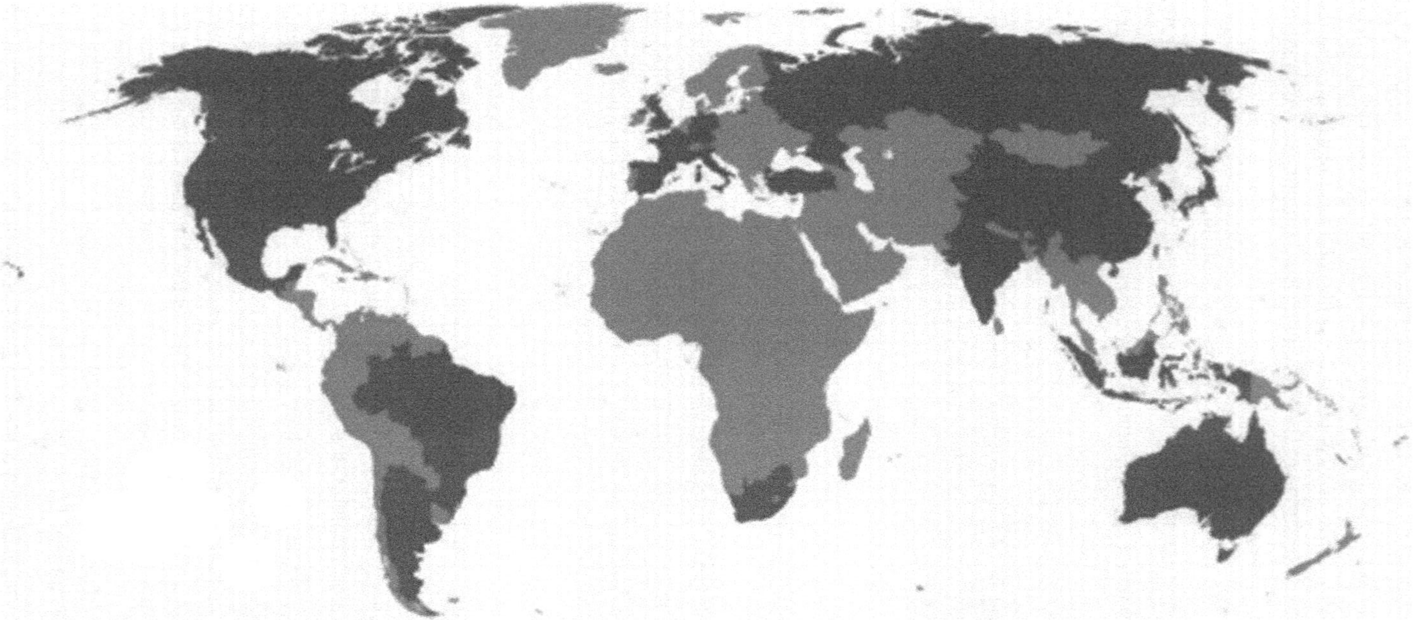

Green Bond Principles and other frameworks, standards and guidelines

Progress achieved in developing the green bond market to date has been significant, but challenges to further scaling up the green bond market remain, including the ongoing development of credible, verifiable and generally accepted market standards and efforts to increase awareness and understanding of the market. As the green bond market develops, so does the risk of greenwashing, as issuers seek to take advantage of investor demand for issues labelled as green.

CASE STUDY

How green is a green bond from an oil and gas company?[10]

The Green Bond Principles (GBP) are a set of voluntary process guidelines that make recommendations on transparency, disclosure and reporting for market participants to promote integrity in the market and enable its development. The GBP are a collaborative project and provide a flexible approach, which has been criticized by some stakeholders for failing to exclude use of proceeds for projects of questionable environmental benefit or sustainability.

A bond that was recently issued by Repsol Energy, for example, fits with the GBP definitions of green but was not viewed as green by some investors as the proceeds finance energy efficiency improvement to oil and gas refineries. It would not qualify under the Climate Bonds Standard and is not included within the Bloomberg or other green bond indices, and the issuance attracted much commentary in the financial press.[11]

This example clearly illustrates the challenge of trying to establish clear expectations and standards for a new product or asset class like green bonds. Labels including the word green have been used for many years by a wide range of financial products. There is a high risk of confusion among investors and of frustration and negative publicity from market participants and other stakeholders where it is felt labels are used in a misleading manner, or in a way that allows less green projects and products to compete with others that adhere to higher or more stringent requirements. There is a risk of misallocation of capital, as well as a risk to the credibility of individual products and to the market as a whole.

Even aside from standards and labelling, the credibility and integrity of issuers is critical. Without this, it is hard for investors to trust that issuers will implement commitments and will have robust and reliable verification, audit and disclosure processes in place.

Another example of the challenges of green bond labelling, assurance and credibility can be seen in the case of the first green sovereign bond, a Polish Government €750 million issue in 2016. The proceeds were earmarked for a range of climate change mitigation projects, including renewable energy, clean transport infrastructure and sustainable agriculture. The first sovereign green bond issue met with a generally positive response, but some environmental groups and investors expressed concerns.

Poland is highly dependent on coal power and has been criticized by some environmental groups for a lack of commitment to tackling climate change and achieving a green energy transition. Whilst the details provided to potential bond investors were considered to be quite comprehensive by analysts (including the investment research service, Sustainalytics), the recent record of the Polish Government, combined with a perceived lack of clear and enforceable controls on the projects for which the proceeds can be used, was viewed by some as cause for caution and close scrutiny.

The investment firm Lombard Odier (an investor in green bonds) declined this issue due to its concerns that Poland was also borrowing money to develop more coal power plants. Lombard Odier also rejected the Repsol green bond highlighted in the case study above. This again highlights the way in which the credibility of the issuer of a green bond and the clarity and level of assurance provided by the standards according to which a bond is structured and monitored are critically important for the success of individual issuances and the further development of the green bond market as a whole.

QUICK QUESTION

What are the costs and benefits of having more stringent standards and requirements on use of proceeds and disclosure in order to secure green bond labelling or certification?

Green Bond Principles

The Green Bond Principles (GBPs), issued by the International Capital Markets Association (ICMA) in 2014 and widely adopted by issuers and investors, are voluntary process guidelines that recommend transparency and disclosure and promote integrity in the green bond market by clarifying the approach for issuance of a green bond.[12] The GBPs aim to provide issuers with guidance on the key components involved in launching a credible green bond; they aid investors by ensuring availability of information necessary to evaluate the environmental impact of green bond investments; and they assist underwriters by moving the market towards standard disclosures that will facilitate transactions.

The GBPs recommend a clear process and disclosure for issuers, which investors, banks, investment banks, underwriters, placement agents and others may use to understand the characteristics of any given green bond. They emphasize the required transparency, accuracy and integrity of information that will be disclosed and reported by issuers to stakeholders.

The GBPs have four core components:

1 Use of proceeds

The cornerstone of a green bond is the utilization of the proceeds of the bond for green projects, which should be appropriately described in the legal documentation for the security. All designated green project categories should provide clear environmental benefits, which will be assessed and, where feasible, quantified by the issuer. Eligible projects should contribute to one or more high-level environmental objectives, defined in the 2018 revision of the Green Bond Principles as climate change mitigation, climate change adaptation, natural resource conservation, biodiversity conservation, and pollution prevention and control.

2 Process for project evaluation and selection

The issuer of a green bond should outline a process to determine how the projects fit within the eligible green projects categories identified above; the related eligibility criteria; and the environmental sustainability objectives. The GBPs encourage a high level of transparency and recommend that an issuer's process for project evaluation and selection be supplemented by an external review. In addition to information disclosed by an issuer on its green bond process, criteria and external reviews, green bond investors may also take into consideration the quality of the issuer's overall profile and performance regarding environmental sustainability.

3 Management of proceeds

The net proceeds of green bonds should be credited to a sub-account, moved to a sub-portfolio or otherwise tracked by the issuer in an appropriate manner and attested to by a formal internal process linked to the issuer's lending and investment operations for green projects. So long as the green bonds are outstanding, the balance of the tracked proceeds should be periodically adjusted to match allocations to eligible green projects made during that period. The issuer should make known to investors the intended types of temporary placement for the balance of unallocated proceeds. The GBPs encourage a high level of transparency and recommend that an issuer's management of proceeds be supplemented by the use of an auditor, or other third party, to verify the internal tracking method and the allocation of funds from the green bond proceeds.

4 Reporting

Issuers should make, and keep, readily available up-to-date information on the use of proceeds, to be renewed annually until full allocation, and as necessary thereafter in the event of new developments. This should include a list of the projects to which green bond proceeds have been allocated, as well as a brief description of the projects and the amounts allocated, and their expected impact. Where confidentiality agreements, competitive considerations, or a large number of underlying projects limit the amount of detail that can be made available, the GBPs recommend that information is presented in generic terms or on an aggregated portfolio basis (eg percentage allocated to certain project categories).

Transparency is of particular value in communicating the expected impact of projects. The GBPs recommend the use of qualitative performance indicators and, where feasible, quantitative performance measures (eg energy capacity, electricity generation, greenhouse gas emissions reduced/avoided, number of people provided with access to clean power, reduction in the number of cars required, etc) with the key underlying methodology and/or assumptions used in the quantitative determination. Issuers with the ability to monitor achieved impacts are encouraged to include those in their regular reporting.[13]

The Green Bond Principles were most recently revised in June 2018. The four core components set out above remain unchanged, but additional guidance on the use of external reviews is now provided. The importance of timely reporting of material developments is also stressed. In addition, the development of additional guidance and taxonomies for better defining green projects by regulatory and industry bodies is noted, examples of which (Climate Bonds Standard and EU Taxonomy) are discussed below. As we saw in the previous chapter, the 2018 Green Loan Principles draw heavily on the approach of the Green Bond Principles.

READING

Despite the best of intentions, green use-of-proceeds bonds are a distraction and a false hope

Ben Caldecott, Director, Oxford Sustainable Finance Programme[14]

Debt capital markets, particularly bond markets, will play a critical role in financing large parts of the transition to global environmental sustainability.

These deep pools of low-cost capital are well suited to the capital-intensive projects and technologies that need to be deployed to implement both the Paris Agreement and the Sustainable Development Goals.

Enter green bonds. These should help sustainable and financeable activities access lower cost capital, thereby improving their economics, and enabling more projects to happen. This would help the world become greener and cleaner.

The green bonds that now dominate the conversation in ESG and responsible investment circles are the kind issued by a sovereign, multilateral institution or company as use-of-proceeds bonds. For example: a government issues a green bond and says it will spend the money raised on funding environmental activities; a multilateral development bank (MDB) issues a green bond and says it will use the funds to finance its climate change projects; an oil company issues a green bond and says it will spend the money on making its business more energy efficient; a railway company issues a green bond to finance the construction of a new railway or to refinance existing debt. According to SEB, approximately 88 per cent ($50 billion) of total year-to-date green bond issuance was for green use-of-proceeds bonds and there have been recent issuances from Apple ($1 billion) and the French Government (€7 billion).

This sounds promising. Green activities are being financed through these green use-of-proceeds bonds. The sovereign, multilateral institution or company issuing the bond feels good and gets to highlight how green it is. The investor buying the bond gets to say it is supporting green activities. The organizations involved in the market can say they're helping to finance the transition to sustainability. What's not to like?

Unfortunately, this is the point at which superficiality meets reality and where it gets uncomfortable for the green bond advocate. Here are some reasons to think that green use-of-proceeds bonds are a real problem and not a solution:

First, there is no cost of capital benefit for the issuer and consequently no economic advantage. The bonds are priced the same as other similar bonds issued by the same issuer. The government, MDB, oil company and railway company are not accessing lower cost capital. The cost of capital is the same as if they just borrowed normally in the debt capital markets. In fact, as they must pay for the bond to be verified there is an extra cost of issuance. That in effect increases the cost of capital, albeit by a small amount. At best there is no cost of capital benefit for the issuer and at worst it is more expensive.

Second, the activities would be financed anyway. The green use-of-proceeds bond is financing activities that would have happened and been successfully financed. The government spends money on the environment that would be funded by either taxation or borrowing, the MDB finances climate mitigation projects and would issue bonds to fund these activities as it does normally, the oil company was going to improve its energy efficiency and finance this from its cash flows or borrowing, and the railway company was going to get its new railway financed and successfully refinance its debt obligations. None of these things happened because a green bond was possible. They were going to happen anyway and in the absence of green use-of-proceeds bonds would have been financed at the same cost of capital.

Third, there is a substantial risk of greenwashing and this seems to be happening already. Poland, arguably the least green country in Europe and the country that persistently undermines EU action on climate change, managed to become the first sovereign issuer of a green bond. There are other examples. In the end this is a material risk for investors holding green use-of-proceeds bonds. A scandal or two, where the funds are being used for non-green activities, will almost certainly happen. The mere prospect of this may introduce liquidity risk for some types of green use-of-proceeds bonds. It would not surprise me if they trade with an illiquidity discount in the future. Remember, this happened in the international carbon market when the market started to discount (due to reputational and then policy risk) Certified Emission Reductions (CERs) generated from large-scale hydro and industrial gas projects.

Fourth, green use-of-proceeds bonds suck up time and energy – they are a dangerous distraction given the scale of the sustainability challenges we face. So much time has been dedicated to this area. You just have to look at the number of conferences and events organized with sessions focused on green use-of-proceeds bonds and the incessant lobbying of governments by their advocates to secure tax incentives and other benefits.

Fifth, because of the staggeringly high hype to environmental impact ratio and the risk of greenwashing, they could quite possibly undermine broader efforts to mainstream sustainable finance and investment. Green bond advocates claim that green use-of-proceeds bonds will help mainstream sustainable finance and investment by getting investors used to green. I disagree. Labelling does little to help investors become familiar with underlying cash flows and activities; in fact it seems to encourage complacency. Scandals and greenwashing could undermine interest in anything green. Poor performing clean tech funds in the late noughties and the collapse of the carbon market at around the same time scarred many institutional investors. The same could happen as a result of green use-of-proceeds bonds.

Green bond advocates need to be honest about what a green use-of-proceeds bond does and does not do. While green use-of-proceeds bonds don't directly support the transition to sustainability, they might do indirectly through encouraging issuers to think about green activities and by creating market momentum towards green. These benefits are hard to define and capture, but they might be significant. Though few green bond advocates seem to spend time pinning down and understanding these possible positive contributions.

But even if such benefits existed they must also be assessed in the round together with the arguments against. On balance, even being generous with the hypothesized benefits, I think that green use-of-proceeds bonds are a marketing gimmick and have very little (if any) positive impact on the real economy. They will likely suffer from liquidity issues in the future. The hype surrounding them will backfire (probably through a series of greenwashing scandals) and this will then hold back the development of sustainable finance and investment more generally. Hence this article and my warning.

Instead of green use-of-proceeds bonds, we should be talking about green infrastructure bonds or green asset-backed securities used to refinance operational cash-flow producing assets. Such refinancing actually lowers the average cost of capital for green activities by creating an exit for early stage capital and by turning equity and bank loans into cheaper long-term debt. They also free up capital that can be recycled back into construction and development. There needs to be a torrent of such issuance in the coming years as the stock of low-carbon infrastructure in Europe and elsewhere is refinanced to free up capacity on company and bank balance sheets. It is an imperative that this market develops quickly. Issuers, investors and governments should put the green infrastructure bond agenda at the very top of their priority list and dump green use-of-proceeds bonds before they do any more damage or distract further attention from the things we actually need to do to deliver on Paris and the SDGs.

QUICK QUESTIONS

Would the things being financed by green use-of-proceeds bonds have been successfully financed anyway and, if so, does it matter?

The wide market acceptance of the Green Bond Principles since their publication in 2014 has certainly helped promote consistency, transparency and market integrity. Their status as voluntary, best practice guidance rather than formal, regulatory standards means that there may, however, be some inconsistency in their application. In particular, the GBPs have been criticized for a lack of detail as to what constitutes a green project that may be financed by the proceeds of a green bond – providing a broad range of project categories, without the level of detail necessary to fully determine their environmental benefits.

Climate Bonds Standard

For this reason, the Climate Bonds Initiative has developed the **Climate Bonds Standard,** fully aligned with but building on the Green Bond Principles, and which detail sector-specific criteria for projects and assets that may be certified by Approved Verifiers as green.[15] The Standard is separated into **pre-issuance requirements,** which need to be met by issuers seeking certification ahead of issuance, and **post-issuance requirements,** which need to be met by issuers seeking continued certification following issuance. Investors benefit from certification by an Approved Verifier (overseen by the Climate Bonds Standard Board – CBSB), and by not having to conduct their own, potentially costly and complex monitoring and verification of use of proceeds.

Issuers benefit from being able to demonstrate the certified nature of the bond to potential investors. The green bond market benefits overall from enhanced consistency and integrity.

The Climate Bonds Standard aims to ensure, through certification and verification, that proceeds from bond issues are consistent with climate change mitigation and adaptation. Criteria have been developed, or are being developed, for sectors including water, solar, wind, forestry, low-carbon buildings, bioenergy, geothermal energy, marine energy and low-carbon transport. The Standard has been developed over time, with version 2.1 valid until June 2020 when it was superseded by version 3.0, designed to align more closely with the 2018 revision of the Green Bond Principles.

The key aspects of the Climate Bonds Standard are:

- identifying qualifying projects and assets, using the Standard's eligibility criteria for low-carbon and climate-resilient projects and assets;
- arranging an independent review, and disclosing the results of that review;
- ensuring that use of proceeds is tracked and reported, at least annually; and
- a robust and effective certification system.[16]

The main differences between the Climate Bonds Standard and the Green Bond Principles are that the former provides more detailed criteria on the use of bond proceeds (ie helping to identify truly green projects), and sets out these and other criteria as requirements rather than the GBP's principles, guidelines and recommendations. The Climate Bonds Standard, therefore, sets a more rigorous standard for green bonds, but offers less flexibility to issuers.

EU Taxonomy for Sustainable Activities and Green Bond Standard

In March 2018, the European Union (EU) published its Action Plan: Financing Sustainable Growth, which established a Technical Expert Group on Sustainable Finance (TEG) to:

- establish an EU Taxonomy for Sustainable Activities (classification system) to determine/define whether an economic activity is environmentally sustainable;
- introduce EU labels for green financial products, including an EU Green Bond Standard;
- introduce benchmarks for low-carbon investment strategies; and

- improve guidance regarding corporate disclosure of climate-related information.[17]

Given the EU's scale and influence, the development and implementation of the Action Plan is likely to have a significant global impact on the green finance market by bringing greater regulatory backing to existing, voluntary market standards including the Green Bond Principles and the Climate Bonds Standard.

The development of the EU Taxonomy for Sustainable Activities is seen by many as the most important and, potentially, far-reaching activity in the Action Plan. It is intended that the classification system, which in effect will define and provide examples of what is and isn't green, will be embedded in EU law and provide a framework for many other aspects of the Action Plan. The Taxonomy will be used, for example, to determine which investments will qualify as being green in the context of the proposed EU Green Bond Standard. Bonds that finance cleaner coal currently labelled as green by some issuers would be unlikely to qualify once this is introduced.

The proposed EU Green Bond Standard, which will draw on the Taxonomy, is intended to explicitly define an EU Green Bond and to enhance transparency, integrity, consistency and comparability of EU Green Bonds. Proposals from December 2018 draw heavily on the Green Bond Principles discussed above, containing the same four core components (use of proceeds, process for project evaluation and selection, management of proceeds, reporting). Independent review by an expert, external reviewer will also be required. Until the EU Taxonomy is published, the proceeds of use of an EU Green Bond must align with either the Green Bond Principles Project Categories and/or the Climate Bonds Standard, demonstrating the extent to which the EU is seeking to build on existing market standards. Unlike those standards, once they come into effect, the EU Taxonomy for Sustainable Activities and Green Bond Standard will have legal force and may diverge, over time, from voluntary market standards if these were to develop at a faster pace.

China's green bond guidelines

One notable recent step is the move by China to establish guidelines for green bonds at both corporate and local government (provincial) levels, as part of a wider programme to promote and expand green finance in China. Like other countries, China recognizes that traditional sources of capital are insufficient to meet the investment needs of a green transition, and so is prioritizing green bonds as a key tool to access large pools of capital from institutional investors. China has become one of the world's largest green bond markets, and the new guidelines are intended to support harmonization around international standards to promote cross-border investment, including between China and European markets. There are concerns, however, that the rapid and recent rise in green bond issuance in China may lead to instances of greenwashing; hence the need for guidelines to ensure market consistency and integrity.

CASE STUDY

China's green bond market practice[18]

While the integrity of the international green bond market is based largely on voluntary principles, in China the market is regulated by different government bodies. For a green bond to be issued on the onshore market, it must be approved by the relevant regulatory authorities, such as the PBoC, NDRC and CSRC. Approval requires that bonds meet guidelines covering: eligible green projects, management of proceeds, disclosure requirement and external verification.

Currently, green bond guidelines differ between regulatory authorities as they focus on different aspects of green. The PBoC guidance focuses on categorization of green projects, and provides more detailed requirements on project categories, eligibility criteria, management of proceeds, information disclosure and third-party verification. It is applicable to both the interbank bond market and exchange markets.

The NDRC guidance provides more detail about the key green sectors that green bonds should support and puts forward several policy incentives. A summary of the two guidelines is provided below.

Eligible green project categories

Both the PBoC and NDRC broadly outline the types of projects that are eligible for green bond funding but use different criteria. The NDRC guidance identifies 12 project categories, while the PBoC catalogue outlines six. The PBoC catalogue was China's first guidance document defining eligible green projects, and provides more detail at sub-sector levels of project classification and eligibility criteria within each of the six broad categories. The country's two stock exchanges both use the catalogue as a reference when determining the scope of green projects. Both sets of guidelines are dynamic and can be altered over time as necessary.

Management of proceeds

Both guidelines have set up some requirements for management of proceeds. The PBoC requires issuers to use ring-fencing or earmarking to track the use of proceeds. The NDRC guidance lays out some requirements for allocation of proceeds during the bond term. For example, issuers can use up to 50 per cent of the bond proceeds to repay bank loans and invest in working capital. However, it does not establish rules for management of proceeds and tracking.

Requirements on information disclosure

The PBoC requires that reporting is published on a quarterly basis and that the issuer discloses detail on the use of proceeds in the annual report and special auditor's report from the preceding year, as well as details on the use of proceeds in the first quarter of the year before 30 April each year. The annual report on use of proceeds must be reported to PBoC. NDRC does not have any specific rules.

Requirements on third party verification

While the PBoC does not require external reviews within its green bonds regulation, it has been made clear to issuers that a review is expected. As a result, reviews have become the norm. Issuers are also encouraged to publish an annual third-party verification/assessment report during the bond term. Reviewers are a mix of international and domestic agencies.

Policy incentives

The PBoC and NDRC both provide incentives to develop the green bond market. The PBoC allows green bonds issued by financial institutions to be used as collateral for low interest central bank loans, which gives banks a strong incentive to issue green bonds.

NDRC guidance proposes incentives for dealing with the simplification of the issuance and approval process for corporate issuers, including:

- allowing for private placements and aggregation for certain project types and under certain circumstances;

- adjusting corporate bond issuance approval conditions, for example proceeds can account for up to 80 per cent of the total investment of a project;
- supporting issuers to use green bond proceeds to improve their capital structure: issuers are allowed to use less than 50 per cent of the bond proceeds to repay bank loans and invest in working capital. Issuers with a credit rating of AA+ and good operational performance could use green bond proceeds to replace high-cost debt for existing green projects under construction.

QUICK QUESTION

Why might China be keen to encourage the growth of its green bond market?

Green bond indices

As with other major asset classes, stock exchanges and other investment funds and data providers are now providing indices of green bonds, making it easier for investors to allocate a proportion of their asset portfolio to green bonds. An index enables investors to gain exposure to a selection of assured green bonds from a potentially diverse range of issuers and sectors.

CASE STUDY

Green bond indices and listings[19]

Green bond indices

An overview of the green bond indices in the market and their inclusion criteria is set out in Table 7.1.

Advantages:

- As the bulk of assets under management globally are passive investments tracking indices, green bond indices are an important

Table 7.1 Green bond indices and summary of inclusion criteria

	Min size	Investment grade only	Bond types	Coupon	Maturity	Green criteria
Solactive	$100m	Mixed (non-investment grade and unrated included)	Corporate bank, development bank	Fixed only	> 6 months	Complies with the Climate Bonds taxonomy
S&P Dow Jones	n/a	Mixed (non-investment grade and unrated included)	Corporate bank, development bank, municipal (ex US)	Fixed, zero, step-up, fixed to float, floaters	> 1 year	Complies with the Climate Bonds taxonomy. Separate unlabelled climate project box index
Barclays & MSCI	$250m	Yes	Corporate bank, development bank, municipal (ex US), ABS	Fixed only	Matures in index	Complies with the Climate Bonds taxonomy. MSCI environmental assessment, unlabelled climate bonds are eligible
Bank of America Merrill Lynch	$250m	Yes	Corporate bank, development bank, municipal (ex US)	n/a	> 1 month	Complies with Bloomberg green bond definition

mechanism to ensure green bond investment is accessible to the mainstream, passive funds. This facilitates the green bond market in being scalable, and avoid remaining a niche market.

- Development of a range of green bond indices allows a range of green bond funds to be launched tracking the different indices.
- Another important role for green bond indices is building a performance history for the financial performance of green bonds.

Challenges:

- Potential lack of agreement of a qualifying definition of what is green is a barrier to green bond indices, as an index has to use set criteria for what qualifies as a green bond and therefore inclusion in the index. At present, CBI provides base data for the Solactive, S&P and Barclays MSCI indices, and synchronizes with Bloomberg, the data provider for the Bank of America index. CBI is also now working with CECEP/CCDC on base data for the new CCDC climate bonds index.
- In emerging markets, there are additional challenges to building green bond indices. This includes a smaller scale of market, liquidity, and a less developed investor base.

Suggested improvements on current practice:

- Technical assistance could be provided in emerging economies to encourage the development and use of green bond indices in line with local green bond market regulation.

Green bond stock exchange lists

As of June 2016, Oslo, Stockholm, Luxembourg, Mexico, Shanghai and London stock exchanges have launched green bond lists.

Advantages:

- The green bond lists on stock exchanges are useful in improving the visibility of green bonds to investors, and encourage secondary market trading.
- The lists are playing a role in pushing the market to use external reviews of the green credentials of the bond – which is important to ensure the environmental integrity of the market – as this is a condition the stock exchanges require to include green bonds on their lists.

- The green bond lists can also help push the market to common definitions around what is green in the green bond market, and therefore reduce transaction costs and facilitate trading. In the future, the stock exchanges can make inclusion in the lists conditional on meeting certain green criteria.

Challenges:

- Green bond lists can only play a role in defining what is green by making inclusion in the list conditional on meeting certain environmental criteria when more standardized bonds are available in the market; the stock exchanges are not well placed to be the initial developer of standardized green definitions.

Suggested improvements on current practice:

- Green bond lists should also be established in emerging economies entering the bond market, such as China and India. Mexico's adoption is a welcome step.

Stock exchanges have a vital role in supporting and promoting the market for green bonds. The Sustainable Stock Exchange (SSE) initiative has prioritized green bond markets in its recommendations and works in partnership with exchanges. Some exchanges, as mentioned in the case study on Oslo Børs, are playing an important role in growing the market and providing new guidance and regulation to help ensure that the market develops in a way that fosters trust from investors about the quality of the green assets and the impact of sustainable investments.

CASE STUDY

Oslo Børs' approach to green bonds and climate finance[20]

Over the past two years, Oslo Børs has been expanding its sustainability strategy, which prompted it to become an SSE Partner Exchange in 2015. Of particular note is its climate work, particularly its expansion of green bonds.

Looking to increase attention to green investment choices, in January 2015 Oslo Børs became the first stock exchange to offer a separate list for green bonds. Initially the list included five green bonds, and has since grown to 11 offered by eight issuers and valued at $1.2 billion.

The first company to issue a green bond on the exchange was the Norwegian energy company BKK in October 2014, and in July 2015 the Oslo kommune became the first municipality to join the list. The list is expected to grow, as there is increasing interest in green bonds from the Norwegian banks. Thorodd Bakken, the Head of Nordea Markets in Norway, noted the green bond issued by the energy utility company NordTrøndelag Elektrisitetsverk became oversubscribed in only two hours. Additionally, BKK initially expected to raise $120 million with its issuance, but demand exceeded expectations and they raised the target to $130 million.

Issuers looking to list on Oslo Børs' green bonds list are subject to specific requirements. First, the proceeds from the issuance must be used for an environmentally friendly purpose. A second opinion on the project's qualification as environmental must be provided by research organizations or certification companies and made publicly available. In addition, ongoing disclosure obligations must be made publicly available through stock exchange announcements.

One research organization that could provide the second opinion required to issue on the green bonds list is CICERO, a Norwegian institute for interdisciplinary climate research. It focuses on the following research areas: food and forests, local solutions, the Arctic, China, international climate policy and climate finance. Climate finance is the most recent addition, for which Oslo Børs hosted the launch and the first Advisory Board Meeting in May 2016.

CICERO communicates often and directly about responses to climate change with the private sector, government and civil society. Its objective is to create a meeting place for climate scientists and leading global investors to improve the understanding of climate risk and develop better tools to incorporate climate risk in long-term investments, tailored to investors' needs. The CICERO Climate Finance Advisory Board includes 14 members including Oslo Børs, large international investors such as BlackRock and NBIM, the Norwegian Ministry of Foreign Affairs, and other Nordic investors such as the Swedish National Pension Fund AP2.

Green sukuk

Sukuk are a Sharia-compliant form of financial certificate, sharing many features with asset-backed bonds, and sometimes referred to as Sharia-compliant bonds. Although sukuk were developed to enable financial markets to operate in a way that is appropriate to Islamic culture and laws, they also have some characteristics that proponents argue make them a natural fit for green finance and other sustainable investment portfolios. The Islamic faith and tradition – and Islamic finance – emphasize the importance of environmental stewardship, public benefit and the prevention of harm to people and planet. Like a green bond, green sukuk refers to a security where the proceeds are used to support projects with environmentally focused outcomes, often infrastructure projects designed to mitigate against the effects of climate change, or aid adaptation to climate change.

The green sukuk market has developed more slowly than the green bond market, and is still in its infancy. The world's first green sukuk (RM250 million) was issued in July 2017 by a Malaysian renewable energy firm with proceeds supporting the construction of large solar energy plants. A second green sukuk (RM1 billion) was issued in October 2018 by a separate renewable energy firm to finance the construction of Southeast Asia's largest solar photovoltaic plant. In March 2018 Indonesia issued the first sovereign green sukuk, raising $1.25 billion.

Governments, regulators and the Islamic finance sector are keen to develop the green sukuk market, with the first issuers (Malaysia and Indonesia) very much in the forefront.

CASE STUDY

Green sukuk: Combining the momentum of Islamic finance growth and green bond expansion[21]

The concept of green sukuk is gaining more attention in the financial community. Sukuk are fixed income instruments issued based on the principles of Islamic law and represent an ownership in underlying assets or earnings from those assets. While sukuk are often described as Islamic bonds, there are also types of sukuk that have equity-type risk-sharing structures. Similar to green bonds, proceeds from green sukuk will be utilized to finance green projects that include supporting the preservation or protection of environmental and natural resources, conservation and renewable energy, and climate change. Sukuk, by nature asset-focused and linked to the real economy, have close affinity with responsible finance that also seeks to maximize financial returns and social good.

Given their sustainable and responsible features, sukuk are a natural fit for use in financing a green project. Green sukuk combine the momentum of sukuk and green bond market growth. In addition to offering the same benefits as those of green bonds, green sukuk would bring opportunities that include:

- providing an alternative source of long-term fundraising solutions to address funding gaps that may not be able to be met by conventional financing alone;
- offering a new asset class for risk and investment diversification, targeting investors with a strong appetite for ethical and socially responsible investing;
- providing access to Islamic investors with an appetite for socially responsible investments who are not able to invest in green bonds; and
- raising the profile of the issuer's corporate image as a forward-thinking and innovative organization that supports a sustainable social agenda.

Green sukuk target a wider investor base that includes both Islamic and conventional investors, thus creating higher demand and hence potentially yielding more competitive pricing. Taking Malaysia as an example, Ringgit sukuk issuance attracts lower yield than bonds, with a savings difference of about 4 to 7 basis points.

In accessing an even bigger pool of investors, green sukuk have the ability to capture retail investors seeking responsible investments. Malaysia's Danainfra pioneered the first exchange-traded sukuk issuance of 10 years, creating a new asset class for retail investors in this market. Danainfra constructs and operates Mass Rapid Transit to boost rail-based public transportation to alleviate traffic congestion, contributing to a reduction in carbon emission by motor vehicles; hence, potentially could fall under a green initiative.

The advent of a green sukuk issuance is imminent. The Islamic Declaration on Global Climate Change, published in August 2015, called for action on climate change from governments, business, investors and Muslims around the world. The annual World Islamic Economic Forum held in November 2015 also dedicated a session exclusively to Islamic Finance for Green Technologies. These efforts have garnered new interest in Islamic finance, particularly from traditional markets looking for ethical and socially responsible investing.

As with green bonds, ensuring the consistency and integrity of the green sukuk market is essential to its growth and sustainability. To that end, the **Green Sukuk Working Group** (GSWG) was established by the Gulf Bond & Sukuk Association, the Climate Bonds Initiative and the Clean Energy Business Council of the Middle East and North Africa to develop voluntary market standards and guidance. The eligible assets for green sukuk are defined and certified by the Climate Bonds Standard (see above), as is the case for many green bonds.

Asset-backed securities

Asset-backed securities (ABSs) are a type of debt product, similar to a bond. In this case, an issuer (often, but not always, a financial institution) makes (or buys) a range of loans that will finance green projects or enterprises, bundles together (securitizes) the revenues from those loans, and issues securities backed by that income. Bundling together revenues from such loans allows them to be traded with investors. The individual loans are usually relatively small, illiquid, and cannot be individually traded. Securitization diversifies the risk of investing in the underlying loans, provided the pool of loans is itself sufficiently diversified and not highly correlated.

QUICK QUESTION

What might be the advantages of asset-backed securities for green investors?

This type of structure has some important advantages, in particular the ability to enable smaller projects and borrowers to access capital from large institutional investors. The cost of investing in small projects and the difficulty of assessing credit risk and green credibility for small issuers can be overcome, or at least simplified, thus increasing availability and reducing the cost of capital for borrowers. As noted above, the largest overall issuer of green bonds in 2018 was the US's Federal National Mortgage Association (Fannie Mae), with issues amounting to nearly $20 billion of green mortgage-backed securities; and 2018, National Australia Bank issued the world's first private Residential Mortgage-Backed Securitization, including a certified green tranche of AU$ 300 million meeting criteria for low-carbon residential buildings.

Asset-backed securities are already proving to be a viable debt-financing instrument for residential solar energy in the US. Development finance institutions such as the IFC are providing support to demonstrate that these approaches are also viable in other countries, where they can contribute to reducing energy poverty as well as supporting sustainable development, as described in the case study on rooftop solar power.

CASE STUDY

Securitization to fund rooftop solar power in India[22]

Meeting the Indian government's target of 40 GW of rooftop solar power by 2022 will require significant financial resources, estimated at $34 billion. Even with a more realistic deployment target of 14 GW by 2022, the solar rooftop sector would still need approximately $12 billion, of which $8.3 billion would be debt capital.

Low availability and low quality of debt capital are key barriers to the growth of the sector. These barriers arise because investors lack confidence in the credit quality of rooftop solar system project deals and lack interest in the small deal sizes on offer. In addition, delays in both lending decisions and disbursal of loans are also slowing growth.

The Rooftop Solar Private Sector Financing Facility addresses these barriers by bundling a large number of small projects together into one structured investment so that the aggregate deal size is large enough and of sufficient credit quality to attract more attention from investors, especially institutional investors. In addition, the Facility could demonstrate the commercial viability of the sector, which will reduce the perception risk of the sector. This securitization will help reduce the cost of capital compared to conventional financing and increase capital flows by expanding the investor base.

The Facility would add around 168 MW of capacity in the pilot phase over 2017–19 and around 500 MW by 2022. It could bring an additional $500 million of capital to the rooftop solar sector, reduce the cost of debt by 0.5–3 per cent and create an additional 20,000 jobs over 2017–22. Beyond 2022, the Facility has the potential to raise more capital by demonstrating the commercial viability of the sector and the attractiveness of rooftop solar asset-backed securities, and by supporting solar developers to reach a scale that enables them to attract commercial investment at attractive terms.

Figure 7.2 Example of an aggregation mechanism

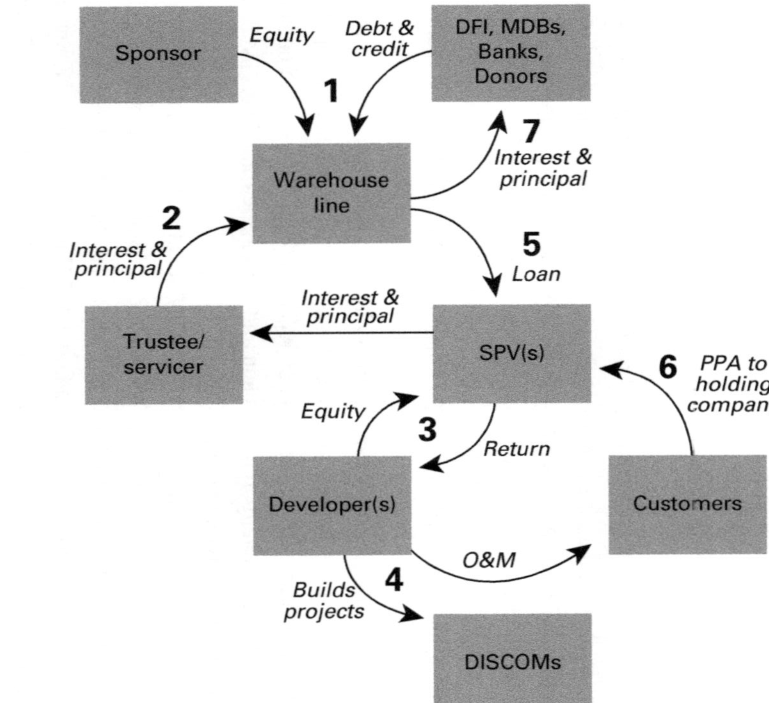

1. The sponsor would create a warehouse line entity with nominal equity capital. The warehouse would be largely funded by financial institutions: Banks, MDBs, donors, etc

2. Assuming that, the trustee/servicer in-houses the warehouse line

3. The developer creates the SPV to house project and capitalizes the SPV

4. The developer builds projects and signs O&M service agreement with the customer

5. The warehouse entity lends the project (SPV)

6. Customers make PPA payments to the SPV. The SPV then makes payments to warehouse to service debt

7. The trustee would payback return to the investor in the warehouse line entity

The proponents of the Facility are in discussions with potential investors and donors to take it forward. Once investors commit capital to the Facility, further work will be done on standardizing the power purchase agreement and loan documents, developing term sheets and prospectus, and selecting developers, customers and projects. This Facility needs around $100 million of capital during the pilot stage from different classes of investors, including banks, development finance institutions and multilateral development banks. This includes $30 million in concessional loans to reduce the cost of funding for rooftop solar projects. In addition, the Facility may need an external credit guarantee from donors.

The Facility has two phases: the aggregation phase and the securitization phase.

The aggregation phase involves building a warehouse line of credit that provides loans to creditworthy rooftop solar projects. The credit line will be available for 24 months, and during this time approved developers and aggregators submit projects. The developer then builds the projects, and signs power purchase agreements (PPAs) with the customers and operations and maintenance agreements with service providers. PPA payments would be used to pay back the investors in the warehouse line of credit. Project developers can draw dividends or redeploy returns as long as they meet certain debt covenants.

The securitization phase includes refinancing the warehouse line of credit by issuing asset-backed security bonds to domestic institutional investors, domestic lenders, or international investors (if currency risk can be managed by the implementing agency). The asset-backed security bond will be securitized against the loan pool. The proceeds from the securitization can be used to pay back the outstanding loans.

In some cases, financial institutions may join forces with a company that wants to raise money to scale up a specific area of business, but for which factors like small company size and large numbers of customers with little or no credit history would make direct access to debt capital markets impossible. In the case of renewable or sustainable energy, for example, this might include a company that provides equipment to customers at reduced or zero up-front cost and receives payment over time for the cost of the equipment as well as any other services provided. This type of funding might be particularly important for a green sector such as off-grid energy generation or energy efficiency provision.

QUICK QUESTION

How can securitization solve the challenge of helping small projects to access finance from large institutional investors?

Key concepts

In this chapter we considered:

- the role of the debt capital markets, and the range of debt products available to green finance investors;
- the main types and features of green bonds, including green sukuk;
- the Green Bond Principles, and how these and other frameworks, standards and guidelines can support the development of the green bond market;
- how asset-backed securities may be used to securitize loans supporting smaller green finance projects, helping these attract capital from institutional investors.

Now go back through this chapter and make sure you fully understand each point.

Review

Debt capital markets play a vital role in allocating capital to finance solutions for environmental, climate change and transition challenges. They can also help investors diversify and manage risk in their portfolio and integrate responsible and ethical investment approaches. Bonds are the largest single asset class in the financial system, with a current value of around $100 trillion. Their importance has increased as capital requirements on bank lending have tightened and equity markets are raising less new capital.

Debt capital is particularly appropriate for financing many green and sustainable projects, particularly those involving renewable energy, because the majority of project costs are incurred upfront, during construction, and ongoing, marginal costs are low. This contrasts with thermal power generation projects, where marginal costs are high relative to construction costs, due to the costs of ongoing fossil fuel inputs.

Green bonds are those where the proceeds raised are allocated to environmental projects or uses, including renewable energy projects, transport infrastructure, sustainable buildings, flood defences, or sustainable forestry and agriculture. Sub-categories of green bonds include climate bonds and blue bonds. Sustainability bonds are similar to green bonds except that proceeds may be used for a wider range of social purposes, often linked to the UN SDGs. Green sukuk are Sharia-compliant financial instruments similar to green bonds.

Beginning in 2007, in recent years the green bond market has developed rapidly, with more than $230 billion of issuance in 2018. To date, corporate, municipal and sovereign issuers from nearly 50 countries have issued green bonds. Green bond indices and funds have developed to improve the visibility of green bonds to investors, and encourage secondary market trading. Investor appetite is high, with high levels of oversubscription for many green bond issuances. The green sukuk market is at an earlier stage of development.

Progress achieved so far in developing the green bond market has been significant, but challenges to further scaling up the green bond market remain. Some green bonds carry a recognized label and/or certification that enables investors to better understand how the proceeds are used, while others may be marketed as green but not carry a specific label (this may or may not in fact indicate a lesser degree or quality of environmental benefit).

As the green bond market develops, so does the risk of greenwashing, as issuers seek to take advantage of investor demand for issues labelled as green. A number of initiatives exist to develop credible, verifiable and generally accepted market standards to ensure market integrity and transparency, the most prominent of which are the Green Bond Principles.

Asset-backed securities are a type of debt product where an issuer (often, but not always, a financial institution) makes (or buys) a range of loans that finance green projects or enterprises, bundles together the revenues from those loans and issues securities that are backed by that income. Securitization, although by no means limited to the green finance sector, can help smaller projects and borrowers access capital from large institutional investors that might otherwise not be available.

Glossary

Asset-backed securities: A type of debt product where an issuer bundles together a range of loans, securitizes the revenues from those loans and issues securities backed by that income.

Blue bond: A sub-category of green bonds designed to support sustainable marine and fisheries projects.

Climate Bonds Standard: Developed by the Climate Bonds Initiative to provide a range of sector-specific definitions for the 'green' use of bond proceeds. Issuers may seek certification against the Climate Bonds Standard to reassure investors of a bond's green credentials.

Climate bonds: A sub-category of green bonds where the proceeds are used to finance projects for climate change mitigation or adaptation.

Debt capital markets: The business of issuing, managing and trading in loans and bonds.

EU Taxonomy for Sustainable Activities: Published in June 2020, the Taxonomy defines and classifies green and sustainable activities, providing a framework for other aspects of the EU's Action Plan: Financing Sustainable Growth.

Green Bond Index: Brings together a range of green bonds to enable investors to gain exposure to the sector from a potentially diverse range of issuers.

Green Bond Principles: Published by the International Capital Markets Association, the GDPs are voluntary process guidelines for green bond issuance that recommend transparency and disclosure in seeking to promote integrity in the green bond market.

Green bonds: Bonds where the proceeds raised are allocated to environmental uses or projects (includes climate bonds).

Green sukuk: A sharia-compliant bond where the proceeds are used to support projects with environmentally focused outcomes.

Project bonds: Bonds backed by a green project's (or projects') assets and balance sheet(s) only, rather than by an issuer's whole balance sheet.

Sustainability bond: Similar to green bonds, with the difference that proceeds are used to fund not only green, but also a wider range of projects intended to have positive social outcomes, often linked to the UN's Sustainable Development Goals.

Notes

1. McKinsey Center for Business and Environment (2016) *Financing Change: How to mobilize private-sector financing for sustainable infrastructure* [Online] http://newclimateeconomy.report/2015/wp-content/uploads/sites/3/2016/01/Financing_change_How_to_mobilize_private-sector_financing_for_sustainable-_infrastructure.pdf (archived at https://perma.cc/GZZ6-M73V)
2. Climate Bonds Initiative (nd) [Online] https://www.climatebonds.net (archived at https://perma.cc/BLZ2-DZVZ)
3. MTA (2016) MTA to issue its first 'Green Bonds' [Online] http://www.mta.info/news-bonds-green-bonds-mta/2016/02/10/mta-issue-its-first-%E2%80%98green-bonds%E2%80%99 (archived at https://perma.cc/8A9P-N2XS)

4 M Jun, C Kamiker, S Kidney and N Pfaff (2016) *Green Bonds: Country experiences, barriers and options*, UNEP [Online] http://unepinquiry.org/wp-content/uploads/2016/09/6_Green_Bonds_Country_Experiences_Barriers_and_Options.pdf (archived at https://perma.cc/RN5L-6RDV)

5 Climate Bonds Initiative (2018) Green bonds market summary: Q1 2018 [Online] https://www.climatebonds.net/resources/reports/green-bonds-market-summary-q1-2018 (archived at https://perma.cc/TH36-ZNFM)

6 S&P Dow Jones Indices (nd) S&P Green Bond Index [Online] https://www.spglobal.com/spdji/en/indices/fixed-income/sp-green-bond-index/#overview (archived at https://perma.cc/N37Q-G8QN)

7 Climate Bonds Initiative (nd) Standard [Online] https://www.climatebonds.net/standard (archived at https://perma.cc/FR68-MLWB)

8 HSBC (2017) HSBC issues world's first corporate sustainable development bond [Online] https://www.hsbc.com/media/media-releases/2017/hsbc-issues-worlds-first-corporate-sustainable-development#:~:text=The%20new%20bond%20builds%20on,financing%20and%20investment%20by%202025 (archived at https://perma.cc/2PEP-B43F)

9 UN Environment (2017) *Green Finance Progress Report* [Online] https://wedocs.unep.org/bitstream/handle/20.500.11822/21608/Green_Finance_Progress_Report_2017.pdf (archived at https://perma.cc/TMS8-36AL)

10 A Whiley (2017) An oil and gas bond we knew would come eventually: Repsol – Good on GBPs, not so sure on green credentials, Climate Bonds Initiative [Online] https://www.climatebonds.net/2017/05/oil-gas-bond-we-knew-would-come-eventually-repsol-good-gbps-not-so-sure-green-credentials (archived at https://perma.cc/64HS-F6S8)

11 For example, https://www.bloomberg.com/news/articles/2017-05-22/first-green-bonds-sold-by-an-oil-giant-find-willing-investors (archived at https://perma.cc/X9NW-9894)

12 ICMA (2018) *Green Bond Principles* [Online] https://www.icmagroup.org/assets/documents/Regulatory/Green-Bonds/Green-Bonds-Principles-June-2018-270520.pdf (archived at https://perma.cc/P9VC-6FNW)

13 ICMA (2018) *Green Bond Principles* [Online] https://www.icmagroup.org/assets/documents/Regulatory/Green-Bonds/Green-Bonds-Principles-June-2018-270520.pdf (archived at https://perma.cc/P9VC-6FNW)

14 B Caldecott (2017) Despite the best of intentions green 'use of proceeds' bonds are a distraction and a false hope, *The Economist* [Online] http://perspectives.eiu.com/financial-services/despite-best-intentions-green-'use-proceeds'-bonds-are-distraction-and-false-hope (archived at https://perma.cc/G8GL-67CT)

15 Climate Bonds Initiative (nd) Standard [Online] https://www.climatebonds.net/standard (archived at https://perma.cc/BLZ2-DZVZ)

16 Climate Bonds Initiative (nd) Standard [Online] https://www.climatebonds.net/standard (archived at https://perma.cc/FR68-MLWB)

17 European Commission (2018) Action Plan: Financing Sustainable Growth [Online] https://eur-lex.europa.eu/legal-content/EN/TXT/?uri=CELEX:52018DC0097 (archived at https://perma.cc/6YKG-82RF)

18 Climate Bonds Initiative (2016) *China Green Bond Market 2016* [Online] https://www.climatebonds.net/resources/reports/china-green-bond-market-2016 (archived at https://perma.cc/G2JD-WV64)

19 M Jun, C Kamiker, S Kidney and N Pfaff (2016) *Green Bonds: Country experiences, barriers and options*, UNEP [Online] http://unepinquiry.org/wp-content/uploads/2016/09/6_Green_Bonds_Country_Experiences_Barriers_and_Options.pdf (archived at https://perma.cc/RN5L-6RDV)

20 D Chesebrough, E Feller, T Grabski, A Miller and M Paty (2016) *2016 Report on Progress*, Sustainable Stock Exchanges Initiative [Online] http://www.sseinitiative.org/wp-content/uploads/2012/03/SSE-Report-on-Progress-2016.pdf (archived at https://perma.cc/8SDS-8C7H)

21 M Jun, C Kamiker, S Kidney and N Pfaff (2016) *Green Bonds: Country experiences, barriers and options*, UNEP [Online] http://unepinquiry.org/wp-content/uploads/2016/09/6_Green_Bonds_Country_Experiences_Barriers_and_Options.pdf (archived at https://perma.cc/RN5L-6RDV)

22 Climate Finance Lab (nd) Rooftop solar private sector financing facility [Online] https://www.climatefinancelab.org/project/rooftop-solar-private-sector-financing-facility/ (archived at https://perma.cc/EZV7-M8CD)

08

Central and development banks

LEARNING OBJECTIVES

On completion of this chapter you should be able to:

- Understand the role of central banks and development banks (national and multilateral) in relation to green finance.
- Describe how central banks assess and seek to manage the risks to financial stability posed by climate change, and support the transition to a low-carbon economy.
- Describe how development banks play a key role in promoting sustainable economic development, and the key products and services they provide in order to do so.
- Cite examples and case studies of central and development banks supporting green finance.

In Chapter 6 we distinguished between four types of banks: retail banks; wholesale and investment banks; development banks; and central banks; these last two being public rather than private institutions. Central banks play key roles in ensuring financial stability and in shaping the regulatory landscape of financial services. Development banks are a major promoter of economic development. Given the very significant risks to the financial system posed by climate change and the transition to a low-carbon economy, along with the need to support sustainable economic development in many parts of the world, both types of banks have a keen interest in green finance in order to contribute to the achievement of public policy objectives.

The role of central banks

Central banks (sometimes referred to as reserve banks) are institutions that oversee the financial system and monetary regime of a country. In most developed countries, central banks are publicly owned, but institutionally independent from the government. Examples of central banks include the US Federal Reserve, the Bank of England, the European Central Bank and the People's Bank of China.

A central bank is not a commercial bank – it is usually not possible for a member of the public to open an account at a central bank or ask for a loan. The role of central banks has varied widely throughout history, but modern central banks typically have two key roles:

- **Monetary policy:** Issue of banknotes and coins, and the conduct of monetary policy to ensure stable prices and confidence in the currency. Many countries have an inflation target that is often set by the government for a central bank to achieve. Setting base interest rates is the main action by central banks in conducting monetary policy.
- **Financial stability:** Supervision of the financial system, with supervisory and regulatory powers to ensure the solvency of member institutions, avoid bank runs, and prevent reckless or fraudulent behaviour by member banks. Also acting as 'lender of last resort' to the banking sector during times of financial crisis.

In some countries, central banks also have wider economic objectives, such as supporting full employment, promoting economic growth and/or maintaining exchange rate stability.

Since the 2007/08 global financial crisis, central banks in advanced economies have expanded their range of tools, and in some of the countries affected most by the crisis they have played a more interventionist role in the economy. This includes the use of quantitative easing to achieve monetary policy objectives and macroprudential policy to achieve financial stability objectives:

- **Quantitative easing (QE):** An unconventional form of monetary policy where a central bank creates new money electronically to buy financial assets like government bonds, thereby aiming to directly increase private sector spending in the economy and return inflation to target.

- **Macroprudential policy:** To prevent the excessive build-up of systemic risk in the financial system resulting from factors such as asset price bubbles or excessive risk-taking by banks. Examples of macroprudential policies include restrictions on certain types of lending, or increased capital requirements for certain types of assets.

QUICK QUESTION

In what ways do you think the activities of central banks could affect the natural environment?

The expanding role of central banks in recent years has triggered a debate about their mandates and objectives, including their role in relation to climate change and environmental outcomes. By intervening directly in financial markets with policies like quantitative easing, central banks arguably may be inadvertently supporting high-carbon industries.

CASE STUDY

Printing money, burning carbon? Why QE may be stimulating more than just the money markets[1]

New research suggests corporate bond purchases by central banks may be inadvertently backing carbon-intensive sectors.

Central banks may be inadvertently prolonging the life of the high-carbon economy, according to new research suggesting measures used by the bodies to stimulate growth may work in favour of polluting market incumbents.

The research, by the Grantham Research Institute on Climate Change and the Environment at the LSE, suggests quantitative easing (QE) – where a central bank creates new money to buy assets and drive wider spending in the economy – may be supporting high-carbon sectors of the economy at the expense of greener alternatives.

The paper looks specifically at a subsector of QE – the purchase of corporate bonds, introduced by the Bank of England (BoE) and the European Central Bank (ECB) last year in a bid to prompt more lending activity in the economy. Although it still represents a relatively small sub-sector of QE programmes, the majority of which are delivered through the purchase of public assets such as gilts, the corporate bond buying programmes of the ECB and the BoE send an important message of confidence in certain sectors to the wider financial market.

According to the report, 62.1 per cent of the ECB's corporate bond purchases under its €82 billion corporate bond purchase programme have been in the manufacturing and utilities sectors, despite the fact they only make up 18 per cent of the Eurozone economy. These sectors produce 58.5 per cent of greenhouse gas emissions in the Eurozone.

Meanwhile, under the BoE £10 billion corporate bond programme, 49.2 per cent of purchases have been made in utilities and manufacturing, where they make up 11.8 per cent of the UK economy and produce 52 per cent of the country's greenhouse gas emissions.

Neither of the central banks has purchased any bonds representing renewable energy companies, whereas oil and gas companies make up 8.4 per cent of ECB corporate bond purchases and 1.8 per cent of BoE corporate bond purchases.

The findings are at odds with the public stance taken by BoE governor Mark Carney, who gave a highly influential speech in 2015 on the risks from climate change's 'tragedy of the horizon' and has urged corporates to be more transparent about their assessment criteria for climate risk.

'This strategy is in direct contradiction with, and may undermine, the signals that financial regulators are making about the risks associated with high-carbon investments and the impact on market efficiency,' the report notes. 'While monetary policy cannot be a substitute for environmental policy, monetary policymakers should be mindful of the impacts on asset pricing, including risks to market efficiency and financial stability.'

The report also points to evidence of a 'disproportionate jump' in the price of eligible assets after the introduction of central bank corporate bond purchasing programmes. This could 'exacerbate existing mispricing' around high-carbon sectors, it warns.

But the QE programmes are meant to be sector neutral to avoid market distortions, and despite warning the wider financial sector of the potential impact of climate change, the central banks have to date maintained that intervening more directly to support the low-carbon transition is outside of their apolitical mandate.

Therefore, their corporate bond choices are made using a strict set of criteria, explains Sini Matikainen, a policy analyst at the Grantham Research Institute and lead author of the report.

'[Buying] corporate bonds is already restricted to certain companies that are issuing corporate bonds. So that already restricts the sectors. Then both banks set an eligibility criteria: that they want to buy something that is investment grade, with a very high credit rating and a certain maturity. So that restricts it as well. And then they take out [the] financial sector because they don't want to be seen as preferentially buying from the financial sector, so they get rid of the bank bonds and so on. So at every stage it takes some corporations out.'

'To a certain extent this is a structural problem – it doesn't appear to be a deliberate attempt by the central banks to focus on manufacturing and utilities,' she concludes.

Added to that, central banks can only purchase available issuances – if there simply aren't the green bond issuances on the market for example, the central bank can't buy.

In response to the report, a spokesperson for the ECB insisted that it is not practically possible for the central bank to start embedding non-monetary policy considerations into its QE corporate bond programme.

'The ECB does not favour specific sectors, it roughly "buys the market",' they said in a statement. 'Given the relatively small size of the euro area corporate bond market, it is not possible to embed non-monetary policy considerations into a large-scale asset purchase programme that is carried out as [a] temporary monetary policy measure over a relatively short time period. They would limit the effectiveness of the programme. A number of assets that are classified as "green bonds" are eligible for the CSPP and have also been purchased by the Eurosystem.'

But Matikainen insists there are measures the central banks can implement without taking direct measures to favour bond purchases in low-carbon sectors.

First, the system currently favours incumbents – the established companies with strong investment histories and good credit ratings that easily meet the central banks' criteria. The central banks could work with other institutions to lend a hand to some of the smaller market insurgents, which low-carbon firms tend to be, to help them clear criteria hurdles larger counterparts sail through.

'We'd like to see the central banks seeing themselves as working with and in collaboration with these other institutions,' she explains. 'If you have a new [renewable energy] company that would like to issue corporate bonds but it can't get the appropriate credit rating because it doesn't have enough credit history or there is uncertainty about the future direction of renewable energy prices, it might be that instead of lowering the eligibility criteria that requires intervention from someone else.'

Matikainen continues: 'So one thing that we mention in the paper is that the European Investment Bank has this project bond investment enhancement tool, which is used to actually increase the credit rating of project bonds. So it could be that you realize there is this skew towards manufacturing and utilities which reflect[s] an overall problem in the financial sector, it could be that the real problem is coming from other areas but it requires some kind of awareness or coordination.'

Such tools could be used to enhanced the credit rating of green projects, she suggested.

To kick this off, the paper calls for the central banks to initiate reviews into their processes to assess the climate impact. The mere act of opening up the discussion on the problem may prompt a much wider awareness of an inherent bias in the system that institutions can collaborate to address, it suggests.

Should the integration of corporate bonds into QE continue in the long term, incorporating climate risk into the eligibility criteria may be an option, particularly now ratings agencies are beginning to do the same and more climate disclosure data is starting to feed through onto the open market.

'By mainstreaming climate considerations into their day-to-day operations and disclosing their approach to transitional risk, central banks would send a strong signal to financial markets and begin to address their own "tragedy of the horizon",' the report suggests.

The paper makes clear that any bias towards high-carbon bond purchases is the result of a set of stringent eligibility criteria that inadvertently favour market incumbents. But the unintended consequences of such corporate bond QE programmes deserve to be investigated more fully, particularly when central banks are beginning to take more of a leadership position in the climate debate. The carbon impact of QE may seem like an obscure topic, but if we aren't careful we may find we are using new money to prop up old, polluting industries.

With responsibility for overseeing financial stability, central banks have a particularly important impact on the way in which banks respond to the physical and transition risks associated with climate change. Even where environmental objectives are not part of a central bank's explicit mandate, the incorporation of sustainability factors may be relevant in order to ensure material risks facing the financial system are identified, disclosed and managed, to achieve price stability and/or safeguard financial stability.

Moreover, with responsibility for overseeing and regulating the creation and allocation of money and credit, central banks can have a particularly important impact on the speed at which the greening of the financial system takes place by incentivizing or directing resources from traditional carbon-intensive sectors towards green investment.

Central banks can (and do) act independently of each other, but often work in a coordinated manner to achieve their objectives, particularly in regard to financial stability. One of the key bodies through which this coordination occurs is the **Financial Stability Board** (FSB), which is comprised of central banks, public international financial institutions (eg World Bank) and international standard-setting organizations. The FSB seeks to strengthen financial systems and promote international financial stability by coordinating the development of strong regulatory, supervisory and other financial sector policies, as well as encouraging consistency in the implementation of these.

The FSB has played a key role in highlighting the risks of climate change to international and national financial stability. In 2015 the FSB established the Task Force on Climate-related Financial Disclosures (TCFD) (introduced in earlier chapters and covered extensively elsewhere in this book, most notably in Chapter 5) to develop recommendations for a consistent international approach to the identification, disclosure and management of climate-related financial risk. The TCFD published its recommendations in 2017, and there has been substantial encouragement and pressure from FSB members in financial institutions and others in their national jurisdictions to adopt the TCFD's disclosure recommendations. By June 2019, over 800 publicly listed firms with a combined market capitalization of more than $8 trillion had pledged to adopt the recommendations.

Some FSB members have begun to consider the inclusion of climate change scenarios in stress tests, which assess the resilience of financial institutions' (usually banks' and insurers') balance sheets to significant shocks. The Banco Central do Brasil, for example, has required banks to conduct stress tests that simulate the impact of climate change on their balance sheets since 2016.[2] The People's Bank of China introduced a green element to its Macro-Prudential Assessments in 2018.[3] Mark Carney, when Governor of the Bank of England (and, until 2018, FSB Chair), proposed in December 2018 the introduction of climate change scenarios in UK bank stress testing. This would go further than current consideration of physical risks (eg the impact of extreme weather events on residential and commercial loan portfolios) already undertaken by banks and model the potential impacts of the transition to a low-carbon economy under different scenarios, adjusted for factors including different rates and levels of global warming and transition speed. As more FSB members adopt this approach, peer pressure and the desire for a coordinated approach to international financial stability will likely see the introduction of climate risk stress testing globally.

In 2017, eight central banks launched the **Network for Greening the Financial System** to provide a more focused forum for sharing best practice and enhancing consistency of approaches. By 2019, the Network had grown to 36 member institutions, representing economies accounting for more than half of global carbon emissions.

Central banks are certainly playing an increasingly active role in supporting the greening of the financial system and addressing the risks posed by climate change. While some central banks are more advanced in this area than others, there has been a general recalibration of traditional tools used by central banks in support of their monetary policy and financial stability objectives (eg credit guidance policies, prudential regulation and supervision) in support of green finance. A number of new instruments have been created to support environmental objectives, which may be divided broadly into four categories:

- green credit allocation instruments that aim to encourage the flow of credit to green sectors;
- green macroprudential instruments for safeguarding financial stability;
- microprudential regulation and firm supervision;
- developing green finance guidelines and frameworks.

Credit allocation instruments

Credit allocation policies, also known as credit guidance policies, direct the creation and allocation of credit towards certain industries or sectors. Historically, credit allocation policies have been used by central banks in advanced and developing countries to guide lending to prioritized sectors deemed essential for economic development. More recently, these policies have been used in some countries to direct credit towards green areas and away from environmentally harmful activities. Today, three main policy instruments are being employed to direct credit towards the green economy.

Firstly, targeted refinancing lines offer central bank finance to commercial banks at reduced interest rates for specified asset classes. In contrast to outright subsidies, they rely on the private sector as a gatekeeper in the allocation of capital. The default risk remains with the banking sector. Targeted refinancing lines have been a common policy tool used by many central banks in emerging and developing economies since the 1950s, and more recently they have been used to direct credit towards green areas in countries such as Bangladesh and China, which introduced low-cost funding to banks (reduced interest rates) to stimulate green lending in 2017.

CASE STUDY

Bangladesh Bank[4]

Bangladesh Bank has created refinancing lines at preferential terms for green loans. Green refinancing lines were launched in 2009 as a revolving refinancing scheme to promote green finance amounting to BDT 2 billion ($25 million) under which Bangladesh Bank refunds commercial banks at a reduced interest rate for loans extended to six specific products. The initial focus of the refinancing lines has been on solar energy, biogas, and waste-treatment projects but has subsequently been expanded and today covers 47 items that are eligible for preferential rediscounting at the central bank. These green refinancing lines are part of a broader refinancing policy initiative that includes priority sectors such as agriculture and garment exporters.

In addition, in February 2015 Bangladesh Bank announced its intention to create a new longer-term refinance window to provide $500 million of funding, of which $200 million will be allocated specifically for green initiatives including water and energy efficiency measures in the textiles industry.

Second, mandatory or minimum credit quotas require banks to allocate a fixed percentage of their loan portfolio to a specified sector. They are also called credit floors, lending requirements, and window guidance. Minimum credit quotas are most often implemented in the form of a priority sector lending programme, where the central bank determines minimum credit quotas and requires commercial banks to lend a specific percentage of their overall lending to specific sectors. Maximum credit ceilings or quotas are used to limit bank lending to less economically desirable sectors or industries of the economy. Whereas minimum credit quotas might be applied to areas such as renewable energy projects, maximum credit quotas could limit lending to carbon-intensive sectors. Quotas have been deployed in some countries, including Bangladesh and India, in order to direct credit towards green sectors.

CASE STUDY

Reserve Bank of India[5]

The Reserve Bank of India's Priority Sector Lending Programme (PSL) has the objective of allocating credit to vulnerable sections of society. The PSL has traditionally focused on enabling access to finance for agriculture, infrastructure, education and micro, small, and medium enterprises (MSMEs), and ensures that 40 per cent of commercial bank lending flows to priority sectors.

In 2012 the RBI reviewed the priority sectors and concluded that access to clean energy should be added. It mandated that loans for off-grid renewable energy solutions, including solar and other clean energy solutions, should be included in the PSL.

Another way for a central bank to influence credit allocation is the use of differentiated reserve requirements. The reserve requirement ratio is the share of reserves that banks must hold in reserve relative to total assets. Reserve requirements have a significant impact on banks' ability to create credit. If the central bank lowers reserve requirements, banks can increase their lending. Allowing lower required reserve rates for certain green assets is one way of incentivizing credit allocation towards green sectors. In 2018, the People's Bank of China announced that it would accept green bonds as eligible collateral in its medium-term lending facility, allowing those financial institutions posting green bonds to increase their lending.[6]

CASE STUDY

Banque du Liban[7]

In 2010, the Banque du Liban, the central bank of Lebanon, exempted banks from part of the required reserve requirement for certain projects related to renewable energy production and energy efficiency in buildings. The Banque du Liban supports the provision of credit to these areas by lowering the reserve requirements of commercial banks by an amount of 100–150 per cent of the loan value if the bank's customer can provide a certificate from the Lebanese Center for Energy Conservation that confirms the energy savings potential of the financed project.

Macroprudential regulation

Since the global financial crisis, central banks in advanced economies have introduced macroprudential policy that aims to prevent the excessive build-up of systemic risk in the financial system. Typically, this is used to suppress credit to certain sectors where excessive lending may pose risks to financial stability, such as real estate. Examples of macroprudential tools include decreasing loan-to-value and loan-to-income ratios for loans.

Some analysts, including the UNEP Inquiry into the Design of a Sustainable Financial System, have explored how macroprudential policy could be used to guide credit towards the green economy, for example by imposing higher risk weightings for carbon-intensive sectors or firms, or by providing a green supporting factor in favour of green assets.

In December 2017 the EU Commission announced, in the context of its Financing Sustainable Growth Action Plan, that it was considering the introduction of a green supporting factor and would lower bank capital requirements for environmentally friendly investments in a bid to boost the green economy and meet its target of cutting carbon emissions by 40 per cent by 2030. Capital relief might be granted, for instance, for green mortgages. More detail on the EU Commission's proposals are outlined in the case study 'Green doesn't mean risk-free' below.

The converse of green supporting factors penalties (eg higher capital weightings) for brown assets such as coal are also proposed by some. In many cases, however, it is much more difficult politically to introduce a penalty on legacy assets and investments than to encourage investment in new, green assets.

CASE STUDY

Green doesn't mean risk-free: why we should be cautious about a green supporting factor in the EU[8]

The European Commission announced this week that the EU is considering lowering capital requirements for sustainable financial products. This means that in future, EU financial regulators would treat green investments as less risky than carbon-intensive investments. So banks would need to hold less capital to buffer themselves against potential losses. The announcement comes as part of the Commission's efforts to support sustainable finance and take action on climate change.

Creating incentives for banks and financial markets to make investments in green assets sounds advantageous for the green economy. However, using regulations designed to reduce risk in the financial system to mobilize investment should be approached cautiously.

A green supporting factor would mean banks have less buffer against losses

In their July 2017 report the High Level Expert Group on Sustainable Finance (HLEG), which reports to the Commission on the opportunities and challenges of sustainable finance, raised the possibility of a green supporting factor. The regulation is designed to boost green investment but the HLEG noted multiple drawbacks.

The amount of risk banks have to factor in when making different types of investments is called risk-weighting. A higher risk-weighting means a bank needs to have more capital to insulate it from potential losses if an investment fails. These regulations are designed to make banks more resilient. Their aim is to avoid another financial crisis where governments have to bail out banks to keep them from failing.

A green supporting factor would mean banks need to hold less capital when making green investments because those investments would have a lower risk-weighting. The Commission hopes that this would encourage sustainable investment, because some European banks have responded to higher capital requirements by reducing lending.

Some banks have been lobbying for the Commission to cut risk-weightings for green assets rather than increase them for carbon-intensive ones, because requiring them to hold more capital to buffer risks can lower their profits. But with less loss-absorbing capital, banks will also be more vulnerable if their investments fail.

Using risk-weightings to motivate investment should be approached with caution.

Green isn't necessarily safer than brown

In the long term, the shift to a low-carbon economy means there will be significant changes to areas like energy generation. As with every kind of technological shift, there will be winners and losers in low-carbon sectors and in carbon-intensive ones, and it's not easy to predict who will be the winners.

For instance, since 2015, more than 200 North American oil and gas companies have declared bankruptcy (mainly due to low oil prices), but so have more than 100 American and European solar companies between 2011 and 2015. In contrast, oil majors like Shell and Exxon Mobil have weathered low oil prices by increasing production efficiency and reducing overhead costs. The shift to low-carbon energy generation will have wider-reaching effects than low oil prices. Some companies may be able to adapt by diversifying their business operations. So it is not a foregone conclusion that the oil and gas sector will disappear, particularly as oil and gas will continue to be part of the energy mix during the transition to low-carbon energy.

In the announcement the Vice President of the European Commission mentioned housing as one of the first areas that could qualify for lower risk-weighting. Efficient homes have lower energy costs. In theory by spending less on energy, green home-owners are better able to repay their mortgage. This makes the risk of them defaulting on payments lower. However, there is little empirical evidence for this – just one study from the US. The lack of evidence suggests it is premature to conclude that green mortgages are categorically lower risk than standard mortgages. More data and research in the EU is needed, and we should be particularly cautious since European banks may already be exposed to risk from overheated property markets.

The case for a brown-penalizing factor is stronger. The financial sector is likely not properly taking account of the climate change risks associated with carbon-intensive assets. Increasing the risk banks need to account for in making carbon-intensive investments could go some way towards correcting this. However, there is still considerable debate about what the right level of risk-weighting would be. There is also discussion of whether other policy tools would be better suited to addressing the risk. More research is needed before moving to concrete policy proposals.

There is no clear evidence that lowering risk-weightings will encourage greater investment

Although the primary purpose of risk-weighting is to reduce the exposure of banks to risk, the Commission has used risk-weighting to try to encourage investment in the past. However, there's no clear evidence that reducing capital requirements on investing in green assets will boost lending to green projects.

The European Commission introduced a 'Small to Medium Enterprise (SME) supporting factor' to decrease the risk-weighting for loans to SMEs. The aim was to encourage banks to lend more. However, there is little evidence that the SME supporting factor has been effective. The European Banking Authority's initial assessment of the policy did not find evidence that it had significantly decreased borrowing costs or increased access to finance for SMEs.

In addition, interviews carried out by the University of Cambridge Institute for Sustainability Leadership with regulators and bank practitioners found that capital requirements only had a marginal impact on investment decisions for green projects. Other studies support the view that capital requirements do not significantly constrain bank lending across the economy.

Without robust evidence for a green supporting factor, the Commission and HLEG should look for other avenues to increase green investment

Giving in to bank lobbying could send the wrong signal to the financial sector. By supporting an unproven regulatory tool without a robust evidence-base, the European Commission could risk damaging the reputation of the concept of sustainable finance as a whole.

Instead of trying to increase the flow of finance towards green assets by hook or by crook, increasing investment should be approached in the light of existing evidence. Regulators can increase the resilience of the financial system through better understanding of climate risks. The HLEG should focus on identifying the most effective policies to scale up green finance, rather than the most politically palatable or convenient ones.

Microprudential regulation and firm supervision

Microprudential regulation is the supervision of individual financial institutions to ensure that they are resilient and solvent. Central banks are often financial regulators too and are responsible for supervising financial institutions in their respective jurisdictions.

The identification and disclosure of climate risks and stranded assets in the supervisory practice of central banks and financial regulators is of significant importance and has encouraged (and required) action from the firms they supervise.

The EU's Solvency II Directive, for example, sets requirements for the capital that EU insurers must hold against risks that might result in insolvency. In the UK, the implementation of Solvency II is overseen by the Prudential Regulation Authority (PRA),which requires that every insurer and reinsurer conducts a Risk and Solvency Assessment (ORSA) and submits this for approval in order to be licensed to operate. In 2015, the PRA noted that climate change may have a substantial impact on insurers, on both the liability and asset sides of their balance sheets. While in the short term physical risks were the most likely to impact these, in the longer term transition and liability risks could also have a significant impact, particularly if climate change increased the impairment and stranding of assets. Consideration of the identification and disclosure of such risks needs to be included, therefore, in ORSAs, encouraging insurers and reinsurers to hold capital against, and do more to accurately price, such risks.

In China, the People's Bank of China (central bank), together with other regulators, announced a series of policy measures in 2016 that were designed to promote a greener financial system. These included the introduction of mandatory disclosure requirements for listed companies as well as mandatory pollution (emissions) liability insurance.

As discussed in the introduction to this chapter, bank and insurer stress testing is another important tool used by regulators. After the financial crisis, many central banks introduced stress testing to model the resilience of the banking sector against certain shocks or scenarios. Currently, in most countries, these stress tests do not consider resilience to environmental factors. Some FSB members, such as the Banco Central do Brasil and the Bank of England, have or plan to introduce climate risk stress testing, and it seems likely that this will become more widely adopted over time.

CASE STUDY

Banco Central do Brasil[9]

The Banco Central do Brasil (BCB) requires banks to evaluate and consider risks to which they are exposed during the year. In assessing their capital needs, banks must demonstrate that they have covered the risk arising from exposure to social and environmental damages via stress testing.

The BCB sets the general framework, including the types of risks that a bank has to consider, and requires banks to submit an annual report to BCB outlining how they assess and calculate risks and the impact on capital adequacy.

It is probably fair to say that in many jurisdictions central banks and regulators have adopted, until recently, a tactical approach to including climate risk considerations into regulation and supervision, for the most part reacting to concerns raised by policymakers. This situation now seems to be changing as regulators adopt a more strategic, forward-looking approach designed to embed the consideration and disclosure of climate risks within financial systems, at global (eg TCFD), national and organizational level.

In the UK, for example, the PRA published a significant consultation paper in 2018, 'Enhancing banks' and insurers' approaches to managing the financial risks from climate change'.[10] This applies to all UK banks, building societies, insurers and investment firms, and sets out the regulator's expectations of how firms should approach managing climate-related financial risk, drawing heavily on the work of the TCFD. Firms and their boards are strongly encouraged to adopt a strategic approach to climate risk and to introduce a specific Senior Management Function in this area, requiring a named individual (or individuals) to be accountable for climate risk.

Firms must:

- embed the consideration of financial risks from climate change in their governance arrangements;
- incorporate financial risks from climate change into existing risk management practice;
- use long-term scenario analysis to inform strategy and risk management;
- develop an approach to disclosure on the financial risks from climate change.

At the same time, the Financial Conduct Authority (FCA) published a discussion paper on climate risk and green finance, and how these were relevant to the objectives of protecting consumers, improving market integrity and advancing competition.[11] The two regulators also announced the establishment of a Climate Financial Risk Forum to help ensure a consistent approach across the financial services sector and regulatory bodies to address and coordinate responses to these issues.

CASE STUDY

Financial regulation in the UK

Financial regulation in the UK is overseen by three main regulators:

- **Bank of England:** The Bank of England is the UK's central bank and aims to deliver monetary and financial stability by setting an interest rate that will enable the inflation target to be met. The Bank's **Financial Policy Committee** (FPC) is responsible for macroprudential regulation of the UK financial system and is charged with a primary objective of identifying, monitoring and taking action to remove or reduce systemic risks – including risks posed by climate change – with a view to protecting and enhancing the resilience of the UK financial system.

- **Prudential Regulation Authority (PRA):** The PRA, which is a subsidiary of the Bank of England, is the prudential regulator for deposit-takers, insurance companies and designated investment firms. Its primary objective is to promote the safety and soundness of those institutions authorized by the PRA by seeking to ensure that their business is carried on in a way that avoids any adverse effect on the stability of the UK financial system. Its secondary objective is facilitating effective competition in the markets for services provided by those institutions.
- **Financial Conduct Authority (FCA):** The FCA is responsible for conduct of business, effective financial markets, consumer protection and for promoting effective competition.

In June 2017 the Bank of England outlined its response to climate change. The Bank's work to assess the financial risks from climate change is focused on two primary risk factors:

- **Physical risks**, which can arise from climate-related events, such as droughts, floods and storms. The frequency and severity of these events can increase as a result of rising global temperatures.
- **Transition risks**, which can arise from the process of adjustment towards a lower-carbon economy, such as developments in climate policy, new disruptive technology or shifting investor sentiment.

The Bank's strategy for mitigating the financial risks from climate change has two core elements. The first involves engaging with regulated firms on climate-related risks through prudential supervision, including augmenting activities in insurance and beginning work in banking. The second involves enhancing the resilience of the UK financial system by engaging with initiatives to support an orderly market transition to a lower-carbon economy. This includes taking a close interest in the FSB's Task Force on Climate-related Financial Disclosures (TCFD), and co-chairing the G20 Green Finance Study Group on behalf of the United Kingdom.

Figure 8.1 The Bank of England's approach to climate change and current activities

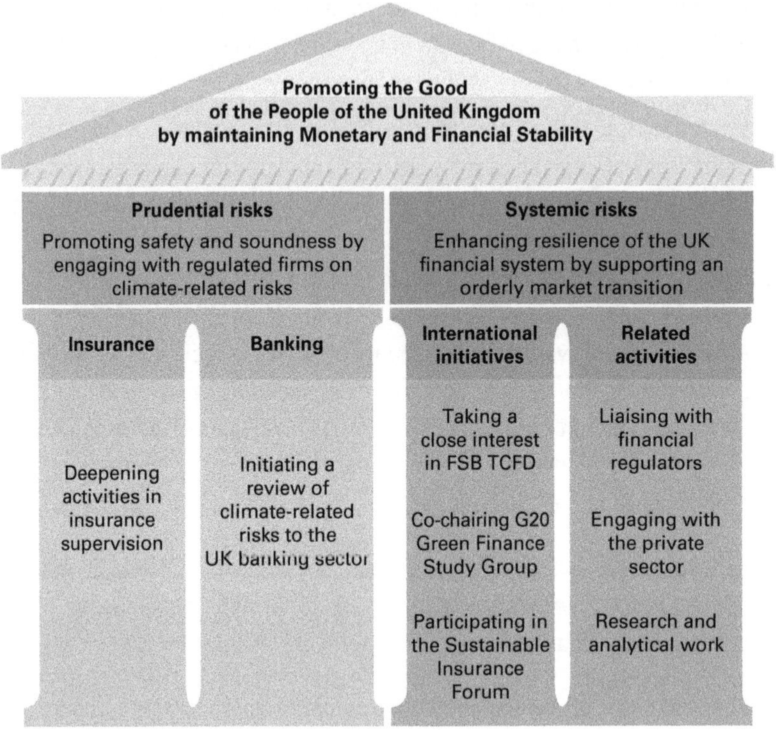

SOURCE Bank of England (2017) The Bank of England's response to climate change, *Quarterly Bulletin*, Q2. https://www.bankofengland.co.uk/-/media/boe/files/quarterly-bulletin/2017/the-banks-response-to-climate-change.pdf?la=en&hash=7DF676C781E5FAEE994C2A210A6B9EEE44879387

In addition to the two risks outlined above, the PRA has identified a third category of risk – liability risk – which is of particular relevance to insurance firms. Liability risks can arise from parties who have suffered loss or damage from the effects of climate change and who seek compensation from those they hold responsible.

The PRA has also identified a number of climate change-related opportunities for insurance firms, including new sources of premium growth, such as renewable energy project insurance, supporting resilience to climate change through risk awareness and risk transfer, investments in green bonds and providing financial sector leadership on climate change.

Guidelines and frameworks

In their role at the centre of the financial system and monetary regime, central banks are in a powerful position to promote green banking guidelines aimed at guiding banks towards greener lending. This might involve voluntary or mandatory green banking guidelines, or steps to support the development of green bond markets. We have covered many of these in previous chapters, including:

- Task Force on Climate-Related Financial Disclosures;
- Green Bond Principles;
- Green Loan Principles.

In many emerging and developing economies, industry-led and central bank-led green finance guidelines have started to emerge. There are also cases where central banks have supported industry-led initiatives by banking associations, thereby rendering them mandatory or quasi-mandatory.

CASE STUDY

The People's Bank of China

The People's Bank of China (PBoC) has become a central agent in mainstreaming green finance in China by working together with other governmental organizations on various measures to develop comprehensive green banking guidelines, as well as internationally through cooperation with the UNEP Inquiry and with other governments under the G20.

In 2006 the PBoC created a countrywide credit database for disclosing information on credit and administrative penalties, as well as information on environmental compliance of firms. In July 2007 the PBoC, the Ministry of Environmental Protection and the China Banking Regulatory Commission jointly launched China's Green Credit Policy. This was a principles-based approach which recommended that banks include environmental compliance and risk assessment as criteria to be considered in the loan origination process, with the overall aim of reallocating credit from high-polluting, energy-intensive firms towards greener projects.

In 2012 the China Banking Regulatory Commission (CBRC) issued Green Credit Guidelines which strengthened this system, and in 2014 this was complemented by a Green Credit Monitoring and Evaluation mechanism and a key Performance Indicators Checklist.

The PBoC has also been involved in the development of a green bond market, introducing the first official green bond guidelines in China in 2015.

SOURCE Volz, 2017[12]

Lastly, central banks can use their soft power to promote the development of new green market segments or products, and nurture of sustainable financial market practices. For example, by including climate and other environmental challenges on the agenda, the central bank can signal the importance of this topic to market actors and encourage them to take it seriously. Similarly, central banks are uniquely positioned to conduct research on green finance, with well-established research departments and access to market data.

The role of development banks

Development banks are public financial institutions tasked with promoting socio-economic development in a country or region. Exact definitions vary, but for the purposes of this course we use the following definition from the World Bank: 'a bank or financial institution with at least 30 per cent state-owned equity that has been given an explicit legal mandate to reach socio-economic goals in a region, sector or particular market segment'.[13] Development banks are sometimes also referred to as development financial institutions and state investment banks.

Development banks play an important role promoting economic development in both developed and developing countries by providing finance and a wide range of advisory and capacity building programmes to clients whose financial needs are not sufficiently served by private commercial banks or local capital markets. Clients typically include SMEs, large private corporations and public bodies.

Development banks vary widely in scale and can take a number of different forms:

- **Multilateral development banks (MDBs):** Supranational institutions set up by sovereign states, which are their shareholders. Their remits reflect the development and cooperation policies established by these states and often include developing countries. Examples of MDBs include the World Bank, International Finance Corporation (IFC), Asian Development Bank (ADB), African Development Bank (AfDB), Inter-American Development Bank (IDB), European Bank of Reconstruction and Development (EBRD) the European Investment Bank (EIB) and the Asian Infrastructure Investment Bank (AIIB).
- **National development banks (NDBs):** Institutions created by national governments to provide financing for the purposes of economic development in the domestic economy. Some national development banks also

provide financing for international development. NDBs tend to have in-depth local knowledge, relationships with, and understanding of, domestic policy and markets. Examples of NDBs include the China Development Bank, the German KfW and the Brazilian BNDES.

- **Export–import banks (or export credit agencies – ECAs):** Public agencies and entities that provide government-backed loans, guarantees and insurance to corporations from their home country that seek to do business overseas in developing countries and emerging markets. ECAs provide loans or guarantees and can also underwrite risks involved in investments in overseas markets. Examples of ECAs include the Export–Import Bank of China, the Export–Import Bank of the United States, and UK Export Finance.

QUICK QUESTION

In what ways do you think development banks have supported the growth of green finance?

The multilateral development banks in particular have played and continue to play key roles in the development and growth of the green finance market. Many have mitigating and adapting to climate change as key policy objectives, with the importance of this compared with other objectives (eg economic development) growing over the past decade.

The European Investment Bank, for instance, which issued the first green (Climate Awareness) bond in 2007, remains one of the world's largest issuers and offers a wide range of green finance products including loans and equity investments. By 2018, the EIB had issued green bonds totalling €23.5 billion, and in September 2018 issued the first Sustainability Awareness Bond, with proceeds earmarked for projects supporting the UN Sustainable Development Goals. In October 2019, the EIB announced that it would end the financing of all oil, gas and coal projects by the end of 2021, and align all future investment decisions with the goals of the Paris Agreement.

The Asian Development Bank (ADB) provided nearly $22 billion of climate finance between 2011 and 2017, with a focus on cleaner infrastructure and technologies, building more resilient communities and helping communities adapt to the effects of climate change. In 2018 the ADB made a commitment that, by 2030, at least 75 per cent of its activities would support climate change mitigation and adaptation, with an $80 billion fund in place to support this.

In 2016 Inter-American Development Bank (IDB) decided to nearly double its operations in the climate finance sector, setting a target for climate finance of 30 per cent of the IDB's overall portfolio by 2020, including loans, grants and equity investments. As well as investments in climate change adaptation and mitigation projects, a key focus for the IDB is capacity building, working with the region's public sector institutions, particularly finance and planning ministries, to help them develop relevant expertise to lead national climate change and resilience activities.

The African Development Bank (AfDB) is more focused on climate change adaptation and resilience than many other MDBs. Africa is not a major emitter of greenhouse gases, but many communities in Africa will be particularly impacted by climate change, whether through rising sea levels or larger tracts of land becoming uninhabitable. The AfDB has a target of 40 per cent of its overall portfolio supporting climate finance by 2020, with equal weighting given to climate change adaptation and mitigation. The AfDB has played the leading role in the development of green bonds in Africa, both through its own issues and in helping to bring other issuers to market (eg the first Nigerian green bonds).

The World Bank works alongside the other MDBs, together with countries and a wide range of other institutions to help coordinate a global response to climate change. The Bank's 2016 Action Plan specifies the organization's objective of increasing the climate finance share of its overall portfolio from 21 per cent to 28 per cent (this target was exceeded in 2018), with total financing planned to increase to approximately $29 billion by 2020. Priorities for the World Bank in the climate finance area have included renewable energy, agriculture and transport. In December 2018 new targets for the period 2021 to 2025 were announced, with approximately $200 billion earmarked for climate finance, which would double current investments in this area. There is an increased emphasis on supporting climate adaptation and resilience, which is to be given equal weighting with investments reducing emissions. This recognizes that other institutions are now playing more significant roles in this area, as well as the policy goal, aligned to the UN Sustainable Development Goals, of supporting countries and communities most impacted by climate change.

In addition to climate finance, the World Bank also plays a key role in developing innovative approaches to combating climate change, facilitating the sharing of best practice and implementing joint projects by bringing together actors from the scientific, finance, policy and other communities. The Bank has also helped to establish many of the international frameworks, organizations and networks supporting the transition to a low-carbon world, and has developed and published a wide range of tools and reports to assist organizations and policymakers with climate change and climate finance, such as the Climate and Disaster Risk Screening Tools, and Climate Adaptation Country Profiles.

While most development banks make a profit, their overarching mandate is typically not to maximize profits but to promote a wider range of economic, social and environmental goals. As the Global Wind Energy Council states:

> The main factor that distinguishes development banks from private sector lending institutions is the ability of development banks to take more risk associated with political, economic and locational aspects. Further, since they are not required to pay dividends to private stakeholders, the development banks take higher risks than commercial banks to meet various national or international 'public good' objectives. Additionally, long-term finance from the private sector for more than a ten year maturity period is not available.[14]

By virtue of their scale, ownership structures and mandates, development banks are well placed to help scale up green finance through a number of channels:

- **Facilitating access to capital:** Development banks can finance green investments directly through the provision of long-term loans and equity investments. In several countries, development banks have been the largest investors in long-term financing for large infrastructure projects involved in renewable and clean energy. Development banks can also facilitate access to capital indirectly via international climate funds public-private partnerships. For example, in 2016, according to the Climate Policy Initiative, development banks were responsible for providing $124 billion of climate finance, making up 89 per cent of the total public sources of climate finance.[15]
- **Reducing risk:** Development banks can de-risk new markets for green assets by providing targeted guarantees and first loss provision mechanisms.
- **New market standards:** Development banks can exhibit leadership through the development of new market standards and in pioneering green practice within the private sector. For example, in 2013, the European Investment Bank decided to limit the financing of coal-fired power plants through the implementation of stringent emissions limits

and the application of a shadow carbon price to energy investments. Development banks were instrumental in the establishment of green bond markets (the first green bond was issued by the European Investment Bank in 2007), and continued issuance can support the deepening of private sector expertise and familiarity with these asset classes in new markets.

- **Fill the capacity gap:** Development banks can provide technical assistance and capacity building to private sector actors in order to aid project development and reduce project risks.

CASE STUDY

Development banking for sustainability[16]

National development banks can play a decisive role in financing the Sustainable Development Goals and the transition to a low-carbon energy future. Given their size and potential, these financial institutions do not receive adequate attention in global financial or development discussions. For the sake of sustainable development, this must change.

To achieve the SDGs, the United Nations estimates that an additional $2 to 3 trillion of investment will be needed per year in energy, infrastructure, agriculture, health and education. Specifically, there remains an annual $1 trillion infrastructure financing gap, mostly in emerging economies, to be filled. Relative to a $110 trillion global economy and over $100 trillion of assets of institutional investors in the Organisation for Economic Co-operation and Development (OECD) alone, this should be manageable. Yet, the critical question remains: what are the right financial institutions to intermediate saving for sustainable investments? National-level development banks are a major part of the answer.

Development banks are financial institutions that provide long-term capital and advisory services for infrastructure projects, businesses, agriculture and other sectors whose financial needs cannot be served solely by the public sector, commercial banks or capital markets.

They are very often publicly funded, or at least initially capitalized, by public resources. They range from international institutions such as the World Bank and the Asian Development Bank, to national level organizations like the China Development Bank, to subnational institutions such as the Chicago Infrastructure Trust or the Connecticut Green Bank in the United States. As these examples suggest, development banks are policy instruments that exist both in the developed and developing world, regardless of the level of economic development.

Although much attention is given to global development banking institutions such as the recently announced Asian Infrastructure Investment Bank, I believe that national level development banking institutions will play an even more critical role in the achievement of the SDGs.

National development banks have played a crucial role in European economic development since the 19th century. In 1852 Credit Foncier and Credit Mobilier were launched in France to accelerate investments in agriculture and manufacturing. They were critical in helping Continental Europe catch up to Great Britain in the industrialization process. More recently in the 20th century, national development banks have helped former colonies to mobilize long-term investments into their economies, from China to India to Ethiopia.

National development banks come in all shapes, sizes and histories. A 2012 survey by the World Bank is quite illuminating. Out of the 90 development banks from 61 countries that responded to the survey, 39 per cent were founded between 1990 and 2011. They represented assets of over $2 trillion, with the China Development Bank, Brazil Development Bank and Kreditanstalt fuer Wiederaufbfau of Germany being larger than the World Bank itself. Over 70 per cent are fully state-owned institutions, whereas others, including the Credit Guarantee Corporation of Malaysia, have part-private ownership.

Despite the expansion of private sector investment vehicles and general deepening on financial markets, development banks remain critical for two reasons: first, the need for public-private partnerships for infrastructure investments, regardless of location, and second, the growing shortage of long-term capital from commercial banks and capital markets due to changes in regulation of pension funds and banks.

First, national development banks must lead on building robust pipelines of bankable projects for infrastructure financing. Institutional investors – namely sovereign wealth funds, insurance companies and pension funds – are looking to significantly increase exposure to infrastructure assets, but are not finding enough opportunities to do so. This is a true public policy failure of global dimensions. National development banks can serve as the critical bridge between the planning of infrastructure investments by government and the proper structuring to crowd-in private capital. They may be the only financial institution that can serve as this bridge.

Second, national development banks should guide local savings pools on how to support and invest in local sustainable development. This is a key modality that has not yet been analysed. The growing savings pools in the developing world must be used to finance domestic development, as opposed to purchasing overseas securities for the sake of diversification. National development banks should engage with domestic pension funds and insurance companies and come up with agreed-to targets for investments.

Third, national development banks should lead on the transition to a low-carbon future. For high-income countries, this means aligning investment with long-term decarbonization strategies. This includes creating new financial instruments – including more aggressive credit guarantees and risk mitigation products – that will attract private capital into low-carbon energy solutions and large-scale infrastructure. For low-income countries, this will mean aligning investment with climate adaptation plans. The growing number of green banks – ranging from the UK Green Investment Bank to the Malaysia Green Bank – shows how this can be done.

Fourth, national development banks must build a presence in the global financial and development discussions. A Global Development Banking Forum, co-chaired by the World Bank and the Asian Infrastructure Investment Bank, should be established with biannual meetings in Washington, DC and Beijing. Such an initiative would accelerate learning and idea sharing between the hundreds of national and subnational development banking institutions. The outcome of this could be tremendous.

National development banks, when structured properly, embody exactly what is needed to finance sustainable development: public-private partnership and long-term capital deployment. Neither the public nor the private financial communities can do this alone. These institutions should be re-examined and elevated in importance to support the coming transitions in our global economy.

While many MDBs and NDBs are active in the provision of green finance, over a dozen national and sub-national governments have created dedicated green development banks (GDBs) for the purpose of providing financing for green projects. According to the OECD, a green development (or investment) bank is a publicly owned entity established specifically to facilitate private investment into domestic low-carbon and climate-resilient infrastructure and other green sectors such as water and waste management.[17] These dedicated green investment entities have been established at national level (Australia, Japan, Malaysia, Switzerland, United Kingdom), state level (California, Connecticut, Hawaii, New Jersey, New York and Rhode Island in the United States), county level (Montgomery County, Maryland, United States) and city level (Masdar, United Arab Emirates). Six of the world's GDBs are now joining forces to scale up private investment to meet sustainability challenges with the launch of the new international Green Bank Network at the Paris Climate Conference.

However, GDBs are still small compared with the green portfolios of most MDBs and NDBs. For example, the European Investment Bank has set a minimum standard of allocating 25 per cent of overall lending to support climate change, equating to €20.6 billion in 2015,[18] while in the same year the German KfW invested €29.5 billion in measures to protect the environment and combat climate change, rising to nearly €33 billion in 2017.[19] In contrast, in 2015 the UK's Green Investment Bank (GIB) invested £770 million, although this amount increased to approximately £3.7 billion including additional private capital mobilized by the GIB.[20]

The products and services offered by development banks vary widely. Some only provide grants or other de-risking instruments. Others offer a wide range of financing options across all categories including loans, equity and guarantees. Many development banks combine instruments to support projects in both the pre-investment stage (grants and technical assistance) and the investment stage (risk enhancements, funding subsidies or other financial tools to attract private capital).

Concessionary loans

Concessional loans are provided at more favourable conditions than those offered by private financial institutions and can be in the form of lower interest rates, longer maturities, longer grace periods or less collateral. The degree of concessionality can be adjusted to the specific needs of a particular project, from highly concessional to just below market terms.

Concessional loans can be used to help develop new markets or policy goals as they address the high cost associated with early market entrants. Used effectively, concessional loans can pave the way for future projects in the sector to be financed on fully commercial terms. Thus, concessionary loans can be an effective way to nurture emerging green sectors.

Bespoke loan products

Many development banks have set targets around the volume of green lending. For example, the European Investment Bank set a minimum standard of allocating 25 per cent of overall lending to support climate change, while KfW has set an objective to make approximately one-third of all new investments in climate change and environmentally sustainable activities. To assist with this, some development banks have developed bespoke products or loan programmes designed to meet the needs of specific customers or environmental problems. These products are typically only available for investments that meet certain green criteria.

CASE STUDY

UK Green Investment Bank (now Green Investment Group)[21]

There are over 7 million street lights in the United Kingdom, which generate over £300 million in electricity costs. The electricity needed to power street lights produces 1.3 million tonnes of CO_2 annually, equivalent to the emissions of 330,000 cars on the road or 674,000 households. Despite the financial and environmental case for improved energy efficiency, fewer than 1 million street lamps are energy efficient.

To encourage municipalities to make the switch to low-energy lighting, the UK Green Investment Bank created an innovative green loan product in 2014 for municipalities that is specifically tailored to help cities upgrade their street lighting to more energy-efficient light emitting diodes (LEDs).

The efficient lighting technology produces energy savings that exceed the cost of the loan payment, allowing borrowers to be cash-flow positive throughout the period of the loan. The product's fixed rates and terms designed to match the payback period allowed cities and towns to enjoy net savings on their street lighting from day one of the project and municipalities save 80 per cent of their lighting costs. By using this product, participating municipalities reduce their operating budgets and take advantage of investment opportunities that otherwise would be left untapped because of competing investment needs deemed to be of higher priority.

QUICK QUESTION

What might be the business advantages of developing bespoke green loan products?

In some cases, close alignment between development banks and government policy has created a powerful synergy between policy, regulation and financing, which has been simultaneously coordinated for maximum impact. New government policies have been complemented with new financing instruments in order to transmit policy objectives more efficiently. One example is the instrumental role that KfW has played in the systemic greening of Germany's economy through the government's Energiewende policy.

CASE STUDY

KfW and the Energiewende[22]

KfW is a German development bank established shortly after the Second World War. Although initially established to support post-war restructuring, the KfW is now involved in a wide range of activities and operates internationally as well as throughout Germany. The organization of KfW's operations has changed over the years and today KfW's activities are focused on three priority megatrends:

- climate change and environment;
- globalization and technical progress;
- demographic development.

KfW's history of investing in energy efficiency and environmental protection dates back to the 1970s, but it was in the 2000s that KfW activities accelerated following the passing of a series of laws promoting renewable energy. This culminated in 2011 with the German Government's Energiewende initiative, which set the goal of phasing out nuclear power sources and of having renewable energy sources meet 60 per cent of Germany's gross final energy consumption by 2050.

In response to the government's decisions to accelerate the energy transition, the KfW launched a suite of new financial products. Among these was a loan programme targeted at large companies with an annual business volume of the group between €500 million and €4 billion. The programme promotes new investment in technologies that consume at least 15 per cent less final energy than the branch average of comparable technologies as well as replacements that lead to a minimum improvement of final energy demand of 20 per cent. This applies to buildings and machines (excluding for residential use), innovations in energy efficiency, production, storage and transmission as well as renewable energy. Technology costs for the following are eligible: heating, cooling, lighting, CHP, building shell, electric motors, pumps, compressed air, process heat and cold, ICT.

The KfW is also playing a key role in the expansion of renewable energies in Germany. For example, the Renewable Energies and Offshore Wind programmes provide low-interest loans and long-term financing for building new power stations and modernizing existing ones.

By financing both the supply side (through the support of green technology firms) and the demand side (through the financing of renewable energy) the KfW has been a key driving force behind the German government's Energiewende policy.

In 2018, 40 per cent of all new investments related to the theme 'Climate change and the environment', representing €30 billion.

Guarantees

A guarantee is when one party commits to being responsible for all or part of the debt upon an event that triggers such a guarantee, such as loan default. Guarantees enable a transaction to move forward by transferring the risk from a party unable or unwilling to bear it to another that will. Most guarantee programmes are established to correct perceived market failures or under-developed markets, in which borrowers are unable to access credit or where the perceived risk to enter a new sector is high, making market-based pricing prohibitively expensive.

Two main types of guarantees are available that aim to cover different risks:

- **Political risk guarantee (PRG):** The principle of a PRG is to insure a borrower against the risks posed by a government's actions that may affect its ability to repay the debt. Specific political risks covered by these guarantees can include currency risks, changes to laws or regulations, nationalization and wars.
- **Partial credit guarantee (PCG):** Credit guarantees are designed to insure against non-payment by a borrower for any reason – political, commercial or otherwise. Guarantees tend to be partial, meaning that they do not cover the entire amount borrowed but only the amount necessary to ensure that the transaction proceeds. The rationale behind this is that by not covering the full amount, the guarantee does not generate moral hazard and ensures that the lender still has an incentive to undertake due diligence on the viability of the borrower and use of resources. Credit guarantees are particularly helpful in improving a project's perceived credit profile, catalysing a wider array of investor interest and better credit terms.

Commercial investors can sometimes be hesitant to invest in projects with a strong environmental impact due to their perceived riskiness or short track record. Green projects can also present technical issues that are often not understood by less sophisticated investors or in developing economies. Development banks therefore often use guarantees to make projects happen that otherwise would not by bearing some of the risk, shifting the balance of risk and reward and crowding-in private investment.

First-loss provisions

First-loss provisions refers to any structure designed to protect investors from the loss of capital that is exposed first if there is a financial loss of security. Development banks may invest first-loss capital into a project or fund that helps to shield investors from a defined initial amount of losses, thereby reducing risk and improving the creditworthiness of the investment.

One example of first-loss provisions being used in conjunction with other structures is the Global Energy Efficiency and Renewable Energy Fund launched by the EIB, which includes a first-loss provision by donors to cushion risk absorption and rebalance the structure of risk and reward for investors.

CASE STUDY

Global Energy Efficiency and Renewable Energy Fund[23]

Climate and development: 'Nobody else has done anything like this in the world'

A ground-breaking fund attracts private investment for climate and development projects

A few years ago, Alastair Vere Nicoll trekked across Antarctica, recreating the adventure of pioneering polar explorer Roald Amundsen. Now he's standing on a spot considerably hotter than those icy southern wastes, and he's part of a project that's as ground-breaking as the great Norwegian's journey to the South Pole.

Beneath his feet, 250 kilometres south of Addis Ababa, is the Corbetti volcanic caldera, part of the Ethiopian Rift. A happy coincidence of geological features sends water through subterranean fissures in the earth where, heated by the volcanic activity around it, the water turns naturally into steam. Vere Nicoll and his colleagues aim to harness the power of that steam to create electricity. 'It's a coal-fired power station without the coal,' he says.

In the dustbowl over the caldera, the renewable energy investment company Berkeley Energy that Vere Nicoll co-founded is building Ethiopia's first independent power project. The pilot stage will be completed in the next two years. Within eight years, Vere Nicoll expects the Corbetti plant to have a capacity of 500 megawatts. That's approximately a quarter of the country's total electricity usage and enough to supply 10 million Ethiopians. 'We've done ground-breaking deals in various emerging markets, but this is the most significant project any of us involved will ever work on,' he says. 'Really, in our entire careers.'

Vere Nicoll's cutting-edge project is typical of the work of one of his main investors, the Global Energy Efficiency and Renewable Energy Fund (Geeref). The Fund started with a big chunk of public money, which it used to entice private investors. The private money followed, as Geeref managers hoped it would – even though they planned to invest in projects that typically are seen as risky.

A cushion against risk

Using the public funds to give private investors a cushion against risk, Geeref has built a unique portfolio of renewable energy investments in developing countries. It has been so successful that Geeref managers will soon be launching a second, bigger fund. 'Nobody else has done anything like this in the world,' says Christopher Knowles, Head of the Climate Change and Environment Division at the European Investment Bank.

Geeref is managed by the European Investment Bank from a single, bustling room in an airy corner of its Luxembourg headquarters. The walls are filled with pictures of the fund managers' children and maps of the exotic places where the Fund invests. A home-baked chocolate cake often takes up space on the small conference table. From this room, the Fund's chief, Cyrille Arnould, a Frenchman with a sardonic sense of humour and a renegade aura, presides over a team that has invested in around 50 separate projects run by first-time managers in developing countries.

'We are proving that you can do social projects with a profit mentality,' Arnould says.

The Fund started in 2008 with €112 million in public funds from Norway, Germany and the European Union. In turn the Fund raised €110 million in private investment. Geeref's targets are ambitious:

- Create 1 gigawatt of clean energy capacity.
- Save 2 million tonnes of carbon dioxide.
- Support energy for 2 million people.
- Support renewable energy without betting [on] the house.

The key to Geeref's structure is what's called a first-loss piece. That means the public money in the fund is used as a buffer to protect the private investors. If the fund has a loss, it comes out of the public money first. That makes private investors more secure and encourages them to invest in a fund that might otherwise have seemed too risky.

Garrie Lette, who runs a €4.5 billion pension fund portfolio in Melbourne, Australia, invested €42 million with Geeref. 'We haven't bet the house on it,' says Lette, Chief Investment Officer of Catholic Super. 'But it's still a significant investment for us.'

'Our investors are expecting high returns, risk-adjusted,' says Aglaé Touchard-Le Drian, a Geeref Senior Investment Officer. The Fund projects returns of somewhat over 20 per cent.

Lette acknowledges that renewable energy in a developing country with first-time fund managers 'doesn't tick all the boxes for us'. It was Geeref's structure that attracted him. 'We're driven by risk and return. The presence of the first-loss capital was crucial in our decision to get involved.'

Leveraging public money with private

Geeref drew essentially the same amount of private investment as its public funding. But once that money is invested, it creates further leverage. For every euro Geeref puts into a project, more than €50 ends up being invested. 'That's amazing leverage,' says Mónica Arévalo Calsina, Geeref's senior investment officer. 'By mitigating the risk of the private sector, we bring much, much greater investment levels.'

That leverage is at work for a series of funds in the Geeref portfolio:

- **Evolution One:** $90 million, renewable energy, energy efficiency, environmental projects and companies in southern Africa, based in Cape Town.
- **Renewable Energy Asia Fund:** €86 million, renewable energy in India and the Philippines, based in Singapore, and managed by Vere Nicoll's Berkeley Energy.
- **Frontier:** €60 million, renewable energy in Sub-Saharan Africa, based in Nairobi and Copenhagen.
- **Emerging Energy Latin American Fund II:** $40 million, renewable energy infrastructure, energy service companies in Latin America and the Caribbean, based in Rio de Janeiro and Stamford, Connecticut.
- **Armstrong:** $164 million, small-scale renewable energy generation and resource efficiency projects in southeast Asia, based in Singapore.
- **MGM Sustainable Energy Fund:** $50 million, energy efficiency and renewable energy projects in Central America and the Caribbean, based in Miami.
- **Africa Renewable Energy Fund:** $200 million, Sub-Saharan Africa renewable energy projects, based in Nairobi, the fund behind the Corbetti project.
- **Solar Arise:** Aims to raise $100 million, solar photovoltaic projects in India, based in 'Gurgaon, in the north Indian state of Haryana.
- **Caucasus Clean Energy:** $100 million targeted, small hydro projects in Georgia, based in Tbilisi and Singapore.

Building projects from scratch

Though Geeref has a broad geographical reach, Arnould sees the best opportunities for growth in the renewable energy sector in Africa. That puts him in agreement with Anders Hauch, investment director of Frontier Investment Management. The 44-year-old Dane and his Frontier colleagues are behind a $45 million hydroelectric project on the Siti River in the remote Mount Elgon area of Uganda.

Currently in its opening stage, Siti aims to produce 5 megawatts of capacity by the end of 2016, with turbines situated at the point where the river first cascades steeply – creating the most force to drive the turbines. That'll rise to a total of 21 megawatts by the end of 2018, when Frontier constructs turbines at the second cascade. That's 2.5 per cent of Uganda's total capacity and very significant to the local area, which is not yet on the country's electrical grid.

Frontier is a typical Geeref investment, in that the fund had no track record, allowing EIB advisers to play an important role in managing it – Arnould heads Frontier's investment advisory board. Importantly, Frontier works on greenfield projects, which means that it doesn't invest in existing projects. It builds all its projects from scratch. That added value is at the heart of what Geeref does.

Frontier's €60 million fund includes a €12 million investment from Geeref. That money was key to raising other financing for Frontier. 'They came with a big investment that helped us bring in other money. Then they gave us a lot of leads for investments that we could make,' Hauch says. 'Geeref was quite essential.'

Now that Geeref has built a track record for its strategy, Arnould and his colleagues are poised for another round of financing. The plan is for Geeref II to be considerably bigger, and for private capital to make up a larger proportion of the fund.

'We expect investors to come back with much more than they did in our first round of financing,' says Geeref senior investment officer Gunter Fischer. The 'first-loss piece' will be smaller proportionately than it was in Geeref's initial financing round.

'We're still mitigating the risk for the private investor,' Arnould says. 'But now we don't need to offer them as much protection, because they can see our track record. We've built a lot of trust.'

Grants

Grants can be used to cover the costs of specific parts of a project, reducing the overall cost of the project in a transparent manner. Grants can be used upfront to accelerate projects, giving them a kick-start, or as a means of reducing the cost of the project over its lifetime. Grants can be particularly important in pilot projects where the associated risks are very high and the returns uncertain. Combining grants with additional support (such as loans and equity) is common – and is sometimes referred to as blending.

Equity investment

Development banks also help to stimulate and catalyse private capital into the green economy by making equity investments. This can be in the form of early-stage risk capital in firms who are working on innovative climate solutions, or undertaking research and development on new green technologies. As development banks often employ significant in-house technical expertise, equity investments can act as a hallmark of quality that helps to crowd-in further private sector capital. Thus, development banks can play an important role as 'investor of first resort' in emerging sectors or firms.

Development banks also make strategic investments in externally managed equity funds that have an environmental focus. For example, the European Investment Bank has invested in a number of green infrastructure funds as well as more bespoke funds focused on issues such as soil decontamination and sustainable agriculture.

In some instances, development banks have set up their own equity investment funds. One prominent example is the UK Green Investment Bank's Offshore Wind Fund.

CASE STUDY

UK Green Investment Bank's Offshore Wind Fund[24]

In 2014 the UK Green Investment Bank (now the Green Investment Group) established the world's first dedicated offshore wind fund. The fund's aim was to attract new capital into the market. By attracting new liquidity into the market, the fund helped to reduce the long-term cost of finance and enabled developers to reduce their stakes and use the proceeds to finance new projects.

The Fund was successful in attracting new and different investors to offshore wind with assets under management surpassing £1 billion. Investors in the Fund included a number of UK-based pension funds as well as international institutional investors, including one of the world's largest sovereign wealth funds and a leading European life and pension company.

The Fund's portfolio consists of interests in six operational wind farms, namely Sheringham Shoal, a 317 MW offshore wind farm located off the North Norfolk coast; Rhyl Flats and Gwynt y Môr offshore wind farms, both located off the coast of North Wales with total capacities of 90 MW and 576 MW respectively; Lynn and Inner Dowsing wind farms, two adjacent operational wind farms with an aggregate installed capacity of 194 MW; and Lincs, a 270 MW wind farm located 5km off the Lincolnshire coast alongside Lynn and Inner Dowsing.

Collectively these projects have a capacity of 1.45GW producing over 4,500 GWh renewable electricity each year, resulting in the avoidance of almost 2 million tonnes of greenhouse gas emissions annually.

Technical assistance and capacity building

Technical assistance and other advisory services are frequently provided by MDBs and their partners as part of a package of investment that can help to improve project preparation, planning and management, as well as the sustainability of the investment and the desired project outcomes. Such assistance can strengthen the economic and technical foundations of an investment and catalyse funding from other sources.

In addition, such services can help to establish an enabling environment for complex projects, promote market awareness among customers and build local capacity and capability to support future green finance projects. Technical assistance facilitates knowledge sharing and dissemination of experience and good practice, but care needs to be taken to ensure that there is a transfer of knowledge and experience to local professionals rather than simply a demonstration effect that has no lasting impact.

CASE STUDY

EBRD Green Cities: Minsk[25]

The EBRD is implementing the first EBRD Green Cities project in Belarus by financing the introduction of state-of-the-art wastewater management systems in the city of Minsk. The project will have significant environmental benefits for the country's largest municipality with a population of more than 2 million inhabitants.

A sovereign loan of €84 million to Minsk Vodokanal (MVK), the country's biggest municipal water utility, will be the largest loan in the municipal sector provided by the EBRD in Belarus to date. It will help finance the rehabilitation and optimization of MVK's wastewater treatment plant and the construction of a cost-efficient, modern, sludge-management facility to ensure the company's compliance with national and EU standards for effluent treatment quality. These measures will improve the city's environment by reducing greenhouse gas emissions by over 130,000 tonnes of CO_2 equivalent annually, which can be compared with removal of 28,000 cars from the streets of the capital.

The project will be co-financed by a parallel loan of the same amount provided by the European Investment Bank (EIB), and will be its first signed project in Belarus. The project is the first transaction under the Minsk Green City Action Plan (GCAP), which is part of EBRD Green Cities. The GCAP is financed by the government of Sweden and supports actions and investments designed to address priority environmental issues in the capital of Belarus. EBRD Green Cities is a €950 million facility that offers a comprehensive business model for green urban development, combining strategic planning with investment and associated technical assistance. The EBRD and EIB will also allocate significant technical assistance funds to support technical, financial, environmental and social implementation aspects of the project. The project is the seventh wastewater treatment plant financed by EBRD in Belarus.

QUICK QUESTION

Why might technical assistance be particularly important for green innovations?

Key concepts

In this chapter we considered:

- the role of central and development banks (national and multilateral) in relation to green finance;
- how central banks assess and seek to manage the risks to financial stability posed by climate change, and support the transition to a low-carbon economy;
- how development banks play a key role in promoting sustainable economic development, and the key products and services they provide in order to do so;

- examples and case studies of central and development banks supporting green finance.

Now go back through this chapter and make sure you fully understand each point.

Review

Central banks are public institutions that oversee the financial system and monetary regime of a country. In most developed countries, central banks are institutionally independent from the government. Since the 2007/08 global financial crisis, central banks in advanced economies have played a more interventionist role in the economy in order to achieve monetary policy and financial stability objectives.

With responsibility for overseeing financial stability, central banks have a particularly important impact on the way in which banks respond to the physical and transition risks associated with climate change. With responsibility for overseeing and regulating the creation and allocation of money and credit, central banks also have an important impact on the speed at which the greening of the financial system takes place by incentivizing or directing resources from traditional carbon-intensive sectors towards green investment.

In many emerging and developing countries, central banks are playing an active role in supporting the greening of the financial system and addressing the risks posed by climate change. In these countries, central banks have recalibrated traditional central bank tools with a green focus, and in some cases, have created new instruments to promote green finance.

Green central banking tools include credit allocation policy instruments, macroprudential policy, microprudential regulation, stress testing, and guidelines and frameworks.

Through global bodies such as the Financial Stability Board (FSB) and the Network for Greening the Financial System (NGFS), central banks coordinate their efforts to manage the impact of climate change on the financial system. The FSB established the Task Force on Climate-Related Financial Disclosures (TCFD) and, through the FSB and individually, central banks have helped set up and support a wide variety of market frameworks and standards for green finance.

Development banks are public (or part-public) financial institutions tasked with promoting socio-economic development in a country or region.

They provide finance and a wide range of advisory and capacity building programmes to clients whose financial needs are not sufficiently served by private commercial banks or local capital markets. While most development banks aim to make a profit, their overarching mandate is typically not to maximize this but to promote a wider range of economic, social and environmental goals. This makes them important actors in the green finance sector. Multinational Development Banks (MDBs) in particular have played key roles in establishing and developing the green finance sector, for example by issuing the first green bonds.

In recent years, dedicated green development banks have been created to provide financing for green projects, working alongside existing development banks but with a specialized mandate. These are still small, however, compared with the green portfolios of the larger and longer established development banks.

Green development banking products and services include concessionary loans, bespoke loan products, guarantees, first-loss provisions, grants, equity and venture capital investment and technical assistance and capacity building. Many development banks combine instruments to support projects in both the pre-investment stage (grants and technical assistance) and the investment stage (risk enhancements, funding subsidies or other financial tools to attract private capital).

Glossary

Central bank: A public institution that oversees the financial system and monetary policy of a country.

Credit allocation policy: A tool used by a central bank to direct the creation and allocation of credit towards certain industries or sectors.

Development bank: A public (or part-public) financial institution tasked with promoting socio-economic development in a country or region.

Financial Stability Board (FSB): The FSB, comprising central banks, public international financial institutions and international standard-setting organizations, aims to strengthen financial systems and promote international financial stability by coordinating the development of strong regulatory, supervisory and other financial sector policies, and encouraging consistency in the implementation of these. The FSB established the Task Force on Climate-related Financial Disclosures (TCFD) in 2015.

Green development banks: National or sub-national banks whose purpose is to provide financing for green projects.

Green supporting factor: Reduces the amount of capital a bank needs to hold in reserve, facilitating the allocation of more capital and lending greater amounts to green projects.

Green tagging: Linking the terms of a loan to the underlying asset's energy performance, fuel efficiency or environmental standard.

Macroprudential policy: Policy aiming to prevent the excessive build-up of systemic risk in the financial system resulting from factors such as asset price bubbles or excessive risk-taking by banks.

Microprudential regulation: Supervision of individual financial institutions to ensure that they are resilient and solvent.

Multilateral Development Banks (MDBs): Supranational institutions established by sovereign states, with aims and objectives reflecting the development and cooperation policies of their sovereign shareholders. MDBs have played key roles in establishing and developing the green finance sector.

Network for Greening the Financial System (NGFS): Established by central banks to provide a forum for sharing best practice and enhancing consistency of approaches to climate risk and green finance. By June 2019, 36 central banks were members of the NGFS.

Quantitative easing: Unconventional form of monetary policy where a central bank creates new money electronically to buy financial assets, like government bonds, aiming to directly increase private sector spending in the economy and return inflation to target.

Stress testing: Assessments conducted (or ordered) by central banks to model the resilience of the banking sector, or individual banks, against shocks and scenarios.

Notes

1. M Cuff (2017) Printing money, burning carbon? Why QE may be stimulating more than just the money markets, Business Green [Online] https://www.businessgreen.com/bg/analysis/3010873/printing-money-burning-carbon-why-qe-may-be-stimulating-more-than-just-the-money-markets (archived at https://perma.cc/P3VX-B2NM)
2. S Dikau (2017) *Green Central Banking in Emerging Market and Developing Country Economics*, New Economics Foundation [Online] https://neweconomics.org/uploads/files/Green-Central-Banking.pdf (archived at https://perma.cc/F8QA-WYJU)
3. U Volz (2017) *On the Role of Central Banks in Enhancing Green Finance*, Inquiry: Design of a Sustainable Financial System, UNEP [Online] http://unepinquiry.org/wp-content/uploads/2017/02/On_the_Role_of_Central_Banks_in_Enhancing_Green_Finance.pdf (archived at https://perma.cc/7SSH-536N)

4 A Barkwai and P Monnin (2015) *Monetary Policy and Sustainability*, Inquiry: Design of a Sustainable Financial System, UNEP [Online] http://unepinquiry.org/wp-content/uploads/2015/04/Monetary_Policy_and_Sustainability_The_Case_of_Bangladesh.pdf (archived at https://perma.cc/J5MA-Y7EC)

5 S Dikau (2017) *Green Central Banking in Emerging Market and Developing Country Economics*, New Economics Foundation [Online] https://neweconomics.org/uploads/files/Green-Central-Banking.pdf (archived at https://perma.cc/F8QA-WYJU)

6 U Volz (2017) *On the Role of Central Banks in Enhancing Green Finance*, Inquiry: Design of a Sustainable Financial System, UNEP [Online] http://unepinquiry.org/wp-content/uploads/2017/02/On_the_Role_of_Central_Banks_in_Enhancing_Green_Finance.pdf (archived at https://perma.cc/7SSH-536N)

7 U Volz (2017) *On the Role of Central Banks in Enhancing Green Finance*, Inquiry: Design of a Sustainable Financial System, UNEP [Online] http://unepinquiry.org/wp-content/uploads/2017/02/On_the_Role_of_Central_Banks_in_Enhancing_Green_Finance.pdf (archived at https://perma.cc/7SSH-536N)

8 Matikainen, S (2017) Green doesn't mean risk-free: Why we should be cautious about a green supporting factor in the EU [Online] http://www.lse.ac.uk/GranthamInstitute/news/eu-green-supporting-factor-bank-risk/ (archived at https://perma.cc/6GQF-864A)

9 S Dikau (2017) *Green Central Banking in Emerging Market and Developing Country Economics*, New Economics Foundation [Online] https://newecnoomics.org/uploads/files/Green-Central-Banking.pdf (archived at https://perma.cc/F8QA-WYJU)

10 Bank of England (2019) Enhancing banks' and insurers' approaches to managing the financial risks from climate change, Policy Statement 11/9 Consultation Paper 23/18 [Online] https://www.bankofengland.co.uk/prudential-regulation/publication/2018/enhancing-banks-and-insurers-approaches-to-managing-the-financial-risks-from-climate-change (archived at https://perma.cc/P332-4MHK)

11 FCA (2018) *Climate Change and Green Finance: Discussion paper DP18/8* [Online] https://www.fca.org.uk/publication/discussion/dp18-08.pdf (archived at https://perma.cc/T6NY-UXBB)

12 U Volz (2017) *On the Role of Central Banks in Enhancing Green Finance*, Inquiry: Design of a Sustainable Financial System, UNEP [Online] http://unepinquiry.org/wp-content/uploads/2017/02/On_the_Role_of_Central_Banks_in_Enhancing_Green_Finance.pdf (archived at https://perma.cc/7SSH-536N)

13 J Luna-Martinez and C L Vincente (2012) *Global Survey of Development Banks*, Policy Research Working Paper 5969, The World Bank [Online] http://documents.worldbank.org/curated/en/313731468154461012/pdf/WPS5969.pdf (archived at https://perma.cc/U2Y2-CWZV)

14 GWEC (2011) *Global Wind Report: Annual market update 2011* [Online] http://gwec.net/wp-content/uploads/2012/06/Annual_report_2011_lowres.pdf (archived at https://perma.cc/FMW2-T8JH)

15 B Buchner, P Oliver, X Wang, C Carswell, C Meattle and F Mazza (2017) *Global Landscape of Climate Finance 2017*, Climate Policy Initiative [Online] https://climatepolicyinitiative.org/wp-content/uploads/2017/10/2017-Global-Landscape-of-Climate-Finance.pdf (archived at https://perma.cc/KDH7-DY74)

16 A Shah (2015) Development banking for sustainability, Devex [Online] https://www.devex.com/news/development-banking-for-sustainability-87333 (archived at https://perma.cc/B7GM-PHSN)

17 OECD (2017) *Green Investment Banks: Innovative public financial institutions – Scaling up private, low-carbon investment*, OECD Environment Policy Paper No. 6 [Online] http://newclimateeconomy.report/workingpapers/wp-content/uploads/sites/5/2017/01/Green-Investment-Banks-OECD.pdf (archived at https://perma.cc/GLD6-52W9)

18 J McDaniels and N Robins (2016) *Greening the Banking System: Taking stock of G20 green banking market practice*, UNEP [Online] http://unepinquiry.org/publication/greening-the-banking-system/ (archived at https://perma.cc/5E2M-FM6P)

19 KfW (2020) KfW at a Glance: Facts and figures [Online] https://www.kfw.de/PDF/Download-Center/Konzernthemen/KfW-im-%C3%9Cberblick/KfW-an-overview.pdf (archived at https://perma.cc/BA9B-NKLU)

20 OECD (2017) *Green Investment Banks: Innovative public financial institutions – Scaling up private, low-carbon investment*, OECD Environment Policy Paper No. 6 [Online] http://newclimateeconomy.report/workingpapers/wp-content/uploads/sites/5/2017/01/Green-Investment-Banks-OECD.pdf (archived at https://perma.cc/GLD6-52W9)

21 OECD (2017) *Green Investment Banks: Innovative public financial institutions – Scaling up private, low-carbon investment*, OECD Environment Policy Paper No. 6 [Online] http://newclimateeconomy.report/workingpapers/wp-content/uploads/sites/5/2017/01/Green-Investment-Banks-OECD.pdf (archived at https://perma.cc/GLD6-52W9)

22 KfW (2016) *Sustainability Report: Facts and figures update 2016* [Online] https://www.kfw.de/PDF/Download-Center/Konzernthemen/Nachhaltigkeit/englisch/Facts-and-Figures-Update-2016.pdf (archived at https://perma.cc/8448-5UQT); KfW (2018) KfW's significant contribution to the energy transition [Online] https://www.kfw.de/KfW-Group/Newsroom/Latest-News/Pressemitteilungen-Details_455616.html (archived at https://perma.cc/5FP3-D38A)

23 M Rees (2016) Climate and development: 'Nobody else has done anything like this in the world', European Investment Bank [Online] http://www.eib.org/infocentre/blog/all/climate-and-development-equity.htm (archived at https://perma.cc/8KK3-6W8E)

24 Green Investment Group (2017) World's first offshore wind fund manager powers through £1bn target [Online] https://www.greeninvestmentgroup.com/news/2017/worlds-first-offshore-wind-fund-manager-powers-through-p1bn-target.html (archived at https://perma.cc/H9ZV-UKF6)

25 A Usov (2018) EBRD extending largest municipal loan in Belarus, European Bank [Online] https://www.ebrd.com/news/2018/ebrd-extending-largest-municipal-loan-in-belarus-.html (archived at https://perma.cc/WD3N-KN3M)

09

Equity markets and investment funds

LEARNING OBJECTIVES

On completion of this chapter you should be able to:

- Understand the differences and similarities between ESG, SRI and other related terms, and explain the growth of the values-based investment sector.
- Describe the role of equity markets within the wider financial system.
- Describe equity products, their suitability for different types of investors, and how they may support green and sustainable finance.
- Understand different types of investment funds and explain how these may support investment in green and sustainable finance.
- Explain portfolio decarbonization as a holistic approach to green and sustainable finance.

Equity markets, including investment funds, have a vital role to play in allocating capital from savers and investors to productive assets and activities in the economy. In order to expand and improve green and sustainable finance it is particularly important that the investment sector is able to support the flow of capital to key sectors such as renewable energy and sustainable infrastructure. It is also important that investment products, services and service providers are able to provide flexibility and a wide diversity of opportunities and risks for investors, including in low-carbon assets. There has been substantial growth in values-based investing, including in green and sustainable funds in recent years, which seems likely to continue to increase.

Introduction to values-based investing

In the context of green and sustainable finance, terms including ESG investing, responsible investing, sustainable investing, socially responsible investing (SRI), ethical investing and impact investing are in common use. All describe investments and/or investment strategies designed to deliver and support positive environmental and social impacts (and/or avoid negative impacts) as well as financial returns. Although the terms are often used interchangeably, there are important differences, which we explore below. We can refer to them in general as **values-based investing** – that is, activities and strategies that take into account investors' beliefs, preferences and values including environmental, ethical, social and other factors alongside their desire for a financial return.

An **environmental, social and governance (ESG)** approach is intended to integrate these factors into traditional financial analysis of investments. The ESG factors may increase the risk profile of an investment (eg if assets are exposed to substantial climate risks) or the potential returns on offer. There is no single method for assessing ESG factors, as we shall see in this chapter, but in general they might encompass:

- **Environmental factors:** Energy use (and mix of renewable/non-renewable energy), emissions, waste production, impact on the natural environment.
- **Social factors:** Human rights, equality, engagement with and impact on communities, employee relations.
- **Governance factors:** Quality of board and senior management, shareholder rights, transparency and disclosure.

ESG is generally seen as a positive screening or inclusive screening approach to investing, as usually investments will be identified that exhibit favourable ESG factors such as those set out above. There is a growing body of evidence that ESG factors have a positive impact on investment returns, which may be due to a range of factors, including the quality of management and corporate stewardship, a longer-term approach to business strategy and value creation, and the avoidance of costs imposed by a negative approach to ESG factors, such as legal liabilities resulting from climate change or poor employee relations, or the costs of carbon taxes.

In green finance, although we focus primarily on environmental factors, social and governance factors are often interlinked with these; for example, the effects of a firm's activities on communities, and its approach to the disclosure of climate-related risk.

Responsible investing as defined by the United Nations-supported Principles for Responsible Investment (PRI), which we describe in more detail later in this chapter, refers to incorporating ESG factors into investment decision-making and strategies.

Sustainable investing generally refers to a more active approach to investing, involving positive selection of investments that deliver environmental and social impacts, and support the transition to a sustainable, low-carbon world. The aim is to reduce risk from ESG factors, such as those set out above, and deliver financial returns as well as a positive impact on the environment and society.

Socially responsible investment (SRI) is also an active approach to portfolios, involving the selection or elimination of investments based on ethical guidelines and SRI screens determined by the investor; for example:

- alcohol and tobacco;
- gambling;
- human rights;
- environmental impact.

Traditionally, SRI approaches were based on negative screening or exclusionary screening, ie the avoidance of stocks, securities, funds and other assets that conflict with the investor's beliefs and personal values, meaning that the investor would be prepared to accept lower portfolio returns. More recently, SRI represents a more positive approach to screening and, with the current growth in green finance investments, white lists of potential investments are becoming more common, rather than black lists of investments to be avoided. SRI approaches may also be referred to as **ethical investing**, as screening and investment decision-making is mainly driven by investors' ethical beliefs.

The objective of **impact investing** is to help investors achieve specific (usually) environmental and/or social objectives, although the term could relate to any form of investing where the primary focus is on non-financial outcomes. In its infancy, impact investing was not particularly concerned with financial returns, and was frequently referred to in the context of investments in not-for-profit activities. In the current context of climate-related impact investing, environmental impact and financial return are often given equal weighting, although many impact investors may be prepared to accept lower returns, compared with alternative investments, in exchange for the positive impacts achieved.

In this short comparison of values-based investing approaches, many similarities are evident, and in practice, combinations of some or all of the elements of all three approaches may be used. For simplicity, the term **values-based investing** is used in this chapter, and elsewhere in this book, to refer to investments, and approaches to investment, that incorporate green and sustainable finance principles and practice, and seek to address climate risks.

QUICK QUESTION

Why might the requirements and needs of investors prioritizing green and sustainable finance be different from those of any other investor?

Growth of values-based investing

Values-based investing has grown substantially over the past decade. According to the Global Sustainable Investment Alliance (GSIA), this now accounts for more than a quarter of assets under management globally (almost $31 trillion in 2018), a 34 per cent increase compared with 2016.[1] Investors integrating ESG factors into their strategies, decision-making and portfolios account for approximately $17.5 trillion of this. Europe and the US accounted for the largest concentrations of sustainable investments in 2018; however, the most rapid growth was in Japan, where sustainable investments grew from 3 per cent of assets under management to 18 per cent between 2016 and 2018, driven by major regulatory changes.

In the specific area of green investment, nearly 400 global asset managers, representing $32 trillion in assets, launched the Investor Agenda in September

2018 to support investors tackling climate change, and to showcase the actions some investors are already taking to improve their climate-related decision-making and risk reporting.[2] The Agenda aims to encourage other institutional investors, asset owners and managers and pension funds, by means of peer pressure and the sharing of good practice, to scale up their green investments to help support the transition to a low-carbon world, and encompasses work in four thematic areas:

- **Investment:** 120 investors pursuing new and existing investments in low-carbon and climate-resilient portfolios, funds, strategies or assets such as renewable energy and energy efficiency projects; phasing out investments in coal; and integrating climate change into portfolio analysis and decision-making.
- **Policy advocacy:** 345 institutional investors with $30 trillion in assets who are urging governments to implement the Paris Agreement and enhance their climate policy ambitions by 2020. This includes calls for bolder action from governments to phase out thermal coal power worldwide, to commit greater investment to low-carbon transition and improve climate-related financial disclosures.
- **Corporate engagement:** 650 investors with $87 trillion in assets backing the Carbon Disclosure Project's environmental disclosure request, and 296 investors with $31 trillion in assets who are signatories to Climate Action 100+.
- **Investor disclosure:** More than 60 investors committed to reporting in line with the TCFD recommendations.[3]

Many commentators believe that values-based investing will continue to grow in prominence, with the emergence and greater impact of millennials (the generation born in the 1980s and 1990s, becoming adults in the 2000s) and female investors as both retail investors and fund/investment managers. A Morgan Stanley report in 2016 demonstrated that nearly 9 out of 10 millennial investors were interested in sustainable investment options that would produce market-rate financial returns alongside positive environmental and/or social returns (ie an impact investing approach).[4] Millennial investors were almost twice as likely as non-millennial investors to invest in assets with specific environmental and/or social outcomes. They were also twice as likely to disinvest from assets harming the environment or society, compared with non-millennial investors. Given that, in many developed markets at least, a significant inter-generational wealth transfer to the millennial and succeeding generations is anticipated, somewhere in the order of $30 trillion, there is great potential for very substantial further growth in the values-based investment sector.

Signatories to the UN-supported Principles for Responsible Investment (PRI) commit to incorporating ESG factors into their investment decision-making. Of more than 2,000 signatories to the PRI (2019), 98 per cent of investment managers in equity markets, and 89 per cent in fixed income markets reported that they incorporated ESG factors into investment decision-making (2019). McKinsey, though, report substantial differences in regional approaches to integrating ESG factors into investment strategies. According to McKinsey, in Europe, Australia and New Zealand, more than half of all investments took account of ESG factors; in the US, approximately a fifth, while in Asia, excluding Japan, only 1 per cent of investments were ESG-integrated.[5]

Another factor supporting the further growth of values-based investment – at least in some markets – is the impact of female investors. According to the Bank of Montreal's Wealth Institute, women now control more than half of private wealth in the US, and will inherit nearly 70 per cent of the $41 trillion expected to be passed on over the next 40 years.[6] Surveys have shown that, in developed markets, up to 80 per cent of female investors expressed interest in values-based approaches to investment; in many cases female investors were twice as likely to show interest in values-based approaches than male investors. In surveys of financial advisers, female advisers have greater interest in advising clients on sustainable investment opportunities than their male counterparts.[7] A 2018 report from Moxie Future encompasses a wider range of markets, including China. Their findings reveal that globally, nearly 70 per cent of women are interested in sustainable investment, if suitable products are available. Interest was highest among women in China (91 per cent), attributable to their exposure to highly visible environmental threats such as air pollution, which may at least to some extent be mitigated by supporting the growth of ESG-focused businesses.[8]

It seems highly likely, therefore, that values-based investment, whether ESG, SRI, impact investing or combinations of these, will continue to grow. Whilst changing social, consumer and investor preferences is part of this, more important will be a clear demonstration of sustainable, financial returns for values-based investments that are higher than returns for traditional investment approaches. In 2015, a substantial meta-study by researchers at the University of Hamburg and Deutsche Asset Management concluded that there was a positive correlation between ESG investing and financial performance.[9] A major 2019 study by Deutsche Bank, which analysed corporate disclosure and media reporting on climate change on 1,600 companies over a 20-year period found that those firms that reported positive impacts and results on climate change experienced, on average, a 26 per cent improvement in their share price over 20 years compared with their peers. Negative impacts and reporting on climate change led to firms underperforming their peers.[10]

As the costs of climate-related physical, liability and transition risks grow, as we have seen in previous chapters, and as the impact of the carbon bubble and stranded assets, described in Chapter 2, becomes more apparent, the balance of financial returns between values-based and traditional approaches to investment seems likely to shift more substantially. Changing demographics and greater awareness of the green and sustainable finance sector is changing investor and fund manager sentiment, promoting a shift towards return-generating impact investing. Policy and regulatory interventions (eg carbon pricing) are also playing their part in strengthening such approaches. In the investment market, a particularly important role has been played by the UN-supported Principles for Responsible Investment (PRI), launched in 2006 by UNEP and a group of the world's largest institutional investors. By 2019, the PRI was supported by more than 2,000 institutions from over 60 countries, representing more than $70 trillion of assets under management.

CASE STUDY

UN-supported Principles for Responsible Investment[11]

The United Nations Environment Programme (UNEP) Finance Initiative and the United Nations Global Compact set up the United Nations-supported Principles for Responsible Investment (PRI) in 2006 with the goal of working with investors to create a set of principles that would support a more sustainable global financial system.

The Principles are voluntary and aspirational, offering a menu of possible actions for incorporating environmental, social and governance (ESG) issues. Signatories to the Principles publicly commit to adopting and implementing them, where consistent with their fiduciary responsibilities.

Figure 9.1 The Principles for Responsible Investment

1 We will incorporate ESG issues into investment analysis and decision-making processes.

Possible actions:

- Address ESG issues in investment policy statements
- Support development of ESG-related tools, metrics, and analyses
- Assess the capabilities of internal investment managers to incorporate ESG issues
- Assess the capabilities of external investment managers to incorporate ESG issues
- Ask investment service providers (such as financial analysts, consultants, brokers, research firms, or rating companies) to integrate ESG factors into evolving research and analysis
- Encourage academic and other research on this theme
- Advocate ESG training for investment professionals

2 We will be active owners and incorporate ESG issues into our ownership policies and practices.

Possible actions:

- Develop and disclose an active ownership policy consistent with the Principles
- Exercise voting rights or monitor compliance with voting policy (if outsourced)
- Develop an engagement capability (either directly or through outsourcing)
- Participate in the development of policy, regulation, and standard setting (such as promoting and protecting shareholder rights)
- File shareholder resolutions consistent with long-term ESG considerations
- Engage with companies on ESG issues
- Participate in collaborative engagement initiatives
- Ask investment managers to undertake and report on ESG-related engagement

3 We will seek appropriate disclosure on ESG issues by the entities in which we invest.

Possible actions:

- Ask for standardized reporting on ESG issues (using tools such as the Global Reporting Initiative)
- Ask for ESG issues to be integrated within annual financial reports
- Ask for information from companies regarding adoption of/adherence to relevant norms, standards, codes of conduct or international initiatives (such as the UN Global Compact)
- Support shareholder initiatives and resolutions promoting ESG disclosure

4 We will promote acceptance and implementation of the Principles within the investment industry.

Possible actions:

- Include Principles-related requirements in requests for proposals (RFPs)
- Align investment mandates, monitoring procedures, performance indicators and incentive structures accordingly (for example, ensure investment management processes reflect long-term time horizons when appropriate)
- Communicate ESG expectations to investment service providers
- Revisit relationships with service providers that fail to meet ESG expectations
- Support the development of tools for benchmarking ESG integration
- Support regulatory or policy developments that enable implementation of the Principles

5 We will work together to enhance our effectiveness in implementing the Principles.

Possible actions:

- Support/participate in networks and information platforms to share tools, pool resources, and make use of investor reporting as a source of learning
- Collectively address relevant emerging issues
- Develop or support appropriate collaborative initiatives

6 We will each report on our activities and progress towards implementing the Principles.

Possible actions:

- Disclose how ESG issues are integrated within investment practices
- Disclose active ownership activities (voting, engagement, and/or policy dialogue)
- Disclose what is required from service providers in relation to the Principles
- Communicate with beneficiaries about ESG issues and the Principles
- Report on progress and/or achievements relating to the Principles using a 'Comply or Explain' approach
- Seek to determine the impact of the Principles
- Make use of reporting to raise awareness among a broader group of stakeholders

Impact of climate change and environmental factors on investment decisions

As we saw in Chapter 2, in 2015 the Economist Intelligence Unit estimated the negative impact of climate change on global assets under management, to the year 2100, at up to $43 trillion. Also in 2015, the University of Cambridge Institute for Sustainability Leadership estimated that the effects of climate change on investments could lead to reductions of up to 45 per cent of the value of global equity portfolios, and of up to 23 per cent losses in fixed income (debt) portfolios.

Investment analysts need to consider, therefore, the negative impacts of climate change on investments, and investment portfolios, in their investment strategies and decisions. There are a wide range of impacts that could have significant effects on investments at the sector, regional, country and/or firm level, including:

- increased costs of physical risks associated with climate change, including the increased frequency and severity of extreme weather events. As we will see in Chapter 10, losses from such events have risen approximately fourfold over the past 30 years to an average of $140 billion per annum – with losses in 2016 and 2017 significantly higher still;
- increased costs of liability risks arising from harmful environmental impacts, and other higher regulatory costs;
- the introduction of realistic carbon pricing – the introduction of globally consistent carbon pricing of around $75 per tonne, as recommended by the IMF;
- changing consumer preferences and investor sentiment;
- reputational risk;
- significant asset impairment and stranding. As we saw in Chapter 2, limiting emissions to limit global warming to 2°C would leave the majority of current oil, gas and coal assets stranded, with the exposure of the European financial sector alone estimated at more than €1 trillion.

Opportunities arising from the transition to a sustainable, low carbon world also need to be considered in investment strategies and decisions. These may have significant, positive effects on investments at the sector, regional, country and/or firm level, including:

- policy and regulatory changes (eg higher carbon prices, or green building codes) making investments in sectors such as clean energy, energy efficiency and clean transport more attractive compared with fossil fuel alternatives;

- technological advances reducing the cost of substitution of sustainable alternatives for fossil fuel based power generation, transportation and products;
- changing consumer preferences and investor sentiment if this shifts substantially towards green and sustainable alternatives.

As we saw in Chapter 1, there is a very sizeable investment opportunity, estimated at $6 trillion per year to 2030, by the G20 and New Climate Economy, to fully fund countries' green infrastructure requirements. This will require a combination of equity and fixed income (debt) finance, with up to 80 per cent of the capital required coming from private sources.

The role of equity markets in the financial system

Historically, equity markets have been the primary source of risk capital for enterprise, with public markets alone including 45,000 companies, with a listed capitalization of around $70 trillion – around one-quarter of global financial assets. However, this has changed in recent years. Large companies tend to use cash flow and debt to fund new investment, in part because in many jurisdictions the interest payments on bonds can be deducted against tax, and this is perceived as creating bias towards debt over equity for businesses raising additional finance.

In the last decade, large and mature markets, including the UK and the US, have seen negative equity issuance, ie more cash being returned to shareholders than capital being raised in new equity issuance. Equity markets remain hugely important, however, both as a source (albeit diminishing in some jurisdictions) of capital and in playing a vital role in terms of corporate governance and stewardship relating to company strategy, performance and capital allocation.

There has been a big shift towards secondary trading of stocks on stock exchanges (ie not raising new capital but buying and selling existing stocks), with exchanges far larger and more complex/diverse in their services and markets experiencing increased trading volumes with a significant role for automated and algorithmic trading. While this has led to the development of new types of products and services, trends have emerged towards increased short-termism and speculative trading.

The diversity of equity markets means there is flexibility and a wider range of investment opportunities for investors with different requirements.

Projects that are important for a sustainable economy represent a broad spectrum of types and levels of risks and returns, and equity markets can match the demand for capital with the supply of funds from investors with a corresponding risk and return appetite.

Equity products

Listed equities

The landscape of equity markets is dominated by listed shares – equities listed on stock exchanges and traded on the public market – and by large institutional investors including asset managers (often investing pension fund money) and insurance companies. Market-weighted indices, like the FTSE 100 (UK), Nasdaq (US), or CAC40 (France), drive investment in these markets, as many large funds (known as passive investors) track the indices rather than using their own analysis and decisions to decide what stocks to buy, sell or hold. Many active investors also mirror indices quite closely and/or mirror sector allocations (eg the proportion in sectors including finance, technology, manufacturing, high-carbon energy, renewable energy, infrastructure, etc) if not the exact composition of indices.

Large institutional shareholders also play a critical role as stewards of companies in which they invest. Stewardship is one of the main responsibilities of equity investors, who hold an ownership stake in a company and have the right (and, some would argue, duty) to play an active role in ensuring that a company is governed responsibly in terms of its impact on all stakeholders as well as in delivering returns to investors in the form of dividends and share value.

Many institutional investors are committed to delivering long-term value for the owners of the assets in which they invest, and these are often linked to individual long-term savings in pensions, for example. This suggests that they might have incentives to be good stewards in terms of supporting or driving companies to avoid excessive risk-taking and to promote environmental and social sustainability, or to invest more in green initiatives and businesses, given the longer-term nature of such investments. Large investors, however, can remain subject to short-termism due to the need for regular reporting and linked remuneration incentives, which undermines their ability to prioritize long-term performance and sustainability.

The situation has been improving in recent years, however. In 2018, for example, 63 per cent of FTSE 100 companies used recognized sustainability reporting frameworks to disclose their impact on the environment and society, and sustainable business practices, according to a report by EcoAct.[12] The adoption of TCFD reporting, especially as this becomes mandatory for large listed firms in major financial markets, as we saw in Chapter 5, will see reporting of climate risks for firms part of standard reporting practices, and included in investment analysis and decision-making.

Equity indices

The dominance of weighted indices is problematic for green and sustainable finance. Indices today for the most part favour high-carbon sectors and create biases against green sectors and low-carbon technologies, which creates an uneven playing field, where institutional investors have a lower level of exposure to the green economy. This represents both a misallocation of capital (towards polluting or harmful sectors and away from green solutions) and an implied financial risk due to the fact that returns from high-carbon sectors can be expected to fall in value as a result of transition to a sustainable, low-carbon world. We have already seen, in Chapter 2, how the carbon bubble can lead to significant asset impairment and/or stranded assets.

Investors and other key players in the investment chain (eg research providers, analysts, investment consultants) have made significant progress in recent years in understanding the risks and opportunities represented by green and sustainable finance, but the largest markets are slow to shift and have a strong bias towards incumbent industries, including high-carbon sectors. In the UK, for example, the benchmark FTSE 100 contained (as of 2019) a significantly higher proportion of high-carbon companies than the UK equity market overall, given the prevalence of oil and gas companies, airlines and other major emitters in the index. This reflects a strong bias in many indices towards the largest companies and incumbent sectors and firms, rather than emerging, low-carbon businesses. This is also reflected in the fact that institutional investment is, in many cases, weighted towards high-carbon investments. In Europe, for example, institutional investors own over 35 per cent of the shares in oil and gas companies, but less than 15 per cent of shares in the green and renewable energy sector.

CASE STUDY

Guidance to issuers on reporting ESG information[13]

As of 2014, only 15 stock exchanges around the world provided voluntary guidance to issuers on reporting ESG information. This gap creates a challenge for investors seeking a comprehensive view of a company's relevant issues. Institutional investors need a higher volume of companies, both public and private, reporting quality ESG information. While different investors have different informational needs, a growing number of investors are incorporating ESG factors into investment decision-making. Globally there is a higher level of understanding that failing to consider ESG information is a failure of an investor's fiduciary duty.

In response to the need for guidance, the SSE initiative, along with a diverse advisory group chaired by London Stock Exchange Group, created a resource for exchanges: the Model Guidance on Reporting ESG Information to Investors. This tool assists exchanges by providing a model, or template, that exchanges can use to develop their own custom guidance.

The spectrum of company approaches to reporting on ESG information is rapidly evolving. While there is no one-size-fits-all method, there are emerging international and local good practices, guidelines and frameworks. Building on these existing resources, the Model Reporting Guidance aims to provide a central set of global principles to consider when companies report ESG information to investors.

In order to promote the use of this Guidance, the SSE collaborated with a member of the SSE Investor Working Group, Allianz Global Investors, on the Campaign to Close the ESG Guidance Gap. This campaign encouraged stock exchanges to voluntarily commit to using the Model Guidance as a basis for introducing their own guidance for issuers. In the first 11 months of the campaign, 23 stock exchanges committed to introducing guidance, more than doubling the number of exchanges in the world with such guidance.

The global support this group garnered from both investors and companies helped exchanges globally make a business case for improving transparency in their markets. Similarly, the World Federation of Exchanges, which endorsed the SSE's model guidance and introduced complementary guidance in October 2015, contributed directly to the success of this past year.

The most common way for stock exchanges to promote green or sustainable equities is by establishing specific green or ESG indices. Thirty-eight exchanges globally (2017) had an ESG index, including all of the major exchanges and index providers (financial research and data provider companies which provide widely-used indices for investors as a part of their core services, including MSCI and Bloomberg). Some have a sector or thematic focus, such as renewable energy, while others are broader or focus on one environmental factor to select stocks for inclusion, such as carbon emissions.

Well-known examples of green and sustainable indices include: the FTSE4Good Index, Dow Jones Sustainability Index, Nasdaq Green Economy Index and Bloomberg Clean Energy. China has been in the forefront of the creation of ESG indices, with a total of 18 green indices launched since 2008, including the CSI AEF Ecology 100 Index and SSE 180 Carbon Efficient Index.

QUICK QUESTION

What are the drawbacks of relying on green equity indices?

READING
Characteristics of green equity indices

Excerpt from OECD's 'Defining and measuring green investments'[14]

The preferences for indices differ across countries and investors. In Japan, there is a focus on environmentally themed indices. Technology and social aspects (eg community investing) are popular in the USA, and in Europe the interest has been generally broad across all responsible investment (RI) approaches. Indices see rising demand for different strands and by all investor groups, driven also by changes in legislation, regulation and government initiatives (eg green ISAs in the UK).

Indices also differ in terms of their approaches to selecting and weighting of the index constituents. There are three basic approaches by index providers:

- **Screening:** Create a green/ESG/SRI subset of a broader market index.
- **Best-of-class:** For example, top 20 per cent within sector or industry (sometimes with neutral sector or country weightings).

- **Re-weighting:** Adjust the weightings of stocks in a standard market index according to a green (carbon) factor (usually keep sector weightings neutral to minimize tracking error).

Index providers use internal and/or external research resources for the determination of their green universes. Given the different approaches, it is no surprise that the definition of green investment varies across different indices.

Some providers select green stocks on a qualitative basis, ie because they operate in certain green sectors or produce green technology. Others take the whole stock market universe and specify greenness quantitatively, eg 50 per cent or more of the revenue needs to be climate change-related, or stocks with the highest contribution to reducing emissions. Finally, in a best-of-class approach, it is all relative, as the top 10–20 per cent of companies of a sector are selected.

As a consequence, not surprisingly, the actual indices all look very different in all dimensions, including the number of stocks, average sizes, liquidity and sector breakdowns. The outcome is a great variety in the constituent companies in the various indices. They range from small, highly specialized niche producers to well-known global players that are deemed to be somehow green or at least greener than others.

There are limitations and weaknesses of green indices. Biases frequently found include (they do not necessarily apply to all indices):

- sector biases (eg overweight in technology, TMT, financials, pharma);
- country biases (eg underweight in Japan, emerging markets);
- size bias (overweight in larger stocks, or small stocks, depending on the index approach);
- cyclicality.

More generally, there are other issues with green indices (again, they do not necessarily apply to all):

- data quality and transparency;
- poor company reporting on ESG or green factors;
- lack of disclosure, eg from SME, emerging markets;
- debates over performance and risk compared to standard indices;
- tracking error relative to general market indices (eg how much should green indices deviate from main-stream market indices?).

One of the challenges faced by green and sustainable indices, several of which have been established for many years, has been a bias towards large companies that report a large quantity and range of information about ESG factors. In the past, compositions and weightings that might seem perverse have appeared. For example, many of the sectors and companies with the highest carbon emissions or linked to negative environmental impacts, such as the oil and gas sector or mining, have appeared in green indices. Such companies disclosed a great deal of information about their environmental impacts, in part because the scale was so great that investors, regulators and other stakeholders felt such disclosure was required.

Environmental groups and others have been concerned that an excessive focus on the level of reporting, rather than on the actual environmental performance of companies (ie is a company cutting greenhouse gas emissions, as well as reporting on them?) compromised the integrity of such scores and weightings. Environmental costs cannot be defrayed by good governance and disclosure. Progress in the quality of reporting and analysis has reduced this problem, but the challenge of verifying the extent to which quality of reporting is matched by high performance and the achievement of positive impact remains one of the hardest for companies and investors to address.

A recent initiative to overcome the limitations of existing sustainable indices is the FTSE TPI Climate Transition index, launched in January 2020 by the Church of England-led Transition Pathway Initiative and FT Russell, a large global index provider. The new index is designed to score more highly those companies who set, disclose and make good progress towards targets aligned to the Paris Agreement, whilst scoring more lowly or excluding those companies that fail to do this. MSCI, another large global index provider, has also recently launched a range of Climate Change Indexes linked to alignment with the Paris Agreement.

Private equity, venture capital and angel investing

Private equity refers to risk capital that is raised outside the public markets, and covers a range of financial instruments that share in the profits and losses of a business. This includes, but is not limited to, ordinary shares, and frequently involves a combination of shares and loans. Private equity fund managers have traditionally charged a management fee in proportion to the amount of funds invested, and a performance fee linked to the returns made. The usual formula has been '2 and 20' – a 2 per cent management fee, plus 20 per cent of any returns realized. There are strong incentives to take greater levels of risk (albeit carefully calibrated and selected risk) and to seek higher returns.

Most private equity investment is conducted by private equity funds, which are normally structured as limited liability partnerships. Institutional investors and wealthy institutions, including endowments, hedge funds and high-net-worth individuals (known as limited partners) invest alongside the private equity fund managers themselves (known as general partners), who put some of their own capital at risk in investments (often described as having skin in the game). It is common for private equity funds to borrow money to finance acquisitions, which are known as leveraged buyouts.

Private equity investors may take either minority or majority stakes in companies, but in both cases tend to play very active roles in engaging with or joining the management team. They tend to seek returns in the form of capital growth in the value of a business, rather than short-term income, as private equity is primarily a buy-to-sell business model, with investors looking to boost value and then sell the assets in (often) a 5 to 10 year timeframe. One consequence of this is that it may be helpful for public equity markets to develop alongside private equity, because when a company is ready to be sold (known as the 'exit'), one option for private equity investors is to sell it into a public market.

The characteristics of private equity investment – such as a higher appetite for risk, multi-year time horizon, and specialized skills in business transformation and innovation – mean that it may be well suited to support some emerging areas of green finance. For example, companies that need to transform their business model to adapt to a green and sustainable economy may need capital, expertise and time in order to do so. Companies in new sectors or technologies including renewable energy or clean technology might have high potential but present risks and uncertainties that more traditional investors cannot take on. In both cases, a private equity investor may have the appetite and the skills to take on the risks and support a period of change or growth in return for the chance to share in substantial capital growth.

Venture capital refers to a specific type of private equity investing, rather than to a separate approach altogether. Venture capital differs in that there is a greater emphasis on investing in and developing new or early-stage businesses, which means the risks tend to be greater and failures more numerous, but the pay-offs can be very large for successful investments. In order for venture capital funds to be profitable, it is considered necessary to deliver a small number of home-run successes, perhaps increasing in value by 10 or even 100 times, in order to outweigh the many failed enterprises. The technology sector is a good example of a sector where this model has been highly influential.

Venture capital funds may be established by private groups of investors (in which case they are very similar to private equity partnerships, except with a focus on investing at an earlier stage). Recent years have seen the growth of venture capital funds established by large corporations, seeking to identify, spur and support innovation that might be difficult to promote within the culture of a large organization. In financial services, we have seen something similar with banks and other financial services organizations setting up or partnering with FinTech incubators rather than trying to match the speed and agility of FinTech innovation in-house.

In the green and sustainable finance sector, corporate venture capital funds have grown considerably in recent years, with many led by utilities (eg EnBW New Ventures, a Euro100 million fund set up by a large German utility company), or other corporations facing significant costs and change from climate risks (eg Alliance Ventures, a €1 billion fund established by Renault, Nissan and Mitsubishi focused on clean and smart transport). Many different funds of different sizes exist, specializing in different areas of climate change mitigation and adaptation and with differing investment strategies. Ecosummit is a Berlin-based organization promoting green venture capital, and publishes a helpful list of many of the key funds operating in this area.[15]

A type of very early stage venture capital investing is referred to as angel investing, where (usually) wealthy individuals, often successful business people, invest financially and offer advice, expertise and contacts to entrepreneurs. Angel investing can be used to help entrepreneurs fund a proof-of-concept, and perhaps a limited trial, following which additional venture capital funds might be sought to build a more substantial business. While there may be an element of impact investing, in many cases angel investors expect to make financial returns, although accepting that – as with venture capital – investments will need to be spread across a wide portfolio, as a small number of highly profitable investments are required to balance the large number that may fail.

Some angel investors act alone; others form investment syndicates to share risk and pool expertise and networks. Many syndicates choose to specialize in particular sectors, and we are beginning to see the emergence of angel syndicates with a focus on climate change mitigation and adaptation projects. One of these is the UK's Green Angel Syndicate, founded in 2013, which focuses on investments in clean energy, water, sustainable transport and smart cities.[16] As well as providing early stage funding for innovative technologies and businesses seeking to support the transition to a greener economy, syndicate members – many of whom have expertise in green and sustainable business, finance and technology themselves – offer guidance, support and access to business networks to help the early stage investments grow.

There are clear advantages to private equity investment in some cases, but there are also concerns and potential drawbacks. Lower levels of transparency in private markets can make it hard for investors or other stakeholders to assess the performance or impacts of privately held companies. Pressure to deliver the high levels of return demanded by investors who are taking on risk through private equity deals can negatively affect decision-making in investee companies, for example by forcing cost cutting that affects wages for workers or encourages over-exploitation of resources or low standards of environmental conservation. Private equity investments have also been associated with the use of complex corporate structures, financing arrangements and tax havens, which bring the risk of negative publicity and reputational damage or regulatory pressure.

QUICK QUESTION

How can the distinctive characteristics of private equity investment be mobilized in support of green finance?

Yieldcos

One of the new equity-based instruments that have emerged (led by the US) as an important channel for investment in renewable energy is the yieldco. Yieldcos, in essence, are publicly listed companies set up specifically to hold (in this case) renewable energy assets that acquire existing assets from a parent company or other sellers. They are structured so as to hold cash-generating assets and to pay out all or nearly all of the revenues to investors in the form of dividends. It is this which gives them their name – the yield referring to the income generated by the asset, rather than any increase in its face value.

One of the attributes of yieldcos that attracts investors is that they are structured to return little, if any, taxable revenue (in terms of Corporation Tax) and, as such, they can provide a tax-shield for investors. There was a boom in the growth of yieldcos, and similar structures, in the US and UK between 2013 to 2015, driven in part by investors seeking ways to deliver stable returns on capital in an ultra-low interest rate environment.

In the US, where their use has been most widespread, yieldcos were kick-started by NRG Yield, while in the UK a similar structure, known as a quoted project fund, was pioneered by Greencoat UK Wind. Between them, these asset classes raised $7 billion in equity finance in 2015, with investors including hedge funds and institutional investors as well as private individuals. There have also been attempts to set up yieldcos holding renewable energy assets in developing countries such as India, Brazil and South Africa.

The terminology describing the array of financial products and instruments used for green and sustainable finance in this area can easily lead to confusion and there is considerable overlap in the use of some terms. For example, many investment products involve setting up a corporate structure (in effect a company) to hold assets. Sometimes these can look and even function in very similar ways under different names in the same or different jurisdictions. In the UK, for example, there are shares listed in companies that hold renewable energy assets in just the same way as a yieldco and are often described as yieldcos, though in fact they are closed-ended, asset-backed funds listed on the stock market, albeit structured as investment companies.

Concerns about the performance and use of yieldcos rose following increasing market volatility in 2015 and subsequent years. Unexpected shifts are not surprising in a new market and there have been demands for steps to be taken to improve the performance of assets and the level of confidence for investors, including greater transparency on asset composition and transactions. There are also demands for stronger corporate governance, as well as the ongoing need for policy and regulation to be consistent and effective in supporting the growth of renewable energy generation and delivery, and energy efficiency.

Funds and collective investment schemes

One of the most common ways to invest in a particular sector or in a specific selection of stocks, rather than passively tracking a stock market index, is to invest in thematic funds, which include both passive funds and actively managed funds. A very wide range of fund types exist, ranging in size, complexity, risk profile, geography, sector and selection criteria. Funds are run by fund managers who decide on the strategy, choose the stocks and securities and manage the portfolio, charging a management fee and sometimes an additional performance-linked fee for their services. In the EU, funds are regulated and referred to as Undertakings for Collective Investment in Transferable Securities (UCITS). A range of the most common types of funds, including open-ended funds (unit trusts), closed-ended funds (investment trusts), exchange-traded funds (ETFs), index funds, carbon funds and hedge funds are described in this section.

As we saw in the introduction to this chapter, there is a growing body of evidence showing that values-based investment funds (and the companies they invest in) – often referred to as sustainable funds as this is the description used by Morningstar, an influential ratings agency – achieve comparable or superior returns compared to the market as a whole. This may be due to a combination of superior returns from fast-growing asset classes (eg renewable energy, clean transport) and the avoidance of costs associated with carbon-intensive industries (eg increasing carbon prices, litigation costs and other crystalizing physical, liability and transition risks).

Open-ended funds (unit trusts)

The growth of interest in and demand for values-based investments has seen a significant rise in the number and diversity of green, sustainable, ESG, SRI and similar investment funds. These often take the form of open-ended funds, such as unit trusts, which are made up of units created by the fund manager when investors want to buy and then cancelled/redeemed when they want to sell. Open-ended funds are viewed as a relatively safe way for less experienced investors to select stocks.

The first environmentally focused, open-ended fund to be launched in the UK was the Jupiter Ecology Fund, established in 1988. By 2018, a very wide range of sustainable and/or green funds had become available in developed markets. Most mainstream fund managers now offer at least one such fund and there are also numerous specialist fund managers taking advantage of increased investor demand. Choice and diversity bring many benefits, including lower costs for investors, greater liquidity, and the ability to diversify green and sustainable investments across a range of funds and sectors.

It can be difficult for asset owners such as pension funds, and even more so for retail investors, to assess and track funds' green, sustainable and ESG performance, as well as their exposures to underlying assets' climate risk, however. Increased levels of transparency have enabled investors and analysts to improve their understanding of the sustainability policies and performance of companies and fund managers are now disclosing more detailed information about the composition and performance of their portfolios. As we have already seen in relation to other asset classes like green bonds, however, there are differing views on the definition of green and/or sustainable, many tools and criteria for selection (from negative screening to positive stock picking), and many different approaches on how to apply selection criteria. This can lead to outcomes in terms of fund allocation that some investors would view as perverse. This should become less of an issue over time as the EU Taxonomy, and other similar taxonomies and related regulatory interventions designed to ensure consistency and avoid greenwashing develop and are implemented.

Specialist ethical or green financial advisers and consultants can help customers find funds that meet their needs and expectations, and it is becoming easier for both professionals and retail investors to gain access to expert advice and a good range of products and services. The UK ethical investment adviser and manager Castlefield, for example, publishes its own analysis of the environmental credentials of social and responsible investment funds each year, illustrating the difference between dark green and light green funds on offer.

The Castlefield example shows how significant challenges are faced by investors, particularly less sophisticated investors, in identifying truly green, sustainable and/or responsible investments. Its leading fund is from a specialist sustainability fund manager (WHEB), and its lowest performer comes from the portfolio of one of the largest mainstream global asset managers (Vanguard). It is not a given that larger asset managers will have less innovative or stringent approaches to green, sustainable and ESG funds, but there is good reason for values-based and impact-driven investors to consider more specialist offerings, given that they are perhaps less likely to compromise on environmental, sustainability and other factors in order to make funds more attractive to a wider investment base.

Big data and data analytics is increasingly being used to help investors understand the green credentials of funds and their underlying investments. In 2017, for example, Climetrics launched a free-to-use tool that investors can use to assess the climate related-risk and impact for some €2 trillion of actively managed funds and ETFs. In 2018, Sustainalytics, a well-established ESG analytics and ratings firm, began to evaluate companies on their exposure to fossil fuels and the risks faced from the global transition to a low-carbon world. Tumelo, a new UK-based start-up, offers a dashboard enabling retail investors and their advisers to see individual holdings within pension and other funds more clearly, to better assess their exposure to fossil fuel or more sustainable investments. Yova, a Swiss FinTech, provides a platform to help retail investors create their own investment portfolio, using their preferences for different aspects of sustainability (eg climate change, reforestation, education) and investment preferences (eg risk).

CASE STUDY

How Climetrics rates funds[17]

Climetrics offers investors a simple means to understand their exposure to climate risks. Climetrics' scoring system is based on three parts: each fund's portfolio holdings, its investment policy, and the asset manager's governance. The purpose is to assess each fund's entire investment process. Climetrics uses market-leading company data from CDP and ISS-climate, but also draws on additional data sources. Its methodology is fully transparent, and independently delivers up-to-date ratings for any fund in the available universe.

The Climetrics rating measures the climate risk and opportunities of a fund against all other funds in its sample. Three quantitative layers of analysis produce an overall climate score for each fund, which is compared to all funds in the coverage and then assigned a final one to five leaf rating, with five being the best. Five-leaf rated funds must adhere to strict threshold criteria. Asset managers do not need to apply to receive a rating. Climetrics independently rates any available fund in the available universe.

A top Climetrics rating (four or five leaf rating) indicates that, on average, the companies in a fund's portfolio are:

- more carbon efficient;
- better at publicly disclosing and managing climate-related risks and opportunities;
- more likely to deploy key technologies supporting the energy transition.

The use of data analytics and the development of ratings services such as Climetrics and Sustainalytics (together with regulatory developments such as the introduction of green and sustainable taxonomies) should, over time, improve market consistency and integrity in the use of green, sustainable and similar terminology in the marketing of investments and funds. If some fund managers, financial advisers and other market participants misuse green labelling, this may amount to greenwashing, which may risk undermining confidence in the whole sector. This becomes less likely (and greenwashing more likely to be exposed) as green and sustainable fund rating analytics and tools become more widely available. In addition, as we saw in earlier chapters, regulators including the FCA in the UK are already taking a more active interest in ensuring that green labelling is applied correctly, and consistently, together with consistent disclosure of climate-related risks.

QUICK QUESTION

What might be the tensions between making green and sustainable funds greener and making those funds more accessible or attractive to large asset owners like pension funds?

Closed-ended funds (investment trusts)

In contrast to open-ended unit trusts, closed-ended funds, sometimes called investment trusts or investment companies, are listed on the stock exchange and their shares can be bought and sold like those of other listed companies. Closed-ended funds often invest in similar ways to open-ended funds, although there is a general perception that they are more complex and less suited to inexperienced investors.

Investment trusts are publicly listed funds that are closed-ended because they raise a fixed amount of money from investors who buy shares in the fund, which are listed on a stock exchange. Investment trusts are usually eligible for inclusion in retail investment products like ISAs, which are tax-efficient for savers and investors. Investment trusts have become a common way of raising finance for renewable energy projects, and as such they have also become an easy and popular way for retail investors to gain exposure to this asset class.

CASE STUDY

Greencoat Capital[18]

Greencoat Capital is a UK-based fund manager specializing in resource efficiency and renewable energy, with more than £1.8 billion under management, over a range of listed and privately owned funds, including the well-established Greencoat UK Wind fund, and the recently launched Greencoat Renewables fund which invests in Euro-denominated assets and whose shares were listed in London in July 2017.

Greencoat UK Wind

Greencoat UK Wind PLC is the leading listed renewable infrastructure fund, invested in operating UK wind farms, with the aim of providing investors with an annual dividend that increases in line with RPI inflation while preserving the capital value of the investment portfolio in the long term on a real basis through reinvestment of excess cash flow and the prudent use of portfolio leverage.

Highlights

- The Group's investments generated 978.1 GWh of electricity, 6 per cent below budget owing to low wind resource.
- Net cash generation (Group and wind farm SPVs) was £49 million.
- Acquisition of an interest in Clyde and the acquisition of Screggagh increased the portfolio to 19 wind farm investments, net generating capacity to 420 MW and gross asset value (GAV) to £900.1 million as at 31 December 2016.
- Issuance of further shares raising £100 million in May 2016 and £147 million in November 2016.
- The company declared total dividends of 6.34 pence per share with respect to the year and targeted a dividend of 6.49 pence per share for 2017 (increased in line with December 2016 RPI).
- There were £100 million outstanding borrowings at 31 December 2016, equivalent to 11 per cent of GAV.

Defining characteristics

Greencoat UK Wind's 2016 Annual Report stated that:

- Greencoat UK Wind PLC was designed for investors from first principles to be simple, transparent and low risk.
- The Group is invested solely in operating UK wind farms.
- Wind is the most mature and largest scale renewable technology.
- The UK has a long-established regulatory regime, high wind resource and £60 billion of wind farms in operation in the short to medium term.
- The Group is wholly independent and thus avoids conflicts of interests in its investment decisions.
- The UK-based, independent Board is actively involved in key investment decisions and in monitoring the efficient operation of the assets, and works in conjunction with the most experienced investment management team in the sector.
- The Group only invests in wind farms that have an appropriate operational track record (or price adjustment mechanism as disclosed in note 14 to the financial statements).

- Low leverage (including no asset level leverage) is important to ensure a high level of cash-flow stability and higher tolerance to downside sensitivities.
- The Group invests in sterling assets and thus does not incur material currency risk.

Greencoat Renewables

Newly listed Irish energy company Greencoat Renewables has said 'heavy demand' from investors at its initial public offering (IPO) was down to Ireland's 'ambitious' 2020 energy targets, as well as the stability of the Irish regulatory regime.

Executives from the fledgling firm, which acquired part of the original Bord Gáis wind portfolio in 2017, gathered at the offices of the Irish Stock Exchange to witness the ceremonial ringing of the opening bell at 8 am. Greencoat Renewables is the first renewable energy infrastructure company to list on the Dublin exchange, and the first euro-denominated renewable energy infrastructure company to list on the London Stock Exchange. It raised €270 million in its IPO, €20 million above target, as the deal attracted strong investor interest.

Addressing the crowd from the stock exchange's balcony before ringing the bell, non-executive chairman Rónán Murphy said it had been a 'long and torturous process' over the past number of months, but that investor demand had 'surprised us all'.

Speaking to *The Irish Times* afterwards, Paul O'Donnell, partner of Greencoat Capital, the investment manager, said conditions were 'ripe' to go public. 'We were very pleased with the demand. We attracted some really interesting investors right across the board, from across European, the UK, and Irish institutions. If you look at Ireland, we set ourselves ambitious 2020 targets and there is significant investment required to deliver those targets. Looking ahead to that, and beyond 2020, these are long-term assets… The need to decarbonize is becoming more and more evident and we expect growth opportunities to continue beyond 2020.'

Investors include the State's Ireland Strategic Investment Fund and AIB, which helped finance the initial portfolio, comprising 137 megawatts of wind farm assets in Munster that the firm acquired in 2017 from Canada's Brookfield Renewable Partners.

Paul O'Donnell said the listing would provide the platform to build upon its initial portfolio of operational wind farms, with a 'substantial pipeline of future acquisition opportunities' in the Irish market.

Exchange-traded funds (ETFs)

Exchange-traded funds (ETFs) act in a similar manner to an index tracker fund and aim to provide investors with a return that matches the return on a set of specified assets, such as an equity or bond index, a basket of currencies or commodities, or almost any other set/combination of assets. In the case of ETFs, however, an investor is buying a promise by the issuer to provide that return, rather than buying any direct interest in the underlying assets themselves. The return may be generated by buying the underlying assets, but is often composed of a wider range of financial products, including futures and derivatives.

Shares in ETFs are listed on an exchange and can be bought and sold at any time, which can lead many investors to assume that ETFs are more efficient for investors (as an investor does not need to buy or sell what might be a large number of underlying assets and shares, just an ETF share). However, there can be tracking errors, as some ETFs use complex combinations of products to try to match the performance of underlying assets. In addition, investors are exposed to credit risk in relation to the issuer of the ETF, as it is the issuer who is ultimately responsible for maintaining the value of assets to back the shares that are issued.

In recent years, the ETF market has grown rapidly, with approximately $4.4 trillion of assets under management in 2017. Research from Ernst & Young noted a rise in ESG investor interest in ETFs in the years to 2017;[19] in 2018, BlackRock, the world's largest asset manager, launched a range of funds that invest based on ESG criteria to meet increasing investor demand for ETFs.

Advantages of ETFs

- **Flexible trading:** ETFs can be traded at any time of the day, with no minimum investment and without the redemption fees and other costs associated with other funds.
- **Variety:** ETFs can be bought and sold anywhere, and can be structured to mimic the performance of a huge range of assets and products.
- **Reduced costs:** Avoiding having to buy and sell underlying securities means that management and trading costs are reduced, and so in theory more of the capital return can be passed on to the investor.

Disadvantages of ETFs

- **Additional fees:** Brokerage commissions are paid each time ETFs are bought or sold.
- **Price spread:** The structure of ETFs means there is sometimes a wider bid/ask spread, meaning investors may have to buy at a slight premium and sell at a slight discount, especially if liquidity is low or market volatility is high.
- **Risk:** As an ETF is effectively a promise by the issuer to pay a return based on a formula, in reality the ETF investor is exposed to counterparty risk in relation to the ability of the issuer to pay (in addition to market risk in relation to the value of the underlying assets of the actual ETF).

> **QUICK QUESTION**
>
> What might be the advantages and/or disadvantages of ETFs for green and sustainable finance?

Many ETFs seek to replicate the return of the underlying asset by using a range of different investments, rather than by actually buying the underlying assets themselves. The relationships between market prices and capital flows mean that it is not simple to judge the impact of ETF investing on the underlying companies or assets. There is a valid question, however, as to whether the claimed trading liquidity and efficiency benefits of ETFs for investors are sufficiently important to choose this form of investment rather than products that invest directly in the underlying shares or other assets. This is relevant to green and sustainable finance as, given the need for investment capital to be channelled to investments supporting climate change adaptation and mitigation if capital is utilized in general financial instruments of this type, it may not be available for green and sustainable investment.

Like many green investment funds, green ETFs often focus on renewable and clean energy technologies. The range of options and issues that underpin selection criteria for the assets are generally the same as for green investment funds. The removal of the need to actually buy the underlying assets (which may be in limited supply) potentially removes some restrictions regarding the supply of green assets that meet funds' criteria. Thus, investors are able to gain access to green assets, without necessarily owning the green assets themselves. Examples of green and sustainable ETFs include:

- iShares ESG MSCI Global Impact;
- iShares S&P Global Clean Energy;
- First Trust Global Wind Energy;
- First Trust Nasdaq Clean Edge Energy.

As with other types of investment funds, ETFs have been criticized for greenwashing, since some funds labelled as green and/or sustainable also, by their nature of following indices, may have significant exposure to fossil fuel and other less sustainable investments.

Index funds

Funds can adopt active or passive strategies across equities, bonds and other alternative assets. Index funds are a popular type of passive fund, where the fund's portfolio tracks the components of a market index (eg the FTSE 100). Many index funds, especially those tracking main market indices, such as the FTSE or Dow Jones, offer diversification and low management fees and operating expenses.

As noted above, in recent years a number of green, ethical, ESG and sustainability indices have been launched. These are developed and provided by stock exchanges (eg FTSE Global Climate, FTSE4Good), financial data providers (eg MSCI ESG Index), or fund managers (eg First Trust Nasdaq Clean Edge Green Energy Index Fund). Although more specialized than main market index funds, and generally with higher fees and expenses, green and sustainable index funds can attract greater investment to this asset class through funds that are simplified, diversified and have reasonable costs and expenses. Also, as we saw above, indices have been criticized, however, for potentially offering a misleading picture of sustainability; some ESG and sustainability indices, for example, include major oil and gas companies, airlines and airport operators. This is because indices may weight factors including disclosure, governance and fair working practices highly, meaning a low E rating is outweighed by high S and G ratings. Furthermore, some of the most significant emitters of greenhouse gases, eg Shell, are also some of the largest investors in clean energy and other low carbon technologies, which might also give them a higher ESG or sustainability rating.

Investors cannot be sure, therefore, without looking at the component stocks in an index, whether investing in an index fund labelled as sustainable is, in fact, the case. As we saw above, however, recent initiatives including the FTSE TPI Climate Transition and MSCI Climate Change Indexes seek to overcome this by overweighting stocks that set, disclose and make good progress towards targets aligned to the Paris Agreement, whilst underweighting or excluding those that do not.

Index funds are not limited to equities. Green bond indices, for example (also described in Chapter 7) have only recently been developed, but already some of the largest fund managers are marketing green bond index funds as a way for investors to access growing green bond markets efficiently, relying on the methodology and analysis of the index provider to select appropriate green bonds and of the fund to package those into a product for which shares can be sold. The use of an index and the aggregation of bonds in a fund can significantly scale up the flow of finance by allowing investors to buy and sell assets easily, hold a more diversified portfolio and reduce credit and default risk.

CASE STUDY

ChinaBond climate-aligned bond index[20]

China, as the leading market for the issuance of green bonds, has also been a leader in the development of green bond indices. China launched the world's first climate-aligned green bond index in 2016. The Index includes 210 bonds with a total value of ¥1.3 trillion. The bonds cover a wide range of sectors from transport, to energy and diversified bond issues, but the main focus is on transport, which accounts for 91 per cent. Hydropower was excluded due to social and environmental impacts, but could be included in future.

The ChinaBond China Climate-Aligned Bond Index is a collaboration between China Central Depository & Clearing Co. Ltd, China Energy Conservation and Environmental Protection Consulting Co Ltd (CECEP) and the Climate Bonds Initiative (CBI). The research process was undertaken by CBI and CECEP to identify bonds that are in line with the Climate Bonds Taxonomy and the China Green Bond Endorsed Project Catalogue.

Bonds where some of the proceeds are used for general purposes, rather than earmarked for specific climate-aligned projects, are only eligible if the company is a 'pureplay' green company – ie over 95 per cent of its revenue comes from green sectors.

Green bond funds are usually structured as listed, closed-ended investment funds with underlying portfolios comprising a wide range of bond sizes, currencies, sector, geography and features. Fund managers collect a fee for their role in selecting and managing the assets. Specialist green bond funds are managed by a range of large investors in several markets, including SEB Asset Management, Nikko Asset Management, BlackRock, Calvert, and State Street. They are listed in the public markets on exchanges, or in some cases are offered to investors privately through private equity or hedge funds. In March 2018, Amundi and the International Finance Corporation (IFC) launched the world's largest targeted green bond fund, focused on emerging markets. The Amundi Planet Emerging Green One (EGO) fund aims to invest $2 billion into emerging market green bonds to 2025.

Green bond funds have proved successful and popular to date. The challenges to further growth are significant, however. Some green bond funds are struggling to find assets in which to invest. The dynamics of modern financial markets means that demand from investors wanting to buy the product (in this case shares in a green bond fund) often outstrips the supply of suitable assets in the shape of eligible and credible green bonds. Green bonds themselves are a relatively new product for which the definitions and sub-categories remain somewhat unclear, although frameworks and standards, including the Green Bond Principles and Climate Bonds Standard, are bringing greater consistency to the market, and helping to promote market integrity and avoid greenwashing.

Carbon funds

The term carbon fund is used widely to describe a range of investments in green and sustainable assets and activities. This includes, but is not limited to:

- funds established by NGOs and others to support climate change mitigation and adaptation projects (eg Conservation International's Carbon Fund, established in 2009, which has raised more than $30 million for forest conservation projects);
- carbon offsetting programmes (not funds in the generally accepted, investment sense) that aggregate funds from individuals and businesses seeking to offset their carbon emissions, and invest these in green and sustainable projects (eg Carbonfund.org);
- funds established and/or supported by development banks and similar international and national institutions to (usually) acquire carbon credits and identify suitable climate change mitigation and adaptation projects to offset greenhouse gas emissions (eg NEFCO Carbon Funds and NEFCO Norwegian Carbon Procurement Facility);

- funds providing an investment opportunity for secondary and retail trading in carbon credits, linked to emissions trading schemes (eg New Zealand Carbon Fund, which enables investors to trade New Zealand Unit (NZU) carbon credits. One NZU represents 1 tonne CO_2e.

In general, however, carbon fund is usually taken to refer to policy instruments and fundraising mechanisms designed to mobilize public and private capital to reduce greenhouse gas emissions and finance climate change adaptation projects and activities, as in the NEFCO examples above. The World Bank established the first carbon fund in 1999; since then it has invested and leveraged more than $6 billion in a wide range of carbon funds and similar initiatives, including:

- Forest Carbon Partnership Facility and BioCarbon Fund Initiative for Sustainable Forest Landscapes, which purchase Reducing Emissions for Deforestation and Forest Degradation (REDD+) carbon credits;
- Carbon Initiative for Development, a fund focused on clean energy in developing countries;
- Green Climate Fund, a global fund established in 2010 by the UNFCCC parties, with the majority of funding coming from developed countries, to support developing countries in developing low-emission and climate-resilient development.

Hedge funds

Hedge funds seek to generate 'alpha', which means outperforming the market by achieving a greater than market risk-adjusted rate of return, rather than seeking to merely achieve or replicate the market returns, as an index tracking fund might. As they are only allowed to accept investments from professional investors, hedge funds, for the most part, are not regulated like banks or other investment funds, which means that, in reality, hedge funds can invest in almost any asset and in almost any way they like.

The freedom that hedge funds have means that they are actively managed and can choose a combination of very specific sectors or assets and/or choose to take a greater level of risk in anticipation of higher returns. This will often involve the use of specialist analysis and market intelligence, and increasingly involves the use of complex algorithmic trading strategies and techniques, such as high frequency trading, that are controversial due to their potential to cause high volatility and because they are accused of obscuring the market for real investments in productive economic activity.

Hedge funds may also adopt strategies more relevant for green and sustainable finance, including private equity investments in new and potentially high-growth sectors such as renewable energy or clean technology, and look for opportunities to trade in new markets such as those for carbon credits. These are good examples of sectors where mainstream financial markets have difficulty investing without the support of development banks or other policy interventions because there may be limited data on historic performance (many financial markets are surprisingly backward-looking in this sense); or because of the stickiness of assumptions and market behaviour. This is due, in part, to the pressure of having to follow overall market sentiment in order to match indices or seek to maintain returns in the short term, rather than having the ability to anticipate transformative shifts and disruptions and to invest in long-term value.

Portfolio approaches to green and sustainable finance

Delivering on the Paris Agreement to achieve the emissions reductions necessary to tackle climate change and mobilizing investment to achieve the UN Sustainable Development Goals will only happen if investors are able to align their entire portfolios with the needs of a low-carbon and sustainable global economy. The green and sustainable finance products and services discussed in this chapter, together with the products and services outlined in related chapters on banking, green bonds and insurance, all have roles to play. We need to consider a more holistic approach, however, if we are to achieve a successful transition to a sustainable, low-carbon world. This implies an approach to green and sustainable finance that is comprehensive both in terms of the products and services available and utilized, and also in the sense that it proactively engages with actions that support a systemic shift in finance and the wider economy towards low-carbon and sustainable goals.

One way of looking at this challenge is in terms of portfolio decarbonization, which encompasses investment in low-carbon assets with disinvestment from high-carbon assets.

> Portfolio decarbonization refers to systematic efforts by investors to align their investment portfolios with the goals of a low-carbon economy. It includes, but is not limited to, efforts to reduce the carbon footprint of investment portfolios, to increase investment in areas such as renewable energy, to withdraw capital from high energy consumption activities and to encourage companies and other entities to reduce their emissions and support the transition to a low-carbon economy.[21]

The balance of investment versus disinvestment, the pace of portfolio decarbonization and the desired objective (zero carbon versus low carbon) will depend on a range of factors, including investors' preferences and values, the size of organization, position in the investment chain (eg asset owner or asset manager) and the types of assets invested in. Portfolio decarbonization is in its early stages, but a range of important strategies and tools are emerging – alongside a set of priority issues to be addressed, as discussed in the next case study, on the Portfolio Decarbonization Coalition.

CASE STUDY

Portfolio Decarbonization Coalition[22]

The Portfolio Decarbonization Coalition (PDC) was established in 2014 as a multi-stakeholder initiative that seeks to mobilize institutional investors to decarbonize their investment portfolios. As of October 2017 it had 32 members representing over $3 trillion in assets under management with $800 billion in decarbonization commitments. The PDC aims to provide a platform that can drive action by investors and also send strong signals to policymakers and companies about investors' commitment to the transition to a low-carbon economy.

All 32 of the member organizations have begun taking steps to decarbonize. Their targets and approaches vary considerably and a wide range of actions are being taken, including:

- engaging (individually and through collaborative initiatives such as CDP) with companies to encourage them to set emission reduction targets, and to strengthen their climate change-related disclosures;
- engaging with their fund managers and other service providers to encourage them to take account of climate change in their investment practices and processes;
- investing in environmental technologies and renewable energies;
- excluding fossil fuels from their investment portfolios;
- supporting the development of the green bond market;
- supporting the development of low-carbon indices;
- playing an active role in policy debates on climate change.

The benefits are already being seen in terms of the carbon content of these investors' portfolios. For some of the investors, this process is new and exploratory, whereas other members are specialists in sustainable investment and already have a lot of experience with these issues and substantially decarbonized portfolios. Many express the belief that they can match the returns of major indices while reducing carbon exposure, while others see significant investment benefits in terms of long-term value and risk management (eg less risk of stranded assets and more exposure to companies that will benefit from a low-carbon shift).

As experience is growing and lessons are learned, the PDC members have identified several priority areas for action:

- improving the quality of information being reported by companies on Scope 1, 2 and 3 emissions and on the wider life-cycle impacts of their products and services;
- developing decarbonization measurement and assessment methodologies;
- developing decarbonization strategies for all asset classes, not just listed equities;
- building the market for decarbonized investment products and investment solutions. This includes increasing asset owner demand for these products, and encouraging asset managers to develop innovative products, across asset classes, that meet asset owner needs;
- developing tools that enable the aggregate effect of portfolio decarbonization efforts on the real economy to be assessed and reported;
- developing the investment case for decarbonization;
- developing understanding of the contribution that portfolio decarbonization can make to the goal of a low-carbon economy and the timeframes over which this contribution can be made;
- sharing expertise and solutions.

QUICK QUESTION

What might be some of the arguments you could use to advocate for portfolio decarbonization inside your organization?

Portfolio decarbonization is having a demonstrable impact on some of the world's largest organizations. In 2018, for instance, Royal Dutch Shell identified divestment, driven by the decarbonization of investor portfolios, as a material risk to its business – the first of the major oil and gas companies to do so. Responding to the identification of divestment as a material risk, and seeking to mitigate climate risk in their business more generally, Shell announced plans to reduce its Net Carbon Footprint by 35 per cent by 2035, and by 50 per cent by 2050. These targets are linked to executive remuneration, to ensure they are fully embedded in business strategy, planning and operations.

Climate Action 100+, a group of investors managing over $47 trillion with the aim of engaging systemically important greenhouse gas emitters to encourage them to shift resources to clean and/or cleaner energy, played a major role in encouraging Shell to identify, disclose and announce its plans for mitigating climate risk. The group is working with more than 100 high emission 'focus companies', seeking to ensure they align their strategies and operations with the Paris Agreement, as set out in the case study below.

CASE STUDY

Climate Action 100+[23]

What is Climate Action 100+?

Climate Action 100+ is an investor initiative to ensure the world's largest corporate greenhouse gas emitters take necessary action on climate change. The companies include 100 'systemically important emitters', accounting for two-thirds of annual global industrial emissions, alongside more than 60 others with significant opportunity to drive the clean energy transition.

Launched in December 2017 at the One Planet Summit by Betty T Yee, a board member of California Public Employees' Retirement System (CalPERS), Climate Action 100+ garnered worldwide attention as it was highlighted as one of 12 key global initiatives to tackle climate change.

Which investors support Climate Action 100+?

Climate Action 100+ requires investors to sign on to the Climate Action 100+ Sign-on Statement. The public statement sets out the investor signatories' commitment and expectations of the companies on the initiative's focus list. To date, it has been signed by more than 450 investors from across dozens of countries, who collectively manage more than $40 trillion in assets under management.

Why was Climate Action 100+ formed?

In 2015, nearly 200 countries around the world signed (and 170 have already ratified) the Paris Agreement, which aims to keep the increase in global average temperature to well below 2°C above pre-industrial levels and to pursue efforts to limit the temperature increase even further to 1.5°C, recognizing that this would significantly reduce the risks and impacts of climate change. The investor signatories of Climate Action 100+ believe that engaging and working with the companies in which they invest – to secure greater disclosure of climate change risks and robust company strategies aligned with the Paris Agreement – is consistent with their fiduciary duty and is essential to achieve the goals of the Paris Agreement.

Climate Action 100+ is designed to implement the investor commitment first set out in the Global Investor Statement on Climate Change in the months leading up to the adoption of the Paris Agreement.

In that statement investors committed to the following:

> As institutional investors and consistent with our fiduciary duty to our beneficiaries, we will… work with the companies in which we invest to ensure that they are minimizing and disclosing the risks and maximizing the opportunities presented by climate change and climate policy.

What are investors asking focus companies to do?

Investors signed on to Climate Action 100+ are requesting the boards and senior management of companies to:

1. Implement a strong governance framework that clearly articulates the board's accountability and oversight of climate change risks and opportunities.
2. Take action to reduce greenhouse gas emissions across the value chain, consistent with the Paris Agreement's goal of limiting global average temperature increase to well below 2°C above pre-industrial level.
3. Provide enhanced corporate disclosure in line with the final recommendations of the TCFD and, when applicable, sector-specific Global Investor Coalition on Climate Change Investor Expectations

on Climate Change[24] to enable investors to assess the robustness of companies' business plans against a range of climate scenarios, including well below 2°C, and improve investment decision-making.

Why do investors choose engagement?

Global collaborative investor engagement sends a powerful signal – directly to companies – that investors are asking for and expect companies to respond to climate change. Climate change is a systemic risk – one that investors cannot diversify away from. As equity investors and universal owners, investors have the ability and the responsibility to address climate risks and seek greater disclosure on how the most systemically significant emitters are aligning with transition pathways, specifically including well below 2°C and 1.5°C and disclosing climate change risks and opportunities to the market.

Key concepts

In this chapter we considered:

- the differences and similarities between ESG, SRI impact investing and other related terms, and the growth of the values-based investment sector;
- the role of equity markets within the wider financial system;
- a wide range of equity products, their suitability for different types of investors, and how they may support green and sustainable finance;
- different types of investment funds and how these may support investment in green and sustainable finance;
- portfolio decarbonization as a holistic approach to green and sustainable finance.

Now go back through this chapter and make sure you fully understand each point.

Review

In the context of green and sustainable finance, terms including ESG investing, responsible investing, sustainable investing, socially responsible investing (SRI), ethical investing and impact investing are in common use. All describe investments and/or investment strategies designed to deliver and support positive environmental and social impacts (and/or avoid negative impacts) as well as financial returns. We can refer to them in general as **values-based investing.**

Values-based investing has grown substantially over the past decade. According to the Global Sustainable Investment Alliance (GSIA), this now accounts for more than a quarter of assets under management globally (almost $31 trillion in 2018), a 34 per cent increase compared with 2016. Values-based investing has grown substantially over the past decade and accounted for approximately 26 per cent of assets under management globally in 2016. There is a growing base of evidence that values-based investing can deliver returns superior to traditional approaches to investing, at least in the longer term.

Equity markets have a vital role to play in allocating capital from savers and investors to productive assets and activities in the economy. The universe of equity markets, investors and investment products, services and markets is very large and diverse.

Equity markets have traditionally been the largest source of risk capital for companies in developed markets. This role has shifted and been challenged in recent years, but equity markets remain hugely important, both as a source (albeit diminishing in some jurisdictions) of capital and in providing a vital role in terms of corporate governance and stewardship relating to company strategy, performance and capital allocation.

In order to grow and mainstream green and sustainable finance, it is particularly important that the investment sector is able to support the flow of capital to key sectors such as renewable energy and green infrastructure, and that it is able to factor in long-term climate and environmental risks as well as prioritize long-term investments. It is also important that investment products are able to provide flexibility and a wide diversity of opportunities and risks that investors can match to their requirements.

The most common way for investors to gain exposure to companies with a positive environmental impact is via green, sustainable and/or ESG funds and indices, of which there is a wide and growing range. Some have a fairly narrow sector or thematic focus, such as renewable energy, while others are broader or focus on one environmental factor such as carbon emissions.

There is a growing range of green and sustainable investment funds (including index-tracking and exchange-traded funds – ETFs) and fund managers (including large global institutions, hedge funds and boutique green investment specialists) providing an increasing range of ways for investors to fund the transition to a sustainable, low-carbon world. This supports a large universe of sustainable investment possibilities. It also creates a potential risk of greenwashing, however, if some fund managers, financial advisers and other market participants misuse green labelling to take advantage of investor demand. The use of data analytics and the development of ratings and other advisory services, together with action by regulators over time, should improve market consistency and integrity.

Private equity and venture capital investors play important roles too. This is partly due to their ability to provide capital for companies and projects where there is a higher (or harder to measure) level of risk but the potential for strong growth and large-scale impact over time, especially in new sectors or technologies. There are some drawbacks, including generally lower levels of transparency and the fact that this market is more difficult to access for many investors and savers compared with public equity markets.

Achieving the emissions reductions necessary to meet the objectives of the Paris Agreement will only happen if investors are able to align investments with the needs of a sustainable, low-carbon economy. One way of looking at this challenge is through portfolio decarbonization – a comprehensive approach to portfolio management by which investors align their investment portfolio with investments supporting decarbonization.

Glossary

Carbon funds: These mobilize private and public capital for use in projects that tackle climate change.

Environmental, social and governance (ESG) investing: An investment approach that integrates ESG factors into the analysis of investments, usually using positive screening.

Equity: Shares in a business, sold to individual or institutional investors who provide risk capital in return for a share of profits and growth and a say in the governance of the business.

Exchange Traded Funds (ETFs): Investment funds listed on stock exchanges that match the return of a specified set of assets but may not invest directly in those underlying assets.

Funds: Selections of assets managed by a fund manager, who charges a fee (including Undertakings for Collective Investment in Transferable Securities). A huge variety of green funds are available to investors.

Hedge funds: Hedge funds seek to pick assets and investment strategies that should outperform the market, rather than match market-rate returns.

Impact investing: Where a positive environmental and/or social objective is the primary focus of, or given equal weighting to, achieving a positive financial return.

Indices: A selection of assets or investment products with similar characteristics, such as size, geographic focus, sector, or impact/purpose. Green indices are selected according to environmental criteria.

Institutional investors: Owners, managers and stewards of large amounts of assets that are invested on behalf of the beneficiaries (often savers or investors).

Listed equities: Shares listed on stock exchanges and traded on public markets.

Portfolio decarbonization: A systematic approach to portfolio management in which investors align their investment portfolio with investment in low-carbon assets and disinvestment from high-carbon assets.

Private equity: Investments in assets that are not listed or traded on public markets.

Responsible investing: Incorporating ESG factors into investment decision-making and strategies, as defined by the UN-supported Principles for Responsible Investment.

Socially responsible investing (SRI): Where investments are selected or eliminated according to ethical guidelines and SRI 'screens' determined by the investor.

Sustainable investing: An active approach to investing, involving positive selection of investments that deliver positive environmental and social impacts, and support the transition to a sustainable, low-carbon world.

Yieldco: A listed company set up to hold assets that generate a stable cash flow for investors. In recent years this has become a popular way to invest in renewable energy, eg solar and wind.

Notes

1. Global Sustainable Investment Alliance (2018) *2018 Global Sustainable Investment Review* [Online] http://www.gsi-alliance.org/wp-content/uploads/2019/03/GSIR_Review2018.3.28.pdf (archived at https://perma.cc/6C6R-ZWSH)
2. UNEP (2018) 400 investors launch joint global investor agenda for climate action, UNEP Finance Initiative [Online] http://www.unepfi.org/news/industries/investment/nearly-400-investors-with-32-trillion-in-assets-step-up-action-on-climate-change/ (archived at https://perma.cc/DT9E-KLWR)
3. UNEP (2018) 400 investors launch joint global investor agenda for climate action, UNEP Finance Initiative [Online] http://www.unepfi.org/news/industries/investment/nearly-400-investors-with-32-trillion-in-assets-step-up-action-on-climate-change/ (archived at https://perma.cc/DT9E-KLWR)
4. Morgan Stanley (2016) *2016 Sustainability Update* [Online] https://www.morganstanley.com/pub/content/dam/msdotcom/about-us/giving-back/sustainability-at-morgan-stanley/2016_MS_Sustainability_Report.pdf (archived at https://perma.cc/EW2E-VPF4)

5 McKinsey & Company (2017) From 'why' to 'why not': Sustainable investing as the new normal [Online] https://www.mckinsey.com/industries/private-equity-and-principal-investors/our-insights/from-why-to-why-not-sustainable-investing-as-the-new-normal (archived at https://perma.cc/28P9-LRWX)

6 Bank of Montreal (2015) *Financial Concerns of Women* [Online] https://bmogamviewpoints.com/wp-content/uploads/2015/04/wealth-institute-financial-concerns-of-women1.pdf (archived at https://perma.cc/JMC5-XHEE)

7 Deutsche Bank (2012) *Gateways to Impact: Industry survey of financial advisors on sustainable and impact investing* [Online] https://www.db.com/cr/en/docs/Survey_of_financial_advisors_sustainable_investing.pdf (archived at https://perma.cc/RT2B-UAMY)

8 Moxie Future (2018) *Understanding Female Investors: Women using capital to change the world* [Online] https://moxiefuture.com/wp-content/uploads/2018/01/Moxie-Future-Understanding-Female-Investors-Report-UFI18.pdf (archived at https://perma.cc/JY2Y-AU7K)

9 G Friede, T Busch and A Bassen (2015) ESG and financial performance: Aggregated evidence from more than 2000 empirical studies, *Journal of Sustainable Finance and Investment*, 5 (4), pp 210–33 [Online] https://www.tandfonline.com/doi/full/10.1080/20430795.2015.1118917 (archived at https://perma.cc/75EQ-UXJ2)

10 Finextra (2010) Deutsche Bank: Prioritising climate change results in share outperformance [Online] https://www.finextra.com/newsarticle/34436/deutsche-bank-prioritising-climate-change-results-in-share-outperformance (archived at https://perma.cc/W7K6-V639)

11 PRI (2016) *Principles for Responsible Investment* [Online] https://www.sedcocapital.com/sites/default/files/downloads/pri_brochure_2016_0.pdf (archived at https://perma.cc/44SK-3LR3)

12 EcoAct (2018) *The Sustainability Reporting Performance of the FTSE 100* [Online] https://info.eco-act.com/hubfs/Reports/SRP%202018/The%20Sustainability%20Reporting%20Performance%20of%20the%20FTSE%20100%20-%202018.pdf (archived at https://perma.cc/KQ2P-PU6U)

13 D Chesebrough, E Feller, T Grabski, A Miller and M Paty (2016) *2016 Report on Progress*, Sustainable Stock Exchanges Initiative [Online] http://www.sseinitiative.org/wp-content/uploads/2012/03/SSE-Report-on-Progress-2016.pdf (archived at https://perma.cc/U8EM-BVFA)

14 G Inderst, C Kaminker and F Stewart (2012) Defining and measuring green investments, *OECD Working Papers on Finance, Insurance, Private Pensions*, No. 24 [Online] http://www.oecd.org/finance/WP_24_Defining_and_Measuring_Green_Investments.pdf (archived at https://perma.cc/25QW-TX22)

15 J M Hess (2019) Smart green VCs you should know, EcoSummit [Online] https://ecosummit.net/articles/smart-green-vcs-you-should-know (archived at https://perma.cc/B4CE-ZYXF)

16 Green Angel Syndicate (nd) Portfolio [Online] https://www.greenangel-syndicate.com/portfolio (archived at https://perma.cc/NV49-7X2Z)
17 Climetrics (nd) The Climetrics rating for funds [Online] https://www.climetrics-rating.org/about-us (archived at https://perma.cc/KU8K-ZMD3)
18 C Gleeson (2017) Newly listed Greencoat Renewables raises €270 million in its IPO, *The Irish Times* [Online] https://www.irishtimes.com/business/energy-and-resources/newly-listed-greencoat-renewables-raises-270-million-in-its-ipo-1.3166241 (archived at https://perma.cc/7WX5-T482)
19 EY (2017) The EY global ETF report 2017: Reshaping around the investor [Online] https://eyfinancialservicesthoughtgallery.ie/ey-global-etf-survey-2017/ (archived at https://perma.cc/4MWJ-EFT4)
20 Climate Bonds Initiative (nd) *World's First Climate-Aligned Bond Index* [Online] https://www.climatebonds.net/files/files/ChinaBond%20Index%20Methodology.pdf (archived at https://perma.cc/66CS-EWBA)
21 Portfolio Decarbonization Coalition (nd) [Online] https://unepfi.org/pdc/ (archived at https://perma.cc/L9DH-KC4G)
22 Portfolio Decarbonization Coalition (nd) *Progress Reports 2016/2017* [Online] https://unepfi.org/pdc/ (archived at https://perma.cc/L9DH-KC4G)
23 Climate Action 100+ (nd) Global investors driving business transition [Online] http://www.climateaction100.org (archived at https://perma.cc/66H2-FXCL)
24 The Global Investor Coalition on Climate Change Investor Expectations on Climate Change sector guides cover oil and gas, mining, utilities and auto manufacturers and provide additional sector specific disclosure recommendations, particularly regarding the oversight of public policy positions.

10

Insurance

LEARNING OBJECTIVES

On completion of this chapter you should be able to:

- Describe the role of insurance within the wider financial system, and how climate-related financial risks are impacting the insurance sector.
- Describe how different insurance activities can affect the quality and functioning of the natural environment and natural systems.
- Understand how different types of insurance products and services can improve the quality and functioning of the natural environment and natural systems.
- Cite examples and case studies of green insurance products and services.

With core competencies in risk management and finance, the insurance industry is uniquely positioned to embed climate and other environmental risks into decision-making in the financial services sector. While many insurers continue to focus chiefly on financial risk management in response to climate change, others are taking a more proactive approach to environmental sustainability by offering new, green products and services. In addition, some insurers now limit and, in a few cases, refuse cover for high-carbon industries, such as thermal coal. Climate risk insurance products such as sovereign catastrophe risk pooling and index insurance have been developed to improve the resilience of communities most impacted by climate change.

The role of insurance in the financial system

The insurance industry's core business is to understand, manage and carry risk. By pricing and creating a market, risk can be pooled, diversified, managed and reduced, so that society is protected and economic development supported. When a person or business takes out an insurance policy, they make regular payments – premiums – to the insurer in exchange for an agreement that the insurer will cover any losses that materialize under certain circumstances. Premiums are pooled with those of other policyholders who have taken out insurance with the same insurance company. Insurance companies are very significant investors, as they invest the money raised from premiums across a range of asset classes, seeking returns to meet claims made and to keep down the cost of insurance premiums to policyholders.

Without insurance, risks would be borne solely by individuals, households, businesses, governments and other societal entities. Insurance removes the fear of catastrophic losses, and allows businesses and individuals to budget without unexpected variations in expenses. When unexpected losses do arise, insurance helps those affected to overcome the resultant financial hardship.

The insurance industry therefore has three key roles:

- **Risk carrying:** Insurance is a financial loss 'shock absorber' that reinforces the financial resilience of businesses and households to deal with unexpected losses, such as those resulting from natural disasters, currency fluctuations, policy shifts, illness or accident. This in turn enables investment and long-term planning.
- **Risk management:** The insurance industry's contribution to managing risk extends beyond the losses it pays out, to identifying risks in the various sectors and assets that can be insured. Insurers facilitate the understanding and reduction of risk through research, advocacy and support at local level. Insurance pricing and other policy terms and conditions can provide clear risk signals and reward risk reduction efforts.
- **Institutional investment:** Insurers' premiums are pooled and become part of a fund of financial assets, which insurers invest to generate additional funds by which to meet their obligations to policyholders. Globally, it is estimated that the insurance industry had nearly $27 trillion in assets under management in 2016, according to the UNFCCC.[1]

QUICK QUESTIONS

How might the insurance industry be affected by climate change and other forms of environmental damage? What risks and opportunities are there for the insurance industry?

The insurance sector and climate-related financial risks

In Chapter 5 we learned that there are three main types of climate-related financial risks, following the classification system used by the Task Force on Climate-related Financial Disclosure (TCFD) and others: **physical** risks, **transition** risks and **liability** risks:

- **Physical risks:** These arise from climate-related events, such as droughts, floods and storms. For insurers, the risks come from the impacts resulting from such events, such as damage to property, and also those that may arise indirectly through subsequent events, such as disruption of global supply chains or resource scarcity. For example, Lloyd's of London estimated that the 20 cm rise in sea level at the tip of Manhattan since the 1950s increased insured losses from Superstorm Sandy by 30 per cent in New York alone.[2]
- **Transition risks:** These arise from the process of adjustment towards a lower-carbon economy, such as developments in climate policy, new disruptive technology or shifting investor sentiment. For insurance firms, this risk factor is mainly about the potential re-pricing of carbon-intensive investment assets, and the speed at which any such re-pricing might occur, leading to asset impairment or stranded assets.
- **Liability risks:** These arise from parties who have suffered loss or damage from the effects of climate change and who seek compensation from those they hold responsible. Where such claims are successful, those parties against whom the claims are made may seek to pass on some or all of the cost to insurance firms.

Insurer/reinsurer Munich Re has developed the NatCatSERVICE, a large, publicly accessible database tracking significant natural disasters (and the costs of these) over the past 30 years, taking advantage of advances in data availability and analytics. According to Munich Re, overall economic losses from weather-related loss events have increased approximately fourfold in the past 30 years to an average of $140 billion per annum in the period 2010–14.[3] Insured losses have also increased from an average of around $10 billion per annum in the 1980s to more than $50 billion per annum over the past decade, and are predicted to continue to rise, creating financial and strategic challenges for the insurance sector as well as their customers and clients. There is strong evidence regarding an increase in the number of weather-related natural disasters, such as hurricanes and floods, attributable to the effects of climate change, there being no similar increase in non-weather-related natural disasters (eg volcanic eruptions) in the same period, 2010–14.

The year 2017 was the most expensive year on record for insurance companies. According to an overview of the global insurance industry published by EY, extreme weather events, including Hurricanes Harvey, Irma and Maria, combined with more than 700 natural disasters recorded in the NatCatSERVICE database, cost an estimated $330 billion in total economic losses, with insured losses estimated at a record $135 billion – substantially higher than the recent averages outlined above.[4] As a result, many large global insurers posted significant losses for 2017, including Lloyd's of London and Berkshire Hathaway. According to Aon Benfield, reported in the Insurance Journal, total economic losses in the US from hurricanes in 2017 were nearly five times the average of the preceding 16 years, losses from wildfires were four times higher, and losses from other severe storms some 60 per cent higher.[5]

A report published by the Sustainable Insurance Forum and International Association of Insurance Supervisors in 2018 demonstrates that there is a strong body of scientific consensus that climate change is having an influence on the frequency and severity of extreme weather events such as droughts, storms, floods and wildfires, including:

- Research by the World Meteorological Organization concluded that 80 per cent of natural disasters between 2005 and 2015 were in some way climate-related.
- Analysis of 59 studies in scientific journals published between 2016–17 reported that 70 per cent of these found that climate change had increased the risk of extreme weather events.[6]

Furthermore, the report points out that climate risks (physical, transition and liability) are likely to continue to have an increasing financial impact on insurers and the global economy more generally. Despite many insurers' advanced risk management systems, and growing appreciation and management of climate risks in particular, the impact of unforeseen physical risks (ie even more frequent and more severe extreme weather events) may impose further significant costs on insurers.

QUICK QUESTION

How might insurance firms help to protect people from the increasing number of climate-related disasters?

The Asset Owners' Disclosure Project (AODP), now part of ShareAction, rates and ranks the world's largest institutional investors and assesses their response to climate-related risks and opportunities. In 2018, it surveyed the world's 80 largest insurers, using the TCFD framework and recommendations as benchmarks. Key findings included:

- Major European insurers were leaders in climate disclosures, compared to their peers in other parts of the world.
- Climate-related issues are mainly viewed by the majority of insurers as a risk related to underwriting and investment portfolios, not as business opportunities.
- Engagement with management of investment holdings is mainly focused on improving disclosures rather than altering business strategies to support the transition to a low-carbon world.
- Only 1 in 10 major insurers were currently using climate scenario analysis, as recommended by the TCFD.
- The most common approach to insurers' portfolio management is via capital allocation – investing in low-carbon assets and divesting from high-carbon assets.
- On average, insurers have invested only 1 per cent of total assets under management in low-carbon investments.
- Less than a third of insurers have measured their portfolio emissions, although this is a significant improvement from 2017, when only a fifth had.
- Insurers are increasingly ceasing underwriting and investing in thermal coal, including some of Europe's largest insurers and reinsurers.[7]

With a clear interest in identifying and mitigating the risks posed by climate change, both as underwriters and investors, the insurance profession has often taken the lead within the financial services sector more widely, promoting action to understand the potential impacts of climate change, and conducting sophisticated climate modelling, data analysis and research. The insurance profession has also acted (and acts) collectively, and was a significant supporter of the establishment of the UN Environment Programme's Finance Initiative (UNEP FI) in the late 1990s.

In 2012 the UN Principles for Sustainable Insurance (UN PSI) were launched at the UN Conference on Sustainable Development. The UN PSI serves as a global framework for the insurance industry to address environmental, social and governance risks and opportunities. Endorsed by the UN Secretary-General, the Principles have led to the largest collaborative initiative between the UN and the insurance industry. By 2018, 120 organizations had adopted the four Principles for Sustainable Insurance, including insurers representing more than 25 per cent of world premium volume and $14 trillion in assets under management.[8]

The four Principles for Sustainable Insurance are:

1. We will embed in our decision-making environmental, social and governance issues relevant to our insurance business.
2. We will work together with our clients and business partners to raise awareness of environmental, social and governance issues, manage risk and develop solutions.
3. We will work together with governments, regulators and other key stakeholders to promote widespread action across society on environmental, social and governance issues.
4. We will demonstrate accountability and transparency in regularly disclosing publicly our progress in implementing the Principles.

The UN PSI provides a forum for insurers to develop frameworks, standards, guidance and tools to promote a sustainable approach to insurance and share best practice. In November 2018 the UNEP FI, together with 16 large, global insurers and reinsurers, announced a partnership to develop a new generation of climate risk assessment tools that would utilize the most up-to-date climate science research, and include the most advanced climate change scenarios. All of this will help insurers to identify, disclose and manage climate risk in line with the TCFD's recommendations, and provide a model of best practice as a basis for a consistent approach to climate risk management and disclosure.

Insurance regulators have also been proactive in promoting environmental sustainability and a more comprehensive approach to climate risk. The Sustainable Insurance Forum (SIF), mentioned above, was launched in 2016 to promote cooperation on critical sustainable insurance challenges, such as climate change. Convened by the UNEP, the SIF is an international network of insurance regulators and supervisors and includes insurance supervisors and regulators from Brazil, California, France, Ghana, Jamaica, Morocco, the Netherlands, Singapore and the UK, as well as the International Association of Insurance Supervisors (IAIS).

Working collectively, the insurance sector has often acted as a powerful voice for action on climate change.

QUICK QUESTION

What might be considered as green insurance?

While many insurers continue to focus on enhancing their climate-related financial risk management, both to better price premiums and to manage their investment portfolios, others are taking a more proactive approach to environmental sustainability by developing new products and services designed to help mitigate the effects of climate change. In the words of Dr Evan Mills of the Lawrence Berkeley National Laboratory:

> Just as the insurance industry has historically asserted its leadership to minimize risks from building fires and earthquakes, insurers have a huge opportunity today to develop creative loss-prevention solutions and products that will reduce climate-change-related losses for consumers, government and insurers.[9]

The types of products that insurance firms offer vary according to the types of insurance services they are providing. Broadly, there are three categories of insurance firm:

- **Life insurers:** Provide benefits in the event of death, retirement or changes in health, and also provide savings mechanisms for households. Products include annuities, conventional life assurance and other long-term savings products.
- **General insurers (also known as non-life insurers or property and casualty insurers):** Provide non-life insurance, which includes property cover, health insurance, liability policies and miscellaneous financial loss cover for individuals, companies and others. Certain real-economy activities require, either contractually or as a matter of public policy, insurance cover to be retained (for example, car insurance, or employers' liability).
- **Reinsurers:** Sell insurance to other insurance companies. They enable the primary insurance companies described above to cede a portion of risks they do not want fully to retain. Reinsurers pursue similar business models to primary insurers, albeit pooling a more diverse set of risks.

Life insurers tend to be more affected by climate and environment risks from their investments on the asset side of their balance sheets, given the need to match assets to liabilities over the longer term, and because their liabilities tend to be less volatile. They rely on investment returns to fulfil the longer-term obligations on their savings, pension and annuity liabilities. As such, the main way in which life insurers can promote environmental sustainability is through their investment portfolios. We have already considered the role of institutional investors in bond and equity markets in previous chapters.

General insurers, on the other hand, face more risks from their liabilities than their assets, which tend to be shorter in duration, predominantly from annual contracts of insurance. As such, an important way that general insurers can promote environmental sustainability and mitigate the impact of climate change is by offering new green products and services that may encourage changes in individual or corporate behaviour.

General insurance products and services are generally split into two categories: personal insurance, where the policyholder is a private individual, and commercial insurance, where the policyholder is a firm or some other kind of organization. New products have emerged in both categories to assist with the transition to a sustainable, low-carbon world, as we describe below.

Environmental, climate and green insurance

Although environmental, climate and green insurance may sound similar, they are in fact quite different. Environmental insurance provides protection from actual/potential liabilities arising from environmental damage; for example, coverage to protect against pollution, oil spills or other forms of environmental damage. Climate insurance (also known as climate risk insurance) provides protection against (usually) extreme weather events such as drought, floods and storms. We look at this in more detail below.

Green insurance, in contrast, seeks to encourage and support sustainable activities and behaviour by individuals, companies and others, and includes green insurance products and services that allow an insurance premium differentiation on the basis of environmentally positive characteristics/behaviour, and products and services that are tailored for promoting green activities, such as the use of renewable energy or other carbon-reducing activities.

QUICK QUESTION

Can you think of any insurance products or services that might fit with our definition of green insurance?

Green personal insurance

Personal insurance helps protect individuals from potential losses they could not afford to cover on their own. Insurance enables people to, for example, drive a car and own a home without risking major financial loss, as well as encouraging individuals to save and invest for the future instead of consuming their income.

Green motor insurance

Road transport is a significant component of the modern economy. There are approximately 1 billion vehicles on the road worldwide, which generate approximately 17 per cent of man-made greenhouse gases.[10] It is generally mandatory for drivers to have third-party liability insurance.

There are several ways in which motor insurers can enhance environmental sustainability. One way is through offering discounts for environmentally friendly vehicles. Some motor insurance companies offer lower premiums for those who drive hybrid vehicles. A similar discount may also apply to hybrid-electric boats and yachts, or cars that use alternative energy sources such as natural gas, hydrogen or ethanol. Some motor policies include an option of adding an endorsement to upgrade to a hybrid vehicle after the loss of the current vehicle. Specific electric vehicle insurance has also been developed, with discounts for purchasers.

CASE STUDY

TD Insurance for hybrid and electric vehicles[11]

TD Insurance (TDI) offers insurance discounts for hybrid and electric vehicles under TDI's Green Wheel Program. By the end of 2016, a total of 17,777 vehicles were covered under the Program. It is estimated that the company's customers have reduced their GHG emissions by over 33,000 tonnes CO_2e (carbon dioxide equivalent) through the use of hybrid and electric vehicles since 2012.

Another way that motor insurers can seek to promote more sustainable vehicle usage is through usage-based insurance (UBI), of which there are two basic types:

- pay how you drive (PHYD), where the insurance premium is based on how a vehicle is driven, taking into account factors including speed, acceleration and braking;
- pay as you drive (PAYD), where the premium is typically calculated based on the distance driven, and perhaps also the type and length of average/typical journeys.

UBI insurance is available to individuals and to organizations managing fleets of commercial vehicles (eg local government, public transport, logistics companies). In the UK, it is estimated that approximately one-third of fleets had adopted UBI by 2018.

In both PHYD and PAYD, devices or sensors embedded in vehicles, or smartphone-based apps, record telemetry tracking vehicle data such as acceleration, braking, distance, speed, journey time, the amount of time engines are idling, fuel consumption and efficiency and many more data points. Many insurers are now using smartphone-based systems, as an easier (and cheaper) way to track vehicles and driving styles, which can use GPS satellites to record usage rather than rely on black boxes and sensors embedded in vehicles. The telemetry recorded can then be analysed by the insurer to price driver premiums more accurately, based on distance driven (PAYD) and/or driving style (PHYD), with lower premiums available for more efficient and/or careful drivers. According to some estimates, UBI subscribers decrease their miles driven by 10 per cent or more, saving drivers money while reducing accidents, congestion and air pollution.

UBI schemes are growing in popularity, not just because of their environmental benefits but also because of the cheaper insurance available to individual drivers and fleet managers. According to a report by Ptolemus, a consulting firm, there are more than 20 million active UBI policies globally, with 372 active UBI schemes in 58 countries (2018).[12] This is still only a small part of the overall motor insurance market, however, accounting for some $15 billion of premiums compared with $715 billion in total. Frost & Sullivan, another consulting firm, estimates that the UBI market will grow to cover nearly 100 million drivers by 2020, with significant growth in the US, Europe and China.[13] Recent regulatory changes in China, enabling UBI, combined with the high penetration of smartphones, means that the growth of UBI in the world's largest automotive market is likely to be rapid.

> **QUICK QUESTION**
>
> Can you think of any emerging trends that may open up more opportunities for motor insurers to promote environmental sustainability?

Green home (domestic) insurance

Buildings are estimated to account for over 12 per cent of global water use, 40 per cent of global CO_2 emissions, and more than 70 per cent of electricity consumption. The benefits of green homes are becoming increasingly recognized. According to the US Green Building Council, green homes use up to 40 per cent less energy and up to 50 per cent less water than comparable standard homes. Moreover, the use of toxin-free building materials helps to reduce indoor air pollution, which in some cases can be more harmful than outdoor air pollution. Passive houses, ie buildings designed without the need for heating and cooling systems, use a combination of positioning, natural ventilation and shading, efficient construction, roof and window design, insulation and solar/other renewable energy to minimize heat loss (in colder climates) and maximize heat gains. Passive houses are estimated to reduce energy consumption by up to 90 per cent, according to the International Passive House Association.[14]

In many countries, national building codes and standards have been or are being updated to encourage or require the building of more energy-efficient homes. The introduction of compulsory Energy Performance Certificates, and similar, also provides a mechanism to promote energy efficiency measures when buying, selling and renovating homes. Many national and local building codes are referenced to the International Green Construction Code (IgCC), which promotes a whole systems approach to the design, construction and operation of buildings, and sets out criteria in areas including energy efficiency, resource conservation, indoor environmental quality and building performance that are designed to improve sustainability.[15]

Insurers are helping to promote green homes in a number of different ways. Some insurers offer lower premiums for homes that meet stringent efficiency and sustainability standards, often based on or linked to the IgCC noted above.

CASE STUDY
Travelers[16]

Insurance firm Travelers offers a premium discount of up to 5 per cent for homes that are certified as green homes by the Leadership Energy and Environmental Design (LEED) organization. LEED is one of the most popular green building certification programmes used worldwide. Developed by the non-profit US Green Building Council, it includes a set of rating systems for the design, construction, operation and maintenance of green buildings and homes that aims to help building owners and operators be environmentally responsible and to use resources efficiently.

Other insurers offer products that cover rebuilding costs for damaged buildings and homes to upgrade them to better environmental standards, as well as insurance products that replace damaged appliances with energy-efficient ones.

For homeowners who generate their own renewable energy and sell surplus energy back to the local power grid, there are now insurance policies that cover both the income lost when there is a power outage and the extra expense to the homeowner of temporarily buying electricity from another source.

Green commercial and corporate insurance

Commercial and corporate insurance protects businesses and other organizations, of all sizes, from potential losses they could not afford to cover on their own, which allows businesses to operate when otherwise it might be too risky to do so. Insurance therefore supports entrepreneurialism, innovation and economic development by managing risks that could deter people from starting and growing businesses.

In terms of climate-related risks, insurance may cover a wide range of risks to which businesses are exposed, including, but by no means limited to:

- catastrophic risks (eg hurricanes and tropical storms);
- direct losses caused by extreme weather events (eg flood damage);
- business and supply chain interruption;
- legal liabilities arising from environmental and other damage caused by an organization's activities.

Policies for these and other climate risks for businesses in developed economies, at least, tend to be developed and underwritten on a bespoke basis, given that the exposure to and risk profile of climate-related risks will vary on a case-by-case basis. A firm's location(s), business activities, supply chains and many other factors will impact on the pricing of risk and insurance. As more organizations adopt the recommendations of the TCFD for identifying, disclosing and managing climate-related risks, and additional guidance is developed to encourage standardized approaches to this in different industry sectors, we are likely to see the development of more standardized commercial insurance products and services in this area too.

In the sections below, we focus mainly on green commercial insurance that encourages and supports the adoption of energy efficiency measures, and helps businesses to manage the risks of investment in new, energy efficiency technologies.

Commercial property insurance

Traditional commercial property insurance covers replacement or repair of damaged property, using similar materials as in the original construction, or basing repayment on the value of the original equipment or building. Insurers now offer green insurance products, which replace standard materials with environmentally friendly or more energy-efficient ones when making repairs. In the event of a total loss, some policies may cover the costs of rebuilding as a green building – this may be required in some countries and regions by national and local building codes.

Renewable energy insurance

Renewable energy generation has increased dramatically in recent years, driven by government policy, changing customer attitudes and advances in technology. A wide range of insurance products has emerged, tailored towards the renewable energy market, including coverage spanning construction and operational risks, business interruption, liability or technical failure, and loss of earnings due to discrepancies in actual versus expected energy generation.

CASE STUDY

Renewable energy insurance - renewed efforts[17]

Global renewable energy capacity grew at record rates in 2016, with investments in solar greater than investment in any other electricity-producing technology during that year. David Adams looks at how the insurance market is responding.

Despite attempts made by some – including former US President Donald Trump – to turn back the clock, renewable energy is booming. Global renewable energy capacity grew by 161 Gigawatts (GW) in 2016, a record annual increase, according to energy policy network REN21. Around half this new capacity came from solar power, which means that investments in this form of renewable energy were greater than investment in any other electricity-producing technology made during 2016.

New renewables capacity installed across the globe in 2016 cost $242 billion, 23 per cent less than was invested in new renewable capacity during 2015; the cost of building and operating solar and wind energy installations has fallen significantly. In the UK, in June 2017, the National Grid announced that a new record for renewables generation meant that for the first time, a combination of solar, wind, biomass and hydropower sources had made a greater contribution to electricity generation (50.7 per cent) than fossil fuels.

Still, it is important to keep these figures in context. Renewables contributed 10 per cent of global energy generation in 2016, still far behind the 80 per cent generated using fossil fuels. Although they contributed almost a quarter (24 per cent) of global electricity generation in 2016, most of this was produced by hydropower. Wind generated 4 per cent and solar 1.5 per cent.

Yet the clear upward trend in the use of renewables and the fall in costs have both been very clear during recent years. So how have insurers responded to the expansion of the renewable energy industry, to cover risks around renewables, from microgeneration to large-scale projects?

Murray Haynes is a partner and a renewable energy risk specialist at Alesco, which arranges multi-line insurance and reinsurance for businesses during construction and operation of renewable energy projects and facilities. He says the core insurance products used to insure renewables are those you would expect to use to insure any construction project or operational facility. For example, during the construction phase there is a need for marine cargo cover, various covers for damage due to natural causes; and delay in start-up insurance, to cover income-loss caused by delayed project completion.

During the operational phase, there would then be a requirement for insurance to cover operational risks, related to damage to property in particular; and business interruption insurance to cover fixed costs during major disruption. Other covers that might be more or less relevant depending on the location of a project, could address risks such as terrorism, sabotage and industrial action.

Cover against other political risks may also be necessary, in case such eventualities as changing tariff rates or outbreaks of civil unrest, for example, prevent access to facilities. It is also not unheard of for a government to seize assets, or to stop businesses using foreign exchange to take money out of the country. None of these issues is unique to renewable energy facilities, of course; more specific risks include those related to offshore projects (the vast majority of renewable projects are onshore). Premiums for offshore projects can be up to five times more expensive than equivalent projects or operations on land, in part simply because of practicalities. If an offshore wind turbine becomes badly damaged, for example, it may be necessary to recover hardware from the seabed, which can be a very expensive undertaking.

Renewable insurance needs can vary significantly. Consider, for instance, the physical conditions that might affect wind turbines in northern Scandinavia, where a build-up of ice on turbines can disrupt operations and/or create additional risks to people or property nearby; or the risks facing facilities in areas prone to extreme weather or earthquakes. Such natural catastrophe perils 'weigh quite heavily on underwriters' minds,' according to Haynes.

However, insurers have also written policies to address more specific requirements around scale or technology. The range of renewables-related products now offered by the broker Lycetts, for example, includes cover for landowners investing in anaerobic digestion technology for waste management and fuel production; insurance for biomass and geothermal generation; and policies tailored for microhydro electricity generation schemes, alongside insurance for solar and wind energy generation projects.

Specialist broker Nviro has also developed policies covering the lesser-known forms of renewables for projects of varying sizes. Its hydro power insurance solutions may suit small projects, including community generation initiatives and watermill renovations. The company also offers insurance for newer renewable technologies, including tidal and wave energy; desalination and osmosis energy generation technologies; kinetic energy generation; fuel cells; and carbon capture and storage.

XL Catlin, meanwhile, is leading the insurance programme for the ITER experimental fusion project, a scientific venture seeking to demonstrate the technical feasibility of using nuclear fusion to develop a limitless source of energy. The organization is currently building a magnetic structure to control and confine fusion processes taking place within plasma heated to 150 million degrees centigrade.

For most renewables-based projects, however, the reality of insurance is a little more traditional. One final group of risks to highlight is that related to series losses, where design or manufacturing defects, or a widely used installation method may result in the same claim being made for many multiples of the same piece of equipment. To counter this, underwriters may insert a series losses clause to limit the number of times they will pay out on claims with an identical cause.

Haynes does not feel there are any particularly striking trends in claims related to renewables at present – many claims are technology-specific, others relate to more generic risks, such as accidental damage of assets in transit or during construction.

He does pick out one trend, however: losses related to cabling used for offshore wind facilities. Cable losses are thought to account for about half of all losses related to offshore wind projects. These problems may include damage to cables that occurs during their manufacture, or in transit – or by the installer, such as over-twisting of cabling. Cables can also easily be damaged during the process of laying them on the sea bed: laying one cable may dislodge and damage another, for example. Sometimes the sea bed erodes under cabling, leaving lengths of cable hanging between rocks, which can also cause damage.

Repairing these cables can be very expensive: the cost of chartering a specialist vessel for several weeks can be extremely high. But it may also be unavoidable, particularly if it is the large export cables, which carry energy back to the shore, that are damaged.

Even those businesses that need to sacrifice more of the potential returns on renewables investments on insurance, at least have the consolation that now is a good time to be buying these policies. 'There's a lot of capacity in the market at the moment,' Haynes points out. 'Underwriters have a commercial imperative to be competitive.'

QUICK QUESTION

With renewable energy set to grow further in the coming years, what more could insurance firms do to encourage take up?

Energy efficiency insurance

Driven by the combination of factors outlined above, including tighter, green building codes and standards, the need to reduce energy costs and greater awareness of the social, environmental and financial benefits of improving energy efficiency, many commercial property owners and managers invest in substantial energy efficiency projects, including replacing windows and insulation, upgrading heating and cooling systems, installing new lighting and other electrical systems and, sometimes, installing solar, wind or other sources of renewable energy. The capital costs of such projects can be high, especially when older buildings require significant retrofitting, but the expectation is that these will be recouped over time by substantially lower annual running costs.

Energy efficiency insurance can reduce the risk to building owners and managers of not achieving the anticipated savings by (usually) providing cover in three areas:

- **Material damage:** The risk of damage or destruction of energy-saving equipment installed, eg solar panels.
- **Business interruption:** The risk of losses in business revenue caused by events associated with the energy-saving equipment installed, eg a power failure causes production stoppages.
- **Energy performance:** The most important and innovative part of energy efficiency insurance, this covers any shortfalls in actual versus expected energy and cost savings.

Energy efficiency insurance is considered key in promoting the uptake of energy efficiency measures, particularly by SMEs in the developing world. According to the Global Innovation Lab for Climate Finance (now the Climate Finance Lab), energy efficiency upgrades can make SMEs more competitive and productive, while reducing their emissions of harmful greenhouse gases.[18] In many developing countries, however, funding for energy efficiency upgrades tends to be limited; SMEs and local banks often lack the technical capacity to assess the potential of capital-intensive energy efficiency investments and confidence in the data that these will generate positive returns.

To address this barrier to investment, the Inter-American Development Bank (IDB), Danish Government and BASE (formerly the Basel Agency for Sustainable Energy) have developed Energy Savings Insurance (ESI), whereby providers of energy efficiency technology, rather than building owners, purchase insurance to back guarantees to their SME clients on the energy performance of and financial savings from their products and services. The Climate Finance Lab has found that this can absorb up to 80 per cent of the underperformance risk and thus incentivize energy efficiency upgrades. A pilot scheme was implemented in Mexico with a target of stimulating $25 million of investment in 190 energy efficiency projects in the agro-industry sector by 2020. Further opportunities are being considered in other developing countries; in the long term it is estimated that ESI and similar schemes could support up to $100 billion in energy-efficient investments.

CASE STUDY

Scaling up energy efficiency with Energy Savings Insurance[19]

The Energy Savings Insurance model aims to scale up investments in energy efficiency, facilitate the flow of financing for these technology solutions and address the untapped market potential.

The challenge

Energy efficiency (EE) presents enormous investment opportunities for businesses with significant potential to reduce greenhouse gas emissions, especially in developing countries. However, many development programmes targeting EE have struggled to catalyse the market. One of the main reasons is that EE is not a priority for many businesses, such as hotels or agribusinesses.

The concept of energy efficiency can be difficult to sell: it requires providers of technologies like air conditioning or boilers to change the way they approach businesses. Instead of simply selling new technology, a provider needs to sell a promise of future energy savings that should be high enough to justify the investment. Businesses are not used to buying future energy savings, especially in developing countries. Many have a lack of trust in the technologies, and often do not see the need to replace a working piece of equipment that they already have.

Many development programmes aim to drive the market for EE by providing financing, but this alone is not enough to convince businesses to invest in promised energy savings.

The solution

In order to motivate SMEs to invest in EE and generate a continuous pipeline of bankable projects, it is fundamental to build trust and credibility among key actors and reduce the risk–return trade-off perception.

With the support of the Inter-American Development Bank and the Danish Government, BASE developed the ESI model that comprises financial and non-financial mechanisms designed to work together to overcome barriers, create trust and reduce the perceived risks for stakeholders. The model consists of risk mitigation instruments, including insurance, standardized contracts, and a simplified validation process, which together help to mobilize financing. BASE has also developed an ESI toolkit that offers step-by-step instructions on how national development banks can establish a programme that is able to catalyse the EE market.

The outcome

The ESI model is being planned, developed or rolled out with different partners in various countries across Latin America, Africa, Asia and Europe.

It was recognized by the Global Innovation Lab for Climate Finance as one of the most promising instruments to mobilize private sector investments in EE. The AM BEST insurance rating agency featured it as one of the most innovative insurance products of 2015, and the Clean Energy Finance Forum at the University of Yale identified ESI as a winning idea and a successful financial vehicle for climate change mitigation. The ESI model also features in the *G20 Energy Efficiency Investment Toolkit*, published in 2017.

QUICK QUESTION

How else might finance help to encourage energy efficiency?

Carbon credit/carbon credit delivery insurance

One emerging area of commercial and corporate insurance with the potential to grow rapidly is in insuring risks related to carbon credits and greenhouse gas emissions reduction.

As discussed earlier, carbon pricing and carbon credit markets are volatile and subject to changing political and regulatory requirements. It may be difficult or impossible, therefore, for organizations wishing to purchase carbon credits to offset against emissions to be certain of the future value or eligibility of those credits, increasing the risk of purchase. Carbon credit insurance offers certainty in terms of future value, in exchange for insurance premiums.

Carbon credit delivery insurance is also related to carbon markets and emissions trading schemes, whereby organizations that reduce carbon emissions gain carbon credits (or can obtain these at subsidized prices) that may then be traded. Organizations can insure the risk that their emissions-reduction activities might fail to achieve the anticipated reductions, and therefore will not receive the anticipated carbon credits and future revenue from these.

Climate risk insurance

We saw in the introduction to this chapter how climate change impacts the insurance sector, particularly large insurers based (at least until recently) in developed, Western markets. Climate change disproportionately affects the world's poorest and most vulnerable communities, however, as we have seen elsewhere in this book. Moreover, when extreme weather events occur or the impact of other climate-related events (eg rising sea levels) are experienced, those living in or close to poverty are the least able to cope due to their lack of savings, government support and other safety nets.

The most vulnerable are the world's 2+ billion individuals reliant on subsistence or small-scale agriculture and fishing, living in those regions most vulnerable to climate change (eg in low-lying coastal areas, or in parts of the world most affected by drought and water shortage). Few such individuals have access to private insurance coverage to protect themselves, their families, their homes, possessions and livelihoods from climate risks. In many cases, poorer communities are more vulnerable to the effects of climate change, because of where they are located, and less resilient to its effects because of the lack of support. As a result, a number of insurance products have emerged in recent years with the aim of mitigating the impact of climate change and enhancing the resilience of individuals and communities in the developing world.

Although insurance may cover a wide range of climate-related risks to which businesses are exposed, the terms climate insurance and climate risk insurance are most often used in relation to providing insurance to individuals, communities and countries in the developing world that are most exposed to climate change. In this section, we look at two approaches to climate risk insurance in the developing world: sovereign catastrophe risk pooling and index insurance.

Sovereign catastrophe risk pooling

Sovereign catastrophe/disaster risk pooling occurs when governments or other organizations (such as humanitarian agencies acting on behalf of impacted communities) take out insurance against natural catastrophes, including extreme weather and other climate-related events. By pooling the risks, countries and communities can create a more diversified portfolio, and reduce the cost of premiums compared to insuring single, high-impact and high-cost risks.

When a catastrophic event occurs, the insurance policy will (usually) provide a rapid pay-out that can be used to fund disaster relief and recovery programmes. The advantage for governments and other agencies is that the pay-out from the insurer enables funds to be released without having to utilize existing budgets. Such funds are more quickly available than through other disaster relief channels, such as appeals and grants.

CASE STUDY

What makes catastrophe risk pools work: Lessons for policymakers[20]

Securing access to financial resources before a disaster strikes by means of sovereign catastrophe risk pools allows countries to respond quickly to disasters and reduce their impact on people and their livelihoods.

This is what islands in both the Caribbean and the Pacific have done over the last decade through regional risk pools – the Caribbean Catastrophe Risk Insurance Facility (CCRIF SPC) and the Pacific Catastrophe Risk Assessment and Financing Initiative (PCRAFI) Insurance Program.

In the aftermath of Hurricanes Irma and Maria, CCRIF SPC provided $29.6 million in pay-outs in less than 15 days to six Caribbean countries: Antigua and Barbuda, Anguilla, Haiti, Saint Kitts and Nevis, the Bahamas, and Turks and Caicos Islands, while in Dominica the CCRIF SPC, along with an existing World Bank disaster reduction project, made a $19 million pay-out.

Likewise, in 2015, just seven days after Cyclone Pam devastated Vanuatu – leaving one-third of the island's population homeless and causing damages equivalent to more than 60 per cent of the GDP – the government received a $2 million pay-out from the insurance policy it had purchased through PCRAFI. While $2 million may not be a large amount of money, it was eight times the government's emergency provision and was critical for funding urgent priorities, such as flying medical personnel to the worst affected areas.

Through sovereign catastrophe risk pools, countries can pool risks in a diversified portfolio, retain some of the risk through joint reserves and capital, and transfer excess risk to the reinsurance and capital markets.

Since it is highly unlikely that several countries will be hit by a major disaster within the same year, the diversification among participating countries creates a more stable and less capital-intensive portfolio, which is cheaper to reinsure.

By putting a price tag on risk, sovereign catastrophe risk pools can also create incentives for countries to invest in risk reduction. This is important because donor assistance is struggling to meet the rising cost of disasters, and insurance coverage remains low in vulnerable countries. At the same time, disaster losses are on the rise, with climate hazards increasing in frequency and intensity, and more people and assets in harm's way.

Already the impact of natural disasters is equivalent to a $520 billion loss in annual consumption, and forces some 26 million people into poverty each year. In the last 10 years, 26 countries in three regions – Africa, the Pacific, and the Caribbean and Central America – have joined three sovereign catastrophe risk pools, thanks in part to contributions from donors, who provided technical and financial resources to support them. They have purchased parametric catastrophe risk insurance for an aggregate coverage of $870 million and an aggregate premium volume of $56.6 million, backed by more than 30 reinsurance companies. The three pools have made $105 million in pay-outs to date.

In November 2017 the InsuResilience Global Partnership for Climate and Disaster Risk Finance and Insurance Solutions was launched at COP23 in Bonn, bringing together 40 developed and developing countries, with the aim of increasing resilience amongst the communities most vulnerable to climate change. In particular, InsuResilience plans to expand climate risk insurance coverage to an additional 400 million poor and vulnerable people in developing countries by 2020, as the case study 'Climate insurance for farmers' below describes.

Index insurance

Index insurance pays out for losses resulting from extreme weather and other catastrophic events on the basis of deviations from a predetermined index of one or more generally weather- or agriculture-related parameters (eg rainfall, water levels, temperature, crop yield, livestock mortality). Advances in satellite, drone, weather station and other monitoring technologies have made it easier and cheaper to track the desired parameters, and pay-outs to small farmers and other insured individuals and small businesses are triggered automatically when data breaches previously agreed thresholds. Combined with the use of smartphones to assist with monitoring and as a mechanism for payment, the settlement and pay-out process is much quicker and cheaper to administer than traditional insurance.

Index insurance is available to individuals (the micro level) and to collective groups such as farm cooperatives that can pool premiums and risks (the meso level), as well as being increasingly used by banks and other lenders in the developing world to insure their micro-finance portfolios.

According to an overview of climate risk insurance published by Results, index insurance dramatically lowers transaction costs. It has made access to insurance for individuals, families and small farmers in the developing world possible, increasing the resilience of those communities most impacted by climate change.[21] By increasing the certainty and speed of settlements and pay-outs, it also supports small entrepreneurs and farmers, encouraging investment that might otherwise not be possible.

CASE STUDY

Climate insurance for farmers: A shield that boosts innovation[22]

New insurance products geared towards smallholder farmers can help them recover their losses, and even encourage investment in climate-resilient innovations.

What stands between a smallholder farmer and a bag of climate-adapted seeds? In many cases, it's the hesitation to take a risk. Farmers may want to use improved varieties, invest in new tools, or diversify what they grow, but they need reassurance that their investments and hard work will not be squandered.

Climate change already threatens crops and livestock; one unfortunately timed dry spell or flash flood can mean losing everything. Today, innovative insurance products are tipping the balance in farmers' favour. That's why insurance was featured as one of 10 innovations for climate action in agriculture, in a new report released ahead of the 2017 UN Climate Talks. These innovations are drawn from decades of agricultural research for development by CGIAR and its partners, and showcase an array of integrated solutions that can transform the food system.

Index insurance is making a difference to farmers at the frontlines of climate change. It is an essential building block for adapting our global food system and helping farmers thrive in a changing climate. Taken together with other innovations like stress-tolerant crop varieties, climate-informed advisories for farmers, and creative business and financial models, index insurance shows tremendous promise.

The concept is simple. To start with, farmers who are covered can recoup their losses if (for example) rainfall or average yield falls above or below a pre-specified threshold or index. This is a leap forward compared to the costly and slow process of manually verifying the damage and loss in each farmer's field. In India, scientists from the International Water Management Institute and the Indian Council of Agricultural Research have worked out the water level thresholds that could spell disaster for rice farmers if exceeded. Combining 35 years of observed rainfall and other data with high-resolution satellite images of actual flooding, scientists and insurers can accurately gauge the extent of flooding and crop loss to quickly determine who gets pay-outs.

The core feature of index insurance is to offer a lifeline to farmers, so they can shield themselves from the very worst effects of climate change. But that's not all. CIMMYT is investigating how insurance can help farmers adopt new and improved varieties. Scientists are very good at developing technologies but farmers are not always willing to make the leap. This is one of the most important challenges that they grapple with. What they've found has amazed them: buying insurance can help farmers overcome uncertainty and give them the confidence to invest in new innovations and approaches. This is critical for climate change adaptation. They're also finding that creditors are more willing to lend to insured farmers and that insurance can stimulate entrepreneurship and innovation. Ultimately, insurance can help break poverty traps, by encouraging a transformation in farming.

Insurers at the cutting edge are making it easy for farmers to get coverage. In Kenya, insurance is being bundled into bags of maize seeds, in a scheme led by ACRE Africa. Farmers pay a small premium when buying the seeds and each bag contains a scratch card with a code, which farmers text to ACRE at the time of planting. This initiates coverage against drought for the next 21 days; participating farms are monitored using satellite imagery. If there are enough days without rain, a farmer gets paid instantly via their mobile phone.

Farmers everywhere are businesspeople who seek to increase yields and profits while minimizing risk and losses. As such, insurance has widespread appeal. Successful initiatives have grown rapidly in India, China, Zambia, Kenya and Mexico, which points to significant potential in other countries and contexts. The farmers most likely to benefit from index insurance are emergent and commercial farmers, as they are more likely than subsistence smallholder farmers to purchase insurance on a continual basis.

It's time for more investment in index insurance and other innovations that can help farmers adapt to climate change. Countries have overwhelmingly prioritized climate actions in the agriculture sector, and sustained support is now needed to help them meet the goals set out in the Paris Climate Agreement.

The balance of responsibility

While climate risk insurance, such as sovereign catastrophe risk pooling and index insurance, can undoubtedly improve resilience to the effects of climate change, some critics have expressed concern about measures that make those (in most cases) least responsible for climate change bear responsibility for its risks and costs. Climate risk insurance also does little to deal with the underlying causes of climate change, while concern has been expressed regarding potential unintended consequences of poorly designed or implemented schemes.

CASE STUDY

Climate insurance: Closing the protection or the resilience gap?[23]

Does climate insurance work as a catalyst for climate risk management and sustainable development? Or is insurance deflecting attention from other disaster risk management solutions?

Insurance can help reduce the impacts of natural disasters and build resilience

Disaster insurance instruments, such as micro/sovereign insurance mechanisms and risk pools, help to manage the risks of disasters.

Immediate insurance pay-outs mean recovery and rebuilding can begin rapidly after a disaster, without waiting for government to reallocate funds. This implies that closing the protection gap could be an important element in a climate risk management strategy.

Experience from developed countries shows that insurance can play a cost-effective role in a country's efforts to increase its disaster resilience. This has spurred efforts to test insurance across developing countries, with a range of new schemes being piloted, and international support money being pledged to increase the use of insurance, such as the G7 InsuResilience initiative.

But does insurance really increase climate resilience of the most vulnerable people?

While disaster insurance offers many opportunities, it is far from clear how insurance schemes improve climate risk management and support climate-resilient development. There is uncertainty about how to monitor and evaluate resilience-building and there are few rigorously designed studies to examine the impact that these insurance schemes have.

A recent study for the Climate Investment Fund warned that climate insurance could also have unwanted consequences and may not benefit the poor nor foster climate resilience. Poorly designed or implemented climate insurance may reduce incentives for risk reduction. This would increase moral hazards and potentially lower resilience through a false sense of security.

This is a key area of concern. Several of the development-aid funded schemes such as sovereign risk pools have to conduct evaluations, but results will take time and are in some cases not publicly available, creating a lack of trust.

A new project, funded by IGA/Rockefeller, plans to address this measurement gap. This work will build upon the expertise of existing resilience frameworks from the Food and Agriculture Organization and Food Security Information Network groups.

The protection gap should not distract from the resilience gap

Insurance is an important tool in managing the impact of disasters. However, prevention and preparedness measures are the most effective ways to reduce fatalities and limit damage from disasters.

To create longer-term solutions, we need to focus on closing the resilience gap between developed and developing countries, while addressing the underlying causes of loss and damage.

Insurance as a risk transfer instrument can play a role. However, there is far bigger potential for bringing in the industry's risk knowledge and expertise. Donors, insurers and NGOs have an opportunity to shape this by embedding climate resilience within their sustainable development agendas.

What about fairness?

Finally, there are equity and fairness dimensions to all of this. Is it fair that those least responsible and least able to pay the premiums should take responsibility for the risk? Subsidies can help to avoid shifting the burden to those most vulnerable, but this also means that insurance may not offer value for money due to high transaction and capital costs. This suggests that international funds might be better spent on other types of safety nets, rather than buying insurance cover from international insurance markets.

It is also important to consider how any insurance mechanism will cope with changing risk levels. The intensity and frequency of climate extremes is increasing and the cost of insurance is rising, which will put pressure on subsidies and other support measures. Above all, it is important to recognize that there is a moral case beyond the economic considerations. For many parts of the world, loss and damage is not a distant threat but a current reality. The political complexities and technical challenges of climate attribution should not distract from this.

QUICK QUESTION

Reflecting on the case studies above, do you think that climate risk insurance of the types outlined in this section are effective tools to mitigate the risks posed by climate change?

Key concepts

In this chapter we considered:

- the role of insurance within the wider financial system, and how climate-related financial risks are impacting the insurance sector;
- how different insurance activities can affect the quality and functioning of the natural environment and natural systems;

- how different types of insurance products and services can improve the quality and functioning of the natural environment and natural systems;
- examples and case studies of green insurance products and services.

Now go back through this chapter and make sure you fully understand each point.

Review

The insurance industry's core business is to understand, manage and carry risk, and by pricing and creating a market, enables risk to be pooled, diversified, managed and reduced, thereby protecting individuals and society and supporting economic development. With these core competencies, the insurance industry is uniquely positioned to embed climate and other environmental risks into decision-making in the financial services sector.

While many insurers continue to focus chiefly on financial risk management in response to climate change, others take a more proactive approach to environmental sustainability by offering new green products and services.

Life insurers tend to be more affected by climate and environmental risks from their investments on the asset side of their balance sheets, and therefore the main way in which life insurers can promote environmental sustainability is through their investment portfolios.

General insurers face more risks from their liabilities than their assets, and so they can best promote environmental sustainability by offering new green products and services.

Environmental insurance provides protection from actual/potential liabilities arising from environmental damage. Climate insurance/climate risk insurance provides protection against (usually) extreme weather events such as drought, floods and storms.

Green insurance seeks to encourage and support sustainable activities and behaviour by individuals, companies and others. Green insurance includes products and services that allow an insurance premium differentiation on the basis of environmentally relevant characteristics/behaviour, and products and services that are tailored to promoting green activities such as the use of renewable energy or other means of reducing carbon.

Green personal insurance products include different types of motor insurance and home insurance. Green commercial insurance products include different types of commercial property insurance, renewable energy insurance, energy efficiency insurance and carbon credit insurance.

A number of insurance products, usually termed climate risk insurance, have emerged in recent years to mitigate the impact of climate change, particularly in the developing world, including sovereign catastrophe risk pooling and index insurance. Some critics are concerned that, despite the benefits of such products, they make those least responsible for climate change bear responsibility for its risks and costs.

Glossary

Climate/climate risk insurance: Insurance to individuals, communities and countries in the developing world most exposed to climate change.

CO_2e: Carbon dioxide equivalent: a standard unit for measuring carbon footprints. It captures the impact of each different greenhouse gas in terms of the amount of CO_2 that would create the same amount of warming; thus, a carbon footprint consisting of different greenhouse gases can be expressed as a single number.

Energy efficiency Insurance: Reduces the risk to building owners and managers of not achieving the anticipated energy and financial savings of capital investment in energy efficiency measures.

Environmental insurance: Insurance that provides protection from actual/potential liabilities arising from environmental damage; for example, coverage to protect against pollution, oil spills or other forms of environmental damage.

General insurers: Insurance companies that provide non life insurance. They provide property cover, health insurance, liability policies and miscellaneous financial loss cover for individuals, companies and others.

Green insurance: Insurance products and services that either allow an insurance premium differentiation on the basis of environmentally relevant characteristics/ behaviour, or are designed to promote 'green' activities.

Index insurance: Insurance products that link pay-outs to changes in a predetermined index or set of parameters.

International Green Construction Code (IgCC): A voluntary code, increasingly widely adopted in national and local building codes and standards, promoting a whole systems approach to the design, construction and operation of buildings. The Code sets out criteria in areas including energy efficiency, resource conservation, indoor environmental quality and building performance, designed to improve sustainability.

Life insurers: Insurance companies that provide benefits in the event of death, retirement or changes in health.

Reinsurers: Insurance companies that provide insurance to other insurance companies, enabling the further diversification of risk.

Sovereign catastrophe risk pooling: When governments or other organizations such as humanitarian agencies take out insurance policies that will provide a pay-out in the event of a defined extreme weather event such as a major drought or hurricane occurring in a country.

UNEP FI Principles for Sustainable Insurance (UN PSI): A global framework for the insurance industry to address ESG risks and opportunities.

Usage-based insurance: Vehicle insurance based on how a vehicle is driven (pay how you drive) and/or the distance driven and type of journey undertaken (pay as you drive).

Notes

1 UNEP (nd) The global insurance industry, UNEP Finance Initiative [Online] https://unfccc.int/files/adaptation/workstreams/loss_and_damage/application/pdf/unep.pdf (archived at https://perma.cc/DTA7-2H63)

2 R Toumi and L Restell (2014) *Catastrophe Modelling and Climate Change*, Lloyds [Online] https://www.lloyds.com/~/media/lloyds/reports/emerging-risk-reports/cc-and-modelling-template-v6.pdf (archived at https://perma.cc/5HT7-CC2M)

3 Munich Re (nd) Data on natural disasters since 1980: Munich Re's NatCatSERVICE [Online] https://www.munichre.com/en/solutions/for-industry-clients/natcatservice.html (archived at https://perma.cc/4Z7R-EGWJ)

4 EY (2018) *Global Insurance Trends Analysis 2018*, EY

5 D Jergler (2018) Report outlines climate change risks faced by insurance sector, *Insurance Journal* [Online] https://www.insurancejournal.com/news/national/2018/08/23/499027.htm (archived at https://perma.cc/L5UV-E4CM)

6 IAIS (2018) *Issues Paper on Climate Change Risks to the Insurance Sector*, Sustainable Insurance Forum [Online] https://docs.wixstatic.com/ugd/eb1f0b_0e5afc146e44459b907f0431b9e3bf21.pdf (archived at https://perma.cc/JRL7-2VFF)

7 Asset Owners' Disclosure Project (2018) AODP Global Climate Index 2018: Insurance [Online] https://aodproject.net/insurance/ (archived at https://perma.cc/L5WW-2V3A)

8 UNEP (nd) The UNEP FI principles for sustainable insurance [Online] http://www.unepfi.org/psi/the-principles/ (archived at https://perma.cc/3FTZ-6EN5)

9 E Mills (2009) A global review of insurance industry responses to climate change, *The Geneva Papers on Risk and Insurance: Issues and practice*, 34, pp 323–59 [Online] https://link.springer.com/article/10.1057/gpp.2009.14 (archived at https://perma.cc/H7UD-K5BV)

10 UNEP (2007) *Insuring for Sustainability* [Online] http://www.unepfi.org/fileadmin/documents/insuring_for_sustainability.pdf (archived at https://perma.cc/LZG4-G66E)

11 TD (2016) Green products, Morningstar Research [Online] https://www.td.com/document/PDF/corporateresponsibility/2016-Green-Products.pdf (archived at https://perma.cc/SHP6-PMMG)

12 Ptolemus Consulting Group (2018) UBI infographic 2018 [Online] https://www.ptolemus.com/ubi-study/ubi-infographic-2018/ (archived at https://perma.cc/C5PU-DZX3)

13 Frost & Sullivan (2018) *Global Strategic Analysis of Usage-based Insurance Market for Passenger Vehicles, Forecast to 2025*, Frost & Sullivan

14 International Passive House Association (nd) The Passive House: Sustainable, affordable, comfortable, versatile [Online] https://passivehouse-international.org/index.php?page_id=79 (archived at https://perma.cc/GH8W-EDS6)

15 International Code Council (2018) Overview of the International Green Construction Code [Online] https://www.iccsafe.org/codes-tech-support/codes/2018-i-codes/igcc/ (archived at https://perma.cc/SXS6-9Z99)

16 Travelers (nd) Home insurance discounts [Online] https://www.travelers.com/home-insurance/discounts (archived at https://perma.cc/4EJR-DH9E)

17 D Adams (2017) Renewable energy insurance: Renewed efforts, CIR Magazine [Online] http://www.cirmagazine.com/cir/renewed-efforts.php (archived at https://perma.cc/48FK-XXZY)

18 Climate Finance Lab (nd) Energy savings insurance [Online] https://www.climatefinancelab.org/project/insurance-for-energy-savings/ (archived at https://perma.cc/HXP8-ETWK)

19 Energy Base (nd) Scaling up energy efficiency with Energy Savings Insurance, Energy Base

20 The World Bank (2017) What makes catastrophe risk pools work: Lessons for policymakers [Online] http://www.worldbank.org/en/news/feature/2017/11/14/what-makes-catastrophe-risk-pools-work (archived at https://perma.cc/DFV6-XBKQ)

21 Results (nd) An introduction to climate risk insurance [Online] https://www.results.org.uk/guides/introduction-climate-risk-insurance (archived at https://perma.cc/TA5S-U74Y)

22 CIMMYT (2017) Climate insurance for farmers: A shield that boosts innovation [Online] https://www.cimmyt.org/news/climate-insurance-for-farmers-a-shield-that-boosts-innovation/ (archived at https://perma.cc/XMH8-HHX5)

23 S Surminski (2017) Climate insurance: Closing the protection or the resilience gap, Oxfam [Online] https://views-voices.oxfam.org.uk/climate-change/2017/07/climate-insurance-closing-the-protection-or-the-resilience-gap (archived at https://perma.cc/TBN6-HDXG)

11

FinTech in green finance

LEARNING OBJECTIVES

On completion of this chapter you should be able to:

- Understand what is meant by FinTech and associated terms.
- Describe FinTech tools and techniques, and how they can support the growth of green finance and support the transition to a low-carbon world.
- Explain the benefits of applying FinTech tools and techniques to support green finance.
- Explain challenges that may arise from using FinTech tools and techniques to support green and sustainable finance.

In this chapter, we explore how financial technology (FinTech) is transforming many aspects of financial services and can support the growth of green and sustainable finance. The combination of FinTech tools and techniques, notably distributed ledgers (blockchain), the Internet of Things (IoT) and big data analysis can support financial inclusion and resilience, improve climate risk management, enhance verification, reporting and regulation, and facilitate access to capital markets. Although FinTech represents a generally positive development for green finance, some negative aspects and consequences of the use of FinTech tools and techniques need to be addressed.

Introduction to FinTech

The financial sector has been one of the earliest adopters and most extensive users of technology throughout its history, and over the past 20 years, especially in the last decade, the effective use of digital, data and internet-enabled technologies has increased significantly across the entire financial services industry. Such technologies are collectively known as FinTech (combining, obviously, the words finance and technology) and have become major enablers and disruptors of the operations of financial services, radically transforming the way finance functions and relates to the economy, environment and society.

FinTech refers to a wide collection of technologies, including, but not limited to, smart phones and banking apps, the IoT, application programme interfaces (APIs), distributed ledgers (blockchain), artificial intelligence (AI) and machine learning, big data and data analytics. Advances in digital technology and data science, new policies and regulations (particularly those aimed at increasing competition in the sector, such as Open Banking in the UK and PSD2 in Europe), wider economic and technological trends (such as a more flexible labour market and the digitization of the economy), as well as evolving customer expectations and behaviours (such as rises in the use of digital payments and falling branch footfall) have all accelerated the pace of change in how the finance sector operates. In the early stages of development, FinTech was associated with new start-up businesses aiming to challenge the position of large financial services firms in the market, but large institutions have since adopted the tools and techniques of FinTech.

QUICK QUESTION

What opportunities might FinTech offer for green finance?

We have already seen some examples of FinTech products and services in earlier chapters, such as Ant Forest in Chapter 6 and 'pay as you drive' insurance in Chapter 10. More generally, well-known FinTech products and services include mobile payment platforms (eg Alipay, ApplePay) retail investment platforms (eg Nutmeg and Robinhood), price comparison sites (eg MoneySuperMarket), peer-to-peer (P2P) lending for individuals and businesses (eg Zopa, Funding Circle), cryptocurrencies (eg Ethereum) and crowdfunding (eg Kickstarter). There is also a wide range of FinTech applications supporting the more efficient and effective delivery of financial services, including **RegTech** (using some or all of the technologies outlined above to better manage regulatory compliance, eg customer identification and onboarding), interbank payments (utilizing blockchain), improving risk identification, analysis and management, and high-frequency and other types of automated, algorithmic analysis and trading. The use of satellite and other remote monitoring techniques (using advanced data analytics) for verifying green outcomes of projects, discussed in Chapter 4, is another example of the application of the digital and data-driven technologies that can underpin FinTech in the finance sector.

FinTech is relevant throughout the financial services value chain. In many countries, payments are increasingly made digitally, generating a wealth of transaction data; customers can download apps that offer price comparisons and switching services, and navigate complex financial markets with the support of robo-advisors. Big data and advanced data analytics are used to tailor products and services to customers and better assess credit and insurance risks, enabling new types of loans to be made and more accurate pricing of insurance premiums. Trading is becoming ever more automated and algorithm-led, and central banks are looking to distributed ledgers (blockchain) to improve the accuracy, efficiency and security of wholesale payments, clearing and settlement infrastructure. Sweden is expected to be the first country to trial a central bank digital currency, with the Riksbank launching a pilot of an e-krona during 2019.

FinTech has the potential to support green finance and sustainable development in a number of ways, including by:

- increasing the provision and transparency of green finance-related data, which can be used to make improved assessments of risks and opportunities;
- decentralizing and increasing access to services and markets, helping more customers, communities and institutions to participate in and engage with green finance;
- lowering the costs, and increasing the speed and efficiency, of providing financial services.

A related term in common use in green finance is **CleanTech** (sometimes also known as **GreenTech**), which covers a wide range of technologies linked to environmental management, climate change mitigation and adaptation, and other related areas, including, but not limited to:

- renewable energy, eg solar, wind and marine, smartgrids, energy storage;
- energy efficiency, eg passive buildings, improving power transmission, improving energy usage;
- resources, eg recycling, reducing/utilizing waste products and packaging, developing substitutes for high-carbon plastics;
- transportation and urban infrastructure, eg public transport, electric and hydrogen-powered vehicles;
- sustainable food production and land use, eg agriculture, aquaculture, forestry.

The CleanTech sector, and renewable energy in particular, can benefit from the application of FinTech tools and techniques. In contrast to old, centralized fossil fuel energy systems, which are a good fit with large, centralized and linear funding models, renewable energy systems may be most effective when structured in a decentralized network of modular and interoperable units. Combined together, blockchain technology and P2P funding models can channel finance towards renewable energy. Blockchain technology can enable the aggregation of distributed community-driven energy generation on a scale where it can connect with energy markets; and P2P funding can mobilize savings and investment capital, connect it to these investment opportunities and help scale up distributed energy generation, as the following case study shows.

CASE STUDY

Community distributed generation[1]

Micro-generation allows consumers to produce energy in-house or in a local community. Trading this micro-generated energy then becomes possible among consumers and 'prosumers'. Blockchain, combined with IoT metering systems and next-generation batteries, has the potential to open the energy market to prosumers via an energy-coin system. Creating blockchain-enabled markets for micro-generated energy would further expand solar PV adoption on rooftops.

Distributed community generation at scale creates significant resiliency to the electrical grid in the case of climatic disasters, as a local Brooklyn-distributed generation implementation clearly demonstrated when hurricane Sandy hit New York in 2012. LO3 Energy start-up, in partnership with Consensys (Ethereum co-founders), is working with local utilities, community leaders and technology partners to create a market where neighbours can buy and sell the local environmental value of their energy generated, which simplifies messaging complexity and ensures that the parties cooperate over their data.

Developments in the CleanTech sector are beyond the scope of this chapter and book, but this is clearly an area of great interest to Green and Sustainable Finance Professionals seeking to support the transition to a more sustainable, low-carbon world, as it encompasses many of the infrastructure and technology investments that are needed for successful climate change mitigation and adaptation.

Applying FinTech tools and techniques in green finance

Over the past five years, there has been significant global interest in applying FinTech tools and techniques to support the growth of green finance, and a considerable number of new start-ups and incumbents have developed innovative, FinTech products and services to support the sector, some of which are presented later in this chapter. Some of the key features and benefits of FinTech for the green finance sector include:

- **Improving access to financial services:** The availability of financial services via ever more widely available smartphones means greater numbers of individuals and small businesses can access services, such as microfinance and insurance, to invest in climate mitigation/adaptation activities and enhance climate resilience.
- **Lowering the costs of delivering financial services:** Process automation, the delivery of financial services via digital channels and the use of advanced data analytics to better understand and price risk can lower the costs of providing financial services, making previously unbanked/uninsured individuals more attractive to providers.
- **Improving access to capital markets:** The combination of FinTech tools and techniques, including digital platforms, data analysis and distributed ledgers, can reduce the cost of issuing bonds and other securities, making

it easier for smaller businesses and projects to receive funding that is currently only accessible by larger issuers.

- **Increasing efficiency:** As well as providing cost efficiencies, the use of FinTech tools, such as smart contracts, can automate services (eg approving and paying out insurance claims) without the need for human intervention.
- **Decentralization:** Distributed ledger (blockchain) and smart contract technology enables the tracking and direct transfer of digital assets without the need for trusted intermediaries, further reducing costs.
- **Improving risk management:** Access to, and analysis of, data over a wide range of green finance-related areas (eg climate data, emissions tracking) makes it easier for financial institutions to identify, assess, manage and disclose risk.
- **Enhancing transparency and market integrity:** Availability of monitoring and verification data from satellites, drones, smartphones and other sources makes the verification and publication of impact data more robust, cheaper and accessible.
- **Promoting competition:** FinTech start-ups can experiment with innovative approaches to providing financial services that might be difficult or impossible for larger institutions.
- **Targeting investors:** Digital platforms and data analytics enable issuers, fund managers and others to target retail or institutional investors with an appetite for green and sustainable finance investment.
- **Changing consumer behaviour:** Apps that can track customer spending behaviour can nudge consumers towards more climate-positive spending and behaviours (eg using public transport).

QUICK QUESTION

Given the key features and benefits of FinTech, what green products and services might best be supported by applying FinTech tools and techniques?

According to BNY Mellon Asset Servicing, FinTech and sustainable finance may become a key driver of financial markets in Europe during the next decade, with FinTech being the key to growing the sustainable development market.[2] By reducing costs and boosting efficiency, digital technologies such as distributed ledger, machine learning, artificial intelligence and the IoT have the potential to:

- mobilize green finance and enable poorer people around the world to access clean energy through innovative projects that offset carbon emissions or fund lost solar power;
- unlock the barriers to greater financial inclusion for those seeking funding for new businesses that will deliver both impacts and financial returns;
- mobilize domestic savings by providing channels or platforms for retail investors to access impact-investing opportunities;
- collect, analyse and distribute information on financial performance and impact performance to achieve better economic decision-making, regulation and risk management;
- provide financial markets with the level playing field and market integrity needed for long-term real economy investments, aligned with the sustainable development agenda.

READING
Greening digital finance[3]

Digital finance has the potential to overcome some of the pervasive barriers to deploying private finance for the wider good, and so to improve environmental outcomes. On the supply side, digital finance reduces costs and increases speed, providing a foundation for identifying and creating profitable green savings and investment opportunities. Trine, a Swedish tech start-up, enables savers in downtown Stockholm to profitably fund distributed solar energy systems in rural sub-Saharan Africa. On the demand side, similarly, reduced financing costs and pay-as-you-go access to clean energy opens up new markets, particularly for poorer consumers. Kenya's M-KOPA is leveraging the hugely successful domestic, mobile payments platform, M-PESA, to open up clean energy to poorer communities.

The prize could be very large. ANT Financial Services, with 450 million users of its mobile payments platform in China alone, has launched a green energy app that rewards users for reduced carbon use, revealed through a set of algorithms that translate individuals' financial transaction data into an estimate of their carbon-foot. To scale up this and other innovative green digital finance initiatives, UN Environment, in partnership with ANT, is launching the Green Digital Finance Alliance at Davos in January 2017. Extending just this single carbon-saving rewards initiative across a number of payments platforms could engage hundreds of millions of individuals in making carbon-saving lifestyle decisions on a daily basis.

FinTech is not a solitary, technological disruptor. It is part of a broader technological ecology that centrally includes the IoT and artificial intelligence. As such, it will increasingly animate the physical world, integrating physical and natural assets by enabling interactions with each other that in turn drive sensing and responding to each other in real time. Just as blockchain technology will create a history to money in revealing where it has been and what it has done, so will the life cycle of products become an easily traceable experience along with its interaction with the environment and its financing. The impact of this technological surge goes beyond enabling new decision-making opportunities based on objective data and new business models. Behavioural norms will also be reshaped as personal and group identities are increasingly shaped through virtual experience. ANT's carbon-saving initiative is closely tied not only to its financial services proposition but also to its social media strategy, in recognition of its potential for eliciting even greater behavioural change.

All revolutions come at a price. Incumbent financial institutions that cannot evolve rapidly, and the people dependent on them for their livelihoods, will be the first to pay as they are cut out of profitable parts of the financial value chain. The eradication of Kodak and Nokia in the face of early-stage digital upheaval comes to mind as minor rehearsals of what is to come. The misuse of new financial technologies is inevitable, although every effort must be made to prevent it. Loss of privacy is the most visible penalty, which is likely despite noble efforts at creating safeguards. Less visible are negative effects of disruption of existing markets. Michael Lewis revealed in his bestselling book *Flash Boys* the negative impacts of high-frequency trading on the financial returns from our lumbering, 20th-century pension funds. Regulation itself will be a casualty, at least for a while, as financial regulators struggle to oversee and guide an ever-more complex, dynamic and virtual financial system. Some commentators, such as the *FT*'s Izabella Kaminski, have argued that the commoditization effects of speed and big data itself undermine the conditions for sustainable development.

It is certain that FinTech will reshape the global financial system and its relationship with both the societies in which we live and the ecosystems on which we depend. Harnessing technology for the greater good has been a challenge throughout history. In that sense, aligning digital finance, and its close cousins, to the imperatives laid out in the Sustainable Development Goals is just another iteration of such efforts. Some solutions will be framed by compliance, some by standards and the rule of law, and others by riding the technological wave through innovation. Here, three, related solution arenas are emphasized:

- First, the digital finance community needs to be rapidly aligned with sustainable development imperatives to prevent the emergence of a new generation of incumbent, problematic financial institutions.
- Second, financial policymakers and regulators need to embrace sustainable development as core to their engagement with the FinTech community, most immediately in their ongoing regulatory sandbox experiments.
- Third, the sustainable development finance community is woefully ignorant of the significance of these developments and needs to wake up and engage now, or it risks becoming irrelevant, or worse.

2017 is the year where green digital finance can come of age. Germany's presidency of the Group of 20 (G-20) is taking on themes of digital and resilience, and is considering FinTech as part of its focus on green finance. At the same time, the G7 under Italy's presidency will explore how to channel finance to green SMEs, including the role played by FinTech-powered financial innovations. Governments from Singapore to Morocco and Argentina can integrate digital finance into their sustainable development financing plans, and coalitions such as the Green Digital Finance Alliance can mobilize collective action by leading financial institutions and their stakeholders.

Given the benefits to the green finance sector of applying FinTech tools and techniques, these may be applied to a wide range of areas, as we have seen in examples given in earlier chapters, and as set out below.

Retail financial services

Some of the most obvious applications of FinTech tools and techniques, at least to the general public, may be found in retail financial services, including services for micro and small businesses, including:

- promoting green and sustainable finance to retail customers, and encouraging and supporting behavioural change by providing products and services, such as current accounts and payments, that nudge and/or reinforce green and sustainable financial and purchasing decisions (eg Ant Forest, as described in Chapter 6);
- providing access to banking, insurance and other financial services, particularly in developing markets, where smartphones with cameras and fingerprint readers can be used to prove identity, onboard customers and deliver financial services, including payments, credit and insurance, that can support climate mitigation and resilience;
- supporting lending via microfinance and other institutions to climate smart agriculture, forestry, fisheries and other sectors, where traditional approaches to credit scoring, loan disbursement and repayment, and monitoring outcomes would require expensive branch networks, but can be delivered much more cost-effectively by utilizing technology;
- utilizing the increasing availability and granularity of data relating to climate risks and opportunities, and advances in data analysis techniques, to better price risk and return for individuals, businesses and communities, enabling financial services firms to offer a wider range of green products and services (eg green mortgages and loans, climate insurance) – although data availability and quality is still skewed towards the developed world;
- channelling retail investors' savings to green and sustainable finance products and services, either through using aggregator apps and sites to promote traditional investment vehicles, or via P2P lending or crowdfunding platforms to enable direct investment in green and sustainable projects, as set out in the case study on Bettervest.

CASE STUDY

Bettervest[4]

Bettervest describes itself as the world's first crowdfunding platform for energy efficiency projects. Trend researcher and futurist Patrick Mijnals came up with this innovative concept in 2006. His vision was to not only use energy efficiency to provide the needed impetus for a climate-friendly economy and society, but that ordinary people should be able to invest in it. During the 2012 event 'Startup-Weekend Rhein-Main', a group of experts in various fields were presented with the opportunity to take this concept further. Over just two days this team took Mijnals' concept and together they drew up a funding model for energy-efficient projects based on the idea of public participation. The model was able to convince a jury of experts and won the team the Startup Award.

Bettervest enables people to jointly invest individual sums of money – from as little as €50 onward – in renewable energy, energy and resource efficiency projects initiated by established enterprises, NGOs and local municipalities. In return, investors benefit financially from the resulting cost and energy savings. The Bettervest platform has thus opened up the energy efficiency market to private investors. With these targeted investments, ecologically and economically viable energy efficiency measures can be implemented, leading to cost, energy and CO_2 reductions.

Eligible projects are conceptualized and calculated by certified energy consultants, and are regularly monitored throughout the investment term. The project owners commit to using the annual cost savings to pay back their investors over a fixed contract period until the initial investment sum plus interest has been paid off. Once the contract period has ended, the savings remain in the project owner's company. The Bettervest platform is financed by a percentage commission (based on the investment sum) and an annual handling fee during the contract period.

Other examples include the Brooklyn Microgrid (United States), a P2P energy exchange that uses blockchain technology to facilitate the decentralized buying and selling of solar power generated by local residents and businesses ('prosumers'). Prosumers and consumers access the Microgrid energy market through an app, which they can use to buy and sell energy from a variety of sources. Vattenfall, a large Scandinavian power utility, has developed a similar scheme to enable residents and retailers to sell surplus electricity, generated by solar power, to the national grid.

QUICK QUESTION

What do you see as some of the key differences between intermediated lending and investment, and peer-to-peer lending and crowdfunding?

P2P lending and crowdfunding platforms have grown significantly in number and in scale in recent years. Both generalist platforms such as Funding Circle and specialist green platforms such as Bettervest can support lending to, and investing in, green and sustainable projects. This approach can have multiple benefits, including cheaper and more flexible funding, increased engagement with potential customers and of customers/investors with green issues and approaches, as well as the capability of sharing risk with other investors and across a potentially wide and diversified portfolio of investments.

However, there have been concerns about the protection of investors in P2P and crowdfunding schemes, particularly if they involve complex projects and financial risks. Do retail investors genuinely understand the risks they are taking, and that their capital may be at risk if a large number of loans or investments default? Some financial regulators are considering how best to balance support for innovative approaches to delivering financial services with investor protection, which raises questions about how far and how fast these approaches might be expanded into riskier or less transparent emerging market segments, such as green finance.

Corporate banking and capital markets

We have already observed how financial institutions can use advanced data analytics to help better identify, assess, manage, price and disclose climate-related and associated risks, as well as monitor/verify green project outcomes (eg when assessing the impact of green bonds or green corporate loans). Such analytics play an important role in encouraging the further development of the green finance market by aiding transparency and reporting, and supporting market integrity. A good example of how FinTech tools and techniques can be used to support the development of capital markets is the Green Assets Wallet initiative, described in the case study below.

CASE STUDY

Green Assets Wallet[5]

The Green Assets Wallet (GAW) initiative aims to scale up the green debt market by bridging green investors with potential investment opportunities through cost-efficient and immutable validation and reporting of green commitments and impact. To stimulate both the supply of and demand for credible green investment opportunities, especially in emerging markets, the initiative has developed a blockchain-based platform for validating green investments, bringing both greater efficiency and transparency.

Launched in December 2017 by Stockholm Green Digital Finance, the GAW initiative brings together climate finance and digital technology expertise in a unique multi-stakeholder consortium including blockchain engineer ChromaWay, the climate research institute and data provider CICERO, the asset management firm Öhman, and the Swedish bank SEB (a leading issuer and underwriter of green bonds).

The first version of the GAW, an open source application for validating, monitoring and reporting of green investments, was launched in November 2018. The blockchain platform provides a system for the validation of green investments and impact reporting via accredited validators (eg auditors, certifiers, regulators) or automated data feeds and evidence points (such as satellite images, engineering reports, audit reports, and electricity generation data). In doing so, it builds trust in the integrity of the green debt market.

The GAW platform makes high impact investment opportunities accessible to potential investors and allows them to efficiently and transparently assess and monitor impact. In addition, it supports emerging market issuers to successfully demonstrate credentials and attract investment for green activities, making the platform valuable for investors, issuers and validators alike.

FinTech tools and techniques, such as the use of digital platforms and blockchains (distributed ledgers), can also reduce the cost and complexity of accessing capital markets, making it easier for smaller businesses and projects to issue, for example, green bonds or other securities. Given the challenges of identifying green and sustainable finance projects of sufficient scale to be financed by traditional means, due in large part to the costs of issue, if technology can support smaller-scale capital market issuances, this may help to accelerate the growth of green finance. As evidenced in the next case study on BBVA, using blockchain technology enabled a €35 million green bond to be issued – well below the more common €0.5 billion to €1 billion benchmark issues.

CASE STUDY

BBVA issues blockchain supported green bond[6]

In 2019 BBVA issued a six-year, €35 million structured green bond via a private placement with MAPFRE, a Spanish insurer, using an in-house, private blockchain platform. The platform allows clients to choose between numerous product configuration options in an entirely digital process in which the negotiation of the structure and prices, and the creation of documentation for the bond, are part of the same tool. This reduces the cost, time and complexity of creating securities, and also ensures that agreements are fully traceable and immutable.

Juan Garat, BBVA's Head of Global Sales states:

> With this deal, BBVA reasserts its firm commitment to both sustainable financing and new technologies. Using DLT – distributed ledger technology – for this transaction allowed us to simplify the processes and streamline the negotiation time frames, which is in line with our pursuit of excellence in customer service.

According to BBVA, the use of the blockchain platform offers the following advantages:

- **It allows all participants to have access to the transaction.** Distributed ledger technology reduces issuing time and ensures that negotiations and agreements reached are traceable and immutable. These features of traceability and immutability make it easier to demonstrate compliance with relevant regulations.
- The platform allows the client to **choose between numerous product configuration options**. This gives clients considerable flexibility in terms of designing the bond that best suits their needs.
- It works for the simplest to the most complex products. This enables a **self-service approach** in which investors who know what product they want to invest in can save time and effort by limiting the definition of the different variables. Investors looking for new investment solutions can quickly and easily explore new products.
- It is an **entirely digital process** in which the negotiation of the structure and prices, and the creation of documentation for the bond are part of the same tool.

QUICK QUESTION

What initiatives can you identify in markets with which you are familiar that seek to apply FinTech tools and techniques to green and sustainable corporate banking and capital markets activities?

Investment

In addition to enabling retail investors to participate directly in investment in and lending to green activities and projects, FinTech tools and techniques may support investment in green and sustainable activities, firms and projects more generally. In particular, the increasing availability and granularity of data related to sustainability, improvements in data quality, standardization and verification, and advances in AI and machine learning applied to data analysis can support the continued growth of ESG investing in general and in green investing more specifically.

The ever-increasing availability of data creates challenges as well as benefits for investors and analysts, however, as it becomes more difficult to separate the truly meaningful and useful data that can provide insights into financial and sustainability performance from noise. A number of technology-driven data analytics and ratings firms have been established and have grown rapidly in recent years, including Sustainalytics (see Chapter 9), TruValueLabs and Arabesque.

CASE STUDY

Arabesque S-Ray®[7]

Arabesque S-Ray® is a proprietary tool that allows investors and others to monitor the sustainability of over 7,000 of the world's largest corporations.

Using machine learning and big data, Arabesque S-Ray® systematically combines over 200 ESG metrics with news signals from over 50,000 sources across 20 languages.

It is the first tool of its kind to rate companies on the normative principles of the United Nations Global Compact (GC score). Additionally, Arabesque S-Ray® provides an industry-specific assessment of companies' performance on financially material sustainability criteria (ESG score). Both scores are combined with a preferences filter that allows anyone to better understand each company's business involvements, and how those activities align with personal values.

GC Score

Arabesque S-Ray® analyses companies based on the four core principles of the United Nations Global Compact: human rights, labour rights, the environment, and anti-corruption. With Arabesque S-Ray®, these principles are quantified for the first time, with the potential to inspire more companies to take shared responsibility and join the Global Compact in its commitment to achieve a sustainable and inclusive global economy.

ESG Score

Arabesque S-Ray® incorporates sector-specific assessments of company performance across financially material ESG issues. Each company is scored within the context of its industry environment, based on factors that have a significant relationship with future financial performance. The result is a proprietary ESG score for each company, providing an assessment of long-term financial performance.

Arabesque S-Ray® is a next generation transparency lens that can empower all stakeholders to make better decisions for a more sustainable future.

Advantages to ESG and green investors of advances in data availability and analysis include:

- developing a more comprehensive view of a company's/investment's exposure to climate risks, impact on the environment, and sustainability more broadly, by enabling multiple – perhaps hundreds of – data sources to be utilized and compared, improving investment decision-making;
- the growing availability of standardized data on environmental performance and sustainability, allowing different potential investments to be more easily and effectively compared;
- enabling real-time monitoring and verification of investment performance in terms of desired green and sustainable outcomes, for instance monitoring emissions data, power usage or the sustainability of supply chains, helping investors manage investments more dynamically;
- using blockchain (distributed ledger) technology to validate and provide an immutable record of outcomes, as in the Green Assets Wallet initiative, and the World Wide Generation G17 Eco Platform;

- developing new ESG, green and/or sustainable investment funds, such as ESG index-tracking funds;
- reducing the costs of investment analysis via automation, particularly important for active investment managers who are under pressure from lower-cost tracker and other passive investment funds.

CASE STUDY

World Wide Generation G17Eco Platform[8]

The World Wide Generation (WWG) is a movement and blockchain-enabled platform that provides an interoperable, transparent marketplace for sustainable investing. As well as a number of leading financial services and investment firms, global FMCG giants such as Unilever are partnering with WWG to drive a more sustainable agenda across industry.

G17Eco uses distributed ledger technology to provide a monitoring, data flow, investment exchange and tech infrastructure that can identify, showcase and scale up sustainable businesses and initiatives across all sectors. Whether it's energy tech businesses, agri-tech exchanges or grass roots education platforms, investors can now put capital to work at scale with not only their targeted financial returns in mind but also with societal good as a clear barometer of success.

G17Eco enables corporates, governments, financial institutions and non-profits to **map, manage, monitor, measure and market** their SDG initiatives from one blockchain-powered platform. It shows via dashboards where investments go and how the financial and impact returns are made in real time. The platform solves the transparency and trusted data challenge that has hindered the matching of the need for investment in sustainable activities and outcomes to the funds seeking suitable investments and returns.

QUICK QUESTION

What data does your organization, or an organization with which you are familiar, provide that might help investors and analysts assess sustainability?

Insurance

In Chapter 10 we saw how FinTech tools and techniques have already been adopted in insurance in both developed and developing markets, including pay-as-you-go (PAYG) insurance, using telematics and smartphone apps to price and pay for insurance based on journeys taken and driving style, as well as blockchain/smart contract-based climate index insurance for farmers and smallholders. As major institutional investors, insurers can also benefit from the application of FinTech tools and techniques more generally, and, as risk managers, insurers can benefit from the increasing availability, granularity and capabilities of analytics.

Perhaps the most significant contribution that FinTech tools and techniques can make in the insurance sector in terms of green finance is by providing access to insurance for communities particularly at risk from climate change and related extreme weather events, in order to enhance climate resilience. In the case of products and services targeted at individuals, smallholders and small businesses in the developing world (referred to as micro-insurance) the combination of lower-cost and wider distribution, and claims management via smartphones with index insurance linked to remote data monitoring and providing automatic pay-outs, provides a new, lower-cost model for climate resilient insurance that can effectively support those individuals and communities most at risk from climate change. In the developing world, insurers such as Ayo and BIMA partner with mobile phone providers to offer a range of insurance services to their customers, using existing distribution channels and giving mobile providers an additional revenue stream.

CASE STUDY

OKO: Bringing crop insurance to emerging markets[9]

OKO is an Israeli InsureTech company supported by the Luxembourg Catapult: Inclusion Africa FinTech incubator and development programme. It combines new technologies in satellite imagery and weather forecasting to simplify and automate claims management, and create low-cost crop insurance for smallholder farms, together with mobile distribution.

Index insurance product creation

OKO partners with the most advanced weather information providers, using satellite or microwave technologies to obtain hyper-local data that can be used to:

- define risk with high precision, and therefore optimize the premium price;
- automate the claim validation process by analysis of the historical data.

Distribution tools

OKO creates innovative tools to distribute insurance in remote areas and to un-banked farmers:

- a USSD menu allowing policy management from any mobile device;
- a mobile app that provides a second-to-none customer experience, and is usable offline;
- an API that lets partners (micro-finance institutions, for example) access relevant information securely.

Working with the Fijian government and the Fiji Sugar Corporation, OKO developed a micro-insurance scheme offering farmers subsidized insurance against drought, floods and hurricanes. Ultra-localized weather monitoring and automated claims management meant farmers could obtain insurance at a low cost.

QUICK QUESTION

How might FinTech-enabled micro-insurance principles be applied to promote green and sustainable finance outcomes in the developed world?

Cryptocurrencies

In addition to the application of FinTech tools and techniques in the retail, corporate and capital markets, investment and insurance sectors, some commentators believe that cryptocurrencies (also referred to as cryptoassets) and digital assets generally, using blockchain (distributed ledger) as a means of exchange for financial transactions without a central issuing authority, can support green finance and sustainable development.

After rapid growth in the availability and value of cryptocurrencies since the launch of Bitcoin in 2009, the value of many cryptocurrencies fell significantly in 2018, from an estimated total market value of more than $800 billion in January to approximately $200 billion in November 2018. Despite this, and the collapse and disappearance of some cryptocurrencies, in 2018 there were more than 1,650 different cryptocurrencies available, according to The Motley Fool, an investment publication, and the number continues to increase.[10] Some of the more established variants, including Bitcoin, Ethereum and Ripple, have a wide base of users and are being increasingly used for real world transactions, rather than speculative investing, and some central banks are experimenting with versions of digital currencies.

Proponents of cryptocurrencies for growing green and sustainable finance suggest that decentralized blockchain and smart contract technologies, linked to the availability of environmental performance and sustainability data, and supported by access to cryptocurrencies through digital wallets, can incentivize more sustainable consumer behaviour. A number of green and sustainable cryptocurrencies have been launched, including SolarCoin, as described in the next case study.

CASE STUDY

SolarCoin hopes to ride the bitcoin buzz[11]

Bitcoin hit a record value of over $4,480 this month [August 2017], and the cryptocurrency's steep rise is attracting copycats – one of which, SolarCoin, hopes to boost solar energy by giving people an incentive to go green. SolarCoins work like a reward programme for solar power generators: people or businesses with solar panels can get a coin for each megawatt hour of electricity their solar panels generate. Users have to send scans of verified meter readings as proof of power generation, which are checked by volunteers.

An average individual producer in Belgium would get about five SolarCoins per year, said François Sonnet, an advisor to the SolarCoin project, who is also co-founder of ElectriCChain, a solar energy generation data project that helps with the disbursement of the digital currency. Unlike bitcoins, SolarCoins aren't yet going to make anyone rich. The average value of a coin is about 18 cents, up from 6 cents at the beginning of 2017. That gives the hypothetical individual Belgian solar power producer an annual windfall of about 90 cents.

But the ambitions are big. The project started in 2014, and its founders set a maximum limit of 97.5 billion SolarCoins that can be claimed over the next 40 years, based on solar power generation estimates from the International Energy Agency, Sonnet said. They are stored in a reserve account owned by the Solarcoin Foundation and will be exchanged gradually as solar panel owners claim them. 'The idea is to create a global network of solar installations so that people can start using this digital asset as a means to buy, trade and sell goods and services into this currency,' said Sonnet.

About 240,000 SolarCoins, worth a total of about €43,000, have gone to solar power producers in 39 countries, Sonnet said. Users can load their coins in an online wallet application, shop online from stores that partner with the project, or trade them for dollars, euros or other currencies on Lykke Exchange, a Swiss-based exchange platform.

'At the moment there are not that many shops doing that,' Sonnet said. A few businesses are accepting SolarCoins. ekWateur, a Paris-based independent renewable energy distributor with about 13,000 customers, began taking the digital currency in March 2017. It has seen three transactions with SolarCoins so far from two different customers, one worth €4 and the other two worth about €100, said Julien Tchernia, president of ekWateur.

Tchernia said he plans to exchange the SolarCoins for euros in the fall. 'If we can't get the euros back, we will have to stop,' he said. 'For now, the risk is very low because we only have small transactions.' 'If demand for the coins goes up, businesses would have to be sure the currency is fully tradable,' said Georg Zachmann, senior fellow at the Bruegel think tank. 'If there are not enough people that believe in SolarCoins, then nobody will take it,' he said.

So far uptake is small. 'It's not very easy for people to trust an application and start exchanging value,' said Eva Kaili, a Greek MEP from the Socialists and Democrats who is interested in the project and the blockchain technology underpinning digital currencies. It's also not simple to register for the coins. 'The application process is too complex,' Tchernia said. 'It is hard for someone to get the system working.'

These halting early steps aren't preventing the project's founders from dreaming of vast riches. 'If things go right and people start to see the digital currency as a store of value,' Sonnet said. 'The value could go up as high as €20–30 per coin once the number of solar power installations registered to the network grows.'

However, the currency is based on a very different model from Bitcoin, which is limited to only 21 million coins, so scarcity has driven up its value. SolarCoins are based on solar power generation, and as the technology has become cheaper and more efficient, its use has skyrocketed. There were only 5.1 GW of installed photovoltaics worldwide in 2005. A decade later that was up to 227 GW, according to the 2016 Renewables Global Status Report, and new facilities are coming online at an ever-increasing pace.

But early adopters are keeping the faith. 'It's the future. I'm sure of it,' said Johan De Beugher, a Belgian investing in SolarCoins. 'Because it's free and because it's ecological.'

As has been widely reported, some cryptocurrencies, particularly those that rely on mining, require huge computing power and energy consumption to function, and so have a negative impact on the environment when they rely on fossil fuels for power generation. This disadvantage does not apply to all cryptocurrencies, however; some, such as SolarCoin and Impact Coin, are designed to be environmentally friendly and sustainable from the outset.

At present, however, cryptocurrencies seem a small niche in green and sustainable finance, and unlikely to grow substantially without greater regulatory and economic certainty in the cryptocurrency/cryptoasset market. The blockchain, distributed ledger and smart contract technologies that underpin cryptocurrencies have many wider applications in support of green finance.

QUICK QUESTIONS

A number of other green/sustainable cryptocurrencies are available, including Bitcoin Green and Energy Coin. Pick one of these, or find another online. What are the similarities and differences as compared to SolarCoin? Which do you believe has the greatest potential to support the growth of green finance?

Policy initiatives to support FinTech in green finance

The potential of FinTech to support a range of international and national policy goals relating to green and sustainable finance, including promoting the transition to a sustainable, low-carbon world, increasing financial inclusion to enhance sustainable development, and encouraging greater competition and innovation in financial services, has been recognized by national and international policymakers. This has led to an increasing range of initiatives designed to support the further growth of green and sustainable FinTech, some of which are presented below.

International initiatives

UN Environment Programme

In 2016, the UN Environment Programme (UNEP) published a key report on the use and potential of FinTech to support green and sustainable finance. It concluded that FinTech offers the prospect of accelerating the integration of the financial and real economies, enhancing opportunities for shaping greater decentralization in the transition to sustainable development.[12]

The UNEP report suggests that both FinTech and sustainable development have the same potential as drivers of change and impact and can create new, sustainable business models. They may, therefore, be mutually reinforcing. Combining the IoT, blockchain technology and artificial intelligence to enhance efficiency and distribution, reduce costs and increase access to finance for individuals and small businesses, particularly in the developing world, can accelerate the green and sustainable finance agenda. The UNEP report includes a wide range of recommendations, such as a three-step programme to accelerate innovative approaches to green and sustainable finance:

- **Step 1:** Create a FinTech for Sustainable Development (FT4SD) challenge fund to provide initial angel/venture-style capital and business support for new FinTechs.
- **Step 2:** Establish regional innovation incubators to bring together start-ups, climate scientists, established financial services firms, regulators and others to develop and build new FinTech solutions.
- **Step 3:** Launch FT4SD venture capital and social impact funds to scale-up the successful, early-stage firms.

UNEP proposes a FT4SD Innovation Portfolio, setting out the areas where it believes FinTech tools and techniques (in particular AI, blockchain and the IoT) might best support green and sustainable finance, and aligning these to what it sees as the five key functions of finance.

Green Digital Finance Alliance

The Green Digital Finance Alliance (GDFA) is a partnership between the UNEP and Ant Financial, the Chinese payments and financial services provider behind Alipay and Ant Forest. Launched in 2017, the GDFA aims to accelerate FinTech innovation applied to address global environmental challenges.

CASE STUDY

Green Digital Finance Alliance[13]

The GDFA will support the purchase of clean lighting and energy, substantial agriculture inputs, and tools. The aim is to stimulate the advancements of digital technology in green finance.

One example is M-KOPA Solar, a Kenyan energy company offering access to affordable solar power. The company now provides solar home systems in Kenya, Tanzania and Uganda and uses technology to allow customers to pay for their energy as they use it in a micro-payment solution. The system uses embedded technology to monitor energy usage and charges customers accordingly.

FinTech4Good

FinTech4Good is a global network (with a particular focus on China and the US) that aims to accelerate the development of FinTech through research, incubation, acceleration and investment.[14] Three key areas of focus are blockchain, big data/AI, and crowd investing, and there is a wide range of incubation and acceleration programmes to identify and support innovative start-ups in these and other areas.

Climate Chain Coalition

The Climate Chain Coalition (CCC) was launched in 2017 to 'cooperatively support the application of distributed ledger technology and related digital solutions to addressing climate change'.[15] As at August 2018, there were more than 140 members – mostly FinTech providers, plus relevant finance sector associations, partners and consultancies. The CCC provides a platform for sharing and facilitating the adoption of new ideas and approaches, and supporting good practice in applying blockchain technology to green and sustainable finance, in areas including renewable energy, agriculture and forestry.

QUICK QUESTIONS

What initiatives to accelerate and support the use of FinTech tools and techniques in green finance are you aware of in the jurisdiction(s) where you live and work? How successful are they?

National initiatives

At national level, a wide range of initiatives has been launched in recent years to encourage the development of innovative, FinTech-led approaches to green finance, including the following examples.

In 2017, Sweden launched **Stockholm Green Digital Finance,** building on an existing FinTech hub and incubator to direct greater focus on, and investment to, digital green finance products and services. Among the first projects is a blockchain-based application (Climate KIC) to help investors monitor and verify green investments – particularly green bonds – which it is hoped will give investors greater confidence in investing in such instruments, and thereby build the market for these further.

The UK's Green Finance Taskforce has proposed the creation of a **Green FinTech Catapult**, which would give FinTech firms access to existing UK capabilities in remote sensing, using satellites and other systems, to support the development of new green finance products and services. This could potentially lead to developments in financial and environmental technologies capable of measuring changing environmental risks in real time using observational data, or systems that could monitor real-time emissions and link these to financing and investment decisions.

In 2018 the UK Financial Conduct Authority (FCA) launched a **Green FinTech challenge** to support innovation and growth in the green finance sector, aimed primarily at start-up and early-stage firms that need specific regulatory support to develop new products and services and bring them to market. Successful firms will benefit from support from the FCA Innovate unit, which will provide help and guidance on authorization and live market testing in the FCA sandbox.

In 2018 the **SDG-FinTech Initiative** was launched in Frankfurt, Germany, bringing together green and sustainable finance start-ups and Frankfurt Main Finance (the financial services trade association for Frankfurt), with the aim of combining top-down approaches by policymakers, regulators and others with bottom-up approaches practised by FinTech start-ups. The initiative is developing a community of NGOs, development organizations, larger financial institutions, policymakers and FinTech start-ups to share good practice, facilitate knowledge-sharing and strengthen links between individuals and organizations working in green and sustainable finance.

Costs and challenges of FinTech

While the application of FinTech tools and techniques to the green finance sector has the potential to bring many benefits, and to support and accelerate the growth of the sector, there are also accompanying costs, challenges and drawbacks. As is the case with many technologies, FinTech is neither good nor bad in itself, and may be applied to support positive outcomes for customers, communities and society overall, or deliver negative outcomes, either intentionally or unintentionally. Green and Sustainable Finance Professionals should, therefore, be aware of its advantages and disadvantages when working with or advising customers or colleagues on the potential of FinTech to support green and sustainable finance.

Some advocates of FinTech claim that it is fundamentally more green than existing financial services as it uses technology, rather than physical resources, to deliver products and services. This may be true in some cases, but not in others. Some cryptocurrency mining, for example, requires substantial energy use to support the computing power required, the majority of which currently comes from fossil fuels. Green and Sustainable Finance Professionals should adopt a balanced, curious and sceptical mindset when assessing the benefits and costs of FinTech solutions to green finance challenges.

QUICK QUESTION

What are the potential costs, challenges and drawbacks of utilizing FinTech tools and techniques in green finance?

Other costs and challenges of adopting FinTech tools and techniques include:

- **Digital exclusion:** The adoption of FinTech products and services requires individuals to own, or have access to, internet-enabled digital terminals, typically smartphones. In 2017, nearly 33 per cent of the world's population were estimated to own a smartphone, but this was only 14 per cent for individuals in the Middle East and Africa.[16] Ownership is predicted to rise, and communities often share phones, but this still means that for many of the individuals in the developing world green and sustainable finance products and services are inaccessible, or at best are only accessible infrequently. Other factors, such as access to the internet itself, may make it difficult or impossible to use products and services.

- **Difficulty in supporting vulnerable customers:** Some groups of vulnerable customers (eg elderly, individuals with learning difficulties or other disabilities) may find it hard to use digital technologies to access financial services. Where these services are only available in digital form, eg via a computer or smartphone, customers are unintentionally excluded from such products and services (eg a green investment platform).
- **Granularity:** The availability of big data and the use of advanced data analytics can ensure the better pricing of risk at more detailed levels. Financial products and services, for instance loans and insurance premiums, can now be priced for the individual or small community. This may be a significant issue if, for example, the use of individual level data means that financial services providers are unwilling to offer products and services to individuals at an affordable price because of the lack of risk pooling and the ability to price risk individually. Some individuals and communities may become uninsurable or otherwise have restricted access to financial services – a particular issue if this hampers individuals' or communities' climate resilience.
- **Unconscious bias in AI and machine learning:** For AI-enabled systems to learn and develop, they need to be trained with data sets. The decisions made by automated systems will depend, therefore, on the quality of the data provided and, if the data comes from existing real world scenarios, there is a risk that the data may contain unconscious biases. Credit scoring data, for example, may show that individuals living in certain locations are less likely to default on mortgages and other loans. An AI/machine learning system may correlate this with numerous factors, including ethnicity, but this may lead to outputs and decisions that discriminate for or against particular ethnic groups.
- **Lack of transparency:** While FinTech tools and techniques can be used to enhance monitoring, verification and transparency in green finance, the use of AI and machine learning to analyse data can lead to a black box scenario, where outcomes and decisions cannot be explained, and this can lead to a loss of trust in such decisions.

- **Loss of data control and privacy:** FinTech is based on the availability and analysis of large data sets. A number of high-profile incidents has occurred of individuals' data being used by technology companies for purposes that these individuals had not consented to, and/or were unaware of (eg Facebook/Cambridge Analytica), as well as significant data losses (eg Experian). Without suitable data governance and control, data obtained for the purpose of supporting climate change mitigation, adaptation and other positive, desired outcomes might be used – intentionally or unintentionally – for other purposes.
- **Social costs:** FinTech tools and techniques, particularly increased automation, can lead to job losses and/or increased job insecurity, as evidenced, for example, in the decline of branch networks in financial services, particularly in developed markets. This can disrupt communities if access to banking and other services becomes more difficult for customers who are not able, or unwilling, to use digital channels. At the extreme, the replacement of large numbers of customer-facing and back-office, processing jobs with automation has the potential to significantly disrupt the finance sector and communities dependent on it.
- **Potential for greenwashing:** The rapid growth, and expected continued growth of FinTech products and services supporting green and sustainable finance means there is an increasing risk of greenwashing, where the benefits of a new product are overstated in order to secure investment and/or grow market share.

Of course, some of the above are not only relevant to green finance – unconscious bias in AI and machine learning may impact many, if not all, aspects of financial services where these are deployed. In some areas, however, such as restricting access to climate insurance because of digital exclusion, or facilitating greenwashing, FinTech tools and techniques have the potential to detract from, rather than support the development of green finance. Green and Sustainable Finance Professionals should take active steps, therefore, when applying or advising on FinTech tools and techniques, to ensure that potential drawbacks are identified early, disclosed and, where possible, mitigated.

Key concepts

In this chapter we considered:

- what is meant by FinTech, and associated terms;
- a range of FinTech tools and techniques, such as blockchain, big data analysis, AI and machine learning, and how such techniques can support the growth of green finance and the transition to a low-carbon world;
- the benefits to customers, communities, financial institutions and to society as a whole of applying FinTech tools and techniques;
- some of the challenges to using FinTech tools and techniques to support green and sustainable finance.

Now go back through this chapter and make sure you fully understand each point.

Review

Enabled by advances in digital technology and data science, FinTech covers a wide range of tools and techniques, including, but not limited to, smartphones and banking apps, the IoT, application programme interfaces, distributed ledgers (blockchain), artificial intelligence and machine learning, big data and data analytics. The combination of FinTech tools and techniques can support financial inclusion and resilience, improve climate risk management, enhance verification, reporting and regulation, and facilitate access to capital markets.

RegTech refers to the use of FinTech tools and techniques to better manage regulatory compliance. CleanTech encompasses a wide range of technologies supporting environmental management, climate change mitigation and adaptation, and other related areas.

FinTech tools and techniques may be successfully applied to support the development of green finance, and the transition to a sustainable, low-carbon world, including improving access to, and lowering the costs of, delivering financial services, particularly in the developing world; improving access to capital markets for green firms and projects; enhancing the identification, assessment, management, pricing and disclosure of climate risks; and, via data-driven monitoring and verification, improving reporting of environmental and sustainable outcomes, enhancing transparency and market integrity overall.

In particular, the increasing availability and granularity of data related to environmental performance and sustainability, improvements in data quality, standardization and verification, as well as advances in AI and machine learning applied to data analysis, can support the continued growth of green finance. These factors can also support the development and delivery of green finance across financial services, in retail and corporate banking, investment and insurance sectors.

National and international policymakers have recognized the potential of FinTech tools and techniques to support policy goals relating to green and sustainable finance, including promoting the transition to a sustainable, low-carbon world, increasing financial inclusion to enhance sustainable development, and encouraging greater competition and innovation in financial services. This recognition has led to an increasing range of policy initiatives designed to support the further growth of green and sustainable FinTech.

While FinTech tools and techniques represent generally positive outcomes for green finance, Green and Sustainable Finance Professionals need to acknowledge that there are also some negative aspects and consequences of the use of FinTech, including the high energy costs of cryptocurrency mining, the potential for digital exclusion and/or lack of access to financial products and services due to granular pricing, and the risk of greenwashing.

Glossary

Artificial intelligence (AI): The simulation of human intelligence by a computer or machine.

Blockchain/distributed ledger: A database of records or transactions that are shared among participating parties, and verified by consensus of the majority of those parties – there is no central intermediary managing the database. Blockchains may be open access or private, with limited access.

CleanTech: A term to encompass a wide range of technologies supporting environmental management, climate change mitigation and adaptation, and other related areas. Also sometimes referred to as 'GreenTech'.

Crowdfunding/crowdinvesting: Raising small amounts of capital from a large number of investors to finance projects or new business ventures, typically via the internet.

Cryptocurrency: A digital asset used as a means of exchange for financial transactions without a central issuing authority, generally using blockchain (distributed ledger) technology.

FinTech: A term combining finance and technology. Enabled by advances in digital technology and data science, it includes a wide range of tools and techniques, including, but not limited to, smartphones and banking apps, the internet of things (IoT), application programme interfaces (APIs), distributed ledgers (blockchain), artificial intelligence (AI) and machine learning, big data and data analytics.

Internet of things (IoT): Connecting objects and devices to the internet with a sensor, allowing the sending and receiving of data.

Machine learning: A form of AI that enables systems to learn and improve from experience without being explicitly programmed. Machine learning encompasses a variety of techniques; most involve the use of large quantities of data for pattern recognition and inference to train the system.

Peer-to-peer (P2P) lending: Lending to individuals, businesses or projects via an online marketplace that matches lenders and borrowers.

RegTech: Using FinTech tools and techniques to better manage regulatory compliance, often, although not exclusively, in financial services.

Smart contract: A self-executing contract between parties where the terms of the agreement are expressed and run as computer code, usually utilizing blockchain/distributed ledger technology to provide verification and ensure trust without the need for a central, legal authority.

Notes

1. UNEP (2016) *FinTech and Sustainable Development: Assessing the implications*, Inquiry: Design of a Sustainable Financial System, [Online] http://unepinquiry.org/wp-content/uploads/2016/12/FinTech_and_Sustainable_Development_Assessing_the_Implications.pdf (archived at https://perma.cc/8AGW-T9TX)
2. P North (2019) FinTech and sustainable finance: Key drivers of Europe's financial future, BNY Mellon [Online] https://www.marketscreener.com/quote/stock/BANK-OF-NEW-YORK-MELLON-C-11848/news/FinTech-and-Sustainable-Finance-Key-Drivers-of-Europe-s-Financial-Future-27933373/ (archived at https://perma.cc/3C84-XRXA)
3. S Zadek (2017) Greening digital finance, IISD [Online] http://sdg.iisd.org/commentary/guest-articles/greening-digital-finance/ (archived at https://perma.cc/K6X5-GZXM)
4. Bettervest (nd) [Online] https://www.bettervest.com/en/ (archived at https://perma.cc/5YRP-YVSR)
5. Green Assets Wallet (nd) About [Online] https://greenassetswallet.org/about (archived at https://perma.cc/Z3YW-PYV3)
6. P M Fariña (2019) BBVA issues the first blockchain-supported structured green bond for MAPFRE, BBVA [Online] https://www.bbva.com/en/bbva-issues-the-first-blockchain-supported-structured-green-bond-for-mapfre/ (archived at https://perma.cc/A37V-A3S2)
7. Arabesque (nd) About the Arabesque Group [Online] https://arabesque.com/about/ (archived at https://perma.cc/Z29Q-28XX)

8 G17Eco World Wide Generation (nd) [Online] https://www.worldwidegeneration.co (archived at https://perma.cc/M6E9-5WTN)

9 OKO Crop Assurance (nd) [Online] https://www.oko.finance/ (archived at https://perma.cc/9AGC-MSJV)

10 M Frankel (2018) How many cryptocurrencies are there? The Motley Fool [Online] https://www.fool.com/investing/2018/03/16/how-many-cryptocurrencies-are-there.aspx (archived at https://perma.cc/MF4B-KACZ)

11 A Gurzu (2017) SolarCoin hopes to ride the bitcoin buzz, Politico [Online] https://www.politico.eu/article/solarcoin-hopes-to-ride-the-bitcoin-buzz/ (archived at https://perma.cc/7W6L-KX7N)

12 UNEP (2016) *FinTech and Sustainable Development: Assessing the implications*, Inquiry: Design of a Sustainable Financial System, [Online] http://unepinquiry.org/wp-content/uploads/2016/12/FinTech_and_Sustainable_Development_Assessing_the_Implications.pdf (archived at https://perma.cc/8AGW-T9TX)

13 J Rosenbluth (2017) Green Digital Finance Alliance, UN Reporter [Online] https://unreporter.org/green-digital-finance-alliance/ (archived at https://perma.cc/T5JJ-AZ8M)

14 FinTech4Good (nd) [Online] https://www.FinTech4good.co (archived at https://perma.cc/Q4ZX-T2M5)

15 Climate Chain Coalition (nd) Charter [Online] https://www.climatechaincoalition.io/charter (archived at https://perma.cc/W8L2-PUTC)

16 S O'Dea (2020) Smartphone penetration worldwide as share of global population 2016–2020, Statista [Online] https://www.statista.com/statistics/203734/global-smartphone-penetration-per-capita-since-2005/ (archived at https://perma.cc/3AFM-LP3A)

12

Mainstreaming green finance

LEARNING OBJECTIVES

On completion of this chapter you should be able to:

- Explain why it is vital for green finance to become part of mainstream finance.
- Articulate the significant opportunities associated with the mainstreaming of green finance.
- Outline some of the positive steps that regulators, policymakers, institutions and organizations can take to support the mainstreaming of green finance.
- Describe some of the challenges to mainstreaming green finance.
- Reflect on the role you can play in promoting and embedding green finance as a Green and Sustainable Finance Professional.

This chapter considers how green finance can become part of the mainstream of financial services, and the societal, economic and organizational benefits that will result from this. This chapter also examines what mainstreaming means, how this might be achieved and assessed, and some of the major shifts already under way that are bringing green finance into the mainstream. Finally, this chapter considers the role you can play, as a Green and Sustainable Finance Professional, in embedding green finance principles and practices in financial services and supporting the transition to a sustainable, low-carbon world.

Why green finance will become part of the mainstream

As we have seen throughout this book, 'greening' finance, and the global economic system overall, is necessary to address climate change and the associated environmental challenges facing humanity. This will also help financial institutions to appropriately identify, disclose and manage risk, improve organizational resilience and that of the entire financial system, and generate significant opportunities for sustainable global growth from which financial services – as well as humanity – will benefit.

In addition, playing a proactive role in supporting (and, at times, leading) the transition to a sustainable, low-carbon world will help demonstrate a positive social purpose for financial services, helping to reconnect banks and society, and contributing to the process of rebuilding trust in the financial sector overall. To put it crudely: banks and bankers can help save the world. It is impossible, however, to tackle climate change, and other environmental and sustainability challenges, without mainstreaming green and sustainable finance principles and practice across the entire financial system.

In 2014 the Global Commission on the Economy and Climate estimated that approximately $93 trillion was required over a 15-year period to fund the transition to a low-carbon world, ie approximately $6 trillion per year, with two-thirds of that deployed in developing countries.[1] UNEP estimates the transition to require capital of 'at least' $60 trillion to 2050, with approximately $35 trillion of this required to decarbonize energy and other carbon-dependent systems; and the remainder to support the climate change adaptation required. We saw in Chapter 1, however, that, according to the Climate Policy Initiative, only some $500 billion per year is currently being deployed to fund climate change mitigation and adaptation projects.

While there may be some dispute over the exact amounts of capital required, it is clear that the sums involved are very substantial. The global economic transition will be the most capital-intensive transition in human history. It involves a fundamental change: moving away from opex-based systems (ie small, upfront capital costs followed by high, variable resource input costs, such as oil and gas) to capex-based ones (ie high, upfront capital costs followed by negligible marginal costs, as ongoing inputs are renewable and (mostly) free, such as wind and sun). For the transition to succeed, the availability of substantial amounts of low-cost capital, particularly for low-carbon infrastructure and technology, is essential, generating significant commercial opportunities for financial services firms as the transition is made.

Public funds are insufficient, by a considerable margin, to finance the transition, and it is estimated that up to 80 per cent of the capital required will need to come from private sources. The pool of global capital is sufficient to fund the transition; PwC estimate that worldwide assets under management will rise to nearly $102 trillion in 2020,[2] driven by high savings rates in many large emerging economies. This is currently invested across a wide range of asset classes, including those contributing to global warming. With the 'right' policy interventions and other incentives to promote climate change mitigation and adaptation, combined with increasing investor awareness of the true costs and risks of climate change and asset impairment and stranding, private capital can be more effectively employed to finance the economic transition required. The problem is not the lack of capital to finance the transition, but rather connecting the available capital with the solutions needed for climate change mitigation and adaptation activities, as well as other environmental and sustainability challenges.

Mobilizing that capital is what the financial services sector can do well – connecting capital seeking financial returns with projects and other investment opportunities to deliver both sustainable returns and a sustainable planet. By facilitating the investment required to deliver the transition, financial services and banking in particular will help us to achieve an environmentally sustainable planet for future generations. It also creates an opportunity to address weak global growth and productivity by putting the large savings balances held – particularly in Asia – to productive use.

Key to this will be reducing the average cost of capital on green investments, through the development of new products, services, structures and asset classes that can significantly reduce the overall cost of the transition. For example, if the average cost of capital for green can be reduced by just 1 per cent on the $6 trillion per annum investment required, this amounts to a saving of $60 billion every year. This could be shared between the providers, facilitators and users of capital, and might also be spent on other societal priorities, generating a wide range of benefits for communities around the world.

READING
Green finance and the global economy[3]

In the Arthur Burns Memorial Lecture on 22 September 2016, Mark Carney, then Governor of the Bank of England, made the case that 'green investment represents a major opportunity for both long-term investors and macroeconomic policymakers seeking to jump-start growth'.

Low rates of investment and productivity growth, particularly in developed countries, combined with a glut of global savings, means that green finance is a major opportunity for the global economy. 'By ensuring that capital flows finance long-term projects in countries where growth is most carbon-intensive, financial stability can be promoted. By absorbing excess global saving, equilibrium interest rates can be raised and macroeconomic stability enhanced. And, by allocating capital to green technologies, the prospects for an environmentally sustainable recovery in global growth will increase.'

Furthermore, if financial markets integrate climate change and other environmental risks into decision-making, it will help financial institutions (and organizations throughout the economy) to better identify, disclose, manage and price risk. This will help reduce the risks and costs of asset impairment and stranding, avoid losses and improve the resilience of the financial system as a whole. It may also help organizations to identify commercial opportunities from supporting climate change mitigation and adaptation.

These are all very important and tangible reasons for supporting green finance, and there are undoubtedly compelling reasons to green global capital markets as quickly as possible. Nonetheless, despite the issues tackled in this course having achieved widespread prominence relatively quickly, we are still only at the beginning of that journey, as the investment gap between climate finance today (approximately $500 billion per year) and the amounts of capital required (approximately $6 trillion per year) demonstrates.

To accelerate progress, policymakers and the financial services sector have established a wide range of global initiatives to support the mainstreaming of green and sustainable finance, including, to name only a few: the UN Principles for Responsible Banking, Principles for Responsible Investment and Principles for Sustainable Insurance; the TCFD; the European Commission Action Plan on Financing Sustainable Growth; the Climate Bond Initiative; the Green Bond and Green Loan Principles; Investor Agenda and Climate Action 100+.

Their success, together with the success of other organizations and initiatives working to mainstream green finance, will depend on understanding what mainstreaming actually means and what this might really entail in practice. Too often, mainstreaming is brandished as an objective in this context without being appropriately defined, making it very hard to track progress or to understand the effects of different efforts to mainstream green finance.

QUICK QUESTIONS

How far do you believe green finance is now part of the mainstream of finance? To what extent is it embedded in your organization, and other organizations with which you are familiar?

Assessing progress towards the mainstream

Mainstreaming has several elements, and does not only relate to green finance (as a term and a concept entering regular discourse), although this in itself can be seen as a sign of progress. As we have seen in earlier chapters, terms such as sustainable finance, green finance, responsible investment, ESG and stranded assets have all achieved a degree of familiarity – both among green and sustainable finance specialists and non-specialist financial services professionals, together with their customers and clients.

Mainstreaming, however, must also be about changing industry, institutional and individual practice – developing, identifying and sharing best practice, as well as ratcheting up the quality of what could be called routine practice. This is a dynamic process, with best practice constantly improving to raise the bar for routine practice, in which institutions and individuals developing the former share their knowledge, skills, experience and expertise with others to raise standards for the benefit of all. This is an aspect of green finance where the role of the individual Green and Sustainable Finance Professional is key, in embedding green finance practice into their professional activities, and encouraging others in their organizations and industries to adopt similar practice.

Mainstreaming should also mean that green finance principles and practices are irreversibly adopted, implemented and embedded across multiple parts of the investment chain and investor decision-making in a wide range of different markets. It is not sufficient for adoption to be fleetingly met in one or two parts of the investment chain and in one or two parts of the world (eg green mortgages). The threshold for success is permanent adoption across the whole global financial system.

Perhaps most importantly, the successful mainstreaming of green finance should be seen through outcomes, when the majority of global capital flows irreversibly to assets and projects associated with climate change mitigation and adaptation, and the transition to a sustainable, low-carbon world, rather than to high-carbon assets.

Therefore, a number of possible success criteria for mainstreaming green finance can be defined:

- green finance concepts and terminology entering regular discourse;
- developing and sharing best practice, leading to the enhancement of routine practice throughout financial services;
- embedding green finance principles and practice across financial services;
- closing the gap between the investment required to support the transition to a low-carbon world and current levels of investment;
- mobilizing the majority of global capital in support of green and sustainable finance aims and objectives.

Tracking the growth of green finance is important, both to demonstrate progress to the mainstream and to monitor the size of the investment gap – and opportunity – remaining. Despite the growth of green finance in recent years to approximately $500 billion annual investment in climate change mitigation and adaptation finance, there is still a very large gap to be filled to reach the estimated $6 trillion per year investment required to support the transition to a low-carbon world.

Evidence of progress towards the mainstream

Although there is undoubtedly much still to do, we have seen significant progress in moving green finance from a small niche to a more substantive part of financial services in recent years. There are at least three major shifts among financial institutions and markets that are real and meaningful, and which highlight how the financial system has the capacity to change remarkably quickly. These provide reasons for optimism and suggest pathways to successfully mainstream green finance at the scale and pace required.

First, by showing sustained interest in climate-related risks, including asset impairment and stranding, and their potential to threaten financial stability, global regulators, led by the Financial Stability Board and the Network for Greening the Financial System, have prompted financial institutions and large corporations more generally, to take steps to identify, disclose and manage such risks. The TCFD is perhaps the best example of global cooperation and progress in this area.

Second, the involvement of central banks and regulators has also helped to shift the terms of engagement with green finance principles and practice within institutions, and across the financial services industry as a whole. Until recently, green and sustainable finance tended to be seen as a specialist niche, with Green and Sustainable Finance Professionals in relatively junior roles, struggling to secure senior management time and sponsorship for the integration of climate-related risks and opportunities into decision-making.

This situation now seems to be changing. In the run up to the Paris Climate Change Negotiations in late 2015, and in the period since then, there has been a noticeable shift in Chairman, CEO and Board-level engagement with climate finance in many financial institutions. In addition, many senior financial services executives have adopted a higher public profile on these issues. Boards and senior executives of financial institutions can ensure that green and sustainable finance forms an increasing proportion (or perhaps all) of the business strategies of their firms, and they can also commit their institutions to international, national and sector-level green finance initiatives, can sponsor and provide resources for the integration of climate-related risks and opportunities into decision-making, and can drive implementation across their organizations, all of which aids the mainstreaming of green finance.

QUICK QUESTIONS

What have senior policymakers, regulators and financial services executives in your jurisdiction said about green and sustainable finance? What have senior executives in your organization said?

As we can see from the following selected examples of recent public pronouncements from senior policymakers, regulators and financial services executives, the understanding of the importance of green finance, and support for its continued growth, is widespread.

- Addressing climate change and environmental pollution has been identified by **Chinese President Xi Jinping** as one of his 'three battles' for the period 2018–21. Developing a national green finance system has been made a national priority by President Xi and the Chinese State Council. The Belt and Road initiative, which includes the building of green infrastructure as a key part of the plan, will require up to $1 trillion per year of green investment, according to **Dr Ma Jun, Chairman of the China Green Finance Committee.** Speaking at the launch of the Hong Kong Green Finance Association in 2018, Dr Ma noted that 'the adoption of green finance has become a growing trend around the world'.[4]
- Announcing the World Bank's 2025 Action Plan, with up to $200 billion committed for climate change mitigation and adaptation project financing, the then **World Bank President, Jim Yong Kim** (speaking in 2018) said: 'We are pushing ourselves to do more and go faster on climate [change] and we call on the global community to do the same. This is about putting countries and communities in charge of building a safer, more climate-resilient future.'[5]
- Prior to the COP24 Climate Summit in December 2018, **World Bank CEO Kristalina Georgieva** said the world 'cannot ignore the new reality of powerful weather events that threaten jobs, homes, food security and other critical areas of our lives… The infrastructure that is built today must be ready to cope with tomorrow's changing climate… We need the right incentives and regulations to urgently accelerate funding to these projects.'[6]
- In November 2018 the **United Nations** launched its draft UN-supported Principles for Responsible Banking, supported initially by 28 banks representing more than $17 trillion in assets. In September 2019 the United Nations launched the Principles for Responsible Banking, with initial signatories comprising 130 banks representing more than $47 trillion in assets.
- **HSBC Chief Executive Stuart Gulliver**, speaking in 2017, announced plans for the bank to support $100 billion of low-carbon and sustainable finance to 2025.
- Speaking in 2017, **Jamie Dimon, Chairman and CEO of JPMorgan Chase** announced: 'Business must play a leadership role in creating solutions that protect the environment and grow the economy.'[7]
- In August 2018 **Sir Ian Cheshire, Chairman of Barclays Bank UK,** said: 'The climate crisis showed that the cost of carbon has become unaffordable. At the same time, transitioning to a low-carbon economy will bring benefits to businesses. It is a national strategic objective and it also plays to our strength as a global financial centre.'[8]

- **European Vice-President Valdis Dombrovskis,** in his keynote speech at the launch of the European Sustainable and Responsible Investment Study in November 2018, said: 'More and more people are realising that sustainable finance is one of the missing links in the fight against climate change, and for a more sustainable economy... as today's report confirms, sustainable finance is going mainstream... Now we need to build on these achievements and accelerate sustainable investments. There is still a lot of work to do, and no time to lose.'
- **Larry Fink, the BlackRock Chairman and CEO** announced in September 2018 that it intended to become a global leader in sustainable investing. 'Sustainable investing will be a core component for how everyone invests in the future,' he said in an interview with the Financial Times, adding: 'We are going to see evidence over the long term that sustainable investing is going to be at least equivalent to core investments. I believe personally it will be higher.'[9]
- Prompted by pressure from institutional investors, in 2018 **Royal Dutch Shell** became the first major oil and gas company to announce that divestment should be considered a 'material risk' to its business. Shell has now set short and long-term carbon emissions targets linked to executive remuneration, aiming to reduce its Net Carbon Footprint by approximately 65 per cent by 2050 and by approximately 35 per cent by 2035 as an interim step.[10]

Third, developments in the practice of managing climate-related risks and opportunities in investment portfolios, and the application of FinTech tools and techniques to green and sustainable finance are supporting its growth. There are significant new possibilities – existing data can be analysed using techniques involving artificial intelligence and machine learning, while new asset-level data can be made accessible from previously unavailable sources, such as remote sensing (eg of land usage), and big data. FinTech can support the development of green finance in retail banking and investment, insurance and corporate banking/capital markets.

These three shifts – the integration of climate-related risk into regulatory frameworks and supervisory practice; green and sustainable finance being driven by senior executives as a strategic priority rather than being a niche activity managed by more junior colleagues; and a period of rapid technical innovation driven by asset-level data, advanced analytics and FinTech – are significant and can support the rapid change urgently needed.

Challenges to mainstreaming green finance

Despite undoubted progress in recent years, we cannot currently say that green finance has been mainstreamed, however. The green bond, green loan, ESG investment and other markets may be growing, and growing quickly, but they still account for only a small proportion of financial services overall. The green and sustainable bond market, for example, is only some 2 per cent of the overall bond market.

Therefore, a number of significant challenges has still to be overcome to mainstream green finance, including policy and regulatory challenges, economic challenges, and the lack of data availability and quality.

Policy and regulatory challenges

Policy and regulatory challenges to the growth of green finance include financial policy and regulation, as well as wider areas of policy and regulation that impact on the willingness of financial institutions to invest in green and sustainable finance projects. In terms of financial policy and regulation, current challenges include:

- lack of clear guidance for investment managers on their fiduciary duty, where, despite some progress in integrating ESG factors into investment decisions (not least through the UN-supported Principles for Responsible Investment), there is a lack of global consistency in regulatory guidance requiring investment managers to incorporate ESG factors;
- existing bank and insurance capital requirements (Basel III and Solvency 2), which, as currently drafted, can restrict the flow of capital to green and sustainable projects due to relative capital weightings;
- no uniform taxonomy/definitions for green and sustainable finance, although there has been considerable progress in recent years.

The introduction of a green supporting factor for banks, and similar incentives for investors (including insurers) to hold green assets – or higher risk weightings for brown assets – would undoubtedly accelerate the mainstreaming of green finance.

Many other areas of policy and regulation (eg subsidies, feed-in tariffs, emissions criteria, building codes) can impact on the willingness of financial institutions to invest in green and sustainable finance projects by shifting the risk/return ratio. In general, financial markets like policy and regulatory stability, and when this is absent it becomes more difficult and expensive to invest, particularly in the longer term. Given that many of the non-financial areas of policy and regulation that may impact on the green finance sector are subject to change, driven by a variety of political, economic and scientific factors, and that many of the investments required in the green finance sector are longer term, this can reduce the attractiveness of such investments relative to alternatives. For example, green lending to solar energy farms may be supported by subsidies, or a change of political leadership may see subsidies reduced or removed, making investment no longer viable and/or returns more volatile. Financial institutions, of course, do factor this kind of risk into investment decisions, but long-term policy and regulatory certainty would improve the viability of many projects and investments.

Economic challenges

Possibly the greatest economic challenge to mainstreaming green finance is the lack of a realistic, global carbon price, although some countries and regions are now making progress in introducing this. Carbon pricing, either through carbon taxes or cap-and-trade schemes, creates incentives for firms to invest in low-carbon technologies, and reduce their carbon use and emissions. It also helps firms to quantify climate-related risks and opportunities. The absence of realistic carbon pricing (until recently it was far too low in many instances) means that high-carbon investments may be favoured over low-carbon alternatives, slowing the growth of green finance.

The need for green and sustainable finance to grow in the developing world, where many of the necessary climate change mitigation and adaptation activities need to take place, is a further economic challenge. Investment in the developing world is hampered by a number of factors, including the lack of developed financial markets and regulatory infrastructure, political instability (in some cases) and higher costs of capital and costs of doing business more generally. Green finance may grow rapidly in Western Europe, but this will not be sufficient to support the transition needed to a sustainable, low-carbon world.

Another economic challenge to the growth of green finance is the current lack of demand, especially at retail investor level. At present, demand is driven mainly by institutional investors, prompted by the need to diversify portfolios, seek long-term sustainable returns, and reflect climate-related risks, while demand from retail investors is growing, but less marked. Similarly, while large firms (eg power and other utility companies) might issue green bonds and other green financial instruments, smaller businesses seem less likely to search out green and sustainable financial products and services without prompting from financial institutions. Demand for green finance products and services needs to grow considerably so that at retail and small business level, green mortgages, for example, or green loans become a substantial part of financial services firms' product offerings, rather than being niche products.

Data availability and quality

Many actors and initiatives are seeking to improve the availability and quality of data to enable better scenario planning, identification and pricing of climate-related risk, and monitoring/verification of project outcomes. Despite undoubted progress, particularly in the availability of data, the current reliance (for the most part) on voluntary standards for disclosure and the lack of standardization between jurisdictions and organizations makes it difficult for investors to make informed decisions, or increases the costs and effort involved in doing so. Another problem is the relative lack of data for developing countries and emerging markets, compared with, for example, the US and Europe, despite the urgent need for green finance to be accelerated in the former.

Your role as a Green and Sustainable Finance Professional

This book has outlined the profound challenges we face as individuals, companies, industries and communities if we are to avoid catastrophic climate change, successfully manage the transition to a low-carbon economy and create a more prosperous, sustainable world. We have seen how vital it is to transform and harness the power of finance to achieve this transition and have considered some of the successes and challenges in mainstreaming green finance.

While international and national institutions, and organizations large and small, have key roles to play, so too do individuals. Finance is built on pillars of financial and human capital. Change is led, ultimately, by individuals – not by organizations. The change we seek in mainstreaming green finance needs to be led by increasing numbers of finance professionals with an understanding of the critical role of financial services in supporting the transition to a low-carbon world, and with the knowledge and skills of finance to be able to develop and deploy products, services and tools that will mobilize capital to support the transition, address climate-related risks, and direct customers and communities towards investments that exploit green finance opportunities.

Developing the green finance knowledge and skills of finance professionals will help support the mainstreaming of green and sustainable finance. This is the motivation behind the Chartered Banker Institute's **Certificate in Green and Sustainable Finance**, the world's first benchmark qualification for green finance, which this book has been written to support.[11] Proposed by the UK's Green Finance Taskforce in 2017, the Green and Sustainable Finance Certificate was launched at the Global Green Finance Summit in London in July 2018, and sets the global benchmark standard for the knowledge and skills required by individuals working in green finance. During 2021, the Chartered Banker Institute will launch a new **Green and Sustainable Finance Professional** designation for individuals who complete the Certificate in Green and Sustainable Finance, supporting a global network of financial services professionals committed to green and sustainable finance.

Another initiative designed to accelerate and support the growth of green finance is **Bankers for Climate**, established by Anders Langworth, a Swedish financial services executive. Bankers for Climate aims to build a global, online community of at least 30,000 financial services professionals, who will:

- engage with senior financial services executives and urge them to take ownership of climate action;
- increase awareness of and action on climate change amongst colleagues in the financial services sector;
- increase awareness of climate change in society as a whole.

For further information, visit Bankers for Climate website, https://www.bankersforclimate.com/

Green finance values

Green finance values – based on stewardship, sustainability and a focus on the longer term – are consistent with what many perceive as the values on which a successful and sustainable financial services sector, and profession, need to be built. Many initiatives in recent years, particularly in response to the 2007/8 global financial crisis, have set out the values expected of financial services professionals in codes of ethics, codes of conduct and similar at national, industry and firm level, including the Chartered Banker Code, to which all members of the Chartered Banker Institute subscribe. There are many similarities between such codes, which commonly include values such as the following.

Integrity

Integrity refers to consistently demonstrating high moral standards. A person who displays integrity will steadfastly adhere to their moral values despite pressure exerted to do otherwise. Integrity is an important quality because laws, rules and codes cannot define every situation or dilemma with which the individual may be faced. In a traditional financial services environment, integrity has to be underpinned by:

- ensuring that those who lead the organization are fit and proper, and comply with relevant legislation and regulation;
- recruiting staff with appropriate personal qualities;
- ensuring that employees have the necessary competence to discharge their duties, and providing training where necessary;
- if appropriate, applying sanctions to those who break the rules, or fail to comply with the desired standards.

In green finance, we might also want to see integrity underpinned by:

- personal commitment (in addition to organizational commitment) to supporting sustainable investments, products and services and activities, and refraining from participating in activities that are not sufficiently sustainable; in particular, avoiding greenwashing (knowingly making claims for the green-ness of products, services and outcomes that are significantly overstated);
- ensuring that staff are given the opportunity to develop their knowledge and skills in green and sustainable finance.

Fairness

This refers to dealing with people and issues in an even-handed way, without favouritism or preference for an outcome based on personal value judgements. Fairness in a financial services environment implies that policies and practices should be applied objectively, without undue influence.

It can be argued that ignoring the environmental aspects of financial activities is incompatible with fairness, since negative environmental impacts affect certain groups disproportionately, such as those living in poverty or those living in areas that are highly vulnerable to climate change. There is also an important intergenerational aspect to fairness – sustainability refers to future generations as well as the current generation, and the outcomes of financing decisions taken today could have positive or negative effects on future generations. Green and Sustainable Finance Professionals should therefore consider these issues when choosing a course of action, and it is hoped that, over time, all finance professionals will adopt a similar approach.

Openness and transparency

This refers to an individual's or organization's preparedness to reveal or make available relevant or appropriate information, and also to not cloud an issue nor conceal relevant details. It is possible to mislead without necessarily telling lies, however, as a false impression can be created simply by omitting material facts. In business, it is essential that a firm's financial accounts provide a true and fair view of the firm's financial situation, presenting the facts as they are, and not omitting important information that investors and other users of the accounts require. Complete transparency is not an absolute duty, however, as commercial decisions sometimes involve a need for secrecy, such as when a new product or service is to be launched.

The extent to which an organization is transparent about its environmental impacts is an increasingly important aspect of transparency. Many environmental advocacy groups research and publish data on the involvement of major financial institutions in fossil fuel extraction or other environmentally harmful activities, and research suggests that many customers would not support this type of investment if they were made aware of it. There are many initiatives to improve disclosure (such as the TCFD) and new FinTech products and services may improve transparency to a wider range of stakeholders, including retail customers.

Responsibility

Responsibility is a duty, obligation or burden. In a work context, it relates to what the individual has to do as part of their job. Taking responsibility refers to accepting and acting on an obligation, which can be difficult when there is an unpleasant outcome for an affected party.

It can be argued that all of us have a responsibility to respect the environment in our personal and professional lives, either because a healthy environment is vital for society to function, or because the environment is seen as a source of value in itself. The Chartered Banker Institute argues that all finance professionals should demonstrate a personal commitment to stewardship in the broadest sense – sustaining customers' communities' and society's resources, not just financial resources, for long-term economic benefit and for the benefit of future generations. As finance professionals, we have a responsibility – a duty – to act in these wider interests, not just our own or our employer's.

Accountability

Accountability is taking ultimate responsibility for a duty, obligation or burden. As the global financial crisis demonstrated, in many cases it has been hard for regulators in many countries to hold senior financial services professionals to account for the failure of financial institutions, and the individuals concerned may not have felt accountable themselves, but rather were part of a system that failed.

For financial services professionals who subscribe to the Chartered Banker Code, or similar codes, or who share a similar approach to the profession of financial services rooted in integrity, fairness, transparency, accountability and responsibility, there is a professional duty to support the continued development of green finance and incorporate green finance principles and practice into the mainstream of finance. This requires developing and deploying professionals' own green finance knowledge and skill within organizations to identify opportunities for supporting clients and communities, as well as generating a return for shareholders, and encouraging others in organizations and industries to embed green finance principles and practice more widely.

As already mentioned, the Chartered Banker Institute will launch a new Green and Sustainable Finance Professional designation for individuals who complete the Certificate in Green and Sustainable Finance in 2021. To support this, the Institute has developed guidance on the Chartered Banker Code, to which all members of the Institute subscribe, relating to the application of the seven principles of the Code in a green finance context.

CASE STUDY

The Chartered Banker Code for Green and Sustainable Finance Professionals[12]

All individuals working in financial services should act in a fair and honest manner. This is to help protect the interests of customers, colleagues and counterparties and the wider interests of society. As a minimum, compliance with legislation, regulation and industry/employer codes and standards is required. The Chartered Banker Institute, the oldest institute of bankers in the world, founded in 1875, believes that to enhance public confidence and trust in banks and bankers, and pride within the banking profession, individuals working in banking should make a personal commitment to a higher standard of professionalism, such as that set out in the Institute's Chartered Banker Code.

The Chartered Banker Code sets out the ethical and professional values, attitudes and behaviour expected of all professional bankers by the Institute. Membership of the Chartered Banker Institute brings with it additional responsibilities. All members are expected to act as role models to others working in the banking industry, leading by example and displaying high standards of professionalism and a commitment to ethical conduct and the public interest at all times. Members are also expected to conduct their affairs in a manner that upholds the name and reputation of the Chartered Banker Institute, and the banking profession more broadly.

In 2018, the Institute developed a version of the Chartered Banker Code for Green and Sustainable Finance Professionals, reproduced below. The seven principles on which the Code is based are exactly the same as those on which the Chartered Banker Code itself is based, with additional guidance provided as to how these principles may apply in the context of green finance. It sets out how individuals may incorporate green finance principles and values into their professional practice.

I will demonstrate my personal commitment to professionalism in banking, and to the principles and values of green finance, by:

1 **Treating all customers, colleagues and counterparties with respect and acting with integrity.**
Acting with integrity requires Green and Sustainable Finance Professionals to take active steps to ensure that their activities and, as far as possible, those of their organizations, are aligned with and support the transition to a low-carbon, sustainable world. It involves ensuring that advice given to customers, colleagues and counterparties is consistent with promoting this transition and that financial activities that may damage the environment are identified and disclosed. Green and Sustainable Finance Professionals have a particular responsibility to avoid greenwashing, and should take active steps to ensure their advice and activities does not in any way damage the integrity of the green finance profession.

2 **Developing and maintaining my professional knowledge and acting with due skill, care and diligence; considering the risks and implications of my actions and advice, and holding myself accountable for them and their impact.**

Green and Sustainable Finance Professionals should take active steps to regularly update their knowledge of the principles and practice of green finance, and of emerging best practice, recognizing that this is a sector developing very rapidly. Considering the risks and implications of actions and advice requires detailed consideration of the climate risks involved, and how these may be appropriately identified, disclosed, managed and priced. Green and Sustainable Finance Professionals should hold themselves accountable for the impact of their activities and advice on the environment, and on communities impacted by climate change, seeking to use their knowledge and skills to support climate change mitigation and adaptation and the transition to a low-carbon world, and avoid activities that damage the environment.

3 **Being open and cooperative with the regulators; complying with all current regulatory and legal requirements.**
Complying with current and emerging regulatory requirements relating to green finance is expected of all finance professionals. Green and Sustainable Finance Professionals should take additional steps to comply with relevant market frameworks and standards, even when these are voluntary. Green and Sustainable Finance Professionals should also, where possible, work with regulators and other stakeholders to shape and develop legal and regulatory requirements to ensure a consistent approach to identifying, disclosing and managing climate risk, and to promoting market integrity in the area of green and sustainable finance.

4 **Paying due regard to the interests of customers and treating them fairly.**
Green and Sustainable Finance Professionals should also pay due regard to the interests of future generations of customers, balancing the needs of customers today and tomorrow for sustainable financial returns, and a sustainable planet. They should treat future generations fairly by acting prudently and professionally as stewards of natural and financial resources for the long term, rather than being motivated by the need to generate short-term returns. Treating customers fairly also requires Green and Sustainable Finance Professionals to present the full details and potential impacts of recommended or suggested products and services to customers, including on climate change and natural systems.

5 **Observing and demonstrating proper standards of market conduct at all times.**
This requires Green and Sustainable Finance Professionals to develop their knowledge of, and act in accordance with voluntary frameworks and standards of green finance practice that go beyond legal and regulatory requirements, for instance the Green Bond Principles and the Green Loan Principles. Where possible, Green and Sustainable Finance Professionals should take active steps to help develop, implement and embed market standards within their own organizations and sectors.

6 **Acting in an honest and trustworthy manner, being alert to and managing potential conflicts of interest.**
Green and Sustainable Finance Professionals should be honest with themselves, with customers and with colleagues about the impacts of financial activities that may damage the environment, or are in other ways unsustainable. Being trustworthy requires that Green and Sustainable Finance Professionals must actively avoid being involved in greenwashing and must not overstate the environmental benefits, or avoid disclosing environmental harm, of financial activities. Conflicts of interest can arise when Green and Sustainable Finance Professionals have to balance the needs of customers, shareholders and others for short-term financial returns with longer-term, sustainable financial and environmental returns. Green and Sustainable Finance Professionals should be aware of this conflict, and should seek to encourage a sustainable approach wherever possible; when this is not possible this should be clearly documented and, if necessary, disclosed.

7 **Treating information with appropriate confidentiality and sensitivity.**
In financial services, maintaining the confidentiality of customer and commercial data and information, subject to legal and regulatory disclosure requirements, is of great importance. This applies equally to Green and Sustainable Finance Professionals. There may be occasions, however, when in order to maintain the integrity of the green finance profession and avoid greenwashing, Green and Sustainable Finance Professionals should disclose information, with appropriate safeguards, where this would be in the public interest. Green and Sustainable Finance Professionals should first seek to work within organizational and industry channels for speaking up before publicly disclosing such information.

Finance is a fast-moving sector where major change and disruption can and does occur; for example, the emergence of FinTech over the past decade and its impact (and the impact of digital technologies and data more generally) on banking, investment and insurance. Mainstreaming green finance is possible, especially if pressure from policymakers and regulators, combined with changing customer and client demographics and preferences, support this. Financial services firms and green finance hubs will play key roles in developing and disseminating green finance products, services and tools that can be copied and shared by others. Individual financial services professionals are vital in determining the future success and mainstreaming of green finance. By implementing green finance principles and practice, such as those outlined in this book, in their organizations, and encouraging others to do likewise in sufficient numbers, the changes required to fully align finance with the transition to a sustainable, low-carbon world are within reach.

Personal reflection

Take some time to reflect on what the challenges and opportunities that have been highlighted here pose to you as an individual. First, think about your own strengths and weaknesses and then think about your role in your organization and other organizations/networks you may be part of, as well as how you can use these to make a positive difference.

In the space below, write down what you think are your main strengths. For example, think about whether you have any applicable subject, product or sector-specific knowledge; if you are good at research; at networking and collaboration; at liaising with senior executives, policymakers or organizations; at finding or creating investment opportunities, or perhaps at assessing risk.

My strengths:

Now, reflect on the main challenges to achieving deep green strategies, visions and principles in your role, organization and the wider industry you are part of, and summarize these below.

Challenges for your role:

Challenges for your organization:

Challenges for your industry:

Next, building on these reflections, imagine yourself in the role of change-maker, contributing to the transition to a low-carbon world, and summarize the opportunities you can take advantage of. Write your ideas below.

Opportunities for your role:

Opportunities for your organization:

Opportunities for your industry:

Finally, to conclude this section, note down some action points and associated deadlines to help you start working towards achieving these aims. For example: research your own organization's green provision and aspirations, prepare a presentation for colleagues to introduce the key concepts of green finance, or develop an action plan to increase customer awareness of green finance.

Action points:

Key concepts

In this chapter we considered:

- why it is vital for green finance to become part of the mainstream;
- the significant opportunities associated with the mainstreaming of green finance;
- some of the positive steps that might be taken by regulators, policymakers, institutions and organizations to support the mainstreaming of green finance;
- some of the challenges to mainstreaming green finance;
- the role you can play in promoting and embedding green finance as a Green and Sustainable Finance Professional.

Now go back through this chapter and make sure you fully understand each point.

Review

In this final chapter, we looked at why green finance needs to move from a rapidly growing specialist area of financial services to become part of the mainstream, and how that may be supported and accelerated. The societal, economic and organizational benefits are clear, and are understood and articulated by governments, central banks, regulators and increasingly by senior financial services leaders. The role of the financial services sector in providing the capital and expertise needed to support the transition to a low-carbon world is key, and the sector's willingness to provide these is rapidly becoming part of financial services firms' strategies and operations. To accelerate progress, policymakers have established many initiatives to try to mainstream green finance.

It is important to understand what is meant by mainstreaming. While the ever-increasing use of terms such as green finance and sustainable finance is one sign of this, true mainstreaming requires green finance principles and practice to become embedded as standard industry practice throughout the financial services sector. The key indicator of success will be when capital flows irreversibly towards projects and activities supporting the transition to a sustainable, low-carbon world.

Three major changes already under way, which demonstrate that progress is being made are: (a) a regulatory focus on climate-related financial disclosure and stranded assets; (b) the engagement and sponsorship of senior financial services leaders in green and sustainable finance, and (c) the use of data analytics for managing climate-related risks and the application of FinTech tools and techniques to green and sustainable finance.

While the roles played by governments, regulators, financial institutions and many other organizations are key in embedding green finance principles and practices, so too is the role played by individuals working in financial services. Increasing numbers of Green and Sustainable Finance Professionals, with the knowledge and skills needed to develop and deploy green finance products, services and tools, will play vital roles in embedding green finance within their own organizations, and in encouraging its adoption more widely. The Chartered Banker Code for Green and Sustainable Finance Professionals sets out how individuals may incorporate green finance principles and values into their professional practice.

Notes

1 World Bank Group (2014) Annual meetings 2014 [Online] https://www.imf.org/external/am/2014/index.htm (archived at https://perma.cc/9XFT-CD6R)

2 PwC (2020) *Assest Management 2020: A brave new world* [Online] https://www.pwc.com/gx/en/asset-management/publications/pdfs/pwc-asset-management-2020-a-brave-new-world-final.pdf (archived at https://perma.cc/7QDD-JJAZ)

3 Bank of England (2016) Resolving the climate change paradox, Speech by Mark Carney [Online] https://www.bankofengland.co.uk/-/media/boe/files/speech/2016/resolving-the-climate-paradox.pdf?la=en&hash=CDFB1640F4635BEC9C08601FF616C842BB975CEC (archived at https://perma.cc/8XBY-QM7B)

4 Global Ethical Banking (2018) China leads global focus on green says top PBOC official [Online] https://www.globalethicalbanking.com/china-leads-global-focus-green-financing-says-top-pboc-official/ (archived at https://perma.cc/QER8-QLBC)

5 C Seekings (2018) World Bank to double climate action investments to $200bn, IEMA [Online] https://transform.iema.net/article/world-bank-double-climate-action-investments-200bn (archived at https://perma.cc/6AKV-9XU8)

6 OECD (2018) OECD, UN Environment and World Bank call for a radical shift in financing for a low-carbon, climate-resilient future [Online] https://www.oecd.org/newsroom/oecd-un-environment-and-world-bank-call-for-a-radical-shift-in-financing-for-a-low-carbon-climate-resilient-future.htm (archived at https://perma.cc/B8UG-7MZ9)

7 H Clancy (2017) Why JPMorgan Chase committed $200 billion to 'clean' financing, GreenBiz [Online] https://www.greenbiz.com/article/why-jpmorgan-chase-committed-200-billion-clean-financing (archived at https://perma.cc/R6F9-C9EF)

8 Barclays (2018) The green finance revolution [Online] https://home.barclays/news/2018/08/the-green-finance-revolution/ (archived at https://perma.cc/DY4L-2XQJ)

9 P Smith (2018) BlackRock stakes claim on 'sustainable investing' revolution, *Financial Times* [Online] https://www.ft.com/content/f66b2a9e-d53d-11e8-a854-33d6f82e62f8 (archived at https://perma.cc/7LHN-GE56)

10 Shell (nd) Our response to climate change [Online] https://www.shell.co.uk/a-cleaner-energy-future/our-response-to-climate-change.html (archived at https://perma.cc/U7CN-NFAD)

11 Chartered Banker (nd) Certificate in Green and Sustainable Finance [Online] https://www.charteredbanker.com/qualification/certificate-in-green-finance.html (archived at https://perma.cc/TY3V-BNP5)

12 Chartered Banker Institute (2018) *The Chartered Banker Code of Professional Conduct* [Online] https://www.charteredbanker.com/uploads/assets/uploaded/bc9e34e1-079e-449f-b7b29f9d6e103b31.pdf (archived at https://perma.cc/4AU8-2RZ7)

INDEX

The index is filed in alphabetical, word-by-word order. Numbers within main headings are filed as spelt out, with the exception of ISO standards and RCPs, which are filed in chronological order; acronyms are filed as presented. Page locators in italics denote information within a table or figure; those in roman numerals denote information within the preface.